THE CAMBRIDGE (
TWENTY-FIRST-CENTURY

Reading lists, course syllabi, and prizes incl.... ... phrase "twenty-first-century American literature," but no critical consensus exists regarding when the period began, which works typify it, how to conceptualize its aesthetic priorities, and where its geographical boundaries lie. Considerable criticism has been published on this extraordinary era, but little programmatic analysis has assessed comprehensively the literary and critical/theoretical output to help readers navigate the labyrinth of critical pathways. In addition to ensuring broad coverage of many essential texts, *The Cambridge Companion to Twenty-First-Century American Fiction* offers state-of-the-field analyses of contemporary narrative studies that set the terms of current and future research and teaching. Individual chapters illuminate critical engagements with emergent genres and concepts, including flash fiction, speculative fiction, digital fiction, alternative temporalities, Afro-Futurism, ecocriticism, transgender/queer studies, anti-carceral fiction, precarity, and post-9/11 fiction.

JOSHUA L. MILLER is Associate Professor of English at the University of Michigan. He is the author of *Accented America: The Cultural Politics of Multilingual Modernism* (2011), editor of *The Cambridge Companion to the American Modernist Novel* (2015), and coeditor of *Languages of Modern Jewish Cultures: Comparative Perspectives* (2016).

THE CAMBRIDGE
COMPANION TO

TWENTY-FIRST-CENTURY AMERICAN FICTION

EDITED BY
JOSHUA L. MILLER
University of Michigan, Ann Arbor

CAMBRIDGE
UNIVERSITY PRESS

CAMBRIDGE
UNIVERSITY PRESS

University Printing House, Cambridge CB2 8BS, United Kingdom

One Liberty Plaza, 20th Floor, New York, NY 10006, USA

477 Williamstown Road, Port Melbourne, VIC 3207, Australia

314–321, 3rd Floor, Plot 3, Splendor Forum, Jasola District Centre, New Delhi – 110025, India

103 Penang Road, #05–06/07, Visioncrest Commercial, Singapore 238467

Cambridge University Press is part of the University of Cambridge. It furthers the University's mission by disseminating knowledge in the pursuit of education, learning, and research at the highest international levels of excellence.

www.cambridge.org
Information on this title: www.cambridge.org/9781108838276
DOI: 10.1017/9781108974288

© Cambridge University Press 2021

First published 2021

Printed in the United Kingdom by TJ Books Limited, Padstow Cornwall.

A catalogue record for this publication is available from the British Library.

Library of Congress Cataloging-in-Publication Data
NAMES: Miller, Joshua L., 1971– editor.
TITLE: The Cambridge companion to twenty–first century American fiction / edited by Joshua L. Miller.
DESCRIPTION: Cambridge ; New York, NY : Cambridge University Press, 2021. | Includes bibliographical references and index.
IDENTIFIERS: LCCN 2021027178 (print) | LCCN 2021027179 (ebook) | ISBN 9781108838276 (hardback) | ISBN 9781108974288 (epub)
SUBJECTS: LCSH: American fiction—21st century—History and criticism. | BISAC: LITERARY CRITICISM / American / General | LCGFT: Literary criticism.
CLASSIFICATION: LCC PS380 .C36 2021 (print) | LCC PS380 (ebook) | DDC 813/.609—dc23
LC record available at https://lccn.loc.gov/2021027178
LC ebook record available at https://lccn.loc.gov/2021027179

ISBN 978-1-108-83827-6 Hardback
ISBN 978-1-108-97870-5 Paperback

CONTENTS

Illustrations   *page* vii
Contributors   ix
Acknowledgments   xiii
Chronology   xv

Introduction   1
JOSHUA L. MILLER

PART I   FORMS

1   Short Fiction, Flash Fiction, Microfiction   21
ANGELA NAIMOU

2   Experimental Fiction   43
DAVID JAMES

3   Speculative Fiction   63
MARK BOULD

4   Graphic Fiction   79
KATALIN ORBÁN

5   Digital Fiction   100
SCOTT RETTBERG

CONTENTS

PART II   APPROACHES

6   Afro-Futurism/Afro-Pessimism   123
    CANDICE M. JENKINS

7   Transpacific Diasporas   142
    JULIA H. LEE

8   Hemispheric Routes   157
    MARY PAT BRADY

9   Transgender and Transgenre Writing   174
    TRISH SALAH

10 Climate Fiction   196
    HEATHER HOUSER

PART III   THEMES

11 Convergence   215
    MARK GOBLE

12 Dissolution   234
    CRYSTAL PARIKH

13 Immobility   251
    DENNIS CHILDS

14 Insecurity   271
    HAMILTON CARROLL

    Further Reading   289
    Index   301

ILLUSTRATIONS

I.1 Google N-gram, "you"   *page* 8
1.1 "Mrs. Dalloway" tweet by Teju Cole (2013)
    (Copyright © Teju Cole, used by permission
    of The Wylie Agency LLC. With thanks to
    Kelsey Sheaffer for image reproduction.)   35
4.1 *Here* by Richard McGuire (Double-page spread
    from *Here* by Richard McGuire, n.p. (unpaginated 190–191).
    Graphic novel excerpt from *Here* by Richard McGuire,
    copyright © 2014 by Richard McGuire. Used by permission of
    Pantheon Books, an imprint of the Knopf Doubleday
    Publishing Group, a division of Penguin Random House LLC.
    All rights reserved.)   87
4.2 Detail from *Vietnamerica* by GB Tran (Graphic novel
    excerpt from *Vietnamerica: A Family's Journey* by
    GB Tran, copyright © 2011 by Gia-Bao Tran.
    Used by permission of Villard Books, an imprint
    of Random House, a division of Penguin Random House LLC.
    All rights reserved.)   92

CONTRIBUTORS

MARK BOULD is Reader in Film and Literature at University of West England, Bristol. A recipient of the SFRA Pilgrim Lifetime Achievement Award for Critical Contributions to the Study of Science Fiction and Fantasy (2016) and the IAFA Distinguished Scholarship Award (2019), he is the founding editor of the journal *Science Fiction Film and Television* and the monograph series Studies in Global Science Fiction. His most recent books are *M. John Harrison: Critical Essays* (2019) and *The Anthropocene Unconscious* (2020).

MARY PAT BRADY teaches at Cornell University and is the author of *Extinct Lands, Temporal Geographies: Chicana Literature and the Urgency of Space* (2002), which was awarded the Modern Language Association's Prize for the Best Work of Latina/o and Chicana/o Literary and Cultural Criticism. She is an associate editor of the seventh edition of the *Heath Anthology of American Literature* (2013) and editor of the *Gale Guide to Twentieth and Twenty-First Century American Literature* (2017). She is currently completing a new study of Latinx literature, *Traffic*.

HAMILTON CARROLL is Professor of American Studies at the University of Leeds. He is the author of *Affirmative Reaction: New Formations of White Masculinity* (2011). He has published widely on topics in contemporary American literature and culture in numerous edited collections and in journals such as *Comparative American Studies, Genre*, the *Journal of American Studies, Modern Fiction Studies, Studies in American Fiction*, and *Television and New Media*.

DENNIS CHILDS is Associate Professor of African American Literature and an affiliate faculty member of the Department of Ethnic Studies at the University of California (UC), San Diego. He is the author of *Slaves of the State: Black Incarceration from the Chain Gang to the Penitentiary* (2015), a work that deals with the connections between chattel slavery and prison slavery from the late nineteenth century through the prison industrial complex. As a scholar-activist, he has worked with various social justice organizations including the Malcolm

X Grassroots Movement, All of Us or None, Critical Resistance, and the Chicano Mexicano Prison Project. He currently serves as faculty advisor for Students Against Mass Incarceration (SAMI UCSD) – a student-run prison abolitionist organization. In 2015, he was a member of the first ever prisoner solidarity delegation from the United States to Palestine.

MARK GOBLE is Associate Professor of English at the University of California, Berkeley and the author of *Beautiful Circuits: Modernism and the Mediated Life* (2010). His essays, articles, and reviews have appeared in *Early Literary History*, *Modern Language Quarterly*, *Modern Fiction Studies*, *American Literature*, and the *Los Angeles Review of Books*. He is currently at work on a book entitled *Downtime: The Twentieth Century in Slow Motion*, which explores the relation between the experience of slowness and the limits of high technology across a range of film, literature, and new media art.

HEATHER HOUSER is Associate Professor of English at the University of Texas (UT) at Austin. She is the author of the books *Infowhelm: Environmental Art and Literature in an Age of Data* (2020) and *Ecosickness in Contemporary U.S. Fiction: Environment and Affect* (2014), as well as many articles. She codirects Planet Texas 2050, an interdisciplinary climate research program at UT Austin, and is an associate editor at the journal *Contemporary Literature*.

DAVID JAMES is Professor of English at the University of Birmingham, before which he was Reader in Modern and Contemporary Literature at Queen Mary, University of London. His recent books include *Modernist Futures* (2012) and *Discrepant Solace* (2019), along with edited volumes such as *The Legacies of Modernism* (2012), *The Cambridge Companion to British Fiction since 1945* (2015), and *Modernism and Close Reading* (2020). He is an associated editor at *Contemporary Literature*, and for Columbia University Press he coedits the book series Literature Now. He is currently completing *Sentimental Activism* (forthcoming), a book about the political dynamics of solicitation both in contemporary writing and in the contours of cultural criticism.

CANDICE M. JENKINS is Professor of English and African American Studies at the University of Illinois, Urbana–Champaign. She earned her BA from Spelman College and her PhD from Duke University, both in English. Jenkins's research and teaching use a critical black feminist lens to consider how a variety of African American cultural texts address evolving questions of racial subjectivity, sexual politics, and class in the United States. Her first book, *Private Lives, Proper Relations: Regulating Black Intimacy* (2007), was awarded the William Sanders Scarborough Prize by the Modern Language Association. That project examined how twentieth-century black women writers articulated the political consequences of intimacy for the already-vulnerable black subject. Her new book, *Black Bourgeois: Class and Sex in the Flesh* (2019), explores the dilemma of black middle-class embodiment in recent African American fiction. Jenkins is now at work on another manuscript, extending her interests in embodiment and racialized vulnerability to contemporary black science fiction and fantasy. Tentatively entitled *Speculative Pessimisms*, the project places Afro-Futurist and black speculative cultural production in conversation with Afro-Pessimist thought.

JULIA H. LEE is Associate Professor of Asian American Studies at UC, Irvine. She is the author of *Reciprocal Representations in African- and Asian American Literatures, 1896–1937* (2010) and *Understanding Maxine Hong Kingston* (2018). She is also a coeditor of *Asian American Literature in Transition*, vol. 1, which is forthcoming from Cambridge University Press. Her book-in-progress is *The Racial Railroad*, which explores the prevalence of the train as a setting for narratives of racial formation and conflict in American culture.

ANGELA NAIMOU is Associate Professor of English at Clemson University and coeditor of *Humanity: An International Journal of Human Rights, Humanitarianism, and Development*. Her book *Salvage Work: U.S. and Caribbean Literatures amid the Debris of Legal Personhood* (2015) won the Association for the Study of the Arts of the Present Book Prize and received Honorable Mention for the William Sanders Scarborough Award by the Modern Language Association. Her current book project is about contemporary literature and international migration regimes. She is also at work on a critical volume, *Diaspora and Literary Studies*, as part of the Cambridge University Press Critical Concepts Series.

KATALIN ORBÁN holds a PhD from Rutgers University. She is Associate Professor at the Institute of Art Theory and Media Studies at Eötvös Loránd University, Budapest, with prior positions at Harvard University, National University of Singapore, and Central European University. Her work on graphic narrative has appeared in *Representations*, *Critical Inquiry*, *The Edinburgh Companion to Narrative Theories*, the *Journal of Graphic Novels and Comics*, and most recently in *Documenting Trauma in Comics* (2020) and *The Routledge Companion to Literature and Trauma* (2020). Her work on cultural memory and narrative includes *Ethical Diversions: The Post-Holocaust Narratives of Pynchon, Abish, DeLillo, and Spiegelman* (2005, 2013).

CRYSTAL PARIKH is Professor of Social and Cultural Analysis and English at New York University, where she specializes in twentieth-century and contemporary American literature and culture. In addition to numerous essays and articles, Parikh has published *Writing Human Rights: The Political Imaginaries of Writers of Color* (2017) and *An Ethics of Betrayal: The Politics of Otherness in Emergent U.S. Literature and Culture* (2009). She is also the editor of the recently published *The Cambridge Companion to Human Rights and Literature* (2019) and coeditor, with Daniel Y. Kim, of *The Cambridge Companion to Asian*

American Literature (2015). Parikh is the director of the Asian/Pacific/American Institute at NYU.

SCOTT RETTBERG is Professor of Digital Culture in the Department of Linguistic, Literary, and Aesthetic Studies at the University of Bergen, Norway. Rettberg is the author or coauthor of novel-length works of electronic literature, combinatory poetry, and films including *The Unknown, Kind of Blue, Implementation, Frequency, The Catastrophe Trilogy, Three Rails Live, Toxi*City, Hearts and Minds: The Interrogations Project,* and others. His creative work has been exhibited both online and at art venues including the Venice Biennale, Inova Gallery, Rom 8, the Chemical Heritage Foundation Museum, Palazzo dell Arti Napoli, and elsewhere. Rettberg is the author of *Electronic Literature* (2019), a comprehensive study of the histories and genres of electronic literature and winner of the 2019 N. Katherine Award for Criticism of Electronic Literature.

TRISH SALAH is the author of *Wanting in Arabic* and *Lyric Sexology*, vol. 1 (2014) and coeditor of special issues of *Transgender Studies Quarterly* on "Trans Cultural Production" and of *Arc Poetry Magazine* on work by trans, Two-Spirit, non-binary, and gender non-conforming writers. She is Associate Professor of Gender Studies at Queen's University.

ACKNOWLEDGMENTS

Editing this volume has been a unique privilege and pleasure. First and foremost, I want to thank the extraordinary contributors, all of whom have brought astonishing storehouses of knowledge and expertise to their chapters. Ray Ryan has been the essential and encouraging voice at every stage, from this project's first glimmerings to its conclusion, while Edgar Mendez wisely and patiently accompanied me through the volume's final stages and emergence, and Victoria Parrin tirelessly oversaw its production.

My colleagues and students at the University of Michigan have been pivotal interlocutors for the conceptual frameworks that have informed how I think, teach, and write about twenty-first-century US fiction. Participants in the Critical Contemporary Studies Workshop have been an ongoing source of inspiration and insight. I am very grateful to Hayley O'Malley and Emily Na for their brilliant and scrupulous research assistance. I would also like to acknowledge the crucial support of the Office of the Vice President for Research and the Department of English Language and Literature at the University of Michigan.

I am completing this manuscript at what I hope will be the apex of the COVID-19 global health emergency. The fact that this volume does not contain a discussion of pandemic fiction merely demonstrates, as if we need reminding, the always-unfinished business of critical contemporary cultural studies.

CHRONOLOGY

1965 Immigration and Nationality Act
      Ted Nelson, "A File Structure for the Complex, the Changing, and
      the Indeterminate"
1966 *Star Trek: Original Series* (series, –1969)
      Tom Phillips, *A Humument* (–present)
1968 John Barth, "Frame Tale"
1969 Creation of ARPANET, forerunner of the Internet
1970 George Jackson, *Soledad Brother: The Prison Letters of George
      Jackson*
1971 World Economic Forum founded
1973 Arthur C. Clarke, *Rendezvous with Rama*
      Donald Goines, *White Man's Law, Black Man's Injustice*
      Thomas Pynchon, *Gravity's Rainbow*
      Kurt Vonnegut, *Breakfast of Champions*
1974 James Baldwin, *If Beale Street Could Talk*
      Angela Davis, *Angela Davis: An Autobiography*
      Theodor Holm Nelson, *Computer Lib/Dream Machines*
      Robert Stone, *Dog Soldiers*
      Thomas William, *The Hair of Harold Roux*
1976 Don DeLillo, *Ratner's Star*
      Maxine Hong Kingston, *Woman Warrior*
1977 Leslie Marmon Silko, *Ceremony*
1980 Marilyn Robinson, *Housekeeping*
      Art Spiegelman, *Maus: A Survivor's Tale* (series in *Raw* –1991)
1981 Assata Shakur, *Assata: An Autobiography*
1982 Theresa Hak Kyung Cha, *Dictee*
      Gilbert, Jaime, and Mario Hernandez, *Love and Rockets*
      (series, –1996)
      John McPhee, *Basin and Range*

1983   *Invisible Seattle* novel project (published 1987)
Toni Morrison, "Recitatif"
1984   Apple Macintosh released
William Gibson, *Neuromancer*
Kim Stanley Robinson, *Icehenge*
1986   US Space Shuttle *Challenger* explodes
Judy Malloy, *Uncle Roger*
Alan Moore and Dave Gibbons, *Watchmen* (series, –1987)
1987   "Black Monday," stock market crash
Gloria Anzaldúa, *Borderlands/La Frontera*
Jay David Bolter, John Brown, and Michael Joyce, *Storyspace* software
Octavia Butler, *Dawn* (*Xenogenesis* trilogy)
Michael Joyce, *afternoon, a story*
Toni Morrison, *Beloved*
William T. Vollmann, *You Bright and Risen Angels*
1988   Kathy Acker, *Empire of the Senseless*
Nicholson Baker, *The Mezzanine*
Octavia Butler, *Adulthood Rites* (*Xenogenesis* trilogy)
NWA, "Fuck the Police" (song)
Peter Straub, *Koko*
Public Enemy, "Black Steel in the Hour of Chaos" (song)
1989   Asia-Pacific Economic Cooperation founded
Berlin Wall falls; end of Soviet bloc in Eastern Europe
Tiananmen Square protest and massacre
Tim Berners-Lee, "Information Management: A Proposal"
Octavia Butler, *Imago* (*Xenogenesis* trilogy)
John Langley and Malcolm Barbour, *COPS* (TV program, –2020)
1990   Iraq invades Kuwait, Persian Gulf War
Jessica Hagedorn, *Dogeaters*
Tim O'Brien, *The Things They Carried*
Kim Stanley Robinson, *Pacific Edge*
Karen Tei Yamashita, *Through the Arc of the Rainforest*
1991   Tim Berners-Lee designs first World Wide Web server
Martin Amis, *Time's Arrow*
Donna Harraway, "A Cyborg Manifesto"
Main Source, "More Than Just a Friendly Game of Baseball" (song)
Stuart Moulthrop, *Victory Garden*
Leslie Marmon Silko, *Almanac of the Dead*

1992   Poppy Z. Brite, *Lost Souls*
        Patrick Chamoiseau, *Texaco*
        Robert Coover, "The End of Books"
        Kim Stanley Robinson, *Red Mars* (*Mars* trilogy)
1993   Bombing of the World Trade Center
        Octavia Butler, *The Parable of the Sower*
        KRS, "Sound of Da Police" (song)
        Kim Stanley Robinson, *Green Mars* (*Mars* trilogy)
1994   Netscape Navigator web browser released
        North American Free Trade Agreement
        Samuel Ace, *Normal Sex*
        Edwidge Danticat, *Breath, Eyes, Memory*
        Don DeLillo, "Videotape"
1995   World Trade Organization (WTO) established
        Oklahoma City bombing
        Askari X, "Gotta Go" (song)
        Charles Burns, *Black Hole* (series, –2005)
        Edwidge Danticat, *Krik? Krak!*
        Rosario Ferré, *The House on the Lagoon*
        Shelley Jackson, *Patchwork Girl*
        Stuart Moulthrop, *Hegirascope*
        Adrian Tomine, *Optic Nerve* (series, –2016)
        Chris Ware, *Jimmy Corrigan: The Smartest Kid on Earth* (series, –2000)
1996   Robert Arellano, *Sunshine '69*
        Linda Hogan, *Dwellings: A Spiritual History of the Living World*
        Jamaica Kinkaid, *Autobiography of My Mother*
        Kim Stanley Robinson, *Blue Mars* (*Mars* trilogy)
        Caitlin Sullivan, *Nearly Roadkill*
1997   Mark Amerika, *Grammatron*
        Don DeLillo, *Underworld*
        Francisco Goldman, *The Ordinary Seaman*
        Shelley Jackson, *My Body & a Wunderkammer*
        Toni Morrison, *Paradise*
1998   Google founded
        Tony Burgess, *Pontypool Changes Everything*
        Octavia Butler, *The Parable of the Talents*
        Nalo Hopkinson, *Brown Girl in the Ring*
        Peter Howitt, *Sliding Doors* (film)
        Gayl Jones, *The Healing*
        Monifa Love, *Freedom in the Dismal*
        Curtis White, *Memories of My Father Watching TV*

1999   Electronic Literature Organization founded
William Gillespie, Frank Marquardt, Scott Rettberg, and Dirk Stratton, *The Unknown*
Gayl Jones, *Mosquito*
Jonathan Lethem, *Motherless Brooklyn*
Stuart Moulthrop, *Reagan Library*
Neal Stephenson, *Cryptonomicon*
Rob Wittig, *The Fall of the Site of Marsha*
Colson Whitehead, *The Intuitionist*

2000   George W. Bush elected president after Florida recount
Michael Chabon, *The Amazing Adventures of Kavalier & Clay*
Mark Z. Danielewski, *House of Leaves*
Dead Prez, *Let's Get Free* (song)
Dave Eggers, *A Heartbreaking Work of Staggering Genius*
Nalo Hopkinson, *Midnight Robber*
Evelina Zuni Lucero, *Night Sky, Morning Star*
Talan Memmott, *Lexia to Perplexia*
Emily Short, *Galatea*

2001   Al-Qaeda attacks on the World Trade Center and Pentagon
Apple releases the iPod
USA Patriot Act passed and Global War on Terror declared
Wikipedia launched
Jessica Abel, *La Perdida* (series, –2005)
Percival Everett, *Erasure*
Jonathan Franzen, *The Corrections*
Neil Gaiman, *American Gods*
Shelley and Pamela Jackson, *The Doll Games*

2002   Sandra Cisneros, *Caramelo*
T. Cooper, *Some of the Parts*
Lydia Davis, *Samuel Johnson Is Indignant*
Jeffrey Eugenides, *Middlesex*
Phoebe Gloeckner, *The Diary of a Teenage Girl: An Account in Words and Pictures*
Nelly Rosario, *Song of the Water Saints*
Emily Short, *Savoir-Faire*
Adrian Tomine, *Summer Blonde*

2003   Human Genome Project completed
US invasion of Iraq
Margaret Atwood, *Oryx and Crake* (*MaddAddam* trilogy)
J. Michael Bailey, *The Man Who Would Be Queen*

Susan Choi, *American Woman*
Don DeLillo, *Cosmopolis*
Nalo Hopkinson, *The Salt Roads*
Edward P. Jones, *The Known World*
Robert Kirkman, Tony Moore and Charlie Adlard, *The Walking Dead* (series, –present)
Jhumpa Lahiri, *The Namesake*
Jonathan Lethem, *The Fortress of Solitude*
Christine Schutt, *Florida*
Craig Thompson, *Blankets*
2004   Facebook launched
Invincible, aka Ill Weaver, "The Door," on *The We That Sets Us Free: Building a World without Prisons*
Edwidge Danticat, The *Dew Breaker*
Don Lee, *Country of Origin*
Aimee Phan, *We Should Never Meet*
Kim Stanley Robinson, *Forty Signs of Rain* (*Science in the Capital* trilogy)
Marilynne Robinson, *Gilead*
Philip Roth, *The Plot against America*
Art Spiegelman, *In the Shadow of No Towers*
2005   Hurricane Katrina
Irish Republican Army declares end to military actions against Britain
Kyoto Protocol implemented
YouTube launched
Charlie Anders, *Choirboy*
Octavia Butler, *Fledgling*
Jonathan Safran Foer, *Extremely Loud and Incredibly Close*
Sesshu Foster, *Atomik Aztex*
Matthew Kaopio, *Written in the Sky*
Cormac McCarthy, *No Country for Old Men*
Nnedi Okorafor, *Zahrah the Windseeker*
Kim Stanley Robinson, *Fifty Degrees Below* (*Science in the Capital* trilogy)
2006   Twitter launched
Julia Alvarez, *Saving the World*
Alison Bechdel, *Fun Home: A Family Tragicomic*
Max Brooks, *World War Z*
Dave Eggers, *What Is the What: The Autobiography of Valentino*

Achak Deng
Alicia Goranson, *Supervillainz*
Reyna Grande, *Across a Hundred Mountains*
Andrea Hairston, *Mindscape*
Ann Jaramillo, *La Línea*
Ana-Maurine Lara, *Erzulie's Skirt*
Cormac McCarthy, *The Road*
Jay McInerney, *The Good Life*
Claire Messud, *The Emperor's Children*
Jason Nelson, *Game, Game, Game and Again Game*
Thomas Pynchon, *Against the Day*
Gary Shteyngart, *Absurdistan*
2007   Great Recession/Global financial crisis
Apple iPhone released
Sherman Alexie, *The Absolutely True Diary of a Part-Time Indian*
Michael Chabon, *The Yiddish Policeman's Union*
Susan Choi, *A Person of Interest*
Edwidge Danticat, *Brother, I'm Dying*
Don DeLillo, *Falling Man*
Junot Díaz, *The Brief Wondrous Life of Oscar Wao*
Mohsin Hamid, *The Reluctant Fundamentalist*
Jonathan Lethem, "The Ecstasy of Influence: A Plagiarism"
Judd Morrissey, *The Last Performance*
Nnedi Okorafor, *The Shadow Speaker*
Joseph O'Neill, *Netherland*
Kim Stanley Robinson, *Sixty Days and Counting* (*Science in the Capital* trilogy)
Helen Schulman, *A Day at the Beach*
Helena Mariá Viramontes, *Their Dogs Came with Them*
2008   Barack Obama elected president
Susan Choi, *A Person of Interest*
Sharon Daniel, *Public Secrets*
Aleksandar Hemon, *The Lazarus Project*
Linda Hogan, *People of the Whale*
Jhumpha Lahiri, *Unaccustomed Earth*
Toni Morrison, *A Mercy*
Jason Nelson, *I Made This. You Play This. We Are Enemies*
2009   Margaret Atwood, *The Year of the Flood* (*MaddAddam* trilogy)
Paolo Bacigalupi, *The Windup Girl*
Jeanine Capó Crucet, *How to Leave Hialeah*

Dave Eggers, *Zeitoun*
Victor LaValle, *Big Machine*
Jonathan Lethem, *Chronic City*
Mark Marino, *The Ballad of Work Study Seth*, *The Loss Wikiless Timespedia*
China Miéville, *The City and the City*
Maggie Nelson, *Bluets*
Thomas Pynchon, *Inherent Vice*
David Small, *Stitches*
Kim Stanley Robinson, *Galileo's Dream*
Jess Walter, *The Financial Lives of the Poets*
2010   Earthquake in Haiti
Largest oil spill in US history in the Gulf of Mexico
Paolo Bacigalupi, *Ship Breaker* (*Ship Breaker* trilogy)
Myriam Chancy, *The Loneliness of Angels*
Don DeLillo, *Point Omega*
Jennifer Egan, *A Visit from the Goon Squad*
Jonathan Franzen, *Freedom*
Rachel B. Glaser, *Pee on Water*
Mira Grant, *Feed* (*Newsflesh* series)
Sheila Heti, *How Should a Person Be?*
N. K. Jemisin, *The Hundred Thousand Kingdoms* and *The Broken Kingdoms* (*Inheritance* trilogy)
Ben Marcus, *The Flame Alphabet*
Nnedi Okorafor, *Who Fears Death*
Gary Shteyngart, *Super Sad True Love Story*
GB Tran, *Vietnamerica*
Karen Tei Yamashita, *I Hotel*
2011   Occupy Movement begins
Syrian Civil War begins
Tōhoku earthquake and tsunami, Fukushima Daiichi nuclear disaster
World population reaches seven billion people
Samiya Hameeda Abdullah, aka "Goldii," "Trap Doors" (song)
Teju Cole, *Open City*
Mira Grant, *Deadline* (*Newsflesh* series)
Andrea Hairston, *Redwood and Wildfire*
N. K. Jemisin, *The Kingdom of Gods* (*Inheritance* trilogy)
Mat Johnson, *Pym*
Matthew Kaopio, *Up Among the Stars*
Ben Lerner, *Leaving the Atocha Station*

Mark Marino and Rob Wittig, *Occupy MLA*
China Miéville, *Embassytown*
Nnedi Okorafor, *Akata Witch*
Amy Waldman, *The Submission*
Jesmyn Ward, *Salvage the Bones*
Colson Whitehead, *Zone One*
2012   Murder of Trayvon Martin
Hurricane Sandy
Rover Curiosity takes a selfie on Mars
Paolo Bacigalupi, *Drowned Cities* (*Ship Breaker* trilogy)
Tobias S. Bucknell, *Arctic Rising*
Samuel R. Delany, *Through the Valley of the Nest of Spiders*
Ceyenne Doroshow, *Cooking in Heels*
Dave Eggers, *A Hologram for the King*
Louise Erdrich, *Round House*
Cat Fitzpatrick and Casey Platt, *The Collection: Short Fiction from the Transgender Vanguard*
Gillian Flynn, *Gone Girl*
Ben Fountain, *Billy Lynn's Long Halftime Walk*
Mira Grant, *Blackout* (*Newsflesh* series)
N. K. Jemisin, *Dreamblood* series
Caitlín R. Kiernan, *The Drowning Girl: A Memoir*
Barbara Kingsolver, *Flight Behavior*
Victor LaValle, *The Devil in Silver*
Toni Morrison, *Home*
Porpentine, *Howling Dogs*
Kim Stanley Robinson, *2312*
Emily Short, *Counterfeit Monkey*
Chris Ware, *Building Stories*
2013   Black Lives Matter Movement founded
Chimamanda Ngozi Adichi, *Americanah*
Margaret Atwood, *MaddAddam* (*MaddAddam* trilogy)
Imogen Binnie, *Nevada*
Wesley Chu, *The Lives of Tao* and *The Deaths of Tao* (*Tao* trilogy)
Teju Cole, "Seven Short Stories about Drones"
Edwidge Danticat, *Claire of the Sea Light*
David Eggers, *The Circle*
Fullbright Company, *Gone Home* (video game)
Ben Katchor, *Hand-Drying in America*

Rachel Kushner, *The Flamethrowers*
Kiese Laymon, *Long Division*
Jonathan Lethem, *Dissident Gardens*
Jason Nelson, *Nothing You Have Done Deserves Such Praise*
Ruth Ozeki, *A Tale for the Time Being*
Thomas Pynchon, *Bleeding Edge*
Nathaniel Rich, *Odds against Tomorrow*
George Saunders, *Tenth of December*
Saïd Sayrafiezadeh, *Brief Encounters with the Enemy*
Zadie Smith, "Meet the President!"
TC Tolbert and Tim Trace Peterson, *Troubling the Line: Trans and Genderqueer Poetry and Poetics*

2014 Fatal shooting of Michael Brown leads to protests in Ferguson, Missouri
Tobias S. Buckell, *Hurricane Fever*
Teju Cole, "Hafiz" and *Open City*
Dane Figueroa Edidi, *Yemaya's Daughters*
William Gibson, *The Peripheral*
Chang-rae Lee, *On Such a Full Sea*
Edan Lepucki, *California*
Ben Lerner, *10:04*
Emily St. John Mandel, *Station Eleven*
Richard McGuire, *Here*
Ottessa Moshfegh, *McGlue*
Celeste Ng, *Everything I Never Told You*
Nnedi Okorafor, *Lagoon* and *Who Fears Death*
Porpentine, *With Those We Love Alive*
Claudia Rankine, *Citizen*
Marilynne Robinson, *Lila*
Merritt Tierce, *Love Me Back*
Jeff VanderMeer, *Southern Reach* trilogy

2015 US Supreme Court strikes down state bans on same-sex marriage
Mia Alvar, *In the Country*
Cameron Awkward-Rich, "The Little Girl Will Never Tire of Confession"
Paolo Bacigalupi, *The Water Knife*
Paul Beatty, *The Sellout*
Danny Cannizzaro and Samantha Gorman, *Pry*
Wesley Chu, *The Rebirths of Tao* (*Tao* trilogy)

Ta-Nehisi Coates, *Between the World and Me*
Jennine Capó Crucet, *Make Your Home Among Strangers*
Sharon Daniel, *Inside the Distance*
Carola Dibbell, *The Only Ones*
N. K. Jemisin, *The Fifth Season* (*Broken Earth* trilogy)
Kendrick Lamar, *To Pimp a Butterfly* (album)
Maggie Nelson, *The Argonauts*
Viet Thanh Nguyen, *The Sympathizer*
Nnedi Okorafor, *The Book of the Phoenix*
Kim Stanley Robinson, *Aurora*
Frank Spotnitz, *The Man in the High Castle*
(TV series, –present)
Neal Stephenson, *Seveneves*
Adrian Tomine, *Killing and Dying*
Vendela Vida, *The Diver's Clothes Lie Empty*
Claire Vaye Watkins, *Gold Fame Citrus*
2016 Central American migrant crisis
Donald Trump elected president
Trans-Pacific Partnership (not ratified)
Campo Santo, *Firewatch* (video game)
Roderick Coover and Scott Rettberg, *Toxi*City: A Climate Change Narrative*
Emil Ferris, *My Favorite Thing Is Monsters*
Yaa Gyasi, *Homegoing*
Andrea Hairston, *Will Do Magic for Small Change*
N. K. Jemisin, *The Obelisk Gate* (*Broken Earth* trilogy)
Kendrick Lamar, *Untitled Remastered* (album)
Victor Lavalle, *The Ballad of Black Tom*
China Miéville, *This Census-Taker*
Gabby Rivera, *Juliet Takes a Breath*
Viet Thanh Nguyen, *Nothing Ever Dies*
Kai Cheng Thom, *Fierce Femmes and Notorious Liars: A Dangerous Trans Girl's Confabulous Memoir*
Colson Whitehead, *The Underground Railroad*
Jia Qing Wilson-Yang, *Small Beauty*
2017 Fyre Festival
Hurricanes Harvey and Maria
Paolo Bacigalupi, *Tool of War* (*Ship Breaker* trilogy)
Gabrielle Bell, *Everything Is Flammable* (comic)

Alan Bigelow, "How to Rob a Bank"
Thi Bui, *The Best We Could Do*
Zinzi Clemmons, *What We Lose*
Ryan Coogler, *Black Panther* (film)
Louise Erdrich, *Future Home of the Living God*
Giant Sparrow, *What Remains of Edith Finch*
(video game)
Mohsin Hamid, *Exit West*
Amira Hanafi, *A Dictionary of the Revolution*
N. K. Jemisin, *The Stone Sky* (*Broken Earth* trilogy)
Stephen Graham Jones, *Mapping the Interior*
Victor LaValle, *The Changeling*
Min Jin Lee, *Pachinko*
Valeria Luiselli, *Tell Me How It Ends: An Essay in Forty Questions*
Viet Thanh Nguyen, *The Refugees*
Nnedi Okorafor, *Akata Warrior*
Jordan Peele, *Get Out* (film)
Gabby Rivera, *America*
Kim Stanley Robinson, *New York 2140*
George Saunders, *Lincoln in the Bardo*
Danzy Senna, *New People*
Angie Thomas, *The Hate U Give*
Jeff VanderMeer, *Borne* and *The Strange Bird*
Jesmyn Ward, *Sing, Unburied, Sing*

2018   Extinction Rebellion movement founded
March for our Lives protests following Parkland, Florida school mass shooting
Sesshu Foster, *City of the Future*
Shelley Jackson, *Riddance: Or: The Sybil Joines Vocational School for Ghost Speakers & Hearing-Mouth Children*
Tayari Jones, *An American Marriage*
Rachel Kushner, *The Mars Room*
Viet Thanh Nguyen, *The Displaced: Refugee Writers on Refugee Lives*
Tommy Orange, *There There*
Daniel Peña, *Bang*
Casey Plett, *Little Fish*
Richard Powers, *The Overstory*

2019   Mueller Report on 2016 election interference released
        Impeachment of Donald J. Trump by House of Representatives
        Laila Lalami, *The Other Americans*
        Ann Leckie, *The Raven Tower*
        Ben Lerner, *The Topeka School*
        Valeria Luiselli, *Lost Children Archive*
        Dina Nayeri, *The Ungrateful Refugee*
        Colson Whitehead, *The Nickel Boys*
        Ocean Vuong, *On Earth We're Briefly Gorgeous*

JOSHUA L. MILLER

Introduction

> It's not about Nao's now. It's about yours. You haven't caught up with
> yourself yet, the now of your story, and you can't reach the ending until
> you do.
>
> Ruth Ozeki, *A Tale for the Time Being*

While teaching a course titled "The Literature of Now: 21st Century US
Fiction," I wondered how undergraduates understood the cultural and social
dimensions of "now." We had been focused on literary uses of temporal
paradoxes, like those suffusing Ozeki's narrative in the epigraph above, but
our discussions broadened into the question of how we could decide what
(and who) were our contemporaries. I improvised an exercise on the first day
of my second time teaching the course and asked the class to answer the
question, "When did the present literary or cultural era begin?" I anticipated
that they would all have similar responses (2000 or 9/11) and that we'd have
a predictable conversation about what constrains our definitions of the
contemporary moment. To my surprise, only a few of the forty students
gave those answers. Their ideas ranged widely across decades (from the
1960s to the 2010s) and historical trends (technology, politics, economics,
and social/demographic). Two students cited the Y2K bug hysteria, leading
me to wonder how they even knew about that nonevent. Another referenced
Civil Rights movements as precursors to Occupy Wall Street, Black Lives
Matter, and hashtag activism.

My inner historicist was euphoric, even as I fumbled through the rest of
that class meeting; my plans for a discussion to reorient the class toward
more complex approaches to cultural periodization were flipped on their
head. Since then I have repeated this poll during the first meeting of each
iteration of the course, with similarly wide-ranging and compelling results,
including the invention of the Internet or digital media; the first Persian Gulf
War; the fall of the Berlin Wall; the end of South African apartheid; the

1990s; the presidential elections of 2000, 2008, and 2016; the subprime mortgage crisis; activism in Ferguson, Missouri after the 2014 police murder of Michael Brown; legalization of same-sex marriage; and mass protest movements deploying digital activism.

These informal surveys have no empirical value, but they offer anecdotal insight into both predictable (iPhones and social networks) and surprising (the rise of fast food, the Fyre Festival) ways current students understand their own historicity. For each self-oriented response (my first smartphone, my high school graduation) I received many others that posited the historical importance of events prior to the student's birth, demonstrating students' generational accounting for divergent historical origins (personal, social group, familial, transnational). The caricatures of Millennials and Gen-Zers as too self-absorbed to study history, obsessed with proliferating screens, and communicating through emoticons, is belied by my surveys suggesting that students are acutely politically sensitized, historically informed, confidently diverse in their social group affiliations, and intellectually independent.[1]

Now

As the second decade of the third millennium comes to a close, the contributors of this volume offer a varied set of perspectives on the present, and readers will find that the chapters hazard as many answers to the question of periodizing contemporary fiction as my students did. Arguments for both long and short twenty-first centuries emerge here (pop quiz: Which chapter makes the case for the earliest start to twenty-first-century fiction?), and they draw similarly diverse implications.

One unavoidable conundrum for this volume is whether and how to address the Trump presidency, which has altered definitions of the "now" by speeding up political time with what journalists have described as a firehose pace of scandals. Following President "No Drama" Obama, Donald J. Trump stepped from the set of a "reality television" show (or a gold-plated escalator) to campaign for the 2016 election.[2] His presidency merged so indistinguishably the techniques of television melodrama and political intrigue that authors of fiction have had to (again) reconsider what fiction can do that so-called reality cannot. Comedian Stephen Colbert anticipated the political trend of "truthiness" as a replacement for fact in the debut episode of *The Colbert Report* in 2005, but Trump took fictional license so far that one of his senior advisors found herself defending what she called "alternative facts" shortly after Trump took office.[3] In a column titled, "I Used to Write Novels. Then Trump Rendered Fiction Redundant," Richard North Patterson writes:

> To me, Donald Trump was more than the prototypical protagonist of a psychological novel – he was a fiction writer run amok, the hero of his own impermeable drama, resentful of editors who would prune his imaginings. He feels little need to heed advice, or to learn anything much from anyone. Most of what he says is provisional, ever subject to change, and based on nothing but his transient and subjective needs.[4]

Others have argued that the implications of twenty-first-century technological and political trends worldwide have rendered particular genres ineffectual. In a *New York Times* op-ed column, "The End of Satire" Justin E. H. Smith posits that the 2015 *Charlie Hebdo* attack in Paris represents a definitive cultural shift from print cultures to digital media amid the global reemergence of the alt-right and white nationalism.[5]

The usual problem of contemporary studies in distinguishing among epiphenomenal, residual, and emergent trends poses unique methodological challenges today when so many urgent crises have unknowable ends. Media and publishing platform transformations are ongoing as are the ramifications for narratives conveyed on paper and screens as well as in film and television. The digital integration of creators/authors, publishers/distributors, and readers/viewers signaled by the rise of Netflix and Amazon Prime/Kindle/Audible may intensify or change course. Copyright law and author compensation models in their current form are unlikely to survive the digital era, whether or not internet corporations are broken up into smaller entities. The gig economy may be the future of labor or a historical footnote. Are we on the cusp of genetically curated foods and humans? Will climate change be our downfall, or a new environmental horizon to which humans adapt? Is the global resurgence of populism and avowed white supremacism a short-term blip or a leading indicator? Will migration crises continue to inflict mass cruelty on those surviving under the conditions of the most severe precarity? At this juncture we cannot know which of these questions will remain exigent or become outdated in a decade or two.

This uncertainty regarding many kinds of precarity raises the stakes for the interpretive analysis of coevality. Is the primary methodological challenge within contemporary literary and cultural studies that we know the objects of study too well or that we cannot know what they mean until later? If we cannot historicize the present, are there more modest, yet illuminating, ways to temporalize it?[6] Are there distinctive problematics of contemporary literary studies in the twenty-first century? Adjusting Karl Mannheim's formulation, what is the problem of microgenerations (Gen X, Millennials, Gen Z)?[7] Authors of fiction are responding in real time to current events, such as regional and global migration crises, climatological collapse, police violence, and political authoritarianisms, using formal experimentation to explore the unknowability of the conclusions to their own stories, as in Valeria Luiselli's *Tell Me How It Ends* (2017).

The oft-cited first sentence of Fredric Jameson's *Postmodernism* (1989) now signals a new paradigm shift yet to be formulated. If postmodernism was "an attempt to think the present historically in an age that has forgotten how to think historically in the first place," perhaps the twenty-first century cultural imperative is to think historically in an age of mass, automated data aggregation in which the present is perpetually suspended between the accessible pasts we pocket (in photographs, texts, and documents in phones or watches, available to hackers, governments, and designated "followers") and futures foretold (by predictive algorithms and genetic testing).[8] The means and matter of literary narrative are in the process of adjusting to an age of information infinity. Similarly, the cultural implications of the machine-curation of knowledge are taking shape, as journalistic institutions are characterized as unreliable by a US president and information arrives on media platforms (television and social networks) that cater to preselected, "like"-minded audiences. The practical utility of navigation, reliable searching, and prioritization of information has become the definition of big business. Small wonder then that one of the largest corporations in 2020 began as an internet search portal. How different might our cultural landscape be if Google had lost the web search engine wars of the '90s to an early entrant, such as WebCrawler, Lycos, or AltaVista? Moreover, the ascendancy of Google (now Alphabet, Inc.) as a megacorporation epitomizes the experience of living awash in digital images, statistics, words, and sounds, to the sensory overload of always-on connections and an ever-increasing pace of everyday life. Even the titles of recent fiction allude to distinctive anxieties regarding numerical and alphabetic resequencing in the time of genetic experimentation, digital storage, and drone surveillance: Paul Auster's *4 3 2 1* (2017), Roberto Bolano's *2666* (2004), Ben Lerner's *10:04* (2014), Haruki Murakami's *1Q84* (2009), and Kim Stanley Robinson's *2312* (2012) and *New York 2140* (2017).

The rapid emergence of screen and device interactivity (text messaging, videophone conversations, photo- and video-sharing social networks, and always-on digital assistants like Alexa and Siri) generate the space-time of distant immediacy. The paradox hides within the etymology of the word *immediate* (occurring right away; direct, not mediated) in that speed has become so conflated with technology that the etymological meaning of im-mediate as unmediated is rarely invoked, while the usage of immediate for mediated speed is omnipresent. An unprecedented compression of space (between physically distant people interacting fluidly) simultaneously reinforces the distance created by the screen itself (drawing attention away from non-digital experience). Distant immediacy facilitates both mass mobilizations of political activism (Occupy Wall Street, #BLM, #metoo) as well as distraction, alienation, and political polarization. Claudia Rankine's *Citizen* (2014) engages these social and political undercurrents through a transtemporal present tense, one that demonstrates how the experiences of verbal or representational violence redraw links between embedded histories of brutality and the present-future of everyday life. Rankine further expands the textual present through each reprinting's ever lengthening list of names of African Americans killed by hate crimes and police violence on page 134.[9] In *City of the Future* (2018) Sesshu Foster represents what Ammiel Alcalay calls "the obliteration of the present": "Gentrification of your face inside your sleep. Privatization of identity, corners, and intimations. Wars on the nerve, colors, breathing …. You can't live here now; you must live in the future, in the City of the Future."[10]

In *Lost Children Archive* (2019), one of Valeria Luiselli's protagonists ponders why "we feel time differently. No one has quite been able to capture what is happening or say why. Perhaps it's just that we sense an absence of future, because the present has become too overwhelming, so the future has become unimaginable. And without future, time feels like only an accumulation."[11] A proliferation of fiction representing alt-temporalities distinguishes twenty-first-century fiction from the historical, futurist, and multitemporal novels of earlier periods: deep futurism without memory of our time (e.g., China Miéville's *Embassytown* [2011]), near futurism (Paolo Bacigalupi's *The Water Knife* [2015]), historical fiction remixed with near futurism (Jennifer Egan's *A Visit from the Goon Squad* [2010]), ongoing anachronism scrambling historical causality (Colson Whitehead's *Underground Railroad* [2016]), counterfactual alt-history (Foster's *Atomik Aztex* [2005]), unresolved parallel times (Aleksandar Hemon's *The Lazarus Project* [2008] and Ruth Ozeki's *Tale for the Time Being* [2013]), and metafictional rewritings of earlier novels (Mat Johnson's *Pym* [2011] and Victor LaValle's *The Ballad of Black Tom* [2016]). Discomfort with representing the present suffuses Ben Lerner's *10:04*, from the temporal themes of its intertexts (Robert Zemeckis's *Back to the Future* [1985] and Christian Marclay's *The Clock* [2010]) to its fictional artist character Alena who "deftly aged" and "distressed" her paintings so they "seemed as if they'd been recovered from the rubble of MoMA after an attack or had been defrosted from a future ice age" contrasted with a smaller, "unaltered" painted selfie that "was so located in the present tense that it was difficult to face."[12]

In some cases, recent works use temporal nonlinearity to signal reconsiderations of historical causality – not viewing history as inevitable, but rather infused with contingency and alternative paths – thus reckoning with the histories that did not take place, but were as likely (or more plausible) than those that did, as Mark Goble discerns in Chapter 11 with reference to William Gibson's *The Peripheral* (2014). Tommy Orange writes sardonically in *There There* (2018) of Native people who envision the irony that they have "been fighting for decades to be recognized as a present-tense people, modern and relevant, alive, only to die in the grass wearing feathers."[13] An earlier example is Ted Chiang's "Story of Your Life" (1998), which is narrated in spliced timelines to represent (spoiler alert) the protagonist's altered consciousness after learning an alien language that activates a nonlinear experience of time. As several contributors (Naimou [Chapter 1], Orbán [Chapter 4], Brady [Chapter 8], and Goble [Chapter 11]) demonstrate, temporal and geographic compression and extension in recent years have led to thoroughly reconceptualized narrative forms from flash fiction and microtemporalities to the definitionally inconceivable breadth of the Anthropocene. For example, Egan's *Visit from the Goon Squad* attenuates and expands temporality through categorically different techniques than modernist novels by Virginia Woolf or William Faulkner, while Luiselli's *Lost Children Archive* cites *Mrs. Dalloway* (1925), among other twentieth-century works, as a source.[14] Ruth Ozeki's narrative experimentation with presentness in *A Tale for the Time Being* is too multidimensional to sum up, but the pun of its young protagonist's name, Nao, broadens into multilingual, transtemporal, and metafictional speculation traversing Buddhist spirituality and physicist Hugh Everett III's "many-worlds" conception of quantum mechanics: "The observer was singular, and now you are plural. You can't interact and talk to your other yous, or even know about your other existences in other worlds, because you can't remember . . ."[15]

You

After today you'll never hear a plane in the same way again. But you don't know that yet.

Mia Alvar, "Esmeralda"

You can tell it any way you want, he said, you can be I or he or she or we or they or you and you won't be lying, though you might be telling two stories at once.

China Miéville, *This Census-Taker*

The recent fiction by Ted Chiang, Jennifer Egan, Sesshu Foster, Ruth Ozeki, and Claudia Rankine referenced in the previous section share another distinctive formal innovation in addition to their representations of mixed temporalities – they also pursue what has been historically a rare narrative trick: emplotting second-person narrative perspective. Data analytics are not necessary to determine that something is afoot. Consider this initial inventory of recent partial or full second-person narratives: Alvar, "Esmeralda" in *In the Country* (2016); Chiang, "Story of Your Life"; Egan, "You (Plural)" and "Out of Body" in *A Visit from the Goon Squad*; Louise Erdrich, *Future Home of the Living God* (2017); Foster, *Atomik Aztex*; Mohsin Hamid, *How to Get Filthy Rich in Rising Asia* (2013); N. K. Jemisin, *The Broken Earth* trilogy (2015–2017); Akil Kumarasamy, "At the Birthplace of Sound" in *Half Gods* (2018); Luiselli, *Lost Children Archive*; China Miéville, *This Census-Taker*; Tommy Orange, "Thomas Frank" in *There There*; Ozeki, *A Tale for the Time Being*; Rankine, *Citizen*; Jeff VanderMeer, *Acceptance* (2014); Vendela Vida, *The Diver's Clothes Lie Empty* (2015); and Ocean Vuong, *On Earth We're Briefly Gorgeous* (2019). In this volume, Angela Naimou (Chapter 1) discusses George Saunders's second-person story "Home" (2011), and Scott Rettberg (Chapter 5) considers second-person narration in digital fiction platforms. A 2013 anthology collected recent essays written in the second person, while the volume *Radical Hope* invited prominent authors to channel Baldwin's *The Fire Next Time* by writing "letters of love and dissent in dangerous times," many of which deploy the epistolary second person, such as Achy Obejas's contribution, "You."[16] Not only has the frequency of these narratives increased, so too have their genres and themes proliferated, as the epigraphs to this section signal. Mia Alvar's "Esmeralda" forebodingly depicts the experiences of a Filipino-American service worker in the World Trade Center prior to September 11, 2001, while China Miéville's spare, post-catastrophe *This Census-Taker* intersperses a third-person narrative of the protagonist's childhood with his second-person perspective as an adult.

Another telling, if unscientific, piece of evidence for the rise of second-person discourse comes from Google's Ngram graph of Google Books, which shows a recent and unprecedented rise in the word "you" in twenty-first-century publications (Figure I.1).

The upward curve of usage since the mid-1960s is notable (and perhaps unsurprising to some, like Tom Wolfe, who famously dubbed the 1970s the "Me" decade), spiking with no signs of a slowdown in the twenty-first century.[17]

Pronominal politics abounds throughout literary history, so that alone is not distinctive, but the twenty-first-century You-narrative form differs in signal ways from its prominent precursors: the Romantic self, the Transcendentalist I, the Lyric I (and apostrophized You), modernist free indirect discourse and shifting third person, literary manifestos, and post-modern metafiction. Although recent engagements with narratorial You are deeply engaged with social and political trends, they are also distinct in kind from prominent twentieth-century literary predecessors, including Ayn Rand's *Anthem* (1938) (narrated in the first person plural because singular pronouns have been banned), Albert Camus's *The Fall* (1956), Jay McInerney's *Bright Lights, Big City* (1984), Italo Calvino's *If on a Winter's Night a Traveler* (1979), and Lorrie Moore's *Self Help* (1985).

However, some twentieth-century works anticipate contemporary literary engagements. James Baldwin's *The Fire Next Time* (1963) famously begins with a second-person address to his nephew, while Jamaica Kincaid's *A Small Place* (1988) draws on multi-genre techniques of life-writing, reportage, and postcolonial theory in a narrative addressed to travelers in Antigua seeking exoticized escapism while overlooking the afterlives of slavery on the present-day tourist economy for Antiguans. The direct address of the narrator led some readers to feel, as the *New York Times Book Review* put it, that *A Small Place* "backs the reader into a corner," unintentionally validating the power of Kincaid's narratorial point of view.[18] Theresa Hak Kyung Cha's *Dictee* (1982) uses second-person narrative form in her "Epic Poetry" chapter to address the narrator's mother across migrant time in the present tense after fleeing the Japanese invasion of Korea: "you are eighteen years old .... The tongue that is forbidden is your own mother tongue. You speak in the dark .... I write you. Daily. From here .... You are here I raise the voice."[19]

If twenty-first-century second-person narratives are also attuned to the distant immediacy of digital interactivity, the contemporary proliferation of You-narratives may be an expression of a new set of relations between artists and audiences, in some cases a copresence between cultural producers and recipients. For example, Facebook, Instagram, and Twitter function as

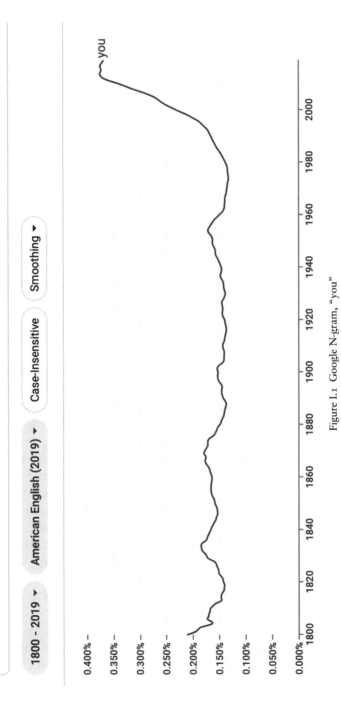

Figure I.1 Google N-gram, "you"

9

serial, long-form self-publishing platforms. Digital environments offer compelling formats for You-narratives to represent simultaneity within an
expanded present tense, as Scott Rettberg points out regarding interactive
fiction in his chapter on "Digital Fiction" (Chapter 5). In addition to the
examples in the previous two paragraphs, another key predecessor is the
Choose Your Own Adventure series (1979–1998) of interactive narratives
that drew on and extended the logics of the 1970s emergence of video
gaming and personal computing.[20] Atari, Inc., for example, was founded
in 1972 as an early game developer, and the first Commodore computer was
sold in 1977 with the model number PET 2001). Edward Packard's original
title for the book series was "Adventures of You," and the prolific Bantam
publications retained the present-tense, second-person narrative form.
Netflix sought to combine the two 1980s trends in a new form of "interactive movie": *Black Mirror: Bandersnatch* (2018) followed by *You vs Wild*
(2019), the former of which was the basis for a lawsuit brought by
Chooseco, the publisher of the *Choose Your Own Adventure* series, as a
violation of trademark law. Although not interactive, the Netflix television
series *You* (2018–present) (adapted from a novel by Caroline Kepnes)
updates the serial killer narrative genre for the social network age.

The twenty-first-century post-privacy era of drone-, cell phone–, and selfie-
surveillance is a media environment perfectly suited to the problematics of
agency in the overlapping arenas of gaming, entertainment, journalism, politics, and everyday life. The faux realism of "reality television," with its winking
confluence of naivete and irony, has roots in the traditions of documentary
naturalism, the French New Wave, and satire (e.g., *This is Spinal Tap* [1984]).
In retrospect, Steven Soderbergh's 1989 debut film, *sex, lies, and videotape*
anticipates the mediatized relations among the ribald, voyeurist, isolating, and
opportunistic. These cultural forces would be used by, for example, *The
Office* (2005–2013), *The Jersey Shore* (2009–2012), and Donald J. Trump.
The latter channeled the rage of white working-class voters in the 2016 presidential campaign through techniques drawn from the soap opera toolkit of
reality television (*The Apprentice*, 14 seasons 2004–2015), including nick-
name insults, hairpin plot twists, and reiterative scandals.

In his 1994 second-person short story "Videotape," Don DeLillo narrates
an experience of visual media fixation on a taped serial murder that anticipates internet-age reiterative viewing of violent scenes: "You sit there thinking that this is a crime that has found its medium, or vice versa – cheap mass
production, the sequence of repeated images and victims, stark and glary and
more or less unremarkable."[21] Soderberg's film and DeLillo's story all but
explicitly challenge their audiences to confront their visual addictions, which

have only been collectively stoked in the decades since by the ever-increasing proliferation and customization of screens that view and track us as we watch them. Having a 1980s-era tabloid fixture–turned reality TV impresario–turned politician in the White House provides a stark contrast of the changing dynamics since the 1970s between privacy/secrecy and public lives such that some observers have paralleled Trump's presidency to the crimes of Watergate, but acted out in public view via Twitter and 24-hour news channels.[22]

Drawing on the ominous forebodings of economic downturns, global crises, environmental disasters, and digital omnisurveillance, Ben Lerner's *10:04* narrates the blackout of a flooded Lower Manhattan, reevoking other harbingers of urban disaster, both foreseen and shocking. The novel concludes with a shift in tense and perspective as Superstorm Sandy submerges a powerless lower Manhattan:

> Sitting at a small table looking through our reflection in the window onto Flatbush Avenue, I will begin to remember our walk in the third person, as if I'd seen it from the Manhattan Bridge, but, at the time of writing, as I lean across the chain-link fence intended to stop jumpers, I am looking back at the totaled city in the second-person plural. I know it's hard to understand.
> I am with you, and I know how it is.[23]

The protagonist distances present experience as material for future memories with the key distinction that the distancing of memory makes one's own prior self into a third-person character of a story ("I will begin to remember ... as if").

Another literary reckoning with imminent violence and tragedy takes shape in N. K. Jemisin's use of the second-person perspective. Beginning with "a personal ending," a son's death, which makes "the end of the world" inconsequential, the prologue to *The Fifth Season* (2015) is titled "you are here" and continues: "But you need context. Let's try the ending again, writ continentally. Here is a land."[24] Chapter one, "you, at the end," begins "You are she. She is you. You are Essun. Remember? The woman whose son is dead ..... Only three people here know what you are, and two of them you gave birth to."[25] Jemison has described her use of second-person narration as a way to represent the "dissociative state" of a woman in the aftermath of her son's murder, who has been "forced through pain and suffering again and again and again, and by a system that isn't going to stop."[26] Jemisin's deep futurism retemporalizes present-day events of police violence, institutional inequality, and ecological precarity. Speculative fiction, she has suggested, can be "a realism" of the contemporary, one in which apocalypse is not a singular event, but a durational experience without end: "This is what the world is for some people. It is the apocalypse again and again and again ... everyone is now suffering this particular apocalypse," which she identifies with "watching Ferguson."[27] In this sense, as Candice Jenkins argues in Chapter 6, Afro-Pessimism draws productively upon the logics of speculative futurism, which Samuel Delany has described as the literature of the present.

The early twenty-first-century efflorescence of second-person narratives cannot be explained by a singular, unified origin, as it draws on a variety of distinct, yet simultaneous trends. Digital media and social networks have generated new interest in dialogic engagements (as both new platforms for conversation and as monologues that simulate dialogue) through the regularization in everyday life of videocalls, tweets, social media posts, videos, videogames, and so on. Digital and electronic fiction have picked up on the distant and screen-mediated simultaneity of twenty-first-century dialogue.[28]

The absence of gender and number specificity in "you" has led authors of transgender narrative to the second-person as well, such as Porpentine Charity Heartscape's Twine works, which Rettberg takes up in Chapter 5.[29] Ann Leckie's *The Raven Tower* (2019) is narrated by a god made of stone who addresses the warrior Eolo, a transgender man who emerges as the novel's central character. In a time of historic social change regarding conceptions of race, gender, and sexuality, conversations over the ethics of engaging difference and/as the homogenizing violence of empathy have yielded a wider sense of modesty about speaking in others' voices. Experiments with the narrative "you" may be a way of respecting the distinct experiences of those who are not the speaker without enacting the homogenizing merger of an undifferentiated "we" or a substituted fictional "I" or "she." Writers have long wrestled with the problematics of narrating characters with social identities and experiences that differ from their own. In the years prior to the Civil War, Herman Melville's "Benito Cereno" (1855) famously represents Babo, the masterful leader of a slave revolt, solely in the performed role of a servant, thus omitting his voice and perspective. You-narratives, by contrast, explicitly acknowledge the limits of intersubjectivity, the boundaries of what one person can know of another's psyche. As dialogic narration that exteriorizes the character, it tells another's story, but does not claim to know her point of view. In Leckie's *The Raven Tower*, a god narrates, but does not represent the interlocutor-protagonist's interior life. What emerges is a divine, but not omniscient, monologue in which the addressee cannot hear because the speaker is both a god and rock. Moreover, the narrative's temporal perspective is geologic, stretching across millennia.

Slip

Jennifer Wortman's 2019 flash fiction "Theories of the Point-of-View Shift in AC/DC's 'You Shook Me All Night Long'" exemplifies fascination with multitemporality and the second-person perspective as well as cross-media intertextuality, mass culture/highbrow, and temporal shifts from 1980 to the present. The story opens by intertwining these concerns in three sentences:

> The speaker – let's call him Brian – is documenting the shift, á la Buber, from I-It to I-Thou relations, from subject-object to intersubjectivity. Confronted with his lover's fast machine and clean motor, Brian can no longer maintain his stance as autonomous male subject gazing upon the Other. He and his lover merge; he is shaken.[30]

Positing a surprising lineage for the twenty-first-century turn to You-narratives, Wortman takes the song's she/you perspectival shift as an opening to link Martin Buber's *I and Thou* (1923) to AC/DC's hit, with perhaps an implicit nod to linguist Emile Benveniste's theorization of pronouns.[31] As it merges techniques drawn from varied genres, the story also plays with non-gendered you and conceptions of the divine, like Leckie's *The Raven Tower*: "Brian understands the vocabulary of masculine and feminine can only be metaphor. As the ultimate You, God transcends material forms and their signifiers. Yet God also inhabits them."

In order to engage the broadest range of contemporary works, *The Cambridge Companion to Twenty-First-Century American Fiction* is divided into three parts – Forms, Approaches, and Themes – but one critical assessment that the volume's contributors share is an awareness that that slipstream is the new mainstream, and genre play has become not exceptional, but the methodological starting point for writers from Egan to Lethem, Miéville, Ozeki, and Whitehead. In her analysis of the rising prominence of recent short and flash fiction, Angela Naimou considers narrative brevity as an opening to geopolitical and temporal expansiveness in her chapter on "Short Fiction, Flash Fiction, Microfiction" (Chapter 1). Measured in major prize awards, sales, or downloads, short and short-short fiction have paradoxically thrived during the spatial and temporal conceptual expansions of, for example, globalization and the Anthropocene. Naimou identifies the techniques of short fiction representing planetary stories of migration, climate crisis, and evolutionary history in works by Teju Cole, Edwidge Danticat, Rachel B. Glaser, Viet Thanh Nguyen, and George Saunders. David James (Chapter 2) takes on another formal challenge posed by contemporary authors, the permeable boundary between modes of literary realism and experimentalism. Marking a shift away from postmodern inaccessibility, irony, and detachment, he argues that twenty-first-century novelists have infused narrative innovation with what he calls "alternative ways of seeing and sensing the world." Delineating a spectrum of literary experimentalism that includes works by Jennifer Egan, Ben Marcus, Cormac McCarthy, Ottessa Moshfegh, Marilynne Robinson, Merritt Tierce, Colson Whitehead, and Joy Williams, among others, James argues that recent novels engage social, economic, and political change and precarity through distinctive modes of aesthetic and formal mimeticism that reflect twenty-first-century contexts.

In a similar spirit, Mark Bould's chapter on "Speculative Fiction" (Chapter 3) begins with Jonathan Lethem's literary critical counterfactual in which the genre border between science fiction and mainstream literature never existed and all novels about science were considered one group. As Bould points out, the very term "slipstream" itself was coined by Bruce Sterling to refer to the disconcerting works of science fiction that played across the edges of varied genre definitions. Heady mixtures of literary conventions have informed all regions of fiction since then, as speculative fiction draws on and critiques archaic and futurist literary movements representing empire, environmentalism, disability, illness, violence, as well as racial, gendered and sexual alterities. Histories of dissolving high/low culture divides also inform Katalin Orbán's discussion (Chapter 4) of contemporary graphic fiction, as she posits the critical and popular emergence of long-form, verbal-visual works that push narrative conventions in new directions, such as spatial-temporal experiments (e.g., by Chris Ware and Richard McGuire), the use of visual metaphors and other conventionally linguistic literary devices, and genre-blurring distinctive to the drawn medium. The material properties of platform and medium figure prominently in Scott Rettberg's examination (Chapter 5) of digital fiction as literary engagements with computer code, video gaming, hypertext, audio and visual plug-ins, and virtual reality. Narratives with multiple or interactive pathways, role-playing and perspectival shifts, and mass authorship reconceptualize postmodern and contemporary literary themes and techniques within digital textualities.

Part II foregrounds methodological approaches to twenty-first-century fiction, starting with Candice Jenkins's analysis (Chapter 6) of Afro-Futurism and Afro-Pessimism as conceptual frameworks within which contemporary African American fiction has represented the past and present during "the Black Lives Matter era." Discerning an inherently speculative quality to the two distinct bodies of thought, Jenkins argues they share a "a certain radicalism – one inclined towards both building and destroying worlds." This speculative radicality infuses the work of a remarkably broad range of writers, including N. K. Jemisin, Jesmyn Ward, and Colson

Whitehead, with the generatively imagined restructured societies derived not from utopianism, but the negative effects of intractable historical racism. Julia Lee (Chapter 7) also identifies temporal, spatial, and affective innovation in twenty-first-century transpacific fiction. Locating formally innovative contemporary Asian American writing in the post-1965 contexts of migration, global economies of labor, environmental anxiety, language difference, and racialized violence, Lee shows how writers have represented new technologies of immediate communication across oceanic flows of migrants, commodities, information, and waste in disjointed, parallel, and nonsequential narrative structures. Childhood trauma lingers across time and geography in a story about a Filipino nurse by Mia Alvar, while novels by Min Jin Lee, Ruth Ozeki, and Thi Bui layer Asian and American modernities, postmodernities, and contemporary present tenses. Mary Pat Brady (Chapter 8) poses an alternative approach to hemispheric fiction by reading not according to the scales of concentric geometries of space (local, regional, national, transnational), but instead reconceptualizing what she terms "pluriversal novels of the twenty-first century." She argues for attending to the complexly mixed geographies, temporalities, and languages of novels that reject the dualism of monoworlds (center/periphery) for the unpredictability of stories anchored in multipolar space-times. While this is not an exclusively twenty-first-century phenomenon, she shows that pluriversal fiction has flourished recently, as works by Linda Hogan, Jennine Capó Crucet, Julia Alvarez, Gabby Rivera, Karen Tei Yamashita, Ana-Maurine Lara, and Evelina Zuni Lucero demonstrate.

The next two chapters examine literary engagements with trends of significant social change that have permeated popular culture, journalism, and everyday life. Trish Salah (Chapter 9) contextualizes the broad post-2010 emergence of transgender fiction in a longer history of earlier trans and queer fiction and theory while arguing that "trans genre writing" has found recent prominence as a new minor literature. Particular challenges have led trans writers to innovate at the levels of language and aesthetics, perspective (collective, but not homogeneous), and genre, among others. Moreover, these works thematize and challenge norms and imperatives of empire, race, history, visibility, and geography. Heather Houser (Chapter 10) considers the conceptual frameworks of a topic that bears on nearly every other chapter in this *Companion*, contemporary "cli-fi" and ecocritical approaches to current literature. When writers presume transformational climate change as a starting point, rather than an abstract possibility, they narrate an "uncanny valley of familiarity and radical alteration" that extends, accelerates, or alters the logics of the present into near or distant futures of drought, warfare, destitution, and superstorms.

Mark Z. Danielewski has distinguished his second novel *Only Revolutions* (2006) as centrifugal, from his first, *House of Leaves* (2000), which he describes as centripetal.[32] This volume's Part III considers four conceptual interpretive frameworks stemming from entropic and neo-structural forces underlying contemporary US cultures. Mark Goble (Chapter 11) uses the concept of convergence to explore the implications of formal and temporal compression, economy, and slowness in an age of unprecedented expansion and speedup. Richard McGuire's *Here* (2014) presents an extreme example of spatial restriction and temporal expansion, while novels by Ruth Ozeki, Richard Powers, and William Gibson juxtapose ecological, scientific, techno-logical, and theological timespans to human ones in ways that echo postmod-ern and science fiction precursors, but with very different aims and warnings in mind for denizens of the Anthropocene. By contrast to Goble's focus on narratives of spatial compression, Crystal Parikh's contribution on dissolution (Chapter 12) takes up narrative fragmentation to thematize outward-moving fictions of "interruption, isolation, suspense, and precarity." Starting with Valeria Luiselli's interviews with migrant asylum-seekers, Parikh argues that a defining feature of contemporary literature is its formal techniques of "dissolution and the fragment as vital aesthetic and stylistic forms to convey the splintering effect that global modernity in the twenty-first century induces." From Luiselli to George Saunders's short stories and novels by Celeste Ng and Jesmyn Ward, among others, Parikh argues that nineteenth- and twentieth-century narrative techniques have been remixed by contempor-ary authors who draw on realism and experimentalism to tell stories of ongoing and unresolved dislocation and vulnerability.

The concluding two chapters take up cultural responses to the ongoing violence perpetuated by mass incarceration and the global cycles of warfare and terror. Dennis Childs (Chapter 13) examines narratives of immobility based on police and state violence, imprisonment, and detention and deport-ation at national borders. He argues that "anti-carceral hip-hop" is the "aesthetic practice [that] represents the quintessential storytelling method for those most commonly targeted for police killing and imprisonment." Reading hip-hop narratives within a "long twenty-first century" of radical literary, political, and musical practices since the 1970s, he links recent works by Dead Prez, Reyna Grande, Ann Jaramillo, Kendrick Lamar, Monifa Love, Main Source, Invincible, and Askari X to those of James Baldwin, Angela Davis, Public Enemy, Chester Himes, George Jackson, Audre Lorde, Toni Morrison, Assata Shakur, and Malcolm X. Hamilton Carroll (Chapter 14) considers shifting trends across nearly two decades of post-9/11 novels from early works grappling with the unrepresentability of terror to recent narratives by Susan Choi, Mohsin Hamid, Joseph O'Neill, and Jess Walter that depict the everyday experiences of racialized precarity in a period of perpetual warfare, nuclear proliferation, migration catastrophes, and neo-ethnonationalisms. Political turmoil and violence by state and non-state entities remain central to twenty-first-century life, even as the events of September 11, 2001, have shifted from recent trauma to historical retrospection.

The chapters in this *Companion* offer literary critical perspectives on pressing social, political, and historical concerns by drawing out the cultural and social implications of formal paradoxes of scale, compression, economy, slowness, decay, and immobility in an era prioritizing aggregation, speed, expansion, productivity, and surveillance.

NOTES

1 Alex Williams, "Move Over, Millennials, Here Comes Generation Z," *New York Times*, September 18, 2015, Style section, 1.

2 For Obama advisor David Axelrod's assignation of "no drama," see Anne E. Kornblut, "Obama Central: Peace, Harmony, and Deep Secrecy," *Washington Post*, August 3, 2008, A15.

3 Stephen Colbert, "The Wørd," *The Colbert Report*, October 17, 2005; and Kellyanne Conway, interview, *Meet the Press*, January 22, 2017.

4 Richard North Patterson, "I Used to Write Novels. Then Trump Rendered Fiction Redundant." *The Atlantic*, March 31, 2019, www.theatlantic.com/ideas/archive/2019/03/richard-north-patterson-i-quit-novels-cover-trump/585901/.

5 Justin E. H. Smith, "The End of Satire," *New York Times*, April 8, 2019, www.nytimes.com/2019/04/08/opinion/the-end-of-satire.html.

6 See Gordon Hutner, "Historicizing the Contemporary: A Response to Amy Hungerford," *American Literary History* 20, nos. 1–2 (2008): 420–424.

7 Karl Mannheim, "The Problem of Generations" (1928) in *Essays on the Sociology of Knowledge*, edited by Paul Kecskemeti (London: Routledge and Kegan Paul, 1952), 276–320.

8 Fredric Jameson, *Postmodernism, or the Cultural Logic of Late Capitalism* (Durham: Duke University Press, 1991), ix. Among many recent discussions of periodizing this present, see Amy Hungerford, *Making Literature Now* (Stanford: Stanford University Press, 2016); Theodore Martin, *Contemporary Drift: Genre, Historicism, and the Problem of the Present* (New York: Columbia University Press, 2017); Rachel Greenwald Smith, ed., *American Literature in Transition: 2000–2010* (New York: Cambridge University Press, 2018); and Michael North, *What Is the Present?* (Princeton: Princeton University Press, 2018).

9 See Abram Foley, "Claudia Rankine, Friedrich Nietzsche, and the Untimely Present," *symplokē* 26, nos. 1–2 (2018): 225–236.

10 Sesshu Foster, *City of the Future* (Los Angeles: Kaya Press, 2018), front dust jacket. Ammiel Alcalay, "Sesshu Foster's *City of the Future*," *Bomb* 144, September 18, 2018, https://bombmagazine.org/articles/sesshu-fosters-city-of-the-future.

11 Valeria Luiselli, *Lost Children Archive* (New York: Knopf, 2019), 103.

12 Ben Lerner, *10:04* (New York: Farrar, Straus and Giroux), 27.

13 Tommy Orange, *There There* (New York: Alfred A. Knopf, 2018), 141.

14 Luiselli, *Lost Children Archive*, 379–380.

15 Ruth Ozeki, *A Tale for the Time Being* (New York: Penguin, 2013), 398.

16 Kim Dana Kuperman with Heather G. Simons and James M. Chesbro, eds., *You: An Anthology of Essays Devoted to the Second Person* (Gettysburg: Welcome Table Press, 2013); and Carolina De Robertis, ed., *Radical Hope: Letters of Love and Dissent in Dangerous Times* (New York: Vintage Books, 2017).

17 Tom Wolfe, "The 'Me' Decade and the Third Great Awakening," *New York Magazine*, August 23, 1976, 26–40.

18 Alison Friesinger Hill, "*A Small Place*, by Jamaica Kincaid," *New York Times Book Review*, July 10, 1988, 19.

19 Theresa Hak Kyung Cha, *Dictee* (Berkeley: Third Woman Press, 1995), 46, 56.

20 In *Electronic Literature*, Scott Rettberg points out that the earliest work of computer-based "interactive fiction was *Colossal Cave Adventure*," initially developed in 1975–1976 and shared electronically in 1977 (Scott Rettberg, *Electronic Literature* [Cambridge: Polity, 2019], 91).

21 Don DeLillo, "Videotape," *Antaeus* 75–76 (Autumn 1994): 59.

22 Barbara McQuade, "Trump May Be Committing Obstruction of Justice in Plain Sight," *Daily Beast*, February 20, 2019, www.thedailybeast.com/trump-may-be-committing-obstruction-of-justice-in-plain-sight.

23 Lerner, *10:04*, 240.

24 N. K. Jemisin, *The Fifth Season, The Broken Earth: Book One* (New York: Orbit, 2015), 1.

25 Ibid., 15.

26 Jason Kehe, "Fantasy Writer N. K. Jemisin on the Weird Dreams that Fuel Her Stories," *Wired*, June 17, 2016, www.wired.com/2016/06/wired-book-club-nk-jemisin.

27 Jessica Hurley, "An Apocalypse Is a Relative Thing: An Interview with N. K. Jemisin," *ASAP/Journal* 3, no. 3 (September 2018): 472.

28 Alice Bell and Astrid Ensslin, "'I Know What It Was. You Know What It Was': Second-Person Narration in Hypertext Fiction," *Narrative* 19, no. 3 (October 2011): 311–329. On gaming and affect, see Paul Wake, "Life and Death in the Second Person: Identification, Empathy, and Antipathy in the Adventure Gamebook," *Narrative* 24, no. 2 (May 2016): 190–210.

29 See also Danielle Clode and Shari Argent, "Choose Your Own Gender: An Interdisciplinary Approach to Studying Reader Assumptions in Second-Person Adventure Stories," *Poetics* 55 (2016): 36–45.

30 Jennifer Wortman, "Theories of the Point-of-View Shift in AC/DC's 'You Shook Me All Night Long,'" *Electric Lit* 56 (2019), https://electricliterature.com/theories-of-the-point-of-view-shift-in-ac-dcs-you-shook-me-all-night-long.

31 Martin Buber, *I and Thou*, trans. Ronald Gregor Smith (New York: Charles Scribner's Sons, 1937); Emile Benveniste, "The Nature of Pronouns," in *Problems in General Linguistics*, trans. Mary Elizabeth Meek (Coral Gables: University of Miami Press, 1971), 217–222.

32 Kiki Benzon, "Revolution 2: An Interview with Mark Z. Danielewski," *Electronic Book Review* (March 2007), http://electronicbookreview.com/essay/revolution-2-an-interview-with-mark-z-danielewski.

PART I

Forms

I

ANGELA NAIMOU

Short Fiction, Flash Fiction, Microfiction

By definition, short fiction does not go on for very long. It could be counted in words, as in Ernest Hemingway's apocryphal six-word story "For sale: baby shoes, never worn."[1] Or it could be measured by the sentence, as in Augusto Monterroso's "El Dinosaurio," widely regarded as one of the world's shortest stories: "Cuando despertó, el dinosaurio todavía estaba allí" ("When he/she/it awoke, the dinosaur was still there").[2] Or in letters and symbols, as in fiction published on Twitter in posts limited to 140 characters. Microfiction has been categorized as fiction less than a hundred words, flash fiction less than 750 words, short-short stories as long as several pages. Words that flash, stories in micro: short fiction forms highlight the relational and seemingly paradoxical experiences of reading as an embodied process in time and space. Short forms have a long history of creating something like a world within a word, or six or seven, a feeling conveyed in the famous slip in a letter from Martha to Henry Bloom: "I called you naughty boy because I do not like that other world."[3]

However defined, shortness is a constraint that may seem inadequate to the complex problems that occupy so much of twenty-first-century fiction. Studies in fiction have tended to center on the novel to track important aesthetic innovations and theorize the relation of fiction to ecological and social time scales so immense they exceed human perception and understanding. How an artwork may render large scales of time and geopolitical space sensible – or at least, imaginable – to human perception has long been a core aesthetic problem. Contemporary art forms and modes of thought attest to the urgency of identifying the global patterns and practices that nourish or degrade our worlds. How can it be that humanity is on the verge of planetary devastation but largely proceeds as though climate change were itself a fiction? How can storytelling illuminate what Rob Nixon has described as the racial-environmental "slow violence" inflicted in devastating but pointedly unspectacular ways, across vast geographies and within microscopic living cells?[4]

This chapter considers how twenty-first-century short fiction has shown itself remarkably powerful in its depictions of the long arcs and wide spans of interrelated problems generated by empire, global racial capitalism, environmental degradation, transnational labor and international migration, land rights, intersectionality, climate change, war, and technology. Short fiction may invoke larger scales of time and space quickly through citation, by making intertextual links to wider bodies of work and broader possibilities within contemporary fiction. Moreover, short fiction can be a major contributor to ongoing debates of the past few decades over literary representation and world-system circulation at large spatial and temporal scales – debates that have relied most heavily on the novel to conceptualize genre fiction and world literary systems.[5] From the short to the flash to the micro, in print and online, twenty-first-century fiction writers have been experimenting with the capacity of brevity to generate new directions in US fiction. Short fiction encapsulates global patterns and stages the interrelationality of time scales through its own narrative acts of scaling.

Short Fiction, Long Scales

The pervasiveness of short forms within twenty-first-century digital environments may seem to reinforce the presumption that short form enables short attention spans, as critics point to the forms of buzzwords, sound bites, talking points, text messages, FB posts, Instagram, GIFs, tweets and retweets that make up an "Age of Distraction."[6] By contrast, novels may require longer spans of attention and construct more complex temporalities by manipulating narrative lengths and reading duration. Reading science fiction novelist Kim Stanley Robinson's nearly 2,000 page–long *Mars* trilogy (1993–1996), for instance, Lindsay Thomas argues that the sheer length of *Mars* enables its narration of climate change as a set of heterogeneous, ongoing, and intersecting human and nonhuman temporalities, in direct contrast to the media of US disaster preparedness scenarios, which represent disasters as discrete and requiring "detached" and immediate responses that maintain the status quo.[7]

Large scales of time and space seem to promise the conceptual power to address big problems, leading to debates over the maximalist novel, systems novel, "mega-novel," encyclopedic novel, modern epic, or the global novel. Consider the related debates over the Anthropocene in contemporary fiction studies: coined in 2000 by a chemist and a biologist, the Anthropocene is a proposed epoch of geologic time to highlight humanity's role in planetary changes, affirming "humanity and planet as interdigitating concepts of time."[8] Both globality and the Anthropocene could be addressed in potentially any literary form. But, as Ursula K. Heise observes in her essay on science fiction and the Anthropocene, "most of these studies" on literary form and large scales of time and space focus on how "literary forms – *the novel above all* – might be able to accommodate the spatial scale and cultural heterogeneity of an entire planet."[9] These big ideas take time, and long-form fiction seems to have more of it.

Compounding the preoccupation with the contemporary novel form is the short story's "long-standing theoretical neglect" in general.[10] Major literary prizes have also participated in the soft devaluing of the short story and short story cycle form. That sentiment is encapsulated in this two-sentence-long story by flash fiction writer Lydia Davis:

> I was recently denied a writing prize because, they said, I was *lazy*. What they meant by *lazy* was that I used too many contractions: for instance, I would not write out in full the words *cannot* and *will not*, but instead contracted them to *can't* and *won't*.[11]

The Man Booker Prize, the Pulitzer Prize, and the National Book Critics Circle award have not had separate categories for novels and short stories, and short story collections overwhelmingly lose against novels. Even sympathetic book prize jurors have written to reflect on why the odds have been stacked against this "little Cinderella genre" from making it to the palace.[12] It has been left to genre-specific prizes in science fiction, fantasy, mystery, romance, or horror to reliably promote short fiction.[13]

The vaunted rise of MFA workshops has been crucial to short fiction genres, especially the short story cycle, a sequence of stories that are both autonomous and interrelated.[14] With MFA programs "steeped" in the short story as their "primary pedagogical genre form," the short story and short story cycles have wide readerships and are ubiquitous to twenty-first-century fiction.[15] Yet short fiction remains under-theorized in contemporary fiction studies: one critic of the short story cycle calls it "the most neglected and the least well understood of the major genres in American literature."[16]

With notable exceptions, authors cross and remix writing across genres more capaciously than genre-based studies and book-classifying markets tend to acknowledge. Meanwhile, writers describe single-authored short story collections as less marketable than novels (though anthologies can be highly profitable, such as Penguin's American short stories list and Norton's *Sudden Fiction* series). Viet Thanh Nguyen has recounted how his breakout reputation as a serious literary author was made with his Pulitzer Prize–winning novel *The Sympathizer*, although he had initially hoped to sell his short story collection *The Refugees*, which he'd spent seventeen years writing:

> My agent had the collection of short stories, and he said "Oh, I love it, but you really need to write a novel to sell in New York," which is what everybody says, so I wrote the novel.

Only after the enormous success of the novel did his agent sell *The Refugees*, knowing it would be more valuable and marketable when it could ride on the novel's success.[17]

After his 2015 novel came the 2016 nonfiction book *Nothing Ever Dies*, his 2017 collection *The Refugees*, and his 2018 edited collection of short essays, *The Displaced: Refugee Writers on Refugee Lives*, which redirects the marketing momentum into humanitarianism, with the publisher's pledge to donate $25,000 minimum to the International Rescue Committee (IRC), a humanitarian aid, relief, and development nongovernmental organization that works with refugees and displaced persons.

Nguyen's story about publishing *The Refugees* resonates with one Amy Tan tells about *The Joy Luck Club* (1989), which she envisioned more as a short story collection inspired by Louise Erdrich's *Love Medicine*.[18] But her publisher insisted it be marketed as a novel: the compromise on the cover identified it as a "first work of fiction."[19]

Perhaps in belated recognition of wider literary trends, 2013 was a notable year for short fiction. Alice Munro won the Nobel Prize for Literature, as the only author to write exclusively short stories to win the prize.[20] And Davis won the Man Booker International Prize that same year. Indeed, short-form fiction has been a key site of literary experimentation in the late twentieth and early twenty-first century, as digital technologies diversify its forms and modes of circulation. Contemporary venues include Twitter, Inc.; Kindle Singles and Audible (owned by Amazon); YouTube (acquired by Google, Inc.); and start-up mobile apps such as Hooked, which promotes "chat lit."[21] Without giving way to technophilia, such developments combine the desire for newness in literature and global capitalism with the potential to change the way we make, circulate, access, and experience an old form – short fiction – in twenty-first-century contexts. And despite genre critics' commiseration over theoretical neglect, short fiction is widely discussed in twenty-first-century literary studies in ways that show less concern with strong genre definitions than in the impressive generic flexibility of short forms and big concepts.

As a verb, scaling transforms: we can scale objects up and down, we can encounter a concept as mammoth and as micro. A devotion to the large and not the small is to miss the full complexity of both. One can look to two recent special issues of the journal *New Literary History* as registers of new attention to scaling and its effects, or affordances, across literary forms, genres, histories, and methodologies. The desire to make social sense of literary scaling leads the editors of "Writ Large" to speculate on intellectual pathologies such as "megalophobia" or "the pervasive suspicion in contemporary intellectual life concerning the big picture."[22] The editors of "In Brief" likewise attempt to make social sense of literary scaling in the frames of pathology ("Brevity seems like a new disease")[23] and futurity ("While the twentieth century's promise of prosperity was often outsized – titanic ships, megahomes, and SUVs – the twenty-first century offers tiny forms for a microsized life: ever-shrinking communication devices, eco-friendly tiny homes, nanoscale robotic particles attached to cancer drugs").[24] Of course, the idea that we attend to either the large or the small is a false choice: one cannot be thought without the other. Scale, after all, engages fundamental questions of writing, reading, form, materiality, and conceptualization.

A Brief History of US Short Fiction

A brief literary history of the US short story may be in order here. Susan Lohafer observes that the modern short story developed within the nineteenth-century print economy as a way for writers to get paid and for newspapers to sell copies and advertising space. Several high points in short story literary history followed: Edgar Allen Poe's 1842 review of Nathaniel Hawthorne's *Twice Told Tales* (1842) established a theory and method for the short story as a distinct genre aimed at achieving a "single *effect*."[25] And the "little" magazines founded in the 1920s US South nurtured short story writers and the New Criticism in sometimes mutually reenforcing ways to make new critical modes of analysis the default for the teaching of literature and the short story form a preferred artifact for literary analysis.

The *New Yorker*, established in 1925 as a highbrow humor magazine, became the preeminent forum for short stories after World War II. Two *New Yorker* stories published in 1948 highlight two major directions for the genre: J. D. Salinger's "A Perfect Day for Bananafish," the story of a war veteran on honeymoon (with a wife and mother-in-law he loathes) who kills himself, and Shirley Jackson's "The Lottery," the story of a small New England town whose annual ritual is to select one of its own to be stoned to death by the community. Lohafer sees the short story as veering at times in the direction of Salinger – "toward the urgency of the lyric ... where form renders feeling"[26] – and at other times, toward Jackson, "the polish of the riddle," chaos economically ordered into "a paradigm of truth."[27] The short story form can gain complexity through compression: it opens realms of psychic interiority and gives shape to a system of power, or pulls at these two directions in formally experimental ways.

In the 1970s–1990s, the short story cycle became crucial to the enormous increase in the publication of multiethnic US literature. One critic credits the cycle's prominence among African American, Native, Latin@, Arab American, and Asian American writers to the way it "invites tensions between reality and fiction and between multiple traditions" of storytelling.[28] Writers of the period include Alice Walker, Toni Morrison (with "Recitatif"), Toni Cade Bambara, Gayl Jones, James Baldwin, Rudolfo Anaya, Leslie Marmon Silko, Louise Erdrich, Sherman Alexie, Sandra Cisneros, Junot Díaz, Edwidge Danticat, Jamaica Kincaid, Julia Alvarez, Bharati Mukherjee, Jhumpa Lahiri, Joseph Geha, Evelyn Shakir, and many more. These writers variously engaged with the post–civil rights movement and histories of racial violence and accommodation within the United States, as well as the rise of the category "ethnic writer," and of neoliberal globalization and diasporic, transnational imaginaries. Susan Koshy's concept of "minority cosmopolitanism," for example, names one way to reconcile ethnic studies and minoritarian critique to world literature and theories of cosmopolitanism.[29] Much of this short fiction grapples with how to accommodate large scales of history and geography via diaspora, migration, ethnic formation and erasure, cosmopolitanism, transnationalism, and the subjects who forge a present amid "imperial debris," to invoke Ann Stoler.

This project continues in twenty-first-century American short fiction. Long Le-Khac points to the formal possibilities the short story cycle offers for narrating transnational communities in his reading of Aimee Phan's short story cycle *We Should Never Meet* (2004), which takes the story cycle form rooted in regionalist fiction emphasizing local community but adapts it "to tell stories of transnational displacement" from French colonization and US war in Vietnam.[30] Such fiction activates potentialities of the form while transforming literary conventions around how to narrate transnational migration. Dina Nayeri's "The Ungrateful Refugee" (2019) reflects on her own refugee migrations through her university course on American "outsider fiction," with short stories by Bernard Malamud, Flannery O'Connor, Bharati Mukherjee, and James Baldwin, as an exercise in theorizing canon formation no less than the burdens of refugee gratitude.[31]

The transnational circulation of twentieth-century short fiction and microfiction in translation has influenced US short-form fiction significantly, if one considers the fiction of Franz Kafka, Bertold Brecht, Italo Calvino, Naguib Mahfouz, Julio Cortázar, and others. Among them, Argentine writer Jorge Luis Borges is a key figure. Written mostly in the 1930s–1950s and gaining international recognition during the so-called Latin American Boom generation of the 1960s and 1970s, Borges's stories conceive of the philosophical and material conundrum that is the universe.[32] In "The Aleph" (1945), the narrator Borges looks into a cellar hole only a "little more than an inch" in diameter, but where every act in the universe could be seen – an experience free from the referential and sequential operation of language:

> In that single gigantic instant I saw millions of acts both delightful and awful; not one of them [...] occupied the same point in space, without overlapping or transparency. What my eyes beheld was simultaneous, but what I shall now write down will be successive, because language is successive.[33]

What follows is a brilliant anaphoric sequence of impossible simultaneity seen in the Aleph. Borges's Aleph is both simultaneous and sequential: "aleph" is precursor to the Greek "alpha" and named for the first letter in Semitic languages of Arabic, Hebrew, Syriac, Phoenician, and Aramaic. Inspired by texts such as *Alf Layla wa Layla* (*1,001 Nights*), the fantasy is an access to the universe that is free of duration.

If the short form depicting long scales tries to "capture" a moment, it will similarly be difficult not to notice how small is the container for such big content. In thinking about the heterogeneity of temporalities and of spatialities that narrative fiction engages, issues operate at global and planetary scales *because* they operate at the small scales of ordinary, lived realities, such as in the activity between a toxic chemical and the living cell in a single body. Short forms, in this analogy, might open up ways to register the global in the cellular.

Short Origin Stories of the Universe

Narrating the enormity of the universe in a short story is a mode of aesthetic compression that has its own tradition in parable or aphorism. To narrate the *origins* of the universe or a similarly Great Thing as a short story, however, raises temporal issues drawn from the longer genres of epic, novel, or tragedy. Science fiction and fantasy writer N. K. Jemisin uses genre mash-ups to activate multiple time scales in her 2016 piece "The City Born Great."[34]

In the story, New York City is actually a living breathing biological entity that gestates for unpredictable durations of time before a chosen midwife helps it get born. Afterward, "the cord is cut and the city becomes a thing of its own, able to stand on wobbly legs and do ... well, whatever the fuck a living, thinking entity shaped like a big-ass city wants to do." Jemisin literalizes metaphors of urban development and renewal to challenge gentrification and the targeting of poor and racialized residents. The city's chosen midwife and avatar is a young, houseless black New Yorker who promises to "sing and paint and dance and fuck and cry the city before I'm done, because it's mine." The city's birth begins when inhabitants and travelers cause enough tears in the fabric of the city to begin the "separation." If it survives its own birth, the city will keep on struggling against ancient forces and eventually grow weary and die. The city is "at war with a cosmic monster" inspired by H. P. Lovecraft's Cthulhu, a "tentacled thing" that in Jemisin's story "takes the form of a cop with too many eyes, arms, and legs."[35] Even as Jemisin vaults the city to a cosmic timescale, the metropolis of millions becomes a single injurable life form inseparable from the human singer of its "birthsong."

Using the short to tell the long is the narrational mode of Rachel B. Glaser's "Pee on Water" (2010). Time shuttles forward in the story, in echoes of Rick Moody's "Boys" (2001), but on a planetary scale. The story is a mash-up of historiographic, scientific, and literary styles that deflate or parody the long-held conventions for representing Grand-Scale History. It reads like a perverse chronicle of evolutionary and technological progress, an unflattering timeline of the development of human complexity delinked from ideas of progress or perfectibility.

The short, present-tense declarative sentences that comprise the story play on the style of Dick-and-Jane readers and parodies the timeline as historiographic genre and progress as political ideology. The story indirectly highlights the imperial, patriarchal, racial, political ideas of the human.

But Glaser doesn't write a counter-narrative to correct the record. What gets told, what gets skipped over, what series of achievements gets included – this is where Glaser plays with the absurdity but also the possibility of telling a coherent narrative of time since the start of Earth: "Atoms bump and lump. Birds have sex. Bears have sex. The sun gets better at setting. Monkeys play with sticks."[36] There's a collation of what we call "telling details," otherwise deemed insignificant but for their ability to make some bigger subject memorable. It becomes a funny way to explain long time scales: the line "The sun gets better at setting," for example, deftly pokes fun at human perception, in which the sun revolves around the human. The sun doesn't get better at moving, of course, but the view that sees a sun "set" or "rise" begins and gets entrenched as the metaphor of scientific observation, telling us more about the observation than it does about the observable object.

The rhetorical thread pulling the short story across long time scales is the biological need for release that can also become an act for marking territory, demonstrating power, disciplining bodies: "They pee on grass. Pee on dirt. Pee on snow …. Early men paint, cry, stare into fire meditatively. Pee on grass. Pee on dirt …. Men feel cool playing the lute. They pee in private" (516–519). The closest moment to a plot development concerns the inventor of the toilet, who "wants a machine that will whirl it all invisible."

But "a smell creeps out of the pipes. The inventor's friends laugh" (520). Infrastructure lags, but soon, "Everyone begins to pee on water," even as people continue to pee on grass (520–521). It is a narrative of human progress told through the organs for sex and waste.

From there comes the strongest urges for power and repression: the short story makes quick shifts between the silliness of learning to urinate on water and the distress of statements describing how humans get educated into sex and sexual assault, as in one sentence about fifth-grade boys showing fifth-grade girls a porn tape featuring an assault, where "A boy laughs. A girl tries it out, laughs a little too" (521). Meanwhile, "On New Year's, everyone looks funny in their 2020 glasses, 2050 glasses, 2086 glasses" (523). The sheer redundancy of "pee on water" gives a long, flat view of humanity as the changing same, resistant to meaningful transformation.

The Long Arcs of a Short Life: Self-Citation, Transnational Labor, and Narratives of Migration

"It took Arnold six and a half seconds to fall five hundred feet." Danticat's opening line to her 2018 stand-alone short story in the *New Yorker*, "Without Inspection," starts with the freefall of Arnold, a Haitian migrant who loses his footing on a scaffold while he works on the construction of a high-rise Miami hotel, his body "sliding out of his either loosened or broken safety harness."[37] Plot development is grim and short: beyond those six and a half seconds, Arnold lands in the drum of a cement mixer truck, is found nearly dead, and holds on to life between morning and the midday news broadcasts. The narration ends with his "half-consciousness" surveying the scene of news crews, bystanders with smart phones, and officials prepared to read statements about his "tragic death."

"Without Inspection" occurs in a short time at one location, it is focalized through one character, and the narration of his thoughts revolve mostly around his life; Darline, the woman who rescued him from shore and became his lover; and her son, Paris. Nonetheless, it is expansive in two major ways: First, it draws on formal techniques used in novels of globalization. Second, it is a stand-alone short story that acts like a linked one in a short story cycle, implicitly referencing the larger body of the author's work so that the short story participates within the bigger fictional world and historical imagination of Danticat's fiction and nonfiction. My reading highlights the intertextuality of minifictions across Danticat's work in ways resonant with Lauro Zavala's concept of "dispersed short stories," where short stories are not stand-alone texts but instead are fictions that can be arranged by readers into different sections or fragments or minifictions across novels or multiple texts.[38] This way of thinking redefines short stories through acts of reading, shaped by "a reader's engagement with a mode of generic textuality that resembles a conceptual art project."[39]

In "Without Inspection," Arnold's narration contains multinational histories, international migrations, and the broad sweep of capitalist investments and hotel industries alongside the uneven modes of precarity created by the racist migration, detention, and deportation regime that migrant and immigrant laborers must navigate. The story links itself to other nodes within Danticat's wider body of writing, sometimes by reconfiguring them. The result is that one short story stands alone yet contains within it the international and transnational threads, recursiveness, and accumulations of meanings that create locales, themes, histories, plots, and characters in her writing.

Its engagement with long scales of time and space happens in a scenario where, according to cliché, one's life is supposed to flash before one's eyes. There is no flashing: Arnold's expansive powers of imagination take their liberty with time – his will can elongate the time so that he feels free to contemplate, to imaginatively visit his beloveds, to recount the moment when Darline rescued him from the shore, to remember when Darline told him about her own harrowing attempt to cross the sea with her husband, who drowned in front of her, and her son, whom she pulled out of the water, the boy forever changed by the experience, whose "mind had been partly lost somewhere between the sea and the beach."[40]

In falling from a great height and thinking to himself, "it was simpler to be free. As free as this fall, which he had neither intended nor chosen," Arnold is linked to the Haitian father character Guy in Danticat's short story "A Wall of Fire Rising" (*Krik? Krak!*, 1995), where Guy launches and then jumps out of a hot air balloon owned by the owners of the sugar mill where he can only obtain occasional work cleaning latrines. Guy's thoughts of emasculation and frustration, his obsession with the freedom of flight, fill the short story before he is in the air: the narration stays on the ground looking up, the story's end focalized through the perspectives of his wife and son who watch in horror. "Without Inspection," by contrast, begins with the laborer falling and finding a kind of freedom in the fall. He may be a partial echo of Guy as well as of the spectacular "falling man" from the Twin Towers in NYC, and of Delillo's 9/11 novel of the same title. Danticat's narration is focalized through the laborer's consciousness in a moment of violence that is spectacularized for a moment – but that, unlike the falling man, will never achieve iconic status or national importance.

In his reflection on crossing the sea to reach US land, he and Darline become the surviving counterparts to the two unnamed lovers in "Children of the Sea" (*Krik? Krak!*). In that story, the young man, whose radio activism makes him a political target, flees on a boat toward Miami but never arrives, while the woman and her family stay in hiding. In "Without Inspection," Arnold may be the only one who survives a capsized boat. The terror of drowning becomes a defining experience that Danticat evokes in describing Arnold's fall: in the drum of the cement mixer, he gasps for air and tries to reach the sanctuary of the cement shaft as his body churns up and down in the drum, threatening to suffocate him with the grout, pebble, and sand, his blood streaking the mix. And yet it's as if Arnold is calling back to the lovers from "Children of the Sea." In an echo of the young lovers' refrain, "My love for you is endless as the sea" comes the line after his death, "There are loves that outlive lovers. Some version of these words had been his prayer as he fell."[41]

Arnold remembers the moment when he is washed up on shore where Darline quickly rescues him: "If you'd stayed, they would have taken you to Krome," she explains, "It's a prison for people like us." Krome is another node in Danticat's oeuvre: it is the detention center she describes in her nonfiction memoir *Brother, I'm Dying* (2007), when her elderly uncle uses his valid travel visa to travel from Port-au-Prince to the Miami International Airport to declare his need for temporary asylum. Instead of refuge, he is interrogated and sent to Krome, denied his necessary medications, and dies in the custody of the Department of Homeland Security, an agency created after September 11, 2001. Again, it is a possible fate that Arnold escapes: having entered the country "without inspection" or official declaration of his intent to apply for asylum, Arnold circumvents immigrant detention.

In Arnold's ability to take his time is something that can only happen as he is dying in a city where he was forced to live as if he did not take up any space. Without "humanitarian parole" or any official status, he learned that "technically, he wasn't even here" (14). His own temporal daring becomes that of the author-narrator's:

> He did not know how long this half-consciousness would last, his being able to think and remember, so he wanted to keep pushing, to see how far he could take it …. Arnold felt the time growing shorter, so he would not be going all the way back to his childhood in Port-de-Paix. (12)

Nonetheless, Arnold pushes against the shortening time by remembering when he was a "child servant in a household, given away by whoever had brought him into the world" (12). Arnold's experience as a child of the restavek system, as an unpaid servant who is supposed to receive care and education by the family in exchange but is in practice vulnerable to abuse, links him to Danticat's characters including Claire from her novel *Claire of the Sea Light* (2013), the daughter of a fisherman who makes his emotionally wrenching decision to send her to live in the care of an important woman in the town of Ville Rose, itself a place that recurs in Danticat's earlier novel *The Dewbreaker* (2004) and *Krik? Krak!*.

Arnold ends his conscious time with a visit to his death site, where he hears reporters broadcasting the official statement issued by the construction company and developer in time for the midday broadcasts: "We are deeply saddened by the tragic death of Ernesto Fernandez," his subjectivity concealed by false corporate feeling and Arnold's false name (17–18).

The "six and a half seconds" of falling expands into most of the narrative duration. Arnold's impossible narration counters the large-scale societal patterns that, broken by design, go "without inspection": migration laws designed and enforced to deny asylum to Haitian nationals; labor and safety laws designed to mean nothing without inspections and enforcement; news media that present the liability-concealing official statement, as if it were reportage of true facts; and the many interrelated histories, large and small scale, international and regional, that vanish from the public acknowledgment of a migrant worker whose official name remains not his own.

Short-Range Vision and Global Militarized Atmospherics

Short fiction convention calls for a small number of characters and minimal background – or atmospherics, to use a different metaphor. It may be that, in exploiting or inverting these expectations, short fiction forms can most provocatively depict the failure to accommodate narrative forms to the systems and practices that organize human life and death-making in the twenty-first century.

The US-led global war on terror – with its complex of war times, war zones, and acts of war not named as such – is among the global forms of violence that exceed the vocabulary and grammar of current political imaginations. US writers are just beginning to reckon with how twenty-first century US militarism is changing the generic scripts of American war fiction, which have reinforced nationalist fantasies of melodrama or revenge from at least the nineteenth-century frontier to contemporary drone killings potentially anywhere. One way to illustrate the aesthetic and political challenge that the global war on terror poses for short fiction is to take up the subject of the war in an explicit way, as a counter to unevenly accessed knowledge about the war on terror in US publics – even by politicians, veterans, drone pilots, intelligence agencies, guards, and private security or service providers that most directly participate in its acts of militarized violence.

The fiction I want to highlight in this section very deliberately refuses documentary realism or melodrama, two main modes in US war fiction focused on the soldier's hell or effects on the home front. Opting out of the explanatory power of fiction, these short stories instead track the after-effects of "9/11" and the "war on terror" as if they were something in the air that can be felt only without clarity, diffuse on a planetary scale but also the stuff we breathe and become – what Teju Cole calls the "cruelties that persist in the psychic atmosphere like ritual pollution."[42] Wars with no clear names (How many times has "Iraq" been conflated with its historical adversary, "Iran"?), no collective memories but as condensed into the iconic "9/11," no justifications that match the official record to its reality. The vague and vast becomes a new non-language for the way war operates with the dim awareness of so many, even those who fight in it. Saïd Sayrafiezadeh's "Paranoia" (2011), George Saunders's "Home" (2011), Teju Cole's "Seven Short Stories about Drones" tweets (2013); his collab-oratively tweeted, single-authored short story "Hafiz" (2014), and Zadie Smith's "Meet the President!" (2013) each contend with the aesthetic, epistemological, and ontological problem of an unjust and undefined war on terror by experimenting with ways to either challenge its vague atmos-pherics or to more exaggeratedly render it.[43]

The opening line to Sayrafiezadeh's "Paranoia" reads: "When April arrived, it started to get warm and everyone said that the war was definitely going to happen soon and there was nothing anybody could do to stop it."[44] The narrator, a young man named Dean, ponders over speculations and disagreements and analogies about "the war" in an accumulation of clichés: the American people are mostly "on the same page" (4) about cheering for the war, news programs keep Americans in the know by reporting false information from military sources as "a deft misdirection to fool the enemy" (27). The obvious media spectacle and nationalist fantasies of "the war" saturate the public discourse: "The channels all showed the same footage, and all the experts agreed: 'Resistance was futile.' 'Ladies and gentlemen,' the newscaster said, 'blink and you might miss this war'" (27). Dean frequently indulges in masculinist hero fantasies of his day as simulations of a soldier at war. Riding a crowded city bus in hot weather, he thinks his ten minutes must be what it was like for soldiers in a foreign land. Watching news of American soldiers who landed at the bottom of ten-thousand-foot-high mountains in order to go up and then down them again, he doesn't think what a Sisyphean or sadistic exercise it was: instead, he wonders what it was like "to reach the summit."

But the motif of "the war" runs through a story that isn't supposed to be about "the war" at all. "Paranoia" recounts the story of a long on-and-off-again friendship between Dean, who describes himself as "blond and white," and Roberto, who is "dark–dark-skinned, dark-haired, from some village in Chile that nobody'd ever heard of," and, importantly, "alone and illegal" (5). Dean's quest to visit Roberto in the hospital becomes the occasion for Dean's experiences of Americanness as whiteness. In the end, Roberto is deported, while his immigrant shoemaker with legal status boss proclaims to Dean that the deportation hurts him as much as it must hurt Roberto. And the young black man Dean had earlier met and dragged into an argument over whether there would be a draft suddenly appears in a parade of new military recruits, while Dean condescendingly calls after him, "I told you there wasn't going to be a draft!" (26).

Long before and after Tim O'Brien's The Things They Carried (1990), the veteran has been the central character in US war fiction. The veteran as narrator informs a literary imagination of war that participates in the political fiction that soldiers carry the primary burden and risk of war, with little theorizing or historically informed critique of the modes and logics of contemporary militarized violence.[45] The short-form fiction that follows explores the atmospherics of post-9/11 militarism within and beyond the traditional confines of US war fiction.

Originally published in the New Yorker, Saunders's "Home" (2011) begins with a narrator visiting his working-class mom after some time. We only learn he is a returning veteran when his mother's lover greets him with the question "What's your worst thing you ever did over there?" The two have never met. Mikey gets caught up on old news: his mother's former lover left her, she has cancer, she has a new lover who swears as freely as his mom would if she weren't changing her speech for the sake of her new church job, his sister has a baby and lives somewhere nicer but her husband "is a hitter." Ma and her lover Harris turn out to be florid talkers and easy liars. When they visit his sister, she corrects the record and reminds Mikey that he has an ex-wife and children he has not yet visited since his return.

Mikey and his military service become things Ma and Harris can use in their own conflicts: confronting the landlord over an eviction notice, Harris invokes them as "the family of a hero," and the landlord mumbles thanks to

Mikey for his "service."[46] Service is a strange euphemism for the militarism that made his leave and return so difficult. At the story's climax, after the family intervenes to stop his gathering rage, Mikey relents: "Okay, okay, you sent me, now bring me back. Find some way to bring me back, you fuckers, or you are the sorriest bunch of bastards the world has ever known" (204).

In his second-person direct address, "you" could be you the family, you the people, you the state. Saunders recalibrates the figure of the returning veteran haunted by memories of war to ask where have they, and we as publics, been sent? What has changed in the deformations of war since 2001, and what is the line of continuity with the years 1900–2000, when not one year was free of US military missions somewhere in the world (Dudziak)? Can "we" bring ourselves "back," and to what?

Saunders's firm grip on the absurdity of American war is here in the second-person address and the ordinary hurt and failure between people. The formal experimentation of "Home" is quieter than in his absurdist ghost-war novel *Lincoln in the Bardo* (2017), but its distancing techniques highlight the despair, confusion, and deep absurdity that becomes sometimes the truest way to understand war. In this "Home" continues a tradition more akin to Joseph Heller's novel *Catch-22* (1961) or Ben Fountain's novel *Billy Lynn's Long Halftime Walk* (2012) than it does to Tim O'Brien's collection *The Things They Carried*.

Cole brings the absurd into focus most explicitly through brevity in his microTwitter fiction about drone strikes. With every major military operation comes technical innovation in devastation. For the twenty-first-century war on terror, which innovated from the celebrated "smart bombs" and "guided missiles" in the massive aerial bombardment of Iraq in the Gulf War (1990–1991), that innovation has been the weaponized drone. Cole's "Seven Short Stories about Drones" (2013) consists of seven sequentially released tweets (Figure 1.1).

Figure 1.1 "Mrs. Dalloway" tweet by Teju Cole (2013) (Copyright © Teju Cole, used by permission of The Wylie Agency LLC. With thanks to Kelsey Sheaffer for image reproduction.)

Within a month, Cole published the tweeted lines as a single paragraph in his *New Yorker* essay "A Reader's War":

> Mrs. Dalloway said she would buy the flowers herself. Pity. A signature strike leveled the florist's. Call me Ishmael. I was a young man of military age. I was immolated at my wedding. My parents are inconsolable. Stately, plump Buck Mulligan came from the stairhead bearing a bowl of lather. A bomb whistled in. Blood on the walls. Fire from heaven. I am an invisible man. My name is unknown. My loves are a mystery. But an unmanned aerial vehicle from a secret location has come for me. Someone must have slandered Josef K., for one morning, without having done anything truly wrong, he was killed by a Predator drone. Okonkwo was well known throughout the nine villages and even beyond. His torso was found, not his head. Mother died today. The program saves American lives.[47]

"Seven Short Stories about Drones" is limited to Twitter Corporation's 140 maximum allowable characters per tweet. This compression highlights the boundary between genres of war and peace by disregarding it: the endings, like the drones, seem to come out of nowhere. The compression also encapsulates the experience of social media content more generally, as the jarringly incongruous content of the opening and the ending words in each story is ready for an almost-simultaneous moment of reading.

Each "short story" also foreshortens what should be longer (as a novel) and what should have been longer (as a human lifetime). Each story opens with a line from canonical novels: Virginia Woolf's *Mrs. Dalloway*, Herman Melville's *Moby Dick*, James Joyce's *Ulysses*, Ralph Ellison's *Invisible Man*, Franz Kafka's *The Trial*, Chinua Achebe's *Things Fall Apart*, and Albert Camus' *The Stranger*. Each get cut violently into short stories by the intrusion of a weaponized drone. The "short story" is one where narrative development cannot happen because a US-initiated program to freely kill people anywhere in the world scrambles the ending and cuts it short. Cole relocates the drone killings from the Global South onto the coordinates of canonical novels that circulate widely in US and European university courses and are likely read by the same *New Yorker* and *The New York Times* subscribers he identifies as part of his readership.

The stories have a beginning and an end – but their extreme brevity violate the rules of a storyworld not only in terms of character and story development but in terms of a violent death that comes down from a zone of power silently hovering miles above the ground, with not even the sound of a war plane audible to the people below. It highlights the cruel grotesquery of weaponizing spatial and temporal disjuncture itself – so that a pilot sits in a suburban strip mall office cubicle in somewhere-town USA to remotely fly a weaponized drone above the heads of people in Afghanistan, Libya, Yemen, Somalia, or Pakistan. As people show up on screen, the pilot releases the bomb that instantly wreaks the most horrific brutality on human bodies.

This digital microfiction project plays on high literariness and Cole's lived relationality to drone killing, as he makes clear in response to an interview question about his "particular interest in drones":

> I know someone whose brother was a drone pilot and it didn't kill him – but it messed up his mind completely. You're killing people. And you're seeing them. We do something called double tap – we go back and kill the rescuers. That's policy.[48]

In interviews and commentary, Cole suggests that "Seven Short Stories about Drones" variously affirms literary community and criticizes its assumed ethical center, and that it reiterates literary writing and writing on social media as distinct registers that can inhabit the same space. Our "comfort zone" appears to be a dark zone of disavowal: Cole's account of his project sees Twitter as a way to have small units of text not only transport us out of our collective comfort zones but also to do so by circulating those units of text at the global network scales made possible by Twitter and its users.

Cole's microfiction – including "Hafiz," the short story he wrote and then had a network of Twitter users tweet, line by line, with coordinated timing to keep the story's original narrative sequence – can be understood in a wider literary experimentation with social media, where writers "have an audience." Lisa Siraganian's reading of modernist Twitter poetics, however, points out that "commercial platforms such as Twitter" put the poetry that emerges there into "a commercial and legal gray area in which an individual writer's creation helps generate capital for massive companies without that writer receiving reimbursement for her work." The point holds for prose as well as poetry. And, as she points out, the very term "platform" – something we usually describe as being given to a speaker to elevate her visibility and better project her voice – obscures the profit and copyright dynamic that is really at work between the writer whose artistic output gets monetized and commoditized into Twitter profit (206).

Cole released these first lines of "Seven Stories about Drones" to an online community constituted by social media networks in order to spotlight an untouchable program of high-tech corporeal violence encapsulated in the stories and in public discourse by the single word "drones."

Cole's literary conceptualization of the Internet and of the novel form in his 2014 *Open City*, whose publication occasioned his taking "a break" from Twitter, are deeply linked. Maria Bose argues that his digital storytelling projects on social media carry a political affirmation of "the network society" that is further complicated by what Bose reads as the novel's analogy of "traumatic memory to the technological unconscious as two species of with-held information, each working beneath the surface of consciousness."[49]

The virtual reality and instant data collection and streaming capacities of a near-future networked society that also enforces global apartheid on the right to move or make a life with resources, dignity, and political participation, and that hides the devastation of drone attacks: this is the nightmare of Zadie Smith's 2013 *New Yorker* short story, "Meet the President!" (reprinted in Marcus). It is a bleak storyworld where a fourteen-year-old boy of extreme wealth and privilege, appropriately "unused to proximity," loiters during one of his father's inspections of the areas deliberately kept in extreme deprivation. Bill Peek "had hit every mark that Pathways expected of its pupils – walking, talking, divesting, monetizing, programming, augmenting." He inhabits the cacoons of total institutional privilege and high-tech virtual reality. And so it becomes "all the more shocking" to find himself in close proximity with an abject young girl in the condemned zones. Aggie, the girl, is abandoned there by her old woman companion while en route to see her sister Melly's body being "laid out." The girl, Aggie, intimates that she is a target:

> "So it was all a lie," Aggie said, throwing her head back dramatically to consider the sky. "Plus one of them's got my number. I've done nothing wrong but still ... one of them thing's been following me, since the pier – even before that."

The boy pedantically corrects Aggie: what is vaguely called "the Program" is "a precise business," "they don't track children," and "if you've done nothing wrong ... you've nothing to worry about."[50] The narrative focalized through him echoes the mendacious public discourse on "smart" weapons and drone killings, and the reasoning that collateral damage was a minimized if unavoidable result of the fight against "those with bad intent."

Eventually, the boy finds himself helping the young girl get to her destination, all the while uploading videos of himself with Aggie for school credit. The boy merges his schoolwork and his virtual game – Meet the President! – with the material world he shares however unequally with the girl, until the climactic scene in which he is pushed forward toward the girl's sister's driftwood coffin, amid keening, jostled as he continues to play his game. Trapped amid the crowd, the girl grieving her sister, it ends with the sensing of an ominous surveillance from the sky.

The ominous surveillance from the sky in "Meet the President!", the drone-cut narratives of Cole's stories about drones, and the god-view that the narrator of "The Aleph" attains by seeing in the space of a single instant the "unimaginable universe" in all its simultaneity: short fiction can encapsulate long time scales and cascades of spatial scale, unhindered by the longer sequential form of narrative fiction in a struggle against its own entropy. In short fiction, flash fiction, and microfiction, there can be the flash of recognition that also transforms what and how we recognize life, violence, and collectivity through story.

This chapter has tracked the productive tension in twenty-first-century fiction between short forms and big troubles. This tension generates new relationships of fiction to a political and historical imagination, to citational modes that enlarge the fictional worlds of short stories, and to the repertoire for narrating labor, migration, and war – not only as experiences, but also as forces actively disavowed, willfully misunderstood, able to jump temporal and spatial scales.

NOTES

1 On Hemingway's apocryphal story in genre criticism, see Zack Wortman, "Daily Shouts Ernest Hemingway's Six-Word Sequels," *New Yorker*, September 11, 2016. See also Luisa Valenzuela, "Introduction: A Smuggler's Sack," in *Sudden Fiction Latino: Short-Short Stories from the United States and Latin America*, edited by Robert Shapard, James Thomas, and Ray Gonzalez (New York: Norton, 2010), 19. See also Diana Fuss, "Flash," *New Literary History* 50, no. 3 (Summer 2019): 405–410.

2 Augusto Monterroso, "El Dinosaurio," in *Obras completas (y otros cuentos)*. (Mexico City: UNAM, 1959; Mexico City: Ediciones Era, 1990), 71. See also Frederick Luis Aldama, "A Scientific Approach to the Teaching of a Flash Fiction," *Interdisciplinary Literary Studies* 16, no. 1 (2014): 127–144.

3 James Joyce, *Ulysses: The Gabler Edition* (New York: Vintage Books, 1986 [1922]), 63.

4 Rob Nixon, *Slow Violence and the Environmentalism of the Poor* (Cambridge, MA: Harvard University Press, 2011).

5 See, for example, theories of reading world literature by Wai-Chee Dimock, David Damrosch, Franco Moretti, Pheng Cheah, Bruce Robbins, Gayatri Spivak, and work by David Palumbo-Liu and Nirvana Tanoukhi, as part of the influence of Immanuel Wallerstein's world-systems theory on literary studies. See Ursula K. Heise, "Science Fiction and the Time Scales of the Anthropocene," *English Literary History* 86, no. 2 (2019): 275–304.

6 Several dozens of academic and mass-market lifestyle books published since
2000 offer diagnoses and prescriptions for everything from knowledge produc-
tion to everyday conversations, spirituality, reading, business leadership models,
and more. See, for examples, Alan Jacobs, *The Pleasures of Reading in an Age of
Distraction* (New York: Oxford University Press, 2011); P. M. Forni, *The
Thinking Life: How to Thrive in the Age of Distraction* (New York: St.
Martin's Press, 2011); Adam S. Miller, *The Gospel according to David Foster
Wallace: Boredom and Addiction in an Age of Distraction* (London: Bloomsbury
Academic, 2016); Robert Hassan, *The Age of Distraction: Reading, Writing, and
Politics in a High-Speed Networked Economy* (New York: Routledge, 2017);
Derek Thompson, *Hit Makers: The Science of Popularity in an Age of Distraction*
(New York: Penguin, 2017); Meghan Cox Gurdon, *The Enchanted Hour: The
Miraculous Power of Reading Aloud in the Age of Distraction* (New York:
Harper Collins, 2019).

7 Lindsay Thomas, "Forms of Duration: Preparedness, the *Mars* Trilogy, and the
Management of Climate Change," *American Literature* 88, no. 1 (March 2016): 162.

8 Heather Houser, "Human/Planetary," in *Time: A Vocabulary of the Present*,
edited by Joel Burges and Amy Elias (New York: New York University Press,
2016), 146. Proposed starting dates for this yet-unofficial epoch range from
50,000 BCE, when human hunting first contributed to species extinction, to the
colonization of the Americas beginning in 1492.

9 Heise, "Science Fiction and the Time Scales of the Anthropocene," 276,
emphasis added.

10 Victoria Patea, "The Short Story: An Overview of the History and Evolution of
the Genre," in *Short Story Theories: A Twenty-First-Century Perspective* (New
York: Bodopi, 2012), 7.

11 Lydia Davis, "*Can't* and *Won't*," in *Can't and Won't: Stories* (New York: Farrar,
Straus, and Giroux, 2014), 46, emphasis in original.

12 Caroline Adderson, "Globe Books 2013: Long Story Short, It Was a Remarkable
Year for Short Fiction," *The Globe and Mail*, December 27, 2013, www
.theglobeandmail.com/arts/books-and-media/globe-books-2013-long-story-
short-it-was-a-remarkable-year-for-short-fiction/article16116522.

13 Lincoln Michel lists the major genre fiction awards for "science fiction (Hugo and
Nebula), fantasy (World Fantasy Award), mystery (Edgars), romance (RITA) and
horror (Bram Stoker and Shirley Jackson Awards)." Lincoln Michel, "Should
Literary Awards Do More to Recognize Short Stories?" *Electric Lit*, April 19,
2016, https://electricliterature.com/should-literary-awards-do-more-to-recognize-
short-stories.

14 Jennifer J. Smith, "Born in the Workshop: The MFA and the Short Story Cycle"
TriQuarterly, January 30, 2012, www.triquarterly.org/craft-essays/born-work
shop-mfa-and-short-story-cycle.

15 The Editors, "MFA vs. NYC," *N+1 Magazine*, no. 10, Fall 2010, https://
nplusonemag.com/issue-10/the-intellectual-situation/mfa-vs-nyc.

16 James Nagel, *The Contemporary American Short-Story Cycle: The Ethnic
Resonance of Genre* (Baton Rouge: Louisiana State University Press, 2001), 246.

17 Michael LeMahieu, Angela Naimou, and Viet Thanh Nguyen, "An Interview
with Viet Thanh Nguyen," *Contemporary Literature* 58, no. 4 (2017): 444–445.

18 Wang quoted in Jennifer L. Smith, *The American Short Story Cycle* (Edinburgh: Edinburgh University Press, 2018), 90.

19 Dorothy Wang, "A Game of Show Not Tell: *The Joy Luck Club*," *Newsweek*, April 17, 1989, 69; Barbara Somogui and David Stanton, "Amy Tan: An Interview by Barbara Somogui and David Stanton," *Poets and Writers* 19, no. 5 (September–October 1991): 26, quoted in Smith, *The American Short Story Cycle*, 90.

20 Adderson, "Globe Books 2013."

21 Hooked, www.hooked.co.

22 Krishan Kumar and Herbert F. Tucker, "Introduction," *New Literary History* 48, no. 4 (2017): 610.

23 Irina Dumitrescu and Bruce Holsinger, "Introduction," *New Literary History* 50, no. 3 (2019): vii.

24 Ibid., ix.

25 Edgar Allan Poe, "Poe on Short Fiction," in *The New Short Story Theories*, edited by Charles E. May (Athens: Ohio University Press, 1994), 61, emphasis in original.

26 Lohafer, Susan, "The Short Story," in *The Cambridge Companion to American Fiction after 1945*, edited by John N. Duvall, Cambridge Companions to Literature (Cambridge: Cambridge University Press, 2011), 68–82.

27 Ibid.

28 Smith, *The American Short Story Cycle*, 90.

29 Susan Koshy, "Minority Cosmopolitanism," *Publications of the Modern Language Associations of America* 126, no. 3 (May 2011): 592–609.

30 Long Le-Khac, "Narrating the Transnational: Refugee Routes, Communities of Shared Fate, and Transnarrative Form," *MELUS: Multi-Ethnic Literature of the U.S.* 43, no. 2 (2018): 107.

31 Dina Nayeri, "The Ungrateful Refugee," in *The Displaced*, edited by Viet Thanh Nguyen (New York: Abrams Press, 2018), 146.

32 See Ilan Stavans, "El Boom and Its Aftershocks in the Global Marketplace," *Los Angeles Review of Books*, October 25, 2016, https://lareviewofbooks.org/article/el-boom-and-its-aftershocks-in-the-global-marketplace.

33 Jorge Luis Borges, "The Aleph," in *The Aleph and Other Stories* (1933–1969), ed. and trans. Norman Thomas Di Giovanni (New York: E.P. Dutton & Co., Inc., 1970), 26.

34 Originally published online at tor.com, "The City Born Great" appears in her anthology, N. K. Jemisin, *How Long 'Til Black Future Month?: Stories* (New York: Orbit Books, 2018), 14–33.

35 Lisa Shapiro, "For Reigning Fantasy Queen N. K. Jemisin, There's No Escape From Reality," *Vulture*, November 29, 2018, www.vulture.com/2018/11/nk-jemisin-fifth-season-broken-earth-trilogy.html?fbclid=IwAR1gsj6htnsCMwmihdNunHTEkj_k2orN5cz176uELCMghx3zbRMarjGDLoY.

36 Rachel Glaser, "Pee on Water," in *New American Stories*, edited by Ben Marcus (New York: Vintage Books, 2015), 517.

37 Edwidge Danticat, "Without Inspection," *New Yorker*, May 14, 2018, www.newyorker.com/magazine/2018/05/14/without-inspection.

38 Lauro Zavala, "The Boundaries of Serial Narrative," in Patea, *Short Story Theories*, 295.

39 Michael Trussler, "*Short Story Theories: A Twenty-First-Century Perspective* ed. by Victoria Patea (review)," *ESC: English Studies in Canada* 40, no. 2 (2014): 203.

40 Danticat, "Without Inspection."

41 Ibid.

42 Teju Cole, *Known and Strange Things: Essays* (New York: Random House, 2016), 261. Originally published as Teju Cole, "A Reader's War," *New Yorker*, February 10, 2013, www.newyorker.com/books/page-turner/a-readers-war.

43 Teju Cole, @tejucole: "Seven short stories about drones." Twitter, January 14, 2013, 12:02pm., https://twitter.com/tejucole/status/290866560309030913?s=20.

44 Saïd Sayrafiezadeh, "Paranoia," in Marcus, *New American Stories*, 3.

45 See Yến Lê Espiritu, "The 'We-Win-Even-When-We-Lose' Syndrome: U.S. Press Coverage of the Twenty-Fifth Anniversary of the 'Fall of Saigon,'" *American Quarterly* 58, no. 2 (June 2006): 329–352; see Vasuki Nesiah, "Human Shields/Human Crosshairs: Colonial Legacies and Contemporary Wars," *All Unbound* 110 (2016): 323–328.

46 George Saunders, "Home," in Marcus, *New American Stories*, 187.

47 Teju Cole, "A Reader's War," in *Known and Strange Things: Essays* (New York: Random House, 2016), 259.

48 Adnan Khan, "Teju Cole Is Way Better at Twitter Than You," *Vice*, August 27, 2013, www.vice.com/en_us/article/9bz9q8/teju-cole-wants-to-keep-us-on-our-toes.

49 Maria Bose, "Virtual Flânerie: Teju Cole and the Algorithmic Logic of Racial Ascription," *C21 Literature: Journal of 21st-Century Writings* 7, no. 1 (April 2019), https://c21.openlibhums.org/article/id/772.

50 Zadie Smith, "Meet the President!," in Marcus, *New American Stories*, 310.

2

DAVID JAMES

Experimental Fiction

"What fiction is not experimental?" By the lights of Marilynne Robinson's frank question, my title might appear to be a misnomer, or at least something of a tautology.[1] The modifier's exact purpose has indeed been notoriously hard to define. And yet, however redundant or distracting *experimental* can seem, this has done nothing to alter the epithet's purchase over time, whether for critics who use it as a byword for aesthetic esteem or for writers for whom it is a badge of honor awarded in recognition of their eschewal of the marketplace in favor of the fringe. Beyond this avant-garde romance of marginalization, though, the category of experimentalism continues to evade capture, escaping neat typologies, formal stratifications, and generic quarantining. Given this, we might wonder, as Robinson rightly does, "[w]hat fiction does not work in delicate signals, flickers of sensation evoked by language that simulate the ways in which we know what we know?"[2] Sensation, language, simulation, knowing. Such are the raw materials of novelistic innovation, reminiscent certainly of modernism's idiomatic fusions of style and sensation, structure and epistemology, but no less current for American fiction today. To extend and intensify language's intimacy with experiences of sensing and knowing the world, and to simulate those experiences in the very anatomy of a novel's form, is often the (deceptively simple) essence of what experimentation means for writers who otherwise rarely rub shoulders in the stories criticism tells about them.

Popular perceptions of experimentation in the twenty-first-century American novel have often relied on its enduring kinships with postmodernism. For fiction to be experimental, according to this model, it typically bears the hallmarks of labyrinthine involution (Mark Z. Danielewski), encyclopedic exhibitionism (Ruth Ozeki), or bravura maximalism (David Foster Wallace). While offering useful coordinates for thinking about metafictional, linguistic, and generic aspects of invention after postmodernism, these views of experimentalism have infiltrated a critical discourse on literary innovation that privileges radical transgressions in mode, structure, or syntax, while privileging too the readerly workouts these disruptions supposedly entail. Workouts can be good for us, of course; but hermeneutic rock climbing is not the only way of apprehending what experimentation now does in fiction or why it can move readers as much as exhaust them. Indeed, it would surely be sanctimonious to insist that only formally forbidding fiction can rouse audiences from their middlebrow comforts, as though strenuous, perplexingly enigmatic narratives offer superior solutions to unreflective consumption and bovine escapism. To broaden the range of what counts as "experimental," as I hope to do across this essay, is to grant the term itself something of a reprieve. In what follows, I thus consider a number of twenty-first-century novels that wouldn't, at first blush, appear to be especially extravagant in their handling of language, event, or genre, and which operate at some distance from modernist and postmodern experimentalism's conventionally unfavorable reputations of opacity, exhibitionism, and difficulty. I choose this somewhat counterintuitive route in order to entertain varieties of experimentation that apply to inconspicuous moments of feeling as much as they do to the acrobatics of heterodox narration, which lead us down the affective avenues of ordinary experience as much as they dazzle us with flamboyancies of stylistic transgression. If, in the final decades of the twentieth century, postmodernism and experimentation came to be seen as virtually interchangeable, recent American writers have confronted that conflation and require, as a result, some adjustment in the very vocabularies with which we describe the affective impact and political import of adventuresome fiction, in all its multiple, unexpected incarnations. Their concerns, as the coming pages will reveal, often come to revolve around the precarity of overlooked, disenfranchised, or otherwise marginalized lives; and doing arresting justice to the emotional and social quiddity of those lives defines the aesthetic challenges American fiction now sets itself.

Experimentalism and Its Others

The temptation to posit innovative fiction in tenuous opposition to a cultural "mainstream" and the putatively acquiescent readers it allegedly nurtures is one that writers themselves have courted. Consolidating what we might call experimentalism's negative eminence, Raymond Federman declared in the mid-1970s that no writer "ever says to himself: 'I am now going to experiment with fiction'" because the label is typically bestowed by others – namely, "middle men" commentators, who deploy it "out of despair" in order to "brush aside" adventurous writing – while Ronald Sukenick caustically suggested a decade later that experimental fiction in practice "means something like 'no sales of subsidiary rights.'"[3] Across our postmillennial era, however, American writers have been expanding innovation's critical and creative valencies, extending the ways in which literature experimentally responds to cultural, social, and economic currents, while thereby provoking reflection on the very condition of fiction's artistic development and political efficacy. Whereas postmodernist fiction mobilized a self-conscious preoccupation with the narrative construction of history, overtly disclosing the novel's mimetic pretensions and limits in ironic (and often self-ironizing) displays of linguistic self-anatomization, the twenty-first-century scene has witnessed more aesthetically capacious and politically purposive reassessments of the potential for realism to converge with formal innovation. If the products of experimentation no longer seem synonymous with all that's purportedly inaccessible, then the procedures of experimentation no longer appear so wedded to subverting realist conventions in pursuit of avant-garde majesty. Consequently, novelists appear to have shifted away from the vaunted demonstration of metacompositional self-dissection or ludic self-parody toward a renewed interest in representation's possibilities (rather than its deficiencies or betrayals). In the process, they have sought to occupy multiple modes of expression, to span rather than strictly comply with genre models, and to synthesize styles in ways that defy stable classification – all the while soliciting equally agile forms of affective response.[4]

Before we get to twenty-first-century writers in detail, it's worth pausing to ask what experimentation itself might now designate. Tempting though it can still be to link literary experiment to a modernist ethos of making things perpetually new, in contemporary writing it may be as applicable to works that model alternative ways of seeing and sensing the world as to those that radically overturn conventions and generate formidable hermeneutic difficulties.[5] When viewed not only as a matter of stylistic athleticism, but as a purposeful extension of fiction's emotive and epistemic capacities, experimentation "proves there is always more to think and feel, always another mind to engage and enter, always intensities we did not know existed."[6] Not Robinson this time, but Ben Marcus; and on the basis of his defense of experimentalism as essentially less about formal elaborateness than about "the possibility of syntax as a way to structure sense and feeling," he sounds well in tune with her account of the capacity of fictional language to simulate alternative ways of perceiving and knowing.[7] In making the case for appreciating how experimental writing "leav[es] us ever hungrier to encounter sentences we've never seen before," Marcus had reasons to be more vociferous than Robinson, polemical though she often is when emphasizing the indispensability of literature's spiritual and epistemic vitality.[8] Marcus's target in defending experiment was Jonathan Franzen, who over time (and most cuttingly in a 2002 *New Yorker* piece, "Mr. Difficult") had questioned both the artistic purpose and readerly value of what he dubbed "status fiction." Precious, self-involved, unapologetically dense – the inventiveness of status novels, in Franzen's indictment, revolves around demonstrating that only the sort of "[p]leasure that demands hard work, the slow penetration of mystery, the outlasting of lesser readers, is the pleasure most worth having."[9] As the self-anointed legislator of that "compact between the writer and the reader," Franzen pictured the reciprocity between novelists and their audiences as a "contract" based on the cultivation of trust rather than alienating impenetrability. He thus concluded that as "the decades pass, the postmodern program, the notion of formal experimentation as an act of resistance, begins to seem seriously misconceived."[10]

Yet as Marcus subsequently observed in his 2005 riposte, what's actually misconceived in Franzen's image of readers longing to have "a good time with a novel" is the very nature and consequence of experimentalism itself.[11] And the problem is that this misconception has gone viral: "everywhere are signs that if you happen to be interested in the possibilities of language" and in "new concoctions of language that set off a series of delicious mental explosions – if you believe any of this, and worse, if you try to practice it, you are," concludes Marcus, "an elitist."[12] Abusing his privilege as an essayist and reviewer with immense cultural capital, Franzen has propagated this equation of innovation with elitism and in so doing has "managed to gaslight writing's alien artisans, those poorly named experimental writers with no sales, little review coverage, a small readership, and the collective cultural pull of an ant."[13] Realism not only rules; it also remains a lodestone for denigrations of formal adventurousness, where originality is situated as the enemy of "storytelling pleasure."[14]

And Marcus is not alone among twenty-first-century novelists in bemoaning the extent to which realism remains "by far the reigning style of contemporary literature, the incumbent mode, however loudly its adherents might claim underdog status."[15] An equally spirited opposition to mimetic conventions holding sway would detonate in Zadie Smith's much-discussed "Two Directions for the Novel," where "lyrical realism" is diagnosed as something of a postmillennial epidemic.[16] This dominant "breed" of writing, argues Smith, is "so solidly established" as to incite "a powerful, somewhat dispiriting sense of recognition," precisely because the mode "has had the freedom of the highway for some time, with most other exits blocked."[17] The latest blockers, though, may not actually be realist novels themselves, in all their linguistic multifariousness and affective complexity, but rather those advocates who perpetuate the "fallacy," as Marcus calls it, that "realists have some privileged relation to reality," and who thereby assume that "reality can be represented only through a certain kind of narrative attention." Such suppositions leave unquestioned the premise that "any movement away from [realism's] well-tested approach toward representing the lives and minds of people would be a compromise."[18]

For Marcus, antidotes to this delusion are offered by writers as different as Denis Johnson, Joy Williams, and Marilynne Robinson: such novelists "are keen to interrogate the assumptions of realism and bend the habitual postures around new shapes."[19] Realism itself, according to this argument, needs conceptually overhauling in ways that would view it as integral rather than antithetical to the transgressions conventionally allied with experimental fiction. Liberated from the perceived shackles of transparency, unselfconsciousness, linearity, or rhetorical moderation, realism could then be "conferred" on any narrative "that actually builds unsentimentalized reality on the page, matches the complexity of life with an equally rich arrangement in language," providing us with a term that might "be assigned no matter the stylistic or linguistic method, no matter the form." Within a revisionary framework of that sort, predicts Marcus, "Gary Lutz, George Saunders, and Aimee Bender would be considered realists right alongside William Trevor, Alistair MacLeod, and Alice Munro."[20] We may of course want to ask whether those "assumptions of realism" comprise something of a covert – and evaluatively convenient – fallacy in their own right, one that allows Marcus to redeem realist fiction for a new century only by making it something other than it supposedly is (or has been). Realism can make a comeback, in other words, thanks to its postmillennial departure from "habitual postures" that may turn out to be straw men: for on closer inspection, realism's "well-tested approach," from *Middlemarch* through to Munro, is far from predictable or stultifying in its consistency.

Nonetheless, it's difficult not to feel enthused by this vision of renewed rapport between realism and experimentation, because rumors of their divorce have rumbled on for decades and still periodically resurface in conversations about how we alternately affiliate and distinguish contemporary writers' formal aims.[21] Where "experimentalism" alone is concerned, synonyms – innovation, invention, originality – don't exactly resolve the conundrum it faces: a truly ingenious renovator of popular romance need not aspire to the avant-garde; dictional or structural inventiveness can be as at home in "social fictions" of chronic precarity as in neo-Impressionist novels of abandonment. Which is why, as we'll later see, a laconic treatment of workaday toil from Merritt Tierce may actually have things in common with a lyrical elegy of orphanhood by Christine Schutt, whatever the *process* of experimenting means respectively for these writers in practice. With such taxonomical tussles aired, how liberating would it be not to invoke such apparently fossilized epithets at all. And yet, they seem as durably persistent for novelists describing their own techniques as they are historically unavoidable for any reader interested in the critical construction of a field like contemporary American fiction studies.[22] All flexible, temporally motile designations have their drawbacks; they also, though, have their interpretive uses, if only as prompts for recognizing how agilely novelists vandalize our expectations.

Cataloging Innovation, Refurbishing Genre

Just as Robinson encourages us to wonder whether it's not the case that all fiction to some degree embarks upon experiments in language so as to simulate our complicated efforts to "know what we know," so Marcus pointedly asks why it should be called "an experiment to attempt something artistic" in the first place.[23] To take our cue from these dovetailing positions is to welcome rather than bemoan experimentalism's own categorical roominess, its omnivorous applicability beyond narratives that happen to be cognitively forbidding or constitutionally iconoclastic. And paradoxically, experimentation's generous embrace of a variety of stylistic strategies and historically contingent motivations is yet another facet of its filial bond with realism, capaciously understood. With that bond in mind, radically distinct novels come into conversation. My oncoming, oversized catalog bears the burden of proving this point, winging its way over the last two decades in an effort to draw otherwise unrelated works under experimentation's ample spotlight. Veins of affiliation are too numerous to collate here, of course; but certain threads stand out, especially in the way style and structure embody the emotional, ethical, and philosophical contours of plot, not simply reflecting but materializing diegetic action in the fibers of expression.

In one strand, language's very materiality and apparent tactility gains prominence: think of the propulsive phrasal torsions and grippingly delineated viscera of Colson Whitehead's zombie-thriller *Zone One* (2011), a novel that at once suavely and macabrely reanimates the dead, a reanimation that begets a more grief-struck mode in George Saunders's *Lincoln in the Bardo* (2017), with its generic cross-pollination of historical supernaturalism and vivacious switches in typography, an impulse taken to its maze-like extreme by the font-cavorting petition for investigative reading in Mark Z. Danielewski's *House of Leaves* (2000). Experiments in tone, meanwhile, fuel the delicate tightrope walk Ben Lerner attempts in *10:04*, where his granular chronicle of New York balances irony and sincerity, producing through (rather than despite) its narrator's interminable self-inspection moments that would otherwise seem like "anachronistic blossoms" in Lerner's realm of reflexivity, reparative moments where we're invited to learn what it means "to become one of the artists who momentarily made bad forms of collectivity figures of [the city's] possibility."[24] The dazzling chorus of *A Visit from the Goon Squad* (2010) enables Jennifer Egan to sustain a level of rhetorical flamboyance from one vignette-like episode to the next, which scarcely detracts from her poignant meditation on the onrush of time. In this multi-protagonist extravaganza, there are searing moments of pause, where Egan touchingly deploys prolepsis to foil precious recollections with devastating futures. Charlie, for instance, "feels" her brother's "self-consciousness miraculously fade" as they take to the dance floor on a trip to Africa, a time she will later "think longingly of" "as the last happy moment of her life." Seemingly unexceptional, it is nonetheless an episode "she'll return to again and again, for the rest of her life, long after Rolph has shot himself in the head in their father's house at twenty-eight: her brother as a boy, hair slicked flat, eyes sparkling, shyly learning to dance."[25] This tragedy's apparent inexorability is replicated within a sentence here that unravels without subordination, so that the moment Charlie longs to retrieve and preserve feels like it is already, grammatically, hurtling toward its catastrophic eventuality.

Catastrophe, albeit of a whole other scale, is the verbal motor too of Cormac McCarthy's *The Road* (2006), whose style forlornly retains a quantum of lyricism that confronts the novel's utter bleakness. In this post-apocalyptic environment, McCarthy's bare syntax on one level seems viscerally mimetic of the wasteland it evokes, while in another sense marshalling all that's left of description – a wrenching experiment in its right own, pitted against ecological and bodily enervation – to offer intermittently luminous retorts to despair that tease its reader's affective and aesthetic responses apart. If not in length, *The Road* is certainly epic in horror. And epic proportions suit the transcontinental reach of Ruth Ozeki's *A Tale for the Time Being* (2013), whose topically encyclopedic detours occasion gymnastic leaps in voice and perspective. Equally expansive and impishly self-reflexive, the intertextual density of Junot Díaz's *The Brief Wondrous Life of Oscar Wao* (2007) "anticipates its own audience," as María del Pilar Blanco has observed, while also mobilizing Oscar himself "as a cipher for an alternative reading of Antillean history." A paean to genre-fiction, the novel refracts Díaz's own "proclamation of the Antilles," in Blanco's phrase, "as a sci-fi space."[26] Díaz calibrates this politico-generic provocation against the radical precedents of Toni Morrison and Octavia Butler who, in his view, are "the most dangerous of artists," to the extent that they have "shown the awful radiant truth of how profoundly constituted we are of our oppressions" and "how indissolubly our identities are bound to the regimes that imprison us."[27]

49

Such a cluster of emblematic contenders has an inevitable whiff of hermeneutic heresy about it. A baldly catch-all conceit, this assembly of texts pulls under the liberally conceived banner of innovation writers who are, for the most part, too formally, ethnically, generationally, thematically, and politically diverse to be legitimately aligned for long. Then again, they do divide and regroup in their world-making (Danielewski, Egan, Díaz) and world-deforming (Whitehead, McCarthy, Lerner) designs, their experimentalism manifesting in emplotment as much as in prose, through their alternative environmental conjurations and demolitions. Either way, that's "experimentation" for you: sufficiently pointed, whenever required, to propel certain estimations about the fortunes of originality; adequately roomy for us to entertain artistic collectivities based on narratologically comparable ambitions, whose affinities might otherwise seem outlandish; and thereby so amply multitiered as to accommodate novelists whose idiosyncratic commitments stress-test even the most permissive methods of comparative reading.

Whichever way we select our optics of affinity, though, such groupings surely evidence that shared "embrace of the long-neglected storehouse of genre models," an embrace that epitomizes "the post-postmodern turn," as Andrew Hoberek observes: "models built up over the years when experimentalism and realism were understood, to varying degrees, to constitute the literary." One way of understanding this genre turn would be as a response to a historical moment in which "neoliberal capital" has itself become "obsessed with innovation." If entrepreneurial neoliberalism has made the "drive for aesthetic innovation" more or less "internally untenable and externally compromised" for American novelists, genre models have "reemerged as a kind of archive of conventions capable of providing a renewed backdrop for individual artistic expression." Far from leaving contemporary fiction still further implicated in the machinery of neoliberal self-cultivation, this scene is one in which "authors can just as easily use genre conventions," advises Hoberek, "to open up new formal possibilities not present in the realist/experimental matrix of twentieth-century modernism."[28] Released from that needless and now-redundant dichotomy, generic reformation becomes in itself an experimental venture, one that no longer depends on the ring-fencing of artistic innovation as an iconoclastic deconstruction of all that has gone before.

Beyond the symptomatic expression of changing political times and generic temperaments, however, what my focal writers in the coming pages have in common is perhaps something more straightforward but no less ponderable: namely, an impulse to evoke experience in such a fashion that structurally "matches the complexity of life," to recall Marcus's phrase, including life's precarities, "with an equally rich arrangement in language."

Just how varied that arrangement is in recent fictions that aren't, at first sight, overtly avant-garde is something that will hopefully become apparent in my following cross-section of established and emerging writers alike. Notwithstanding their differences, I mean to show how purposeful their acts of experiment can be; hardly cosmetic, modes of innovation expose rather than distract from their fiction's ethical and political ligaments.

Grammars of Vulnerable Life

To notice how the complexities of existence find purchase in style we need consider, as this section does, novels that offer slow-motion, particularizing accounts of social deprivation and existential fragility. In these works, expressive experimentation is oriented toward the experiential grammar of what Kathleen Stewart calls "[p]recarity's forms" – forms that "magnetize attachments, tempos, materialities, and states of being."[29] Among the most unflinching exposés of those states in recent years is offered by Merritt Tierce, whose *Love Me Back* (2014) tracks the psychic and familial costs of economic insecurity. The novel centers on Marie, a single mother in Dallas who tolerates long nights waitressing at an upmarket steakhouse, the toil of which she compensates with the obliterative help of risky highs and casual sex. The challenge Tierce sets herself is to extract stylistic vivacity and variation from the monotony of representing unending service work, revolving as the narrative does around the slog of "[d]oing the same thing every day. Same territory, over and over. Watching mammals eat."[30] As a result, *Love Me Back* exploits a brilliant discrepancy between syntactic rapidity and the plodding predictability of Marie's daily grind, a discrepancy that of course embodies the coexistence of inner freneticism and pristine self-presentation that she has to sustain while catering to the incessant requests of wealthy clients. Recalling the multiple challenges of working at the "Dream Café" – "somewhere with stairs, steps, ramps, outdoor seating, small water glasses," and "kids' menus"[31] – Marie attends to an impeccable family who were among the "regular people who spent more than two hours a day working out."[32] After settling the bill, they discover that she has lost their credit card:

> Excuse me, miss, he said, after I had dropped off the check, picked up the check, run the card, stuffed the vouchers back in the book, and dropped it off again with a Thanks so much, take care, and they had begun the process of packing up their baby, who was undoubtedly beautiful too but could barely be found in the middle of a gigantic machine that looked more like a Bowflex than a stroller. I was seating a table behind them when I felt a light touch on my elbow. I turned around. Yes sir? I said.[33]

For a seemingly unremarkable incident, Tierce ratchets up the sense of anticipation by increasing syntactic space between the man's initial appeal and Marie's eventual response through an intermediate, paratactic description of actions. Accretions of percussive verbs ("dropped," "picked," "stuffed") – compounded acoustically by telescoping assonance ("dropped off) and fricative slant rhymes ("off," "stuff") – are punched out in equally staccato clauses, which simulate Marie's unrelenting task of moving rapidly yet with poise from one customer to the next. Meanwhile, the embedded dialogue ("Thanks so much, take care") is quoted as the well-rehearsed and recyclable caption that it is – a rhetorical correlative to routine proficiency, not less indispensable for being so predictable. That single, periodic sentence thus not only creates a miniature moment of suspense within what might seem, at first sight, like a relatively inconsequential recollection of Marie's mishap; it also advertises to us, *through* its very construction, the mental, physical, and discursive tenacity required to keep going at this job, not least with the deftness for which she is poorly rewarded in light of the hours she has to put in.

If *Love Me Back* is lean, barbed, and clipped, then that shouldn't discount it from consideration as experimental. With a prose that's ferociously compact, displaying a zero-tolerance approach to embellishment, Tierce joins those "prominent minimalists who," in Mark McGurl's account, "pointedly reverse the seeming affinity of minimalism with silent masculinity, making it work to record and manage the trauma of female experience."[34] The kind of minimalism Tierce sustains is by no means an exclusively twenty-first-century phenomenon; but her effort to materialize through the leanly articulated velocity of her syntax the affective ramifications of insecure labor does encapsulate, in its purposeful braiding of content and form, a distinctly emergent mode of socially engaged experimentalism. As we've seen, Tierce's innovations lie in modulating diction and grammar so that any given "sentence," in Christine Schutt's phrase, "might sound as it means."[35] Language in *Love Me Back* becomes emotionally mimetic in this sense by doing less, as the novel closely reads precarity's ramifications by duplicating in its very style the embodied sensation of "being hard and relentlessly dazzling in spite of whatever shit," regardless of "any remorse or anguish" Marie harbors within.[36]

Schutt herself is a connoisseur of this variety of performative narration, whereby grammar and lexis become at once dramatically shaped by, while also formally encapsulating, "the scrim of memory and incessant excursions into the past," as she calls them. In this context, syntactic experimentation means equipping fiction to "construct a world" by "stitch[ing] together sensations of it."[37] Schutt's *Florida* (2003) epitomizes this mission. Sensory memories are captioned in a crystalline succession of vignettes, as Alice Fivey becomes her own storyteller to recount a childhood uprooted in the wake of her mother's desertion and a "mysteriously dead and only ever whispered about father."[38] The work of reconstructing episodes from an itinerant upbringing becomes both the novel's topic and its structural engine, as Alice announces that "[a]t ten, eleven, twelve, even older, I wanted everyone to know my story – to know it sharply, as one who rings the wounded might, with me, as its center, reciting: My father is dead, and I am only waiting for my mother to be well enough to take me away from these houses chapped by winter."[39] Adverbs (*sharply*) and adjectives (*chapped*) are collocated in striking terms with their objects (implied listeners, houses). These dictional decisions exemplify Schutt's conviction that just as "banging together unlikely words" constitutes "the fun part of writing" so thereby "[h]earing story is part of reading's pleasure."[40] *Florida*'s reader, inevitably, has to acknowledge that this same aesthetic pleasure is entangled with the rawness of dispossession, as Alice remembers one winter when "Mother never left the house but waved at me from windows to come in":

> "Come in, please! Come in!" she called from the house, the one I put my mouth to. Lip-prints or breath against the mirrors and windows, in such ways I could taste myself and loose-earth taste of the house. We conversed lovingly, the house and I. Everything was in its place and sensate and easily hurt. The front stairs often felt neglected, and the basement knew itself as ugly. Whatever was empty or kicked or slammed shut wept. I heard my father's closet mumbling.
>
> I knew this house.[41]

Home is figured as a refuge but also as a fellow intimate, enduring in "sensate" ways the twinned traumas of perennial loneliness and domestic disarray. Hence, if there's a certain "pleasure," as Schutt hopes, in admiring Alice's facility for entwining sensations by hearing verbally unorthodox combinations, then that gratification coincides with the reader's anguish at witnessing her effort to accumulate these lyrical shards of familial desolation in the first place. "*Stringent* and *inviolate* are words" that "students should learn,"[42] we're later told, leaving us to wonder whether they might not also be watchwords in the end for *Florida* itself. For this is a novel that enunciates everything lyricism cannot compensate or render inviolate, however stringently words labor to ameliorate damage with felicity, as though its own style registers the unsustainability of literary redress – knowing all too well that the "world is a comfort and then it is a discomfort."[43] Stringency would appear to be Schutt's motto, too. She attests that her prose "calls for close, hard readers of fiction,"[44] readers who confront in *Florida* a second-order commentary on its own fractal composition, as the novel fosters rather than resolves the tension between the consolation of collecting segments together and the consequences of replaying those vulnerabilities they memorialize.

Marilynne Robinson has also called for close and hard readers, as her "Gilead" series feels no less demanding for replicating the same story over and over again, landing on different sociopolitical issues and theological arguments each time. In the 2014 addition to this series, we encounter another orphan, the eponymous Lila: until recently homeless, she has for years endured an itinerant life until finding refuge in Rev. John Ames's small-town church. Now in old age, Ames discovers a partner in Lila, an astonishing turn of events that has "enlarged" his "understanding of hope," as he puts it in *Gilead*, "just to know that such a transformation can occur."[45] The couple have a son, Robby, whose very presence has "greatly sweetened my imagination of death, odd as that may sound" (231), just as his feelings for Lila have amounted to "a foretaste of death, at least of dying" (233). Precarity is the essence of what Lila and Ames share: destitution was one reason for her meeting him at all; anticipations of oblivion now intersect his astonishment at feeling "more alive than I have ever been" (60), knowing as he does that the "dream of life will end as dreams do end, abruptly and completely" (118).

Precarity is also the thematic frame and affective catalyst for Robinson's syntactic experiments in *Lila*, strange though it feels to call them that, given how composed and pellucid her free indirect discourse remains. "Fear and comfort could be the same thing," ponders Lila, well acquainted as she is with what it means to seek unlikely recesses from within unrelieved hardship.[46] But if she's expert in "[f]inding comfort where there was no comfort,"[47] Lila also knows the risks of impermanent consolation well. Because early conversations with Ames, for instance, "made a change in her loneliness, made it more tolerable for her," she intimates "how dangerous that could be."[48] The promise of amelioration is one that she has trained herself to ward off; but she assesses that "change" nonetheless and the tentativeness with which she eventually registers what it could mean is reproduced stylistically in a delicate progression from self-instruction to cautious resolve:

> She had told herself more than once not to call it loneliness, since it wasn't any different from one year to the next, it was just how her body felt, like hungry or tired, except it was always there, always the same. Now and again she had distracted herself from it for a while. And it always came back and felt worse. But she began to think about getting herself baptized. She thought there might be something about that water on her forehead that would cool her mind. She had to get through her life one way or another. No reason not to

take any comfort the world seemed to offer her. If none of it made sense to her now, that might change if she let it. If none of it meant anything, after all, no harm done.[49]

Lila second-guesses the implications of accepting "any comfort." This reflection's poignancy finds a grammatical vehicle here in the double negatives and partially anaphoric phrases of those closing three sentences, where Lila's sense of resolution – about committing herself to a course of action that just might offset the "loneliness" to which she's habituated and prefers not to name – competes with hesitation. She has to argue the point, it seems, in order to penetrate the armor of emotional vigilance she's accustomed to wearing and that would normally deflect any intimation of how life "might change," thereby shielding herself from false consolations. That she has to argue the case at all evinces its very own pathos. For the reader knows by the end of this halting decision to reach out to the church in the hope of "get[ting] through her life one way or another" that perseverance has scarcely been a choice or virtue for Lila. Year on year, she has rarely been able to take anything other than precarity for granted. If Robinson's style is experimental, then, it is partly because its texture captures, condenses, and restages in miniature the personal backstory of that vulnerability her plot as a whole unfolds.

Grammatically uncomplicated, undemonstrative, yet affectively loaded, Robinson's lambent prose enacts the principles she holds dear. Although the passage above is conspicuously economical, there's an underlying ambition about what it aspires to communicate through the slender musculature of style, which strives to endorse Robinson's warning that we often "forget to find value in the beauty of a thought."[50] At the same time, this scene, like so many in *Lila*, also holds a mirror up to its reader: Robinson alerts us to the ethically freighted distance implied by our appreciation of cerebral beauty and the material conditions endured by a character who surely has little time for cultivating such appreciations, a character who more often finds blunt recognitions rather than beauty in the thought that she "had the likeness of a woman, with hands but no face at all, since she never let herself see it," acknowledging in turn that she "had the likeness of a life, because she was all alone in it."[51] Experimentation here is a far cry from "virtuosity regaling itself with its own brilliance," to borrow Robinson's own phrase,[52] however admiringly critics have spoken about her lissom narration. What's innovative is precisely her refusal of verbal exhibitionism, her effort to limn microportraits of insecurity and trepidation, to cultivate between grammar and diction an intimacy with the perception of Lila's accustomed precarity, where everyday isolation is so often confirmation of what it means to possess something resembling "a life."

Styles of Freedom

"A primary symptom of vulnerability," observes Ottessa Moshfegh, "is subtlety created by a disruption in the dream of the fiction. What might look at first like the writer's error can carry a great deal of meaning, like when you think you see the voice speak out of character. A stutter, a moment of skewed perspective, something that rings wrong, makes the reader pause, wonder, feel, engage."[53] Errancy would be a premise, even the prerequisite, for experimentation in Moshfegh's model, where apparent imperfections solicit our affective involvement in and appreciation of literary innovation's volatility. This reach for an untutored, serendipitous variety of technical exertion prizes the "disruption" of the creative "dream" of well-wrought form and seamless characterization. Making experimentation more vulnerable, even authorially self-exposing, seemed to be Moshfegh's mission after the tautly executed psycho-historical crime novella *McGlue* (2010). For in a way, that was an exquisitely distancing, depersonalizing text, thanks in part to its setting aboard a ship in the 1850s; yet also due to its immaculate rendition of the first-person perspective of an injured, alcohol-fogged man who struggles to recollect whether or not he has killed his best friend. Without wishing to imply that Moshfegh's imperatives are exclusively suited to historical fiction, the work of making readers "pause, wonder, feel, engage" by means of perspectival shifts and altered voices is nonetheless central to the horrifying antebellum world of Colson Whitehead's *The Underground Railroad* (2016), whose own generative vulnerabilities will occupy me now in closing.

This is not an extravagantly experimental novel by Whitehead's standards, especially if we compare it to the bracingly cumulative sentences, artful nomenclature, and acrobatic world-making of the aforementioned *Zone One*. Instead, *Railroad*'s "quietly radical" renovation of the novel of slavery, as Adam Kelly observes, reveals how the "flippant and ironic tone" of Whitehead's earlier work "has been replaced with a new tone, one for which the term 'irony' – or at least 'postmodern irony' – does not sit altogether comfortably."[54] In this sense, *Railroad* offers a purposeful kind of self-exposure that nonetheless departs from metafictional exhibitionism, uncovering what feels in retrospect like a deliberate compositional transition in Whitehead's writing. This shift in style enables his politically charged and tangibly urgent response to a cultural moment in which the precarity, systemic inequities, and disenfranchisement of African American people were brought to the forefront of public consciousness by the Black Lives Matter movement. For some critics at the time, Whitehead's appalling material was a pretext for literary innovation, highlighting the ethical implications of finding in the trauma of Black history an occasion for generic refurbishment that opened up new vistas for his own artistry. "The matter-of-factness of Whitehead's prose," claimed Thomas Chatterton Williams, "allows him to have his Southern Novel of Black Misery and stand ironically apart from it too. One can't avoid the impression that, for Whitehead, the subject matter is always in service of the intellectual and narrative dexterity on the page."[55] But that may have been precisely Whitehead's point: to subject his own linguistic agility to the ultimate test of history by turning so inventively to an environment of atrocity for which anything other than self-effacing, assiduous modes of representation seem unconscionable. The novel paradoxically seems to offer this acknowledgment, even as it also acknowledges that to do justice in fiction to the experiential violence of slavery demands extraordinary modalities of depictive ingenuity.

As *Railroad* embraces this paradox, we can discern in its very "matter-of-factness" Whitehead's own exposition of inevitably insufficient means, a self-examination of the thresholds of what's possible to describe that none-theless resists the luxury of metafictional confession, where formal self-referentiality equates to ethical self-exoneration. He's able to offer that kind of exposition – itself an experiment in meditating on the challenges of recreating an agonizing past – without detracting from the dramatic immediacy of events. *Railroad* often achieves this by embedding aphoristic observations about what is an indescribable landscape of systemically sanctioned trauma into the prevailing free indirect discourse: "What a world it is, Cora thought, that makes a living prison into your only haven. Was she out of bondage or in its web: how to describe the status of a runaway?"[56] How indeed. The question reiterates the creative problematic Whitehead has posed for himself in *Railroad*, as he anatomizes a seemingly indefinable perception of "freedom" as "a thing that shifted as you looked at it, the way a forest is dense with trees up close but from outside, from the empty meadow, you see its true limits" (179).

This is a novel that's therefore mindful too of its own representational limits, even as it strives to orchestrate moments that contest the existential and material limits imposed by enslavement. One such episode – itself "a moment of skewed perspective," to recall Moshfegh's account of writerly exposure that precipitates readerly enthrallment – occurs in the novel's final stages, in a sequence devoted to Cora's mother, Mabel. We learn that Mabel did not intend to abandon her daughter (as Cora is left to assume) by making her own solitary escape. She plans to return, but a fatal snakebite terminates her journey back to the plantation. Wading into bogs, Mabel comes to rest amid "noises of the swamp" (294). Here there are "[n]o patrollers, no bosses, no cries of anguish to induct her into another's despair. No cabin walls shuttling her through the night seas like the hold of a slave ship" (294). Against the reparative sonic backdrop of "[s]andhill cranes and warblers, otters splashing," Mabel's "breathing slowed and that which separated herself from the swamp disappeared. She was free" (294). "This moment," suggests Whitehead, isn't simply embalmed by the iridescence of naturalistic impressions; it resolves into and frames a clear, purposeful recognition of liberation. The moment's remission is inevitably fugitive: Mabel knew "[s]he had to go back," as Cora "was waiting on her", so the brief pause "would have to do for now" (294). Nonetheless, she

> would keep this moment close, her own treasure. When she found the words to share it with Cora, the girl would understand there was something beyond the plantation, past all that she knew. That one day if she stayed strong, the girl could have it for herself. The world may be mean, but people don't have to be, not if they refuse. (294)

The experimentality of this episode applies as much to structure – to the scene's late placement in the novel, its shimmering "constellations wheeling in the darkness" counterweighing the horrors we've hitherto encountered (294) – as to its style, daringly lyrical though Whitehead's prose undoubtedly is here, when set against the appallingly violent succession of foregoing events. By virtue of this chapter's position at the end of "a text whose temporal structure seems to refuse at every turn the notion of progress," a great deal of its "power stems," as Kelly remarks, "from Whitehead's ironic depiction of her moment of freedom," with the irony itself no longer functioning as a "rhetorical, cynical, or postmodern" idiom but one that's "structural, dramatic, and tragic."[57] Other affective dynamics are in play, though, and reactions needn't be steered or subsumed by irony. In that moving collision of Mabel's misery-born memories and immediate scenic descriptions, the acoustic sinews of Whitehead's language permit pathos to commingle rather provocatively with nascent solace, when the horror-inflected sibilance (*bosses, cries, shuttling, seas*) is counterpointed by the equally sibilant yet consolatory sound of ecological vitality ("Sandhill cranes and warblers, otters splashing"). This might seem like a superficial contrast between comparable phonematic elements; but once spotted, it's hard to overlook the potential of such linguistic connotations to match in microcosmic ways the novel's larger purposes. Style, that is, creates sonic correlatives for Whitehead's overarching effort "to offer a model of resistance, a small gleam of hope," even in circumstances, as reviewers have noted, that "are almost unbearably poignant."[58] What's more, not only does Whitehead offer "[t]his moment" as a sliver of "treasure" before the novel's close, a brief interval that suspends the aftermath and expectation of incessant traumas; he also allows the message at the heart of the scene to assume an extra-diegetic resonance, yielding for the reader those "words" to "keep this moment close," to discern what they briefly yet insistently imply, even as we recognize that the episode's uplifting translucence is ephemeral, recognizing too the devastating discrepancy Whitehead suddenly inserts between what we've been shown and what Cora will never know about her mother's fate. The words in question ("The world may be mean, but people don't have to be, not if they refuse") comprise an asseveration that is also a plea for resistance, allowing Whitehead to enunciate an authorial interjection that spryly masquerades as free indirect style. It is a sentence that does indeed speak somewhat out of character, but strategically so, if only for a beat – precisely in order to speak up instead against our own resurgently racist, nationalistically protectionist, geopolitically divisive present. What better reason to experiment.

*

From grammars of precarity to styles of freedom, formal experimentation in twenty-first-century American fiction does tough, critical work. Rarely an occasion merely for aesthetic showmanship, rarely entailing too the spurning of technical conventions or perceived traditions for iconoclasm's sake alone, experimentalism has arguably turned into a distinctly more affirmative venture – one that extends fiction's expressional facilities with palpably ethical, arrestingly emotional, and urgently political results. For readers, this means that nowadays experimentation is perhaps more likely to spell involvement and enchantment than estrangement or bewilderment. This doesn't make such novels any less difficult to experience, of course, but it does enable them to become a different sort of cultural force.

And that force seems all the more necessary today. To claim so, of course, is to run two inevitable risks at once: inviting accusations of myopic pre-sentism, while flouting the likelihood of sounding imminently dated. But some things can't be ignored as pressing factors with the potential to shape the future scope, urgencies, and justifications of experimental fiction. For as I gather my final thoughts on this chapter, protests against the global scandal of sluggish government responses to climate change have been taking place across Europe. One branch of this movement, "Extinction Rebellion," saw people of all ages take to London's streets in efforts to raise public awareness of looming environmental catastrophe. This existential crisis, which one former – and obscenely negligent – occupant of the Oval Office dubbed a hoax, is surely set to become a primary representational challenge and conditioning historical catalyst for novelistic innovation in years to come.

For Amitav Ghosh, this challenge is so great as to suggest that the "Anthropocene resists literary fiction" altogether. However, it may be in this "very resistance to language itself" that climate change provides the sort of politico-aesthetic crucible from which "new, hybrid forms will emerge."[59] Such is the formidable test that looks set to exercise the generic elasticity and planetary imaginary of writers who push the envelope of fiction as a resource for thinking, and existing, otherwise.

NOTES

1 Marilynne Robinson, "Grace and Beauty," in *What Are We Doing Here? Essays* (London: Virago, 2008), 104.
2 Ibid.
3 Raymond Federman, "Surfiction: Four Propositions in Form of an Introduction," in *Surfiction: Fiction Now and Tomorrow*, edited by Raymond Federman (Chicago: Swallow Press, 1975), 7; Ronald Sukenick, *In Form: Digressions on the Act of Fiction* (Carbondale: Southern Illinois University Press, 1985), 55.
4 Rachel Greenwald Smith has drawn attention to the hurdles we face in trying to classify writers who have emerged over the first two decades of the twenty-first century with reference to their perceived departures from the literary postmodernisms of the 1970s and 1980s: "while tracing the formal genealogy from the postmodernists to the post-postmodernists is fairly straightforward, drawing any categorical conclusions about the influences and innovations of this new cluster of writers is much more difficult. That they have all read and digested postmodernism is clear, but responding to postmodernism either in the affirmative or negative does not seem to be of primary interest to them" (Rachel Greenwald Smith, "Afterword: The 2000s after 2016," in *American Literature in Transition, 2000–2010*, edited by Rachel Greenwald Smith [New York: Cambridge University Press, 2017], 387).
5 As Adam Kelly has shown, the preservation rather than overturning of certain conventions has itself attracted considerable creative investment. He identifies "a self-conscious ethos among a significant set of American novelists, an ethos that found its aesthetic manifestations in such prominent literary trends as the revival of narrative realism, the enthusiastic adoption by celebrated authors of standard genre forms, and the boom in historical fiction," a trend that for some critics amounts to a "dampening of experimentation, estrangement, and difficulty in favor of conventionality, accessibility, and communicative stability" ("Formally Conventional Fiction," in Smith, *American Literature in Transition, 2000–2010*, 47).
6 Ben Marcus, "Why Experimental Fiction Threatens to Destroy Publishing, Jonathan Franzen, and Life as We Know It: A Correction," *Harper's Magazine* (October 2005), 51.
7 Ibid., 40.
8 Ibid.
9 Jonathan Franzen, "Mr. Difficult," *New Yorker*, September 30, 2002, www.newyorker.com/magazine/2002/09/30/mr-difficult.
10 Ibid.

11 Ibid.

12 Marcus, "Why Experimental Fiction," 40.

13 Ibid., 44.

14 Ibid., 46.

15 Ibid., 41.

16 Problematic though the term remains, not least in Smith's overtly schematic discussion, there is a case for recuperating it: see David James, "In Defense of Lyrical Realism," *Diacritics* 45, no. 4 (2017): 69–91.

17 Zadie Smith, "Two Directions for the Novel," in *Changing My Mind: Occasional Essays* (London: Hamish Hamilton, 2009), 71.

18 Marcus, "Why Experimental Fiction," 41–42.

19 Ibid., 42.

20 Ibid.

21 For a historically sensitive account of the realism–experimentalism dichotomy, see Julia Jordan's "Late Modernism and the Avant-Garde Renaissance," in *The Cambridge Companion to British Fiction since 1945*, edited by David James (New York: Cambridge University Press, 2015), 145–159. Chiming with Marcus's technically and thematically capacious view of what realism can do, Deak Nabers urges us "to consider what the study of the novel looks like in the absence of such a form," in order for us "to engage form in its full range of vitality, to approach it as an intellectually and historically vibrant process rather than a taxonomic designator" ("The Forms of Formal Realism: Literary Study and the Life Cycle of the Novel," in *Postmodern | Postwar – and After: Rethinking American Literature*, edited by Jason Gladstone, Andrew Hoberek, and Daniel Worden [Iowa City: University of Iowa Press, 2016], 154, 162). See also Jed Esty and Colleen Lye's introduction to their special issue of *Modern Language Quarterly*: "Peripheral Realisms Now," Special Issue, *Modern Language Quarterly* 73, no. 3 (2012): 269–288.

22 One influential construction of this field is offered by Mark McGurl, via a "typology" of aesthetic reformations in late-twentieth-century fiction, in which he coins the overlapping domains of "techomodernism," "high cultural pluralism," and "lower-middle-class modernism" as a categorizations that, respectively, "correspond roughly to what is more casually called 'postmodernism' ... 'ethnic literature' ... and 'modernism'" (*The Program Era: Postwar Fiction and the Rise of Creative Writing* [Cambridge, MA: Harvard University Press, 2009], 68).

23 Marcus, "Why Experimental Fiction," 42.

24 Ben Lerner, *10:04* (London: Granta, 2014), 108.

25 Jennifer Egan, *A Visit from the Goon Squad* (London: Constable & Robinson, 2011), 87, 86, 87.

26 María del Pilar Blanco, "Reading the Novum World: The Literary Geography of Science Fiction in Junot Díaz's The Brief Wondrous Life of Oscar Wao," in *Surveying the American Tropics: A Literary Geography from New York to Rio*, edited by Maria Christina Fumagalli, Peter Hulme, Owen Robinson, and Lesley Wylie (Liverpool: Liverpool University Press, 2012), 53, 54.

27 Junot Díaz, "The Search for Decolonial Love," interview by Paula M. L. Moya, *Boston Review*, June 26, 2012, http://bostonreview.net/books-ideas/paula-ml-moya-decolonial-love-interview-junot-d%C3%ADaz.

28 Andrew Hoberek, "*Literary Genre Fiction*," in Smith, *American Literature in Transition, 2000–2010*, 70–72.

29 Kathleen Stewart, "Precarity's Forms," *Cultural Anthropology* 27, no. 3 (2012): 524.

30 Merritt Tierce, *Love Me Back* (New York: Anchor, 2015), 61.

31 Ibid., 58.

32 Ibid.

33 Ibid., 59.

34 McGurl, *The Program Era*, 69.

35 David Winters, "The Christine Schutt Interview," *The Quarterly Conversation*, December 2, 2013, http://quarterlyconversation.com/the-christine-schutt-interview.

36 Tierce, *Love Me Back*, 108.

37 Winters, "The Christine Schutt Interview."

38 Christine Schutt, *Florida* (New York: Harcourt, 2004), 34.

39 Ibid., 26.

40 Winters, "The Christine Schutt Interview."

41 Schutt, *Florida*, 35.

42 Ibid., 132.

43 Ibid., 156.

44 Winters, "The Christine Schutt Interview."

45 Marilynne Robinson, *Gilead* (London: Virago, 2006), 231.

46 Marilynne Robinson, *Lila* (London: Virago, 2014), 240.

47 Ibid., 74.

48 Ibid., 34.

49 Ibid., 34–35.

50 Marilynne Robinson, "Reformation," in *The Givenness of Things* (London: Virago, 2015), 28.

51 Robinson, *Lila*, 68.

52 Marilynne Robinson, "Humanism," in *The Givenness of Things*, 13 (Robinson's emphasis).

53 Lorin Stein, "Ottessa Moshfegh," *BOMB Magazine*, October 28, 2014, https://bombmagazine.org/articles/ottessa-moshfegh.

54 Adam Kelly, "Freedom to Struggle: The Ironies of Colson Whitehead," *Open Library of Humanities* 4, no. 2 (2018), 20.

55 Thomas Chatterton Williams, "'Fried Fish,' Review of The Underground Railroad, by Colson Whitehead, *London Review of Books* 38, no. 22 (November 17, 2016): www.lrb.co.uk/v38/n22/thomas-chatterton-williams/fried-fish.

56 Colson Whitehead, *The Underground Railroad* (London: Fleet, 2016), 179.

57 Kelly, "Freedom to Struggle," 20.

58 Alex Preston, "Review of *The Underground Railroad*, by Colson Whitehead," *The Guardian*, October 9, 2016: www.theguardian.com/books/2016/oct/09/the-underground-railroad-colson-whitehead-revie-luminous-furious-wildly-inventive.

59 Amitav Ghosh, *The Great Derangement: Climate Change and the Unthinkable* (Chicago: The University of Chicago Press, 2016), 84.

3

MARK BOULD

Speculative Fiction

In a 1998 *Village Voice* article, Jonathan Lethem proposed an alternative history in which Thomas Pynchon's *Gravity's Rainbow* (1973), rather than Arthur C. Clarke's *Rendezvous with Rama* (1973), won the 1974 Science Fiction Writers of America's Nebula Award for the best science fiction (SF) novel of the year, with Don DeLillo's *Ratner's Star* (1976) winning three years later.[1] In a subsequent email exchange with Lethem, published in *The New York Review of Science Fiction*, Ray Davis suggested a different counterfactual: what if the 1975 National Book Award had not been shared by Thomas Williams's *The Hair of Harold Roux* (1974) and Robert Stone's *Dog Soldiers* (1974) but Samuel R. Delany's *Dhalgren* (1975) and Joanna Russ's *The Female Man* (1975)? That is, what if, instead of the insular world of SF fandom embracing mainstream literary fiction that just happened to be about science, the insular establishment of mundane literary fiction acknowledged the accomplishments of SF that just happened to be literary?

James Patrick Kelly and John Kessel's edited collection *The Secret History of Science Fiction* (2009) begins from the premise that Clarke's triumph was not, in Lethem's words, "a tombstone marking the death of the hope that science fiction was about to merge with the mainstream." Instead, they write, "at the same time that, on one side of the genre divide SF was being written at the highest levels of ambition, on the other side, writers came to use the materials of SF for their own purposes, writing fiction that is clearly science fiction, but not identified by that name."[2] In a footnote, the editors jokingly use that most reliable of measures to determine which of their nineteen authors are literary writers: have they been published in the *New Yorker*? Yes, DeLillo, Lethem, Margaret Atwood, T. C. Boyle, Michael Chabon, Ursula Le Guin, Steve Millhauser, George Saunders, and Gene Wolfe have; but no, not Kelly, Kessel, Thomas Disch, Karen Joy Fowler, Molly Gloss, Maureen F. McHugh, Carter Scholz, Lucius Shepard, Kate Wilhelm, or Connie Willis. This arbitrary test produces anomalies: Le Guin and Wolfe have spent almost their entire careers publishing SF and fantasy; and although Gloss and Fowler often return to the genre in which their careers began, they are much better known for mainstream literary novels, such as, respectively, *The Jump-Off Creek* (1990) and *The Jane Austen Book Club* (2004). Together, these surprise appearances and absences are perhaps less indicative of the merger between genre and literary fiction Lethem imagined than of the increased and increasingly visible traffic between categories that are nonetheless perpetuated.

They perhaps also signal that in the new millennium, after decades of postmodernist claims about the erosion of high–low cultural boundaries, a new sense of cultural capital has emerged.[3] Take, for example, Pynchon's *Against the Day* (2006), an enraptured, monumental recapitulation of the genres composted in dime magazines and early pulps: airship adventures, Edisonades, extraordinary voyages, future wars, hollow earths, lost races, rags-to-riches, sadomasochistic soft porn, scientific romances, spy thrillers, utopias, westerns, and so on. Or such Pulitzer prizewinners as Chabon's *The Amazing Adventures of Kavalier & Clay* (2000) and Junot Díaz's *The Brief Wondrous Life of Oscar Wao* (2007), both of which articulate a knowledge-able love of SF and fantasy; or Cormac McCarthy's post-apocalyptic *The Road* (2006); or Colson Whitehead's fantastically counterfactual *The Underground Railroad* (2016). Indeed, in 2012, as if to confound Kelly and Kessel, the *New Yorker* published a special SF issue, with fiction and essays by Atwood, Díaz, Lethem, and Whitehead among others.

Such trends did not go unnoticed in the world of speculative fiction. Cyberpunk Bruce Sterling devoted his July 1989 *SF Eye* column to outlining what he called "slipstream" fiction, a grab bag mostly of postmodernist SF and fantasy by genre and non-genre authors, dating back to the 1950s, which he described as the "kind of writing which simply makes you feel very strange; the way that living in the twentieth century makes you feel, if you are a person of a certain sensibility."[4] In a pair of essays from 2002, SF critic Gary K. Wolfe identified similar developments from a different per-spective. In "Malebogle, or the Ordnance of Genre," he cites Lethem, Jonathan Carroll, Patrick O'Leary, and Stephen King's *Dark Tower* sequence as examples of the increasingly free flow of "genre materials ... into one another."[5] He also comments upon a parallel and "even more peculiar development: the non-genre genre story" (15), by which he does not mean

> those attempts at using genre material by writers from "outside," such as the occasional ill-conceived science fiction novel by ... John Updike ... or Paul Theroux, but rather those stories so closely informed by genre-based structures and sensibilities that they may convey the *feel* of a particular genre, and may

open up to genre readings in a way different from how they open up to
conventional readings, even though they lack traditional genre markers. (15)

His examples include Peter Straub's non-supernatural Vietnam War/serial
killer/horror novel *Koko* (1988), which won the World Fantasy Award, and
Neal Stephenson's Locus Award–winning *Cryptonomicon* (1999), which
interweaves a fictionalized account of the World War II efforts of Bletchley
Park codebreakers and tactical deception operatives with the story of their
descendants in the 1990s establishing a data haven and an internet currency.
As Wolfe notes,

> now we have a situation in which novels containing no material fantasy at
> all ... receive fantasy awards [and] novels with little or no science fiction
> content gain a huge following among science fiction readers who recognize in
> them something of their own; in which growing numbers of writers view the
> material forged in genre as resources rather than as constraints; in which the
> edges of genre themselves bleed into one another. (16)

In "Evaporating Genres," Wolfe argues that the "post-genre" writer whose
work is grounded in but pushes beyond the genre destabilizes and thereby
revitalizes it: "a healthy genre ... is one at risk, one whose boundaries grow
uncertain and whose foundations get wobbly."[6] His examples include
Straub and King (horror), Geoff Ryman and Jane Yolen (fantasy without
fantasy), Connie Willis and Patricia Anthony (SF historicals), Gregory
Benford (SF thrillers), and Sheri S. Tepper and Sean Stewart (science fantasy), all of whom continued to publish in the new millennium.

The New Weird

Of the various new movements that proclaimed themselves around the turn
of the millennium – post-genre fiction, interstitial fiction, new wave fabulism,
bizarro fiction, and so on – the New Weird has had the greatest traction. The
term originated in the United Kingdom, in a discussion thread instigated by
New Wave SF veteran M. John Harrison and involving China Miéville,
Steph Swainston, Justina Robson, and others.[7] It leaked out into the public
in 2003, with Miéville's "Long Live the New Weird" guest editorial in *The
Third Alternative* 35, and quickly spread. Initially, it was used to describe a
(mostly) new generation of writers, including the Americans Michael Cisco,
Thomas Ligotti, Kelly Link, and Jeff VanderMeer, who remixed and mashed
up genre materials not from ignorance or disdain but with understanding,
respect, and exuberance. In 2005, in probably the nearest thing to a manifesto the movement produced, Miéville declared it "post-Seattle fiction,"
identifying in it an affinity with the alterglobalization movement's daring

and joyful opening up of social horizons after two decades of dreary, devastating neoliberal hegemony.[8] Since then, a second, overlapping meaning has become dominant: the recovery, regeneration and extension of a tradition of weird fiction associated in the United Kingdom with Arthur Machen and William Hope Hodgson, and in the United States with H. P. Lovecraft and the *Weird Tales* pulp magazine (launched 1923). Jeff and Ann VanderMeer's anthology *The Weird* (2012), which reprints 110 stories from two dozen countries published since 1907, exemplifies this project of recuperation. While the haute Weird of the early twentieth century has been largely associated with the cosmic horror and lurid adjectival frenzy of Lovecraft, the New Weird – more interested in monsters and grotesquerie than in scaring anyone – tends toward a rather studied literariness, a preciousness of tone, at times even whimsy. Whereas Lovecraft's fever dreams were grounded in adherence to the "certainties" of bigoted hierarchies of race, gender, class, and sexuality, the New Weird is typically shaped by a rather more progressive politics, embracing uncertainty, welcoming difference and thriving on ambiguity.

Perhaps unsurprisingly in this "post-genre" conjuncture, the first major US New Weird novel came from outside of traditional genre publishing. Mark Z. Danielewski's vast ergodic *House of Leaves* (2000) contains multiple narrative strands, typically distinguished from each other by their position on the page and/or the font in which they are printed (other typographical experiments attempt to match the physical form of the text to the narrative it recounts). Johnny Truant, an unpleasant and self-confessed unreliable narrator, pieces together a manuscript written by recently deceased Zampanò about a documentary film, *The Navidson Record*, which might not actually exist. As Zampanò's detailed critical and at times speculative account of the film reveals, the Navidsons' new family home in Virginia possessed uncanny spaces and impossible dimensions: its interior is an inch larger than its exterior, and gradually expanding; a closet space appears between two rooms; a hallway extends outwards from an external wall, but does not appear in the garden into which it should project. Will Navidson makes a short film, "The Five and a Half Minute Hallway," about these topographical impossibilities and then sets out to explore them. He finds massive halls, twisting labyrinths, and a spiral staircase that seems to descend forever, with more hallways, rooms, and mazes branching off its many levels. Everything is ash-gray in color and unlit; the only sound is a sinister, intermittent low growl. With others he tries to map and record this anomaly – madness, murder, and death ensue – and eventually edits the footage into *The Navidson Record*. Zampanò's exegesis of the film – which, being blind, he could never have seen – is adorned with footnotes (by him and by unknown editors) and appendices, and is interrupted, or accompanied, by Truant's autobiographical ramblings as he becomes increasingly obsessed with Zampanò's work and by other occasional voices.

Danielewski blends the kind of post–Gothic Weird material one might find in Lovecraft – the dread manuscript of a sightless madman, found documentation, pseudo-scholarship, spatial anomalies, non-Euclidan geometries, vaulted chambers, unseen horrors, descents into vast caverns and into insanity – with the kind of epistemological destabilization and ontological uncertainty found in both literary metafiction and the SF of a Philip K. Dick or Barry Malzberg. The overall effect is of a Borgesian conceit hijacked by an author of Melville's encyclopedic appetite and disdain for narrative norms (with a hint of Charles Bukowski in the Truant sections). It is also steeped in genre traditions – the haunted houses and hotels of Shirley Jackson and Stephen King – but unlike them it refuses any climactic encounter or revelation, instead generating a frisson of terror through its absolute refusal of such cathartic comforts. The house, like the text that both depicts and comprises it, troubles any sense of rational propriety, resists stability and meaning. Spaces, actions, events, narrating voices, and explanations simply do not – cannot – add up.

A similar – if less showily experimental – destabilization of haute Weird matter can be found in Caitlín R. Kiernan's *The Drowning Girl: A Memoir* (2012). Narrator India Morgan Phelps knows that she suffers from schizophrenia, and that her experience of reality is authentic even if others do not perceive it as she does. She switches between first and third person as she recounts – and sometimes depicts herself typing – the story of an encounter, which happened either in July or November, with a woman called Eva, who is either a siren or a wolf, depending on which version of their encounter is the one that happened. Eva might also be the ghost of the model who inspired a late nineteenth-century artist, or the mysteriously unaging priestess of a cult that committed collective suicide two decades previously. This tension between either/or, between identity and fluidity, binds every level of the novel together, from the sensitive construction of characters – India's schizophrenia is not consistently medicated or under other forms of control, her new girlfriend Abalyn is a transgender woman – to the careful layering of shifting narratives. While the novel does not require the reader to choose among possibilities – what if they are all true? – India eventually collapses them into the July/siren version of events (which remains haunted by the others). The story ends, but nothing seems resolved: the world remains unstable, full of uncanny potential. Words cannot pin it down.

Jeff VanderMeer's *Southern Reach* trilogy – *Annihilation* (2014), *Authority* (2014), *Acceptance* (2014) – elaborates upon the weirdness of landscape and environment as anthropogenic climate destabilization accelerates. Set over a period of thirty years, it charts the biological and ecological transformations of Area X, an expanding zone of mutations on the southeastern seaboard that threatens to breach the barriers placed around it. Various expeditions have been sent in to record the changes; anyone who returns dies of a mysterious cancer. In *Annihilation*, characters are never called by their real names; they are hypnotized, lied to, and lie to each other; some disappear; motives and agendas remain murky; suspicions surface, along with lost journals and other texts; a spiral staircase descends into a dark pit that is repeatedly called a tower, almost demanding that something ascend it from below; people are driven to madness, murder, and suicide; bodies transform, there is something ominous about the fungus, and a creature stalks the land. *Authority* shows that the Southern Reach Agency, tasked with investigating Area X, is just as impenetrable, unfathomable, and contradictory. *Acceptance* fills in missing back story, seemingly answering questions raised by the first two volumes. However, its revelations mean that those questions arose from partial knowledge and are thus perhaps not the ones to have asked. This escalating play of epistemological uncertainty set against a patient unfurling of genre elements formally captures the experience of climate change: while scientists cannot predict with the precision demanded by denialists the effects of the complex, non-linear climate system, we can nonetheless know – on some levels, and with a high degree of certainty – what is going to happen as atmospheric carbon levels increase. VanderMeer's repeated rejection of the thriller's more formulaic payoffs to generic situations builds this contradiction into the very structure of the novel, even as it depicts the weirdly different, emerging ecologies of which we are a part.

Climate Change and Other Catastrophes

Amitav Ghosh argues that the serious literary novel developed in such a way as to be incapable of addressing climate change. With its early commitment to depicting the regularity of bourgeois life – rational, orderly, statistically normative, and free from exceptional moments – came the "deliberately prosaic world of prose fiction."[9] Some major nineteenth-century writers – Eliot, Tolstoy, Zola, Melville – might have had the necessary scope to tackle world-historical transformations, but throughout the twentieth century the focus of the novel narrowed considerably, preferring the distinctiveness of a finite social and physical setting. Consequently, "connections to the world beyond are made to recede,"[10] and with them those "forces of unthinkable magnitude that create unbearably intimate connections over vast gaps in time and space"[11] and other forms of nonhuman agency.

68

Adam Trexler comes to a similar conclusion when examining the contemporary literary novel's more sustained attempts to engage with climate change. In Jonathan Franzen's *Freedom* (2010), a jaded ecologist strikes a deal with a carbon billionaire to create a nature reserve so as to preserve a single species of bird, the cerulean warbler, threatened with extinction from habitat destruction, but it will be financed by highly destructive mountain-top removal coal mining. For Trexler, the novel's strength is its "rich, detailed account of the political, economic, and social milieu," but at the same time it "fails to articulate the things involved in climate change or extinction ... the environment is merely a *psychological* preoccupation, never meaning much to" any of the characters.[12] Barbara Kingsolver's *Flight Behavior* (2012) focuses on a small Appalachian town suddenly host to millions of monarch butterflies whose migratory route to Mexico has been disrupted by altered weather patterns. They are unlikely to survive the Tennessee winter, possibly driving the species to extinction. While the novel delineates the tensions and conflicting interests within the community, and embeds them within local, regional, and national politics and media, it remains, according to Trexler, "unable to imagine political innovations or new ways of living that could address the challenges of the Anthropocene."[13]

In contrast, speculative fiction has tended to eschew the kinds of particularity typical of the literary novel or, rather, to relativize the personal in relation to spatial and temporal magnitudes and ecological complexities. Its relationship to science ensures a secular materialism and a technical language with which to engage with climatology and other relevant disciplines. This realism is always also mediated by the genre's roots in romance forms, from which it derives an appetite for the exceptional, the vivid, and the sublime. Moreover, its development from and arguably replacement of the historical novel,[14] its long affiliation with utopian and other political visions and projects, and its typical focus on the consequences of technological innovation and social change all equip it to address the shortcomings Ghosh and Trexler associate with the literary novel. It also has a well-developed repertoire of methods and images for depicting large-scale catastrophes and transformed worlds.

Furthermore, SF's metaphorical capacities enable fictions that are not explicitly about climate change to be very precisely about climate change. A particularly clear example is Neal Stephenson's *Seveneves* (2015), in which a mysterious phenomenon shatters the moon into seven pieces. While scientists try to fathom the cause, two of the pieces collide, breaking one of them in half. Astronomer Dubois Harris promptly realizes that such collisions will increase exponentially. In a pointed swipe at climate change denialists, who demand direct linear cause-and-effect chains, Stephenson straightforwardly assumes the self-evident nonlinear dynamics of chaos science, and that correlation and probability are just as persuasive to reasonable people. Indeed, Harris explains what "exponential" means with a hockey-stick curve and outlines the mathematical issues of predictions involving complex systems, both familiar from climate science. While he cannot predict exactly when it will happen, colliding moon fragments will grind each other into countless smaller rocks, trillions of which will crash into the Earth (the others will enter orbit, giving the planet Saturn-like rings). This "Hard Rain" of meteorites will burn the sky, boil away the oceans, and sterilize the planet of all life, rendering it uninhabitable for perhaps ten thousand years. The scale and pace of this catastrophe far outstrips any serious projections about anthropogenic climate destabilization, just as the speed with which plans to preserve humankind by establishing a small space colony taunts utterly inadequate political responses to the real-world climate crisis. But the novel's long view – after the hectic days, weeks, months, and years of its first two parts, the final part starts bluntly, brilliantly, with the heading "FIVE THOUSAND YEARS LATER"– creates a space in which the reader can play with the variables involved in calculating the quantities and complex consequences of atmospheric carbon, contemplating the devastation it has already caused and the further devastation that is already locked in, and entertaining the possible methods of amelioration, repair, and survival.[15]

Although the greenhouse effect was discovered in the mid-nineteenth century, with Svante Arrhenius in 1896 predicting the effects of doubling atmospheric carbon dioxide, the science of global warming did not really come together until the 1970s or register in public consciousness until the 1980s. Climate change – as an element of near-future world-building and as a driver of narratives – began to feature regularly in SF from the late 1980s, with Octavia Butler's *The Parable of the Sower* (1993) and *The Parable of the Talents* (1998) among the earliest major examples. The preeminent author of climate change SF, however, is Kim Stanley Robinson. Stories about the engineering and maintenance of biospheres, which if untended generally find an equilibrium unfavorable to human needs, let alone desires, feature in *Icehenge* (1984) and, more centrally, the *Mars* trilogy (1992–1996), *2312* (2012), and *Aurora* (2015). Related concerns about the nature and extent of acceptable intervention into environments that precede us and of which we are a part can be found in *Pacific Edge* (1990) and *Galileo's Dream* (2009). They are presented more urgently in the *Science in the Capital* trilogy (2004–2007), later condensed as *Green Earth* (2015), in which a US senator, duly elected President, and his science advisor drive efforts to mitigate and adapt to climate change. Despite proposing various technological solutions, it acknowledges that they are little more than sticking plasters – and the unlikelihood of achieving such immediate fixes in the real world. *New York 2140* (2017) is set among the skyscrapers and canals of Manhattan after two catastrophic icecap collapses have seen the sea level rise fifty feet. It is unabashed in identifying capitalism – particularly deregulated finance capital – as the primary cause and explores the potential benefits of a return to a more Keynesian capitalism. Such reforms and regulation provide at best provisional solutions that will not go unchallenged by the existing economic structure and its adherents, but they also provide a space in which the hope of building a better world can be born.

On August 17, 2018, veteran cyberpunk William Gibson tweeted that "All imagined futures lacking recognition of anthropogenic climate-change will increasingly seem absurdly shortsighted [and] to have utterly missed the single most important thing we were doing with technology."[16] And newer writers – such as Paolo Bacigalupi, whose novels include *The Windup Girl* (2009), *The Water Knife* (2015), and the dystopian YA *Shipbreaker* trilogy (2010–2017) – have certainly embraced climate science as a key determinant of imagined futures. Grenadian Tobias S. Buckell's *Arctic Rising* (2012) and *Hurricane Fever* (2014) feature a post-peak oil world of melted ice caps, and thriller narratives in which Bond-like villains attempt to save the planet through geo-engineering projects and viral genocides. Taiwanese-American Wesley Chu's *Tao* trilogy (2013–2015) features climate change, but only as a rather throwaway element in an extraterrestrial takeover narrative. It offers a vital corrective to Eurocentric global histories and depicts the fossil fuel economy as a key part of the aliens' attempt to engineer the habitability of the terrestrial atmosphere for them, regardless of the lethal consequences for humans. There is metaphoric potential in connecting this geo-engineering project to the global transformations wrought by Capital, but Chu's romping adventure does not pursue it. This suggest that if SF were to default, as Gibson suggests, to climate change scenarios, the crisis would be rendered ordinary – safe, uncritical, comforting even, like the rain-washed streets of film noir.

Authors not usually or only occasionally associated with the genre have also turned to "climate fiction" or "cli-fi," such as Canadian Margaret Atwood's *Maddadam* trilogy (2003–2013) or Nathaniel Rich's *Odds Against Tomorrow* (2013). Such fictions are often weak on world-building logic – as Ghosh might predict – and more focused on rendering limited worlds in a prosaic manner. For example, Edan Lepucki's *California* (2014) avoids depicting the catastrophe that causes Cal and Frida to flee to the wilderness and instead delineates the role of personal and family histories in shaping their encounters with other survivors, including a childless community governed by Frida's brother, a political activist/terrorist who faked his own death some years previously. This lends specificity to an otherwise quite conventionally cosy catastrophe and enables a gradual working through of the hysterical, world-damaging logic of gated communities. The environmental disaster is similarly obscure in Claire Vaye Watkins *Gold Fame Citrus* (2015), but its depiction of the observable, inexorable expansion of a Southwestern desert at times achieves a Ballardian imagist intensity capable of upsetting any complacency about humanity's capacity to halt catastrophic environmental transformations.

Although not widely considered "climate fiction," zombie narratives featuring large, mobile "unwanted" populations – such as the Canadian Tony Burgess's *Pontypool Changes Everything* (1998); Robert Kirkman, Tony Moore and Charlie Adlard's *The Walking Dead* comic (2003–); Max Brooks's *World War Z* (2006); Whitehead's *Zone One* (2011); and the *Newsflesh* series (2010–2016) by Seanan McGuire writing as Mira Grant – cannot *not* be read as fiction about climate refugees, of which it is commonly estimated there will be 150–200 million by 2050. That such fictions – including a genuinely global and ongoing cycle of movies since *28 Days Later …* (2002) – typically rework colonial fictions about settlers besieged by to-be-slaughtered indigenes, focus on the violent defense of resources, and feature turn-on-a-dime willingness to kill former allies, friends and family, does not bode well.

Contagion narratives[17] can likewise increasingly be understood as mediating anxieties about climate change: they upset more geographically rooted conceptualizations of space, distance, and temporality; they make visible the precarious infrastructure of daily life in a globalized world; and they render mass mortality proximate and undeniable. Carola Dibbell's *The Only Ones* (2015), set in a future in which deadly pandemics repeatedly sweep the world, features an impoverished, marginalized protagonist called "I" with an unusual degree of immunity. Surviving by selling her teeth, her blood, her eggs, she agrees to be cloned by a grieving mother, who then decides she does not want the resulting child. The narrator must single-handedly raise a daughter in a world that has long since fallen apart. The focus on this relationship grounds the novel's mapping of a global economy in which the core and peripheries are no longer – to the extent that they were – distinctions between colonizer and colonized, but typical of economic, and thus social and political, relations within both core and peripheral nations. In Canadian Emily St. John Mandel's *Station Eleven* (2014), a virulent flu kills 99 percent of the world's population in just two weeks. One strand of the novel is set prior to and during the catastrophe; the other, twenty years later, follows an overlapping cast of characters as a theater troupe travels the southern borderlands of eastern Canada, bringing entertainment, hope, and connectedness to communities of survivors. Although, as Trexler might note, *Station Eleven* lacks any capacity to address the challenges of the Anthropocene, it does present a world that, from the largest scale of global catastrophe down to the smallest scale of individual choices, is haunted by alternatives: other ways things could have been, or could be. In this, at least, it indicates spaces in which hope can operate, and the need to act, to avert, to build better tomorrows.

New Futures

For most of its history, SF has been popularly, if inaccurately, perceived as a genre primarily by and for straight white men. And despite its vocation of imagining change, some strands of SF are indisputably conservative, suspicious of difference and anxious about anything that challenges white heteronormative patriarchal capitalism. But the earliest SF pulps contain stories by Marxist feminists questioning gender roles, reproductive heterosexuality, and the color line. A left-liberal tradition can be traced back at least to the Futurians, a group of fans in the 1930s, many of whom went on to become influential authors, editors, and agents, and in the 1960s and 1970s supported the development of countercultural New Wave SF and overtly feminist SF – movements that included the preeminent African American SF writers, Samuel R. Delany and Octavia Butler. In 2012, Delany returned to SF after a twenty-year hiatus with *Through the Valley of the Nest of Spiders*, which extends several decades into the future but keeps SF elements in the background of its narrative about the life-long relationship of two gay black men. Butler's final novel, *Fledgling* (2005), is a science-fictionalized vampire narrative that, like many of her novels, can be understood as a neo-slave narrative about agency and constraints, sexual diversity, the cultural construction of race, the vitality of hybridity, and the importance of affective ties and mutual aid to survival.

These two novels appeared at a particular conjuncture. Although there had been other African Americans publishing fantastic fiction in genre and non-genre venues – including Amiri Baraka, Steven Barnes, Tananarive Due, Jewelle Gomez, Charles Johnson, Walter Moseley, Phyllis Perry, and Charles R. Saunders – in the new millennium the floodgates seemed to open. Whereas Delany and Butler defined themselves in and against a largely straight white SF, the generation that emerged with the new millennium had role models and increasingly a community that included people of color and feminist and queer writers, editors, and fans. They were not required to break new ground or be representative figures in quite the same way as earlier generations. Jamaican Canadian Nalo Hopkinson's

Brown Girl in the Ring (1998), set in a cyberpunk-influenced, post-economic-collapse Toronto, is imbued with Obeah belief systems and Caribbean rhythms. *Midnight Robber* (2000), a coming-of-age adventure set on the Carib-colonized planet Toussaint, rewrites the planetary romance as an ambiguous, vernacular enterprise. Her most accomplished novel, *The Salt Roads* (2003), tells the stories of three women – Mer, an eighteenth-century slave in a French colony on Hispaniola; the Haitian Jeanne Duval, the actress-singer who became Baudelaire's mistress; Thais, a Nubian slave in fourth century Egypt – all of whom are possessed by the Ginen fertility goddess, Lasirén. Caribbean selkies appear in *The New Moon's Arms* (2007), while *Sister Mine* (2013) returns to Toronto for a story of magical conflicts, monsters, and haints. Hopkinson maintains throughout a distinctive voice, rich in Caribbean lore, language, and perspectives, producing a diasporic, intersectional post-genre SF that never defaults to whiteness or heteronormativity. Sheree R. Thomas edited a pair of substantial anthologies, *Dark Matter: A Century of Speculative Fiction from the African Diaspora* (2000) and *Dark Matter: Reading the Bones* (2004), the first devoted to recuperating the past, the second to opening up the future. Andrea Hairston's *Mindscape* (2006) features a post-catastrophe Earth split into separate zones, literalizing the collision of cultures from a postcolonial perspective. *Redwood and Wildfire* (2011) depicts the early twentieth-century journey from Georgia to Chicago of a young black woman and an Irish-Seminole man, possessing hoodoo powers. A sequel, *Will Do Magic for Small Change* (2016), set in 1980s Pittsburgh, features their granddaughter who, having read about an alien who first appeared in 1890s Dahomey, sets out to reunite its fragmented parts. Africa is central to the work of Nigerian American Nnedi Okorafor. *The Shadow Speaker* (2007) is set in the early twenty-first century after the world has been transformed by nuclear war and the Peace Bomb, a magical device exploded by a Haitian eco-terrorist intending to mutate the world so that everyone will have the same skin, thus destroying racism. *Zahrah the Windseeker* (2005) features a similar African future of surreal vegetable technologies and superpowers. Okorafor continues to write YA fiction – *Akata Witch* (2011), *Akata Warrior* (2017) – but turned to adult fiction with the harrowing *Who Fears Death* (2010). Set in a post-apocalyptic Sudan in which the dark-skinned Okeke are oppressed by the light-skinned Nuru, it tells of an Ewu girl, conceived when a Nuru raped her Okeke mother, who sets out on a quest to kill her father, who is a sorcerer. A prequel, *The Book of the Phoenix* (2015), confronts America's own history of colonial violence, slavery, and weaponized rape. *Lagoon* (2014) is lighter in tone and features a Weird alien splashlanding in Lagos lagoon and transforming the world around it – a world, it turns out, that is already populated by gods, monsters, superhumans, and other mythical beings.

This new wave of Afrodiasporic authors from North America and the Caribbean includes Victor Lavalle, Deji Bryce Olukotun, Dexter Palmer, Sofia Samatar, Nisi Shawl, Barbadian Karen Lord, and Canadian Minister Faust. Perhaps the greatest popular success, though, has been achieved by N. K. Jemisin, author of the *Inheritance* trilogy (2010–2011) and the *Dreamblood* series (2012). With *The Fifth Season* (2015), the opening volume of the *Broken Earth* trilogy (2015–2017), she became the first African American to win the Hugo Award for best novel; with its third volume, *The Stone Sky* (2017), she became the first person ever to win the award three years in a row (and for every book in a series). Nestled somewhere between fantasy and SF, the trilogy features a world repeatedly wracked by cataclysmic geological upheavals and their consequent population movements. Too complex and imaginatively rich to be reduced to mere allegory, it nonetheless develops a critical perspective on the colonial logics currently shaping inadequate and racist responses to anthropogenic climate destabilization, while commenting on #BlackLivesMatter, hardened borders, refugee-panics, and postcolonial, intersectional identities.

This Afrodiasporic wave encouraged other communities of color to announce their presence within SF and related genres. Indigenous futurists include such Native American and First Nations authors as Sherman Alexie, Zainab Amadahy, Joseph Bruchac, Stephen Graham Jones, Misha, Eden Robinson, William Sanders, Leslie Marmon Silko, Gerald Vizenor, and Daniel H. Wilson, as well as Australian Aboriginal and New Zealand Maori writers.[18] Their stories and novels are often haunted by a stolen past and the trauma of its erasure, setting the depleted present – a world of fractured communities, stripped of sufficiency, let alone abundance – against alternative worlds and possible futures. The very existence of such fiction can itself can be understood as an act of survivance, "an active repudiation of dominance, tragedy, and victimization,"[19] or of a "returning to ourselves" by "discovering how personally one is affected by colonization, discarding the emotional and psychological baggage carried from its impact, and recovering ancestral traditions in order to adapt in our post-Native Apocalypse world."[20] For example, Hawaiian Matthew Kaopio's *Written in the Sky* (2005) and *Up among the Stars* (2011), a pair of YA novels about a fourteen-year-old homeless Kanaka Maolo, depicts 'Ikauikalani Kealahele learning not only how to survive on the streets of Honolulu but also how to read the night sky, interpret dreams, and talk to animals; amid quotidian hardships and melodramatic perils, he finds fullness and connection. Rather bleaker is Stephen Graham Jones's *Mapping the Interior* (2017), in which twelve-year-old Junior, his seizure-prone younger brother Dino, and his mum are haunted by his dead dad. Initially a ghostly presence, dad manifests not as the dropout and petty criminal he was in life but as the fancydancer he always yearned to be – shaped by a life he never had, just as Junior is formed by absences, including that of the father in relation to whom he is named. Dad begins to take on substance, vampirically draining energy from Dino, and as Junior sets out to save his brother, so Jones's depiction of everyday reservation life sketches in the long, slow apocalypse of settler-colonialism, the endless cycles of poverty and violence – physical and psychological – visited upon the colonized and upon this particular family.

Afro-Futurism and indigenous futurism are not alone in foregrounding the diversity of twenty-first-century American speculative fiction. Chicanxfuturism and Latinxfuturism includes work by Jaime Hernandez, Ernest Hogan, Carlos Mirajelo, Alejandro Morales, Beatrice Pita, Rosaura Sánchez, and Sabrina Vourvoulias, as well as the Canadian Silvia Moreno-Garcia and the Cuban Yoss. Sesshu Foster's *Atomik Aztex* (2005) interweaves multiple realities. In (at least) one, Spanish invaders were promptly defeated over 500 years ago, and half the world is dominated by the People's Republic of Anahuak of the Aztek Socialist Imperium. In it, Zenzontli, Keeper of the House of Darkness, leads sexy socialist Aztek warriors to the aid of Generalissimo Nestor Makhno, to save Russian Social Anarchism – and besieged Stalingrad – from Nazis. In at least one of the other "stupider realities amongst alternative universes offered by the ever expanding–omniverse, in which the Aztek civilization was 'destroyed,'"[21] Zenzontli finds himself spearheading a campaign to unionize the Los Angeles slaughterhouse in which he works. These and other realities bleed into each other, and Foster's delirious prose, full of anachronisms, bathetic falls, and extended lists – whose logic of composition continually shifts as more items are added – further destabilize any ontological certainty.

Intriguingly, although Foster grew up in and always lived in Latinx communities, he is actually Anglo-Japanese, suggesting the extent to which these various alternative futurisms are part of wider cultural fabrics and must be understood as strategic identities, as much political as aesthetic. Other contemporary SF authors of Asian extraction include Chinese Americans Ted Chiang and Ken Liu, Malaysian American Jaymee Goh, Korean American Yoon Ha Lee, Indian American Vandana Singh, Sri Lankan American Mary Anne Mohanraj, and Japanese American Karen Tei Yamashita.

A number of conservative commentators (and others, more overtly racist, misogynist, and homophobic) complained about the ways in which such diversity was "destroying the genre." *Lightspeed* magazine responded in

2013 by kick-starting an all-female "Women Destroy SF" special issue, raising sufficient funds to also publish sister issues "destroying" fantasy and horror; they went on to publish similar trios of "Queers Destroy" and "POC Destroy" issues, and *Uncanny* published a "Disabled People Destroy SF" issue in 2018.[22]

This chapter has outlined some of the key developments, authors, and works in contemporary North American speculative fiction, with a particular emphasis on SF. Even as SF continues as a series of distinct practices, publishing venues and world views, so – as I hope to have demonstrated – it has also mutated and collapsed, embracing materials and perspectives from neighboring speculative genres that traditionally would have been eschewed and denigrated so as to shore up SF's own identity. What is perhaps most unusual about the shape SF's perpetual border crisis has taken in the new millennium is quite how substantial the drive to weaken, subvert, transgress, and gleefully dance across that border has been – and quite how much critical and popular success has been enjoyed by the authors and works that do this. Certainly, such well-established subgenres as hard-SF, space opera, cyberpunk, steampunk, military SF, and apocalyptic SF persist (as do equivalent traditions in fantasy and horror). Nowadays, however, the leading examples are likely to be at the same time critically concerned with colonialism, the social construction of ability and disability, intersectional identity, human–animal relations, the environment, new class formations under global capitalism, and so on. And while the post-Seattle alterglobalization/New Weird confluence may not have played out in the way Miéville hoped, the subsequent decades have nonetheless produced a speculative fiction that is profoundly dissatisfied with the world we have wrought and that urges us to make other worlds possible.

NOTES

1 Jonathan Lethem, "Close Encounters: The Squandered Promise of Science Fiction," *Village Voice Literary Supplement*, April 1998, https://hipsterbookclub.livejournal.com/1147850.html.

2 James Patrick Kelly and John Kessel, "Introduction," in *The Secret History of Science Fiction*, edited by James Patrick Kelly and John Kessel (San Francisco: Tachyon, 2009), 8.

3 Among genre aficionados, the high–low distinction has often been articulated as a defense of robust genre fiction from the affectations of an insipid literary mainstream, of SF from fantasy and horror, of hard SF from soft SF, and of prose SF from media SF.

4 Bruce Sterling, "CATSCAN: Slipstream," *SF Eye* 5 (July 1989): 78.

5 Gary K. Wolfe, "Malebogle, or the Ordnance of Genre," in *Evaporating Genres: Essays on Fantastic Literature* (Middletown: Wesleyan University Press, 2011), 15.

6 Gary K. Wolfe, "Evaporating Genres," in *Evaporating Genres: Essays on Fantastic Literature*, 51.

7 The thread is no longer accessible, but a version of it is included in Ann VanderMeer and Jeff VanderMeer, *The New Weird* (San Francisco: Tachyon, 2008).

8 China Miéville, "New Weird," in *Nebula Awards Showcase 2005*, edited by Jack Dann (New York: ROC, 2005), 50.

9 Amitav Ghosh, *The Great Derangement: Climate Change and the Unthinkable* (Chicago: The University of Chicago Press, 2016), 26.

10 Ibid., 59.

11 Ibid., 63.

12 Adam Trexler, *Anthropocene Fictions: The Novel in a Time of Climate Change* (Charlottesville: University of Virginia Press, 2015), 226.

13 Ibid., 229.

14 See Carl Freedman, *Critical Theory and Science Fiction* (Hanover: Wesleyan University Press, 2000), 44–62.

15 Neal Stephenson, *Seveneves*, (London: Harper Collins, 2016), 569.

16 William Gibson, Twitter post, August 17, 2018, 8:19 PM, https://twitter.com/greatdismal/status/1030655297633697792?lang=en

17 See Priscilla Wald, *Contagious: Cultures, Carriers, and the Outbreak Narrative* (Durham: Duke University Press, 2008).

18 See Grace L. Dillon, "Imagining Indigenous Futurisms," in *Walking the Clouds: An Anthology of Indigenous Science Fiction*, edited by Grace L. Dillon (Tucson: University of Arizona Press, 2012).

19 Geral Vizenor, *Fugitive Poses: Native American Indian Scenes of Absence and Presence* (Lincoln: University of Nebraska Press, 1998), 15.

20 Dillon, "Imagining Indigenous Futurisms," 10.

21 Sesshu Foster, *Atomik Aztex* (San Francisco: City Lights, 2005), 1.

22 On queer SF, see Wendy Gay Pearson, Veronica Hollinger, and Joan Gordon, eds., *Queer Universes: Sexualities in Science Fiction* (Liverpool: Liverpool University Press, 2008). On disability and SF, see Kathryn Allen, *Disability in Science Fiction: Representations of Technology as Cure* (Basingstoke: Palgrave Macmillan, 2008).

4

KATALIN ORBÁN

Graphic Fiction

Beginning with Art Spiegelman's *Maus: A Survivor's Tale* (1980), the last decades of the twentieth century saw a seismic shift in the cultural positioning of American graphic narrative.[1] Along with Alan Moore and Dave Gibbons's *Watchmen* (1986),[2] *Maus* consolidated the earlier emergence of comics' cultural value, demonstrating the seriousness of the medium by focusing on the Holocaust. Spiegelman's thematic choice was a complex genocidal event subject to intricate representational regulations and particularly strict visual protocols, and the prevailing approach to the Holocaust as a limit event set the authenticity of the document and testimony against the sacrilegious insolence of attempts to imagine and aestheticize it. *Maus* ingeniously used the non-photographic visual form of comics to create a transformed view, one that resists the voyeuristic display of dehumanized victims, yet also rejects the denigration of vision and the valorization of silence. *Maus* won the Pulitzer Prize in 1992, and the ensuing decade witnessed a decisive movement of comics into the hallowed institutions of the cultural canon – the bookstore, the library, and the university curriculum. And yet comics remained within a tacit struggle against an assumed stigmatization, the presumption of light entertainment, limited literacy, and childishness. Unlike the Francophone *bande dessinée*, with its much longer history of prestige and institutions, American comics had to make repeated claims to mainstream cultural value, at times to the point of elitist self-denial. In its ambivalent aspirations to art and literary culture and partial break with mass cultural formats and modes of circulation, American comics as *books* became a site of debate over cultural value. This was perhaps best captured by the emergence in critical and popular discourse of the distinctively Anglo-American term *graphic novel*, which erased the semantic connection to the comic and suggested that certain long-form graphic narratives are respectable literary products (while misleadingly subsuming various genres of life writing and reportage under the label of the novel).[3] Embraced most wholeheartedly by the publishing industry, at times

criticized by comics creators as a euphemistic sign of the unwelcome gentrification of comics,[4] but also increasingly recognized as an existing and
lasting type of practice in the medium of comics, the graphic novel label
engendered critical debate about the cultural role and artistic merit of
the medium.

While critics and scholars debated alternative names and definitions of the
medium,[5] the books and new audiences kept coming in, drawn perhaps by a
perceptually rich reading experience that combined immersion with the
attention patterns of an increasingly visually oriented multitasking culture.
Graphic narratives sold through traditional book retailers rather than spe-
cialized comics shops became one of the highest growth categories in the
book market[6] and part of the mainstream reading repertoire. Inventive and
serious graphic narratives and reprint collections were regularly published
by dedicated presses, including Fantagraphics hardcover collections (reprints
of Robert Crumb's work, the Hernandez brothers' *Love & Rockets* series
[1982–1996], and many others) and their European graphic novel line
(2005), Drawn & Quarterly's publications, and McSweeney's issue #13 on
Comics, edited by Chris Ware (2004).

Their readers might still be unsure at times if what they do counts as "real
reading,"[7] but there is now an extensive and varied corpus of American
graphic narrative, stratified in style, theme, technique, and in its producers'
and consumers' cultural identities, which is being read in the way more
traditional literary forms are read. This continuity with contemporary fiction
is based on the discernment of a partly established, yet also variable and
discoverable set of features that requires a primarily aesthetic judgment. It
also demands being attuned to nuanced interpretive possibilities, often
unfolding in a process of deepening narrative relationships and inviting
explorations through rereading. However, this comparable disposition gives
rise to different practices in the case of graphic fiction, because the reader's
attention is intrinsically more divided in processing the comics form, and
discerning relationships is a less exclusively mental exercise and frequently
depends on physical perception, sensory orientation to detail or overview,
which in turn calls for a more material engagement with the medium than
conventional fiction. At the same time, the mainstreaming of graphic fiction
by the twenty-first century allows authors to inhabit the entire spectrum of
convention and innovation: they can rely on the general reader's ability to
appreciate variations and styles on the basis of familiarity with the aesthetic
features of comics, and they can make radical experiments on the foundation
of assumed aesthetic value justifying difficulty.

Another implication of this spectrum is the shifting – nostalgic, ironic,
earnest, or ambivalent – approaches to retaining and cultivating the roots of

graphic fiction in popular culture. Charles Hatfield and later Jan Baetens and Hugo Frey have convincingly argued that an overly sharp division between comic books produced in the economic context of the cultural industry and auteur graphic narratives of a presumed elite culture are not only suspect, but – if the division were to be maintained very strictly – would also be damaging to the graphic novel in the long run: its rarefied isolation would arguably drain it of the energy and inspiration it takes from its roots in popular culture and, quite often, eliminate the financial feasibility of its production through advance or interim serialized publishing.[8] On the other hand, as Baetens and Frey also point out, it is important to recognize the contours of a more nuanced type of graphic narrative[9] and to identify how it contributes to the ongoing adjustments of the understanding of literature in a cultural context where the long-form reading of homogenous texts is no longer the norm.[10] For instance, the heterogeneity of the comics form and the variability of spatial arrangements allows authors to develop a rich constellation of story lines that may unfold either in succession or synchrony, to modulate or suspend the narrative status of what appears (for example, using blatant or obscure visual devices to indicate the real or imaginary, diegetic or extradiegetic status of something, changing focalization, or eliminating verbal temporal markers in "silent" panels to create an opaque narrative context). Given the centrality of arrangement and layout to meaning, searching is an integral part of the dynamic and visually oriented reading process of graphic narrative: in addition to following multiple tracks, the reader of graphic fiction must also scan the field in order to identify and reappraise potentially meaningful elements. These features of graphic fiction often uniquely combine the sustained attention devoted to literary interpretation with the scattered attention and multidirectional alertness of pervasive contemporary nonliterary reading practices. While this degree of complexity was previously absent or a result of the serial accrual of storyworlds, twenty-first-century graphic fiction increasingly displays it in larger complex stories in single works.

The Space of Participatory Reading

The aesthetic, literary quality of graphic narrative resides in the possibilities of the dynamic participatory interaction between author and reader rather than in the independent qualities of either the artwork or the text. Comics combine images and words in a unique hybrid mode of picture-writing[11] that is governed by the sequential logic of the story, the material characteristics of the given format, and by the contingencies of production by the creator's hand – an organic process arising out of the mutual impact of consciousness and gesture in drawing. In other words, the relationship is not illustrative, even when there is an imbalance between the image and word components in either direction. The different perceptual modes of linear writing and looking at images and the necessary alternation of focus between smaller and larger units of composition (for instance, details, panels, pages, or double-page spreads) as well as the constant reliance on negative space created by framing elements call for a dynamic, participatory reading process, which is one of the main pleasures of reading graphic narratives. This dynamism inheres in the necessary oscillation between focal and peripheral views and the mutual enrichment of synthetic global vision and analytical deciphering.[12] In some cases, one follows the development of a story in panels arranged in the traditional reading order, a relatively conventional, even formulaic spatialization of time in sequences of left-right top-down paneling. These panels are, however, also part of the larger space of the page as a whole and are often visually linked to nonadjacent panels through repetition, similarity, or larger continuing shapes. Checking for such connections is an integral part of reading comics. Of course, any story in conventional fiction also spatializes time once it is recorded and materialized in lines, pages, or volumes succeeding each other; yet, even the simplest, most conventional graphic narrative makes this spatial sense of time inherently more complex by not merely translating temporal sequences to spatial arrangements, but also endowing iconic shapes and negative space with temporal significance. Ben Katchor's single-page stories of city life and urban history, for example, thrive on such visualizations of the disparate time scales of the minutiae of ordinary life and the long-term urban memory embedded in a changing and often obsolete material culture, dramatizing the contested significance of small details normally passed over or taken for granted. Even though the vignettes contain brief stories that are simple and ordinary to the point of seeming like non-stories, the spatial sense of time opens them to reflection and significance. At the other end of the spectrum, the medium lends itself to highly inventive arrangements with greater variation in compression and extension, which can resemble nonreading activities like play, puzzle-solving, or daydreaming.

Within the large array of long-form graphic narratives that are redrawing the outlines of contemporary American literature, certain trends have emerged across the genre: the recognition of the long-form, single-story book in print and the dominance of single-author works uniting the roles of writer and artist. In principle, collective or collaborative authorship of a graphic novel entails "a team of people with different roles and degrees of authority" and a complex "distribution of production roles and artistic responsibility" (such as writer, line artist, inker, colorist, editor, and others) subject to change during the life of the project.[13] This is standard practice in mass-art comics, although the visibility of the work and the perception of the relative significance of contributions as constituting authorship have varied. In American long-form graphic fiction, however, single authors with complete creative control have dominated the canon, and literariness and "absolutist constructions of authorship"[14] have been mutually validating. Since creating a long graphic narrative can be extremely laborious, many authors produce a large part of the book serially first. *Black Hole* (1995–2005) by Charles Burns, published in installments over ten years and then reissued as a book, is an example.[15] Yet, even this slow serialization can become a challenge, as Daniel Clowes recalls the effort to cater to the growing new audience for the kind of comics that would evolve into literary graphic narrative: "At a certain point I got so slow that I was taking over a year in between issues and it just – that whole serial nature became absurd."[16] Although such labor-intensive creative work makes the production of inventive, complex large narratives with epic unity and unity of design a major challenge (hence the partial reliance on the traditional economics of the comic book market), they offer rich multimodal, multisensory reading experiences drawing on an aesthetics of intimacy sustained by their embodied production and reading, the author typically drawing and lettering by hand and the reader engaged with the tactile visuality of handling the book object. The most extreme cases of such production and reception are what might be called conceptual works of literary graphic narrative, which foreground, investigate, and test the medium in unique ways and highlight the distinctiveness of its literary potential. Such inspiringly atypical conceptual-philosophical objects – thought-provoking and memorable, but hardly repeatable experiments – include Chris Ware's *Building Stories* (2012) and Richard McGuire's *Here* (2014).[17]

Radical Experiments with Assembling the Narrative

Building Stories is about an unnamed female protagonist and a host of minor characters – human, animal, and inanimate – who knowingly or unknowingly come in contact with her existence.[18] The narrative is a collection of fourteen unnumbered paper and cardboard objects in different print publication formats, including hardcover books, pamphlets, broadsheets, and a folding game board, among others, contained in a big cardboard box. The collection has no marked beginning and end, so the exploratory and participatory reading of comics pages, in which page design creates meaningful connections and paths between panels, has to be replicated in assembling the larger narrative from its cohesive but disparate parts. At some point, the couple struggling with their failing relationship in a

Chicago brownstone are revealed to be the protagonist's downstairs neighbors; a character appearing in *The Daily Bee* newspaper, price 2 pollen, turns out to have been fatally trapped in the basement of the same brownstone. Their stories fall into *place* and *time* in a narrative edifice not unlike the building that ties the events and characters together and appears as a sentient thinking and remembering character in one story, but the variations in the order of reading and rereading will make the participatory discovery of the whole very different for individual readers. The protagonist's own story grows from a similar accrual of temporal layers, prehistories, consequences, and digressions within and between the story-objects. For example, careful observation of an elongated rectangular wordless flip-book reveals that it condenses discontinuous phases over different seasonal changes in the woman's life as a mother in a suburban home as her daughter grows up at a flip-book pace. The differences in reading have subtle effects on interpretation, never jeopardizing the ontological stability and coherence of the diegetic world. The unpredictable order primarily governs the shifting constructions of the familiar and the strange, producing tension and mystery within the familiar, temporally situated context. As signaled by the fusion of narrative and architectural construction in the title, this dispersal of the narrative into things that need to be held, handled, and read differently also anchors the reading experience in a sensuous interaction with three-dimensional material objects rather than viewing words and images flattened to the abstract plane of the page. Due to these requirements of close attention and sensuous, immersive phases of exploration, the work offers a commentary on distraction (most specifically on the distraction fed by network culture in the chapter "Disconnect") while inviting a reading that is everything but distracted.

Building Stories, as both process and object, amplifies the dynamic interplay within the hybrid language of comics, the lively alternation between the closer view of details and their narrative (re)contextualization within the diegetic horizon of the visible page or double-page spread. Different kinds of looking and even different ways of holding or turning the text are required by tiny script; by enormous conjunctions like THUS or AND appearing as large typographical images in narrative sequences; by diagrammatic-analytical overviews, layouts, and grids of the story emphasizing the grammar of picture-writing; and by tracking potentially meaningful visual elements that may be passed over as random or decorative. The resulting typographic and visual awareness not only introduces reading options and variations as visual play, but also emphasizes the materiality of signs and the continuity, rather than opposition, of literary and visual arts.[19] Experimental novels have used comparable typographical and visual strategies to enrich and destabilize the sources of meaning and to halt and derail linear progression, but rather as departures from the undisputed dominance of verbal expression, unlike the far more balanced alternation here, where no mode is the natural *home* of narration from which experimental excursions can be made.

Unlike *Building Stories*, which thrives on the variability of graphic story-telling and its material forms, McGuire's *Here* is based on single-minded repetition, the overwhelming unity of design, while exploiting the unique possibilities of spatializing time in the medium. What Ware's and McGuire's bold experiments share is not so much a general aesthetics of difficulty, but rather an exploration of the limits of the form that presents itself on the scale of a complete work rather than in its processual, serial origin. *Here* is a narrative of the events that occur in a single place – which is a room in a house in the United States – between 3,000,500,000 BCE and 22,175, represented non-chronologically from a fixed point of view. (The twenty-five-year process that took this curious concept from its the original six-page version published under Françoise Mouly and Art Spiegelman's editorship in *RAW* magazine in 1989 to its final version in a hefty novel-shaped hardcover book that nevertheless explodes fundamental narrative assumptions of conventional fiction encapsulates the era in question rather well.) Graphic narrative always represents time as space, typically using panel shapes and arrangements to indicate temporal dimensions, while also creating perspective. A sense of passing time and pace is normally generated by successive panels and the gutter between them, complemented by the often elaborate trans-linear connections of long-form comics, linking panels across page boundaries. *Here* stakes everything on the representation of time, yet almost completely abandons the simultaneously visible panel sequences that are the primary means of temporal ordering in graphic storytelling. This is a radical experiment, because it drastically transforms the two most distinctive features of comics form: sequenced panels and the significance of the page (or double page) as a unit of meaning.

Although the customary means of indicating temporal relations in comics through sequence, shape, and verbal reference are severely reduced, the book interestingly does not dissolve into temporal chaos, but rather establishes an alternative order that cuts through the linear passage of time. Each double page has a small label in the top left corner, indicating the date of the borderless double-page image of the same place from the same perspective; many of the pages also have additional numerically dated smaller panels of varying sizes and number, and the replacement of the gutter with an unobtrusive narrow panel frame turns the double page into an intermittently translucent palimpsest of time with slivers of the past and future embedded or floating within the given here and now. The eternal persistence of a fixed perspective evokes a transhuman and disembodied view – whether divine, cosmic, or geological is undeterminable – rather than an anthropocentric sense of point of view for the states of life observed and the countless microstories developing in parallel over numerous pages. These are not fractured, partial experiences and selves of modernist multitemporality seemingly held together by subjective perspective, urban infrastructure, or standardized time, but rather an array of mutual implications in a vast vision of interconnections that can generate countless stories, some of which appear, while others remain hidden. They nevertheless draw on the tradition of modernist difficulty insofar as the reader's task of assembling potentially connected parts is similarly challenging. The unconventional use of paneling to represent temporal layers puts great demands on the reader to read and remember multiple parts of the timeline, recognizing settings, decors, and characters based on images, dates, and dialogue, but without the help of verbal narration. The unfolding loose set of microstories – of prehistoric and future environmental events, the Native American deer hunter and the politically divided colonial family, residents of the building during its time of existence, and post-human beings – are not arranged as an evolutionary narrative in a flip-book blur of environmental and social change, but rather as coexisting, their connections as much thematic (identical words or concepts, such as loss) and visual (resemblance of shape or color) as narrative and causal, resulting in a rhythmic, rhyming, quasi-musical composition.

The diverse types of connections ensure that the composition is irreducible to a story (however difficult to piece together) or an archeology. Within a double page dated 1986 (see Figure 4.1), the vertical wooden plank held by a couple in 1972 visually rhymes with the tree trunks a Native American woman leans on in 1352 before going for a swim in the lake, and the composition of the landscape painting on their wall rhymes with the forest scene, but there is also a causal relationship (replacement of the tree by industrial wood products in the process of manufacturing and the resulting replacement of landscapes by their visual representations). The large panel including the inserts of both scenes is an almost completely obstructed view of the room in the year supplying the narrative connection between the two scenes: 1986 is the year when members of the local archeological society visit the resident to tell her that her home had been built over an important site of Native American culture, a story developed much earlier in the book. Rather than leaping back and forth in the plot, the juxtaposition of such panels and their representation of multi-temporality can be interpreted as a type of synchronicity and copresence or as the relative absence of successive realities, resulting alternatively in a sense of plenitude and interconnectedness or a sense of ghostly emptiness, the fragility, even mirage of life. What

86

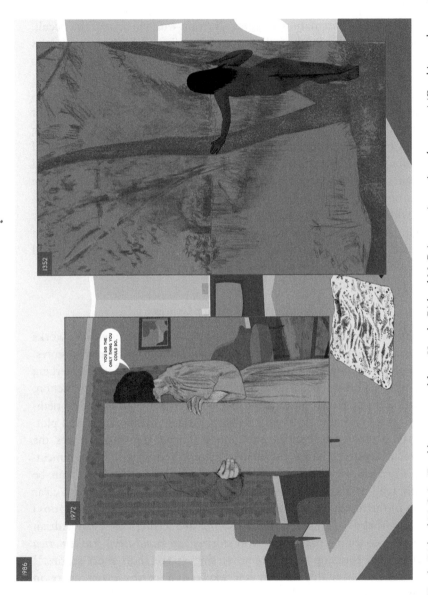

Figure 4.1 *Here* by Richard McGuire (Double-page spread from *Here* by Richard McGuire, n.p. (unpaginated 190–191) (Graphic novel excerpt from *Here* by Richard McGuire, copyright © 2014 by Richard McGuire. Used by permission of Pantheon Books, an imprint of the Knopf Doubleday Publishing Group, a division of Penguin Random House LLC. All rights reserved.)

87

ecological readings identify as the representation of the Anthropocene era on a geological time scale[20] can also be recognized as a transcendental sense of life intimated in hauntings and premonitions, but never fully grasped, for which the non-photographic visualization of drawing serves as a type of magical medium of animation, aligning drawing with magic and the occult.

Experiments of this kind on the scale of Ware's and McGuire's projects not only show that some "cartoonists have started to think of themselves as designers,"[21] planning elaborate physical objects in non-standardized formats, but the willingness of some publishers to risk distribution challenges by allowing authors to make innovatively idiosyncratic decisions about format and page design. While this can create new possibilities of shifting attention between details and contexts – drastically enlarging the span of alternation in *Building Stories*, for instance – variations in format, size, and base material complicate collection in a single book format and increase production costs. It is noteworthy that even these radical long-form experiments with the medium retain the possibility of immersion into the story through the medium-specific sensuous imaginative participation in absorbing narrative sequences, in which the structured time of panel arrangements turns into an immersive experience of time.[22]

Adaptations of Literary Genres

The majority of contemporary American comics fiction, however, works within more moderate adaptations of conventional literary narrative genres. In fact, beside examples of the twenty-first-century trend of genre-merging fiction and the porous borders between literary production and genre fiction, they can seem positively traditional in their revival of familiar twentieth-century genres of literature based on their treatment of characters and plot. This may be the case, because multimodal formal innovation takes the pressure of creative change off strictly textual and generic development. *Jimmy Corrigan, or the Smartest Kid on Earth* (1995) by Ware can be fruitfully read as a graphic novel (an indisputable term for once in a clear revision of the multigenerational *Familienroman*), *La Perdida* (2001–2005) by Jessica Abel as a graphic novella, *Killing and Dying* (2015) by Adrian Tomine as a collection of graphic short stories, and *Hand-drying in America* (2013) by Ben Katchor as a volume of single-page short-short stories.[23] These versions inevitably modify the expression of the given genre in medium-specific ways, but the degree of concentration and elaboration, the variety of components (characters, subplots, and settings) they can hold, and therefore the types of stories they invite and fit, are the same. Tomine recalls that, after publishing a number of short stories in comic book format in the

Optic Nerve series (1995–2016), he "felt obligated to attempt a real 'graphic novel,'" envious of the monumental achievement represented by the "giant tomes" produced by some of his peers. He would soon abandon the project that would limit his ability to shift styles and the scope of which was draining "joy from the work," to remain a short-story writer.[24] Aside from personal authorial preferences or the assumed hierarchy of genres, the development of these independent alternatives indicates the maturity of graphic narrative as a medium of literature.

As comics, the four examples are very different, ranging from the geometric-diagrammatic to the expressive, from completely conventional and uniform paneling to wildly changing unique page designs, and from loquacious narration and dialogue to verbal reticence and long stretches of silent panels. These formal and stylistic choices reflect a literary self-knowing and a sense of tradition and influence in a wide variety of ways. For example, Tomine's short story "A Brief History of the Art Form Known as 'Hortisculpture'" may be identified as using conventional paneling, but that convention is used as a quotation and imitation of the daily newspaper comic strip in cycles of six black-and-white weekday strips and one double-sized Sunday strip in color. Given its publication in a comic book and later in a 128-page-long hardcover book, the story format not only references the daily strip (as a tradition and recognized influence), but also newspaper comic strip *reprint* collections (the recent rediscovery, preservation, and canonization of that tradition). In this sense, the uniform regular arrangement is no less a complex, reflective literary choice than the endlessly changing arrangements in *Jimmy Corrigan*.

Compared to recent non-graphic novels, the share of (auto)biographical works in graphic narrative fiction is striking, though the degrees of fictionalization and the implied distance between the authors and their alter egos can vary widely. Hillary Chute argues persuasively for an affinity between comics and narratives of development and suggests that their inherent formal fragmentation suits reconstructions of traumatic memory: "Through its hybrid and spatial form, comics lends itself to expressing stories, especially narratives of development, that present and underscore hybrid subjectivities."[25] Even so, these types of works seem particularly prominent in contemporary American graphic narrative, falling into various subgenres of life writing, often balancing autobiographical elements with the stories of parents or several generations, sometimes encapsulating whole lives, but occasionally limiting themselves to a few significant years. In their diverse ways, they take advantage of the capacity of graphic narrative to create associative links between events both moments and generations apart, thereby modeling the operations and dysfunctions of memory.

Alison Bechdel's *Fun Home: A Family Tragicomic* (2006) builds a memoir of a father-daughter relationship as gothic as the mansion in which the family lived their complicated lives, whereas Gabrielle Bell's *Everything Is Flammable* (2017) telescopes the history of a mother-daughter relationship into just one intense year of moving back to the scene of her childhood, after her mother loses her home in a fire, making the small nonevents of the everyday luminous with a stark, but darkly hilarious existential reappraisal of life.[26] GB Tran's narrative of self-discovery through the reconstruction of a multigenerational diasporic family history fraught with secrets and silences in *Vietnamerica* (2010) is even larger in scale: the dual journeys of the author's present return and the older generations' prior exile and loss he ends up discovering include a huge cast of characters and multiple locations and storylines in the family history.[27] Craig Thompson's *Blankets* (2003) is a more lyrical bildungsroman, a long flowing account of growing up in the Midwest in a fundamentalist Christian family that denigrates artistic talent and of negotiating the struggle with art and faith in the process of becoming an adult.[28]

While similarly coming-of-age narratives, Phoebe Gloeckner's *The Diary of a Teenage Girl* (2002) and David Small's *Stitches* (2009) are accounts focused on more specific losses and wounds, inflicted by family members as sexual abusers and negligent parents.[29] Gloeckner expands and revises her one-time diary into a trauma memoir interspersed with pictures and comics pages, telling the inextricable stories of her alter ego's sexual awakening and abuse by her mother's boyfriend. *Stitches* ingeniously combines medical autobiography, family history, and bildungs- and *Künstlerroman*, telling the story of young David's loss of voice as a result of an illness suffered through neglect and mistreatment in a dysfunctional family of medical professionals and of his subsequent recovery through therapy and art. A more complicated genre experiment is at work in Emil Ferris's *My Favorite Thing Is Monsters* (2016), set in 1960's Chicago with a subplot in Nazi Germany and narrated as the journal of its young protagonist, a social outcast who imagines herself as a monster. Combining 20 percent memoir, 38 percent mystery and 15 percent historical fiction (by the author's tongue-in-cheek breakdown), the book transforms autobiographical material into Karen's fictional journal through lovingly reworked popular, even pulp genres and a deliberate performance of outsider or novice status (using BIC pens and "ruining" the artwork with the intrusive lines of the lined notebook). These incorporate the effects of both commercial professionalism and nonprofessional authorship into the presentation of literature as art. Finally, a considerable part of graphic reportage, notably Joe Sacco's work,[30] integrates its journalistic subject with the reporter's subjective life experience deeply enough to warrant inclusion in this group of autobiographically based literary works. The distinctive constellation of temporal frames within a space of exploration at a reader-governed pace that makes the medium attuned to memory also "lends it a representational mode capable of taking up complex political and historical issues with an explicit, formal degree of self-awareness."[31] While graphic reportage shifts the emphasis from the family to the public sphere, the often extensive representation and involvement of the authorial alter ego in the metastory of finding, producing, and delivering the news story usually turns these into a type of autobiographical work with the same literary ambitions and qualities as more recognizable memoirs.

Expanding the Language of Contemporary Literature

The literary qualities of contemporary graphic narratives are both like traditional criteria of literary value, such as the significance of implicit meaning available through interpretation and a foregrounding of the aesthetic quality of the text, and unlike them insofar as they are inseparable from the nature of their partly visual medium. In other words, they can be productively treated as literature, if one accepts that they collectively revise what counts as *language* in contemporary literature, extending it to a more complex hybrid language produced and received within the institution of literature. In order to assess how they expand the possibilities of contemporary literature, it is useful to register some notable characteristics in their production of literary value.

The potential for rich and subtle layers of meaning in graphic narrative primarily relies less on verbal or visual stylistic choices alone, but rather on synchronous multiplicity, on the possible confluence of meanings from different sources, some of which are always and explicitly meaningful (narration and dialogue), while others are more ambiguously coded and completely tacit (iconic aspects of the verbal, for instance, in lettering; iconic and non-iconic elements of the nonverbal visual). For instance, a chapter of *Vietnamerica*, which is focalized through the mother character, recounts the death of her step-brother Vinh, killed by a land mine while on patrol shortly after being drafted.[32] As banal and life-altering events unfold concurrently at home and in the war in this six-page sequence, the paneling creates a sense of time affected by delays and differing paces through its composition of multiple sources of meaning. Framed as a failed exchange of letters, the sequence focuses on gaps of knowledge between senders and addressees, both information intentionally withheld and logistically delayed (see Figure 4.2). Thanks to the iconic markers of the sender and the letter

Figure 4.2 Detail from *Vietnamerica* by GB Tran (Graphic novel excerpt from
Vietnamerica: A Family's Journey by GB Tran, copyright © 2011 by Gia-Bao Tran.
Used by permission of Villard Books, an imprint of Random House, a division of Penguin
Random House LLC. All rights reserved.)

(the mother's handwriting and a dog-eared rectangle), messages can hover autonomously in any visual space (for instance, the tranquil empty sea off the coast of Vietnam) and still retain a link to the character and narrative situation. When the mother's message expressing hope for Vinh's safe return and recounting the banal details of a tactfully embellished home life float in panels showing the explosion and impact of the mine, there is a brutal collision of verbal and visual meanings, and its effect is amplified by the visually created mystery of *when* this is taking place. Already unmoored from its moment of composition on its precarious way to a destination, the message hovers over the addressee's destruction in a diegetically impossible space, since the unfinished letter shown falling into the black space of the page background has obviously exploded along with its reader. Consequently, the time that fuses the second-by-second anatomy of the moment of catastrophe with the eternal reflection on a message and life lost forever, never happened except here in the book. Graphic narrative, thanks to its capacity for narrating by showing, is capable of creating such imaginative spaces that exploit the conflict between visual evidence and narrative counterfactuality. Importantly, these paces are created visually, through panel shapes, color, and technique: large reflective panels in graded watercolor wash with no action alternate with vertical stacks of shrinking panels anatomizing clearly outlined scenes of human interaction governed by measured time, schedules, and decisions. These verbal and visual sources of meaning work in concert without being predetermined; while they involve conventions of the medium, their complex narrative meaning is generated *in situ*, and often in ways that require close attention, rereading, and making connections across pages or even chapters.

Additionally, the reader frequently needs to reevaluate what components of the visible page and what connections between elements need to be factored into this generation of meaning. A hue or texture may fade into the setting or be recognized as carrying information about the narrative status of what is depicted. A shape or size can be regarded rhythmically or referentially. In this example, if we decode the iconic meaning of the panel showing the fateful step on the land mine in extreme close-up, we identify its curled-up corner – hit by the KLIK sound of the land mine from below – as the dog-ear mark of the letter in the book. As the addressee of this "letter," the reader is invited to imagine herself in the same position of delayed and limited understanding as the characters. Finally, the meaning of the letter falling into black space is revised in the last pages of the book, when it is echoed in the climactic representation of the narrow escape of the author's parents in the evacuation: the slow fall of a leaf across nine full pages of black, the impenetrable border between lives before and after, which installs itself at the moment of exile and which the book is in the service of partially dismantling. Narrative relationships can visually manifest themselves in alternating styles, forms, lettering, and color palette, identifying generational differences and family lineages. Even more importantly, the affordances and commitments of the image allow (inter)cultural memoirs to present the density of what is not understood, yet force it to show specific details of represented reality.

Similarly, twenty-first-century graphic narrative literalizes metaphoricity in ways that distinguish it from contemporary (and earlier) prose narrative. Nearly all of the works mentioned in this section prioritize recurring visual metaphors (not infrequently indicated in the title): the house and its teeming ornaments in *Fun Home*, the stitched-up wound and the rabbit hole quoted from *Alice in Wonderland* in *Stitches*, the tree leaves and roots and packing boxes in *Vietnamerica*, the blanket in *Blankets*, and fire and the animal in *Everything Is Flammable*, for instance. Some of these metaphors can easily be translated into the conceptual mapping of one thing understood in terms of another, drawing on both verbal and visual elements of their context. However, the use of visual metaphor in a multimodal text can undermine the strict hierarchy of the metaphorical substitution of one term for another, as visualization pulls what is figured into the material plane of the image surface. Instead of making a metaphorical projection from embodied experience, it produces an altered, transposed embodiment. This is analogous to Baetens and Frey's observation that the clear distinction between narration and description in conventional fiction cannot be maintained in graphic narratives, because narrating inescapably entails describing.[33]

The elaborate metaphor of the house as the crafting of life and identity in *Fun Home* (the concepts of technique and invention drawn from the myth of Daedalus and Icarus) is also counter-metaphorically dismantled from the start, as the home is explained and shown as the crafting of a closeted life that both is and is not true, lived falsely but also actually. "It's tempting to suggest, in retrospect, that our family was a sham. That our house was not a real home at all, but the simulacrum of one, a museum. Yet we really were a family, and we really did live in those period rooms." When performing the duties of the ideal husband and father, in fact, merges *seeming* and *being* an ideal husband and father, it is the actuality of the figural from which there is no escape. Even when the verbal elaboration of the metaphorical understanding of life processes and relationships is so strong – thanks to a web of correspondences to myths and literary works and Bechdel's subtle narrative voice – and even when it internally, verbally critiques its own figuration, the specific images (of the house and its ornaments) affirm the embodied and concrete while opening different, pictorial figurative possibilities. Visuality also creates potentially less determined target-source hierarchies of meta-phor – in other words, it allows more ambiguity in terms of what is figured as what: house as life or life as house. Consequently, the metaphorical move is deflected, spreading laterally and idiosyncratically on the surface to asso-ciative links between embodied details.

Bell's *Everything Is Flammable* is punctuated by life's small alarms (strangers suddenly and inexplicably inviting themselves to the yard or cucumbers overpowering tomatoes in the container garden), as the narrative develops the grand metaphor of fire as existential peril: "The blanket was one of those synthetic flammable kind and it went up just like that .... I didn't know something could catch fire so quickly," reports the mother during the first phone call after the fire.[34] This figure of sudden overwhelm-ing loss, which is announced in the title and developed throughout the text, guides the reading of countless scenes of anxiety-ridden contemporary life presented with affectionate, but mordantly satirical self-analysis. Less notice-ably, through visual pairings of existential threat and animals in various panels, the animal also slowly emerges as its metaphorical counterpart. Pets and wild animals, which appear in the narrative either as terrifying feral creatures encroaching on the areas of habitation or, conversely, as the bedrock of affection, companionship, and intimacy that renders these areas minimally habitable, become the "animal," metaphorically understood as the residue of unnumbed experience, the dreaded and desired *heat* that only sporadically returns into life experienced as dish rack purchase and plumbing repair. In fact, it is only this visually underwritten metaphorical understanding of linked motifs over the whole narrative that permits a metaphorical understanding of the "synthetic flammable" object. These are not pictorial metaphors – for one thing, the generic concept of the animal is too abstract for visual representation – but a metaphorical understanding created through interlinked images and text, which is undetectable in any single one of the individual details (textual or visual) contributing to it.

One example of figuration that is particularly common in stories of trauma and illness, but is relevant to the medium as a whole, is the recurrent figurative connection between the book and the body. A connection predi-cated on the perceived intimacy of the hand as a mark of embodied writing and drawing in comics and on a sense of the body as potentially legible and decipherable, some version of this body-book is at work in Small's *Stitches* and Gloeckner's *The Diary of a Teenage Girl* among others. *Stitches* creates a relationship between the book and the body as a site of experience, in which the book comes to stand for the body without reducing it to meta-phor. Frequently representing embodied subjectivity as an interior architec-tural space and an imagined or imaged body cavity, the work maps this depth onto the book itself as a three-dimensional physical object, for instance, in fantasy sequences of David escaping his world by literally diving through the plane of the page and finding himself inside his body. There are correspondences between stitching wounds and panels, between physical voice impairment and long wordless stretches in the book. Yet there is a metonymic rather than metaphorical logic at work here too, in the process of transmitting David's experience to the reader through multiple mediated reembodiments of experience from handwriting and drawing to the reader physically touching the book.

This is a far more uncomfortable and ambivalent figuration than in Gloeckner's *Diary*, in which the book similarly comes to stand for the author's body, a kind of surrogate container for experiences, a connecting node but also a protective proxy between the external observer and the self. The child alter ego often seems to think of her diary "as a body or, at least, a metaphysical extension of her own body" and dreaming about "destroying the textual object she has composed as a register of self-effacement."[35] Opening the book becomes inseparable from exposing the body (of experience) represented in it and, given the theme and particularly the graphic sexual imagery with which Gloeckner confronts the reader, this puts the reader in the uncomfortable position of witness-voyeur. We are invited to reimagine with the adult author the experience of the child-author of the original diaries in a textual body they co-constructed, responding to their different perspectives and contradictory statements of consent (Gloeckner approves, but her child alter ego prohibits it).[36] This figure of the book-body relies both on the idea of the diary as intimately connected to the diarist and, once again, on the "affordances of labored embodiment through the line,"[37] represented by drawings and comics rather than typed text in the unusual generic mixture of the work.[38]

Graphic Narrative in the Contemporary Mediascape

While the importance of this "labored embodiment" is particularly obvious in works that focus on the body thematically, it is also important for understanding the place graphic narrative has in the new understanding – even rediscovery – of *reading* in a rapidly shifting contemporary media environment. Many of the insights into reading complex multimodal texts in the digital era are applicable to reading graphic narrative, even though its emerging canon is published in print and even foregrounds the book as a physical object. By contrast, the cultural implications of recent "deep changes in the forms and functions of writing," the change from a *world told* to a *world shown*, which will undoubtedly have "profound effects on human, cognitive/affective, cultural and bodily engagement with the world, and on the forms and shapes of knowledge"[39] are nearly always identified with a shift to the screen. Where does this leave graphic narrative in relation to reading and to literature?

Graphic fiction, I would argue, has become a rich and successful medium for the early twenty-first century precisely at the time when the natural relation between book, page, text, and reading can no longer be taken for granted, but can still be intimately inhabited. It creates an intersection between the finite and enduring material objects and the new reading practices and literacies in our increasingly digital lives. Comics as a finite, carefully designed multimodal construction is positioned somewhere between the kind of reading in which readers "follow the pregiven complexities of the syntactic reading path" and the one asking "that the reader establish a reading path on the basis of criteria of her or his relevance," a cognitive characteristic of reading multimodal texts, especially more open-ended ones.[40] This latter type of reading is rarely united with the affordances of labored embodiment, with the sensory modalities of reading non-ephemeral tangible objects with dimensions and weight independent of the reading process (the material properties of the book), as it is in the "giant tomes" of graphic narrative. Long-form graphic narrative seems to retain some capacity for deep reading, for being transported into a storyworld without the interruptions and interventions often required by manipulating electronic text or the need to exercise a degree of authorial control,[41] while also meeting new cognitive expectations of screen-habituated readers. It appears that graphic fiction *as* literature is an attractive proposition of dynamically multitasking our way to a renewed sense of absorption and psychological investment in unified texts in a largely post-print culture.

NOTES

1 Art Spiegelman, *Maus: A Survivor's Tale*, vol. 1, *My Father Bleeds History* (New York: Pantheon, 1986); *Maus: A Survivor's Tale*, vol. 2, *And Here My Troubles Began* (New York: Pantheon, 1991).

2 Alan Moore and Dave Gibbons, *Watchmen* (New York: DC Comics, 2008).

3 Although there are some earlier sporadic documented instances of the term, Will Eisner is widely held to have introduced the concept of graphic novel (in addition to sequential art) in order "to stress the literary ambition of the 'art' comics." Jan Baetens, "New = Old, Old = New," *Electronic Book Review*, January 1, 2001, http://electronicbookreview.com/essay/new-old-old-new.

4 Spiegelman calls it a "Faustian deal," risking the work becoming "arid and genteel." W. J. T. Mitchell and Art Spiegelman, "Public Conversation: What the %$#! Happened to Comics?: May 19, 2012," *Critical Inquiry* 40, no. 3 (Spring 2014): 24.

5 The debates about names and definitions, which responded to the challenge of the broad formal variety of works and at times to the embattled legitimacy of comics, eventually subsided even to the point of arguments questioning the usefulness of defining the medium, as in A. Meskin, "Defining Comics?," *The Journal of Aesthetics and Art Criticism* 65, no. 4 (2007): 369–379. The issue has resurfaced with the appearance of digital comics, which are not always easily distinguishable from games, apps, and animation, for example, in the context of library collection and preservation. See Jen Aggleton, "Defining Digital Comics: A British Library Perspective," *Journal of Graphic Novels and Comics* (2018): 1–17.

6 "Comics and Graphic Novels One of Highest Growth Categories in Publishing, Reports NPD," *The NPD Group*, October 6, 2017, www.npd.com/wps/portal/npd/us/news/press-releases/2017/comics-and-graphic-novels-one-of-highest-growth-categories-in-publishing-reports-npd/.

7 Jennifer M. Smith and Kathryn Pole, "What's Going On in a Graphic Novel?" *The Reading Teacher* 72, no. 2 (2018): 1; Stergios Botzakis, "Adult Fans of Comic Books: What They Get Out of Reading," *Journal of Adolescent & Adult Literacy* 53, no. 1 (2009): 50–59.

8 Charles Hatfield, *Alternative Comics: An Emerging Literature* (Jackson: University Press of Mississippi, 2005); Jan Baetens and Hugo Frey, *The Graphic Novel: An Introduction* (New York: Cambridge University Press, 2017), 18.

9 Baetens and Frey, *The Graphic Novel*, 18.

10 Anne Mangen and Adriaan van der Weel, "The Evolution of Reading in the Age of Digitisation: An Integrative Framework for Reading Research," *Literacy* 50, no. 3 (2016): 118.

11 Hillary L. Chute, *Disaster Drawn: Visual Witness, Comics, and Documentary Form* (Cambridge, MA: The Belknap Press of Harvard University Press, 2016), 69–71.

12 Thierry Groensteen, *The System of Comics*, trans. Bart Beaty and Nick Nguyen (Jackson: University Press of Mississippi, 2007), 19.

13 Jan Noel Thon, "Who's Telling the Tale: Authors and Narrators in Graphic Narrative," in *From Comic Strips to Graphic Novels: Contributions to the Theory and History of Graphic Narrative*, edited by Daniel Stein and Jan-Noël Thon (Berlin: De Gruyter, 2013), 88.

14 Maaheen Ahmed, "Comics and Authorship: An Introduction," *Authorship* 6, no. 2 (2017), DOI 10.21825/aj.v6i2.7702, 4.

15 Charles Burns, *Black Hole* (New York: Pantheon, 2005).

16 Charles Burns, Daniel Clowes, Seth, and Chris Ware, "Graphic Novel Forms Today: Panel Moderated by Hillary Chute," special issue, *Critical Inquiry* 40, no. 3, "Comics & Media," edited by Hillary Chute and Patrick Jagoda (2014): 167.

17 Chris Ware, *Building Stories* (New York: Pantheon, 2012); Richard McGuire, *Here* (New York: Pantheon, 2014).

18 For an extensive analysis of slow reading as an enhancer of haptic visuality in *Building Stories*, see Katalin Orbán, "Closer Than They Seem: Graphic Narrative and the Senses," in *The Edinburgh Companion to Contemporary Narrative Theories*, edited by Zara Dinnen and Robyn Warhol (Edinburgh: Edinburgh University Press, 2018), 239–255.

19 Johanna Drucker, *The Visible Word: Experimental Typography and Modern Art, 1909–1923* (Chicago: The University of Chicago Press, 1996).

20 Mahlu Mertens and Stef Craps, "Contemporary Fiction vs. the Challenge of Imagining the Timescale of Climate Change," *Studies in the Novel* 50, no. 1 (2018): 134–153.

21 Burns, Clowes, Seth and Ware, "Graphic Novel Forms Today," 154.

22 Tom Gunning, "The Art of Succession: Reading, Writing, and Watching Comics," special issue, *Critical Inquiry* 40, no. 3, edited by Chute and Jagoda "Comics & Media," 40.

23 Chris Ware, *Jimmy Corrigan, or the Smartest Kid on Earth* (New York: Pantheon, 2000); Jessica Abel, *La Perdida* (New York: Pantheon, 2006); Adrian Tomine, *Killing and Dying* (Montreal: Drawn & Quarterly, 2015); Ben Katchor, *Hand-Drying in America* (New York: Pantheon, 2013).

24 Adrian Tomine, "'Optic Nerve' 2011: An Interview with Adrian Tomine," interviewed by Jorge Khoury, *CBR*, November 29, 2011, www.cbr.com/optic-nerve-2011-an-interview-with-adrian-tomine/.

25 Hillary L. Chute, *Graphic Women: Life Narrative and Contemporary Comics* (New York: Columbia University Press, 2010), 5.

26 Alison Bechdel, *Fun Home: A Family Tragicomic* (Boston: Houghton Mifflin, 2006); Gabrielle Bell, *Everything Is Flammable* (Minneapolis: Uncivilized Books, 2017).

27 GB Tran, *Vietnamerica: A Family's Journey* (New York: Villard, 2010).

28 Craig Thompson, *Blankets* (Marietta: Top Shelf, 2003).

29 Phoebe Gloeckner, *The Diary of a Teenage Girl: An Account in Words and Pictures* (Berkeley: North Atlantic Books, 2015); David Small, *Stitches: A Memoir* (New York: Norton, 2009).

30 See especially Joe Sacco, *The Fixer: A Story from Sarajevo* (London: Jonathan Cape, 2004).

31 Chute, *Graphic Women*, 9.

32 Tran, *Vietnamerica*, 173–178.

33 Baetens and Frey, *The Graphic Novel*, 180.

34 Bell, *Everything Is Flammable*, 17.

35 R. Miller, "Keep Out, or Else: Diary as Body in The Diary of a Teenage Girl and Cruddy," in *Comics Memory: Archives and Styles (Palgrave Studies in Comics and Graphic Novels)*, edited by Maaheen Ahmed and Benoît Crucifix (London: Palgrave Macmillan, 2018), 116.

36 Gloeckner, *Diary*, xv, xix.

37 Miller, "Keep Out, or Else," 104.

38 Some essays on Bechdel's *Fun Home* make a similar point: Chute, *Graphic Women*, 195, 197; Robyn Warhol, "The Space Between: A Narrative Approach to Alison Bechdel's 'Fun Home,'" *College Literature* 38, no. 3 (2011): 6. For a critique of this opposition between handwriting and typewriting, see Aaron Kashtan, "My Mother Was a Typewriter: Fun Home and the Importance of Materiality in Comics Studies," *Journal of Graphic Novels and Comics* 4, no. 1 (2013): 92–116.

39 G. Kress, *Literacy in the New Media Age* (New York: Routledge, 2003), 1.

40 Ibid., 58.

41 See Anne Mangen and Adriaan van der Weel's perceptive analysis of the nearly complete failure of hypertext fiction, mistakenly expected to become the new form of fiction for readers of the digital era. Anne Mangen and Adriaan van der Weel, "Why Don't We Read Hypertext Novels?," *Convergence: The International Journal of Research into New Media Technologies* 23, no. 2 (2017): 166–181.

5

SCOTT RETTBERG

Digital Fiction

The first two decades of the twenty-first century represent an American era framed by shock, anger, sadness, and increasing cynicism. From the attack on the Twin Towers to the election of President Trump, the United States has lived through a period of interminable background war punctuated with moments of hope and slowly creeping fear, capped with a pandemic. Over this span the United States has seen the rise of the security state and deteriorating conceptions of personal privacy. In terms of our cultural engagement with technology, it has been a time of both ever-increasing connectedness and ever-expanding paranoia. It has also been the period in which the global network became ubiquitous and pervasive. We have gone from the wild west and wide-eyed utopianism of the early World Wide Web of the 1990s to an age of smartphones, tablets, networked watches – screens everywhere we turn – and Alexas listening for every utterance. Computational devices are tethered to every step we take and every sound we make, mediating many aspects of our engagement with culture, politics, and society.

Since 2000, a substantial corpus of work exploring the literary potential of digital media has been written. The field of electronic literature (e-lit), focused on born-digital literary practice, was largely defined as a recognizable area of academic research, rather than as a niche area of interest, during this twenty-year period. The Electronic Literature Organization, which I founded along with Robert Coover and Jeff Ballowe in 1999, has provided e-lit with an institutional center of gravity and an advocate for twenty years. Its conference series, the three volumes of the *Electronic Literature Collection*, the exhibitions and performance events it has produced, its archiving initiatives, the international consortium (CELL) of research databases it coordinates, and its social media community have all been essential to the production of a dynamic international field of creative and critical research.[1]

This chapter will largely be written in the margins of my book *Electronic Literature* (Polity, 2019), a comprehensive introduction to the histories and genres of e-lit. In it, I trace the emergent forms and techniques of e-lit including combinatory poetics, hypertext fiction, interactive fiction, kinetic and interactive poetry, and network writing, among others. Here I will focus specifically on those forms of electronic literature that can be defined as fiction and that, to a great extent, emerge in conversation with trends in late twentieth and early twenty-first-century American print fiction, such as literary postmodernism and conceptual writing. These forms also emerge from particular technological and cultural circumstances – we can regard the use of specific technological platforms as constraints that have distinctive effects on the form and style of works written in digital media.

Hypertext Technology and Hypertext Fiction

Hypertext fiction, the form of digital fiction most often addressed by literary criticism, had a substantial history before the turn of the millennium, marked by landmark classics such as *Uncle Roger* by Judy Malloy (1986) and *afternoon, a story* (1987) by Michael Joyce.[2] A series of important classics such as *Victory Garden* (1991) by Stuart Moulthrop[3] and *Patchwork Girl* (1995) by Shelley Jackson had been published on disk by Eastgate system in Storyspace software. Hypertext fiction had also already garnered a substantial body of important theoretical work from authors such as Jay Bolter, George Landow, and N. Katherine Hayles, and had even gained a place in the public discourse through Robert Coover's "The End of Books" (1992) published in the *New York Times Book Review* and subsequent articles in print newspapers and online publications.[4]

The core ideas of hypertext technology, such as associative indexing and universal knowledge access systems extend back to the thinking of Paul Otlet, Vannevar Bush, and Ted Nelson, who first introduced the term "hypertext" in his 1965 paper "A File Structure for the Complex, the Changing, and the Indeterminate."[5] Otlet developed a number of information classification systems and conceived of the "Universal Bibliographic Repertory," a notecard database of facts that eventually reached 15,000,000 entries, which has been described as an analog search engine. Bush was the director of the Office of Scientific Research and Development, the forerunner to DARPA, the agency responsible for the Manhattan Project and other advanced scientific projects organized by the US government during World War II. In an essay he published in *The Atlantic* in 1942, Bush speculated on how the type of collective scientific energy applied to the war effort might be applied toward peacetime advancement of civilization, and he proposed a number of potential scientific innovations, including the "memex," a microfilm-based technology that would serve as an "enlarged intimate supplement" to the user's memory, where the user could store all his books, records, and documents and, importantly, create "trails" through different series of documents. The idea was that indexing and connections between texts could be multiple and associative.[6] Theodor Holm Nelson described hypertext "to mean a body of written or pictorial material interconnected in such a complex way that it could not conveniently be presented or represented on paper."[7] In "Computer Lib/Dream Machines" (1974), Nelson extended this to a more expansive definition of "hyper-media" as "branching or performing presentations which respond to user actions."[8] From the 1960s (with the HES developed by Andries Van Dam, Ted Nelson, and students at Brown University) forward, a number of different hypertext authoring platforms emerged that could organize and link texts and media objects in nonlinear networked ways. Apple's first Macintosh computer shipped with HyperCard (1987), a hypertext system based on a metaphor of programmable punch card stacks that could be scripted in a variety of ways. Storyspace, initially developed by Jay David Bolter, John Brown, and Michael Joyce (1987) would prove particularly important for early work in hypertext fiction, as the software was designed specifically for the purpose of writing narratives in hypertext form. Storyspace included a number of features, such as visual mapping of story structure and "guard fields" to present a different version of text on subsequent visits to the same node, which were in many ways more technically advanced than the hypertext system that would eventually become the dominant standard: the World Wide Web.

In 1989, Tim Berners-Lee wrote the white paper "Information Management: A Proposal," proposing the development of a hypertext markup language standard, and in 1991 set up the first World Wide Web server.[9] Initially the community of hypertext researchers was lukewarm to Berners-Lee's proposed standard – after all the system he proposed was remarkably simple in comparison to many hypertext systems that had already been developed. The simplicity of HTML (Hypertext Markup Language), however, worked to its advantage. Little training was required to learn HTML, which allowed users to link together documents online in a common format that could be accessed from any standard hardware platform. After the launch of the first Web browsers, hypertext began to find its first mass audience. If hypertext fiction was (and largely remains) a niche literary form, by the turn of the millennium, reading nonlinearly through linked documents was no longer anything unusual, but a daily activity for millions on the World Wide Web.

Hypertext in the Context of (Post)modernism

The poetics and sensibilities of early hypertext fiction did not only emerge from experiments with technological innovation in hypertext, but in response to aesthetic moves made by modernist and postmodernist authors during the twentieth century.[10] Many of the characteristics of modernism, such as intertextuality, fragmentation, and attempts to represent the flow and associative movement of human thought are hallmarks of hypertext works such as Judy Malloy's *Uncle Roger* and Michael Joyce's *afternoon, a story*. The stylistic experimentation, rapid point-of-view shifts, and spatialized storytelling of James Joyce's *Ulysses* (1922) are recapitulated in many works of hyperfiction.[11] From postmodernism, hypertext adopts many different forms of self-conscious reflexivity: resulting in fictions that reflect critically on aspects of form, authorship, conditions of production, and mediality. In *Electronic Literature*, I identify four forms of reflexivity present in modern and postmodern fiction, in particular, works of meta-fiction that are reiterated and developed in hypertext fiction, including authorial, intertextual, and generic reflexivity.

Authorial reflexivity involves the appearance of the author of a work, or a very similar character to the author, in the fictional world of the text itself, in order to question the ontological barriers between the imagined world of the fiction and the lived experience of the writer. Reacting in some ways to the poststructuralist "Death of the Author" theorized by Roland Barthes and Michel Foucault, works that exhibit authorial reflexivity reclaim space for the reactive consciousness of the author at the time of writing, highlighting the fact that any fiction is the product of a recursive process between a text, the person writing it, and the interpretative experience of the person reading it.[12] At the same time, this move often highlights the fact that the identity of the author may itself be a fiction. Just as novelists such as John Barth, Paul Auster, Kurt Vonnegut, and David Foster Wallace inserted themselves or their doppelgangers into their works to play with the relationship between author and text, many early hypertexts were similarly reflexive. Two of Shelley Jackson's landmark hypertext works, *Patchwork Girl* and *My Body & a Wunderkammer* (1997), involve considerable play with the author persona.[13] In *Patchwork Girl*, a feminist retelling of Mary Shelley's *Frankenstein* (1818), readers move between the narratives of the female monster, stitched together from body (and personality) parts of many dead women, the author of Frankenstein (Mary) Shelley, and Shelley (Jackson), the young female author of the hypertext.[14] In *My Body & a Wunderkammer*, the text navigates readers through a (semi-fictionalized) memoir told through stories bound to her individual organs and their connections to each other. Jackson's postmodern use of fractured identities calls into question the veracity of memory against imaginative self-invention, such as representing the protagonist having a tail, raising questions of interspecies being.

Intertextual reflexivity grows out of modernist and postmodernist inter-textuality, the deep layering of references to other texts within a literary work. Intertextuality codes a work as emerging from a wider discourse network – what Ted Nelson described as "a literature" in his *Literary Machines* (1981).[15] Intertextuality is essential to hypertext's nature as a text technology – the main element of hypertext after all is the link, which can both connect nodes within a given work and connect to other texts outside the boundaries of the given work. But intertextuality in the literary sense as represented, for example, in postmodern fictions such as Kurt Vonnegut's *Breakfast of Champions* (1973) or Kathy Acker's *Empire of the Senseless* (1988) was also quite common in early Storyspace and web-based hypertexts.[16] Michael Joyce's *afternoon, a story* was laden with references to Greek mythology and the *Odyssey*, to James Joyce's *Ulysses*, Goethe, the Brothers Grimm, and Tolstoy. Jackson's *Patchwork Girl* is written on the bones of *Frankenstein* but also fleshed out with elements of Frank L. Baum's *The Patchwork Girl of Oz* and a variety of theoretical texts, such as Jacques Derrida's *Dissemination* (1983), Donna Haraway's "A Cyborg Manifesto" (1991), and Barbara Maria Stafford's *Body Criticism* (1991).[17] William Gillespie, Frank Marquardt, Scott Rettberg, and Dirk Stratton's *The Unknown* (1999)[18] includes overwriting and parodies of works written by authors such as John Barth, Nelson Algren, Jack Kerouac, and Edgar Alan Poe. The literal linkage of hypertext seems to encourage this kind of post-modern intertextual play and pastiche of texts and styles across literary history. This new literary form, in its process of becoming, often turned back toward print fiction, as if reflexively seeking its own rhizomatic roots in connections to older forms.

A number of works of postmodern fiction could be characterized as generically or formally reflexive in the sense that they called out and tested the limits of particular elements of the textual apparatus and form of the text. John Barth's "Sentence" was, for example, a story written in the form of a very long single sentence, calling into question the minimal conditions under which a text can be considered a story. Authors such as David Foster Wallace and Mark Danielewski embedded not only references but core plot elements within footnotes. Barth's "Frame Tale" (1968) is simply the words "once upon a time there was a story that began" along with instructions to cut out the text and form it into a mobius strip, creating an infinite loop.[19] Many hypertext fictions similarly play conceptually with the textual apparatus. Given a completely new system of communicating stories, with structural potentialities different from those of the book, it is no wonder that a frequent concern of hypertext authors should be reflecting on the constraints and affordances of the environment in which they were writing, to ask not only "what am I meaning?" but also "*how* am I meaning?" or even more simply "how does this text-machine work?" Many of Stuart Moulthrop's groundbreaking works have simultaneously engaged with the political discourse and media environments of the times in which they were produced while simultaneously testing and reflecting on the media technologies used to produce them – for example, *Hegirascope* (1995) was both a fiction that explored "hot" and "cold" media in McLuhan's terms and an experiment in using "push" media then new to the Web.[20] His *Reagan Library* (1999) meditated both on degrading cultural memory and political discourse and reflected on the nascent (and now largely forgotten) technology of QuickTime VR.[21] Moulthrop's *Pax: An Instrument* (2003) both reflected the uncertainty, fear, and paranoia of the period immediately following 9/11 and explored the idea of a textual instrument – a work that could convey meaning only through interaction with a human "player" who was not only navigating, but also playing the work in a way similar to a musician playing a musical instrument.[22]

Another form of reflexivity present in works of American postmodern fiction that later inflects hypertext and other forms of digital storytelling is medial reflexivity – texts that consider the relation of print fiction to other art and media forms. Examples of this impulse include works that take techniques or materials from other forms: Donald Barthelme's use of visual collages of images from nineteenth-century books in his twentieth-century fictions, or Tom Philips's technique of selectively painting over the pages of *A Humument* (1966) to create a new literary/artistic work.[23] A number of authors also explicitly considered the conventions and styles of other forms of storytelling in fiction: *A Night at the Movies, or, You Must Remember This* (1992) or Curtis White's *Memories of My Father Watching TV* (1998) that mediate fiction through the conventions of cinema and 1950s TV shows respectively. In doing so, these authors exposed the specific affordances of stories on the written page that are not available in the same way in other media.[24]

Media reflexivity coheres with what N. Katherine Hayles (2004) has described as media specificity, which has been a common critical consideration in electronic literature: the basis for comparing or understanding the aesthetics and metaphors of a given work of e-lit cannot rest solely on criteria derived from readings of print literature.[25] Authors communicated multimodally: through images, video, audio, sound, animation, interactivity, and computation, they are working with different registers of meaning. That is not to say that the conventions of print fiction are completely absent or foreign to e-lit – they remain in the author's toolbox, but they are used in concert (or competition) with other ways of meaning making specific the computational context. This complicates the work of the critic: in a form such as hypertext, two readers exposed to the same work will almost certainly have entirely different experiences of that work – not only because they interpret it differently, but because the parts of the text they will be exposed to and the composition of the fragments they read will be based on the choices they make in terms of selecting individual links. The reader's material interaction with the text is as significant a signifier as any of the words that they read. Jay David Bolter and Richard Grusin's theory of "remediation" (1999) has also been an important background idea for e-lit.[26] The core idea is that new media integrate and adapt conventions from older media in the process of developing their own conventions, and in turn, these new media also influence changes in the conventions of the older media that they remediate. Hypertexts engage with and mutate conventions of print fiction, and digital media have also had effects on the material properties of contemporary print books. Some important works of early twenty-first-century hypertext fiction, such as Talan Memmott's *Lexia to Perplexia* (2000) and Mark Amerika's *Grammatron* (1997) highlighted how hypertext, computation, and the global network might be remediating not only the properties of print and other writing technologies, but also reshaping human consciousness, as human thought and communication are increasingly remediated by networked computers.[27]

The five years on either side of the millennium represent the rise of the World Wide Web and the first wave of the mass adoption of internet communication on a large scale and into everyday life. It was also a period in which a number of authors first explored the narrative and poetic potentialities of the Web as a writing medium, publishing hypertext novels directly on the Web. If the publisher Eastgate Systems adopted a brand of modernist high seriousness (as the home of "serious hypertext"), much of hypertext fiction published on the Web during the late 1990s and early 2000s responded as much to the anything-goes postmodern cultural mood and cyber-utopianism of the early Web more than it did to prior models of literary publishing. Although HTML is actually a good deal less technically advanced than earlier hypertext authoring systems – both Storyspace and HyperCard enable more complex programmable behaviors out of the box – HTML on the World Wide Web offered other advantages, including instantaneous networked publication before a potentially global audience. And although simple HTML links are essentially just a way of connecting one location on the Web to another, HTML is extensible, allowing developers to include other code written according to both open and proprietary standards to plug into it. A host of "plug-ins" such as RealAudio, Flash, QuickTime VR, Shockwave and others (many of which are no longer supported), as well as JavaScript code and DHTML, allowed authors to extend the technical capabilities of web-based hypertext.

At the same, of course, authors were only beginning to explore the narrative potentiality of hypertext. There was no ready-to-hand grammar of how links, fragmentation, nonlinearity, or multilinearity might best function within a story. There were also many different ideas of how one could think about hypertextual narrative structure. Certain twentieth-century works of print fiction, such as Julio Cortazar's *Hopscotch* (Spanish: *Rayuela*) (1963) and Jorge Luis Borges's "The Garden of Forking Paths," (1962) as well as the *Choose-Your-Own-Adventure* book series suggested some possibilities, such as branching path structures where reader choices determined alternate versions of a given narrative or narratives that would change substantially by presenting events in alternative reading order, while extensively footnoted novels suggested others.[28] Many authors have further explored other ways of using hypertextual structures, for example, using links to explore cycles of recursion, in which readers will revisit nodes they have already read, to find that they have changed slightly, or opened up new narrative paths.

Web Hypertext Novels: Portfolios of Complexity

Several notable works have treated the hypertext novel as a kind of portfolio of materials that can be navigated via a number of different conceptual reading strategies. Robert Arellano's *Sunshine '69*, probably the first hypertext novel published in HTML on the Web, in 1996, is a historical fiction set in northern California during the 1960s, centering on events leading up and including the Rolling Stones concert at Altamont Speedway on December 6, 1969.[29] The concert was intended to be a kind of West Coast Woodstock, with bands such as Santana, Jefferson Airplane, The Flying Burrito Brothers, and Crosby, Stills, Nash & Young playing along with the Stones. Things went horribly wrong at the concert: four deaths occurred during the event, including the stabbing murder of Meredith Hunter, an LSD-overdose-related drowning, and hit-and-run accident. In representing these events, Arellano tracks the lives of nine characters: Alan Passaro, a Hell's Angel working security at Altamont; Lucifer; the Glimmer Twins (Mick Jagger and Keith Richards); Ali aka Ronald Stark, a shady figure connected with the CIA; Meredith Hunter, a young African American hipster from South Berkeley; Orange Sunshine, alternatively a hippie girl-next-door and a brand of LSD; Norm Cavettesa, a discharged Vietnam veteran; and Timothy Leary, the countercultural advocate of "Turning on, tuning in, and dropping out." *Sunshine '69* presents a range of navigational options to the reader, as well as in-text links between parts of the story. Each screen of the *Sunshine '69* has four buttons linking to "Calendar," "People," "8-Track," and "Map." Each button links to a different navigational apparatus, so that readers could navigate by character, chronologically, according to musical selections, or by a map.

The Unknown (1999), the hypertext novel I coauthored from 1999–2001 with William Gillespie, Frank Marquardt, and Dirk Stratton, also explored alternative ways of structuring a narrative in a nonlinear fashion.[30] We adopted a metaphor from the Chicago El rail system in organizing content into differently labeled "lines" of content that were distinct but interconnected: the red line, a "sickeningly decadent hypertext novel"; the blue line of documentary material; the purple line of "metafictional bullshit"; the orange line correspondence; the brown line of related art projects; and the green line documentation of live readings. In addition, the work included several alternate indexes: a list of notable people with links to scenes in which they were mentioned, a psychedelic map of the United States that readers could use to navigate by location, and an index of bookstores where various scenes of the novel took place. *The Unknown* centers on a book tour that takes on the dimensions and excesses of an epic rock tour. Self-consciously structured as a picaresque road trip novel, our solution to the problem of constructing a nonlinear narrative experience was to author discretely coherent self-standing scenes that could be entered and exited through numerous associative links within the text as well as via these various indexes. Our approach presents the novel as a multivocal body of narrative experiences. Because it provides a large collection of textual materials to be woven together differently by each reader who approaches it, *The Unknown* generates a sense of ineffable infinitude. No matter how much of the story readers encounter, the full potential narrative of events remains forever beyond reach. If one of the compelling aspects of the conventional print novel is that it can offer a sense of closure, a coherent ordering of life impossible in lived experience, hypertext fictions often revel in the mess of fragmented experience, which can never be understood as a singular whole.

Shelley and Pamela Jackson took a different type of portfolio approach in *The Doll Games* (2001).[31] The work is based on narrative games that the two sisters played with their dolls when they were young, but these games have ostensibly become the center of a field of academic study. The section of the work titled "definition" and subtitled "a funhouse mirror" is by J. F. Bellwether, PhD, an invented scholar who is a renowned expert on the "ground-breaking series of theatrical performances by Shelley and Pamela Jackson that took place in a private home in Berkeley, California in the first half of the 1970s." *The Doll Games* uses hypertext more indexically than associatively. Presented as a set of interlinked web pages, the fiction includes sections focused on the dolls, artifacts, documents, commentary, and tapes of transcripts of the two women discussing the games, as well as interviews with others who played similar games. In one part, the dolls themselves become characters, writing to each other. The project draws on a postmodern pastiche of different styles and modes of discourse: an academic study, a psychological analysis, a documentary, a "making of" special, an archaeological investigation, a photo study, and a comic book. Shelley Jackson's interest in exploring varied textual styles and modes of verbal and visual expression bridges her digital and print fictions. Her most recent novel, *Riddance: Or: The Sybil Joines Vocational School for Ghost Speakers & Hearing-Mouth Children* (2018) is consistent with her digital work in its embrace of multimediality and an expansive approach to visual textuality.[32] The novel includes many images: doctored photographs and drawings, maps and diagrams, facsimiles of letters and telegraphs, asemic writing, medical documents, illustrations of exercises, musical notes, and teaching materials.

Hypertext's heyday was brief and essentially over by the mid-2000s. For about a decade in the field of e-lit there was a good deal more activity focused on animated digital poetry. Fewer American fiction writers produced work in this audiovisual software environment, though there were some notable exceptions. Many of Alan Bigelow's works (mainly authored in Flash during the 2000s but developed in HTML5 in more recent years) generally adhere to more linear conventions than most hypertext fictions, but his "web yarns" such as "When I Was President" (2007) and his "Brainstrips" are often quirky and comical works that play with many of the same visual design conventions used by authors of kinetic poetry but within narrative contexts.[33] Many of Bigelow's more recent works are less interactive than much of his prior work but inventively engage with web platforms as storytelling environments. Bigelow's work, such as "How to Rob a Bank" (2017), cleverly reflects changes in the nature of social communication and our lived experience of the world in an era of ubiquitous computing, when smart phones have almost become cyborg prosthetics that mediate our interaction with our environments.[34]

Overall, we can read twenty-first-century hypertext fiction as being in many ways an extension of the aesthetic project and formal concerns of postmodernism with a difference: while postmodernist referentiality, reflexivity, and self-conscious texts were deliberate experimental moves made by postmodern print authors, in many ways these forms of extensibility and interactivity are baked into the form of hypertext itself – they are not only concepts, but text technologies. And while American literary postmodernism from the 1960s onward was largely about constructing a new sort of lens through which to reflect on culture and storytelling, by the turn of the millennium, the culture itself was already postmodern, mediated, and fragmented. By the second decade of the twenty-first century, metanarratives have broken down. It is no longer a bold philosophical move to question the idea of "universal truth": we live in an era when politicians claim that there is no such entity as objective reality, that all information is subjective, that all news is fake news. This situation may call writers to develop new tactics and strategies, and while formal experimentation remains a concern of twenty-first century authors of digital fiction, we can also note a turn in the corpus toward a different manner of engagement with societal challenges that extend beyond play with the nature of the text, and beyond innovation for innovation's sake.

Interactive Fiction: You Can Go Your Own Way

Interactive Fiction (IF) is a genre of electronic literature with a history that extends back to the first popular genre or computer games – text adventures. Games such as those of the *Zork* series (first version developed at MIT in 1978–1979) sold in great number during the 1980s as consumer level personal computers began to become commonplace in middle class American homes. Text adventures were popular during the period before most PCs had powerful graphics cards. Instead of a visual narrative experience, players interacted with these programs via a rudimentary conversational interface: after being offered a description of a given room or environment, commands, such as "go north," "take gold," or "use sword to kill pirate." The software company Infocom was a moderately successful venture for a time, with about 100 employees, but by 1986 had been acquired by Activision and was fully shuttered by 1989, as graphics-based computer games had decimated the text adventure market niche. In spite of this, however, a core group of enthusiasts developed around the genre and this "amateur IF" community went on to develop its own development software, user community forums, open distribution platforms, and awards. This community grew in particular after the launch of the Web, and a quite substantial corpus of work was produced and distributed by the IF community during the 2000s and 2010s. While some of the work is very puzzle-oriented and in keeping with the adventure game conventions that emerged during the commercial era, many of the twenty-first-century works are more interesting from a literary standpoint, particularly in terms of conversational character interactions.

In his book-length study of IF, *Twisty Little Passages* (2005), Nick Montfort describes works of IF as simultaneously functioning as "*programs, potential narratives, worlds* and *games.*"³⁵ The *reader* of the narrative produced by IF is also the *player* of a game. Montfort describes this dual role as being that of an *interactor*. The interactor is usually addressed in the second person in IF (you) and is therefore positioned as a player character in the text. This second-person form of address is formally important in the sense that it places interactors into the same diegetic world as the characters they are reading about. It offers authors the possibility of bringing about new modes of identification, affect, and complicity within the stories they read. While many IF works focus on gameplay through puzzle-solving, some of the most compelling instead focus on the characters in the game – both the non-player characters and often the slowly revealed backstory of the player's own character. While the characters in most of the early text adventure games were essentially flat constructs or types, characters, for example, in the works of Emily Short, are much more dynamic, and the interactor's conversational interactions with them have a significant impact on the experience of the work.

Emily Short's *Galatea* (2000) is one of the most character-driven works in the genre.³⁶ The interactor engages in one long conversation with a living marble statue commissioned by the late artist, Pygmalion of Cyprus. The game is multilinear in the sense that rather than striving toward a clear "win" outcome, the conversation may end in various ways. Over the course of the discussion and through replay, the interactor is able to reveal more of Galatea's story and her troubled relationship with her creator. The objective of the work is primarily to unwind that story. The gameplay involved is largely about finding the right tone and approach to entice Galatea to speak her story openly. In contrast to exploratory works of IF that emphasize directional navigation or object gathering, key commands in *Galatea* such as "ASK ABOUT," "TELL ABOUT," and even "THINK ABOUT" emphasize narration and memory. With *Galatea* Short ramped up her focus on complex conversational interaction. The main character can deliver hundreds of lines in a wide variety of configurations, and the system tracks the conversation, remembering what has already been said and reacting positively or negatively to certain cues. Although *Galatea* is a short work, which can be played through quickly, Short has developed similarly complex characters, character interactions, complex plots, and wordplay in other works that could be thought of as "novel length," such as *Savoir-Faire* (2002), a fantasy set in eighteenth-century France,³⁷ or *Counterfeit Monkey* (2012), an espionage tale set in a fictional Atlantis policed by a "Bureau of Orthography" wherein the player must navigate the world using linguistic tools and sophisticated punning.³⁸

Twine Games for Contemporary Dystopias

While the majority of Short's works and many of the other notable works of IF produced during the 2000s were authored in Inform, a text-parser-based platform conceptually rooted in the model of interactive fiction developed in the Infocom era, Twine is an open-source platform released by Chris Klimas in 2009 that instead hearkens back to hypertext conventions of the 1980s and 1990s. Twine was designed with *Choose-Your-Own-Adventure* stories in mind. It offers a similar set of features to Storyspace software, including conditional links, variables, and path tracking. In contrast to the complexity of parser-based interactive fiction authoring tools, Twine offers a comparatively simple visual authoring environment. Authors do not need to write code in order to start writing in Twine (though those who chose to can integrate complex scripted behaviors). While from a structural standpoint work made in Twine has more in common with hypertext than it does with text-parser based interactive fiction, the authors in the community refer to their outputs as "games." Many Twine games have adopted conventions from IF, such as the second-person form of address to the player character, spatial navigation through the narrative, and a sparse style. Twine represents a kind of merging of hypertext and interactive fiction conventions, a digital fiction genre informed by aspects of both that preceded it. The large writing community that has developed around Twine is largely composed of Millennials, and many of its authors are interested in themes revolving around gender, identity, and economic precarity.

Porpentine Charity Heartscape (Porpentine) is one of the most noted authors who has worked with Twine and has reached a substantial audience online and in the cultural landscape.[39] Porpentine is a transgender artist with a punk sensibility. Her work is both aesthetically challenging and politically charged. Many of her works address themes of gender, the body, fear, and displaced subject positions in disturbing environments, such as a sadist's pit or an alien body. In *Howling Dogs* (2012), the player character lives in a bleak cell and is sustained by consuming bland nutrition bars.[40] The "gameplay" involves often-mundane drudgery. The player character gets tired and needs to sleep, thirsty and needs to drink. The only "escape" offered the interactor from this dreary existence is a VR system. The narratives realized by the interactor's engagement with this system are however just as or more painful than those of her "real" life: in one episode, the player character feels compelled to strangle an abusive partner, in another she is placed into the body of Joan of Arc in the last moments before she is burned alive. While the interactor might achieve some success in these scenarios, Porpentine writes that these moments represent "false catharsis in the form of these victories – but at the end of the day you're still in the black room."[41] Porpentine's works place the interactor in Kafkaesque scenarios that the author describes with the no-holds-barred linguistic sensibilities and intensity of a modern-day Kathy Acker.

In *With Those We Love Alive* (2014), Porpentine uses the second-person point of view to put the interactor proximate to characters in skin-crawling situations of complicity.[42] The player character is cast as a servant charged with crafting weapons for a queen who hunts humans, often using the bones of her victims. To join the human community, the player character must commit a metaphorical act of genocide. Porpentine's work exemplifies the stakes of how interactive elements of IF can model complex moral dilemmas.

If IF represents a genre in which gaming conventions and narrative conventions can be brought together in the production of complex interactive digital narratives, in some cases authors employ commercial game engines to literary ends. The art games of Jason Nelson, such as *Game, Game, Game and Again Game* (2006), *I Made This. You Play This. We Are Enemies* (2008), and *Nothing You Have Done Deserves Such Praise* (2013), for example, are genre-bending works that are part surreal game, part poetry, part fiction, and part philosophical investigations of contemporary cultural phenomena.[43] In recent years, a number of larger commercial game studios have also produced a number of quite successful "walking simulator" games such as *Gone Home* (2013)[44] and *What Remains of Edith Finch* (2017),[45] which adapt the adventure game conventions and spatial exploration of IF in developing richly imagined narratives of mysterious family histories. In these and commercial games of this genre, such as *Firewatch* (2016), rich graphical environments are used to present narrative worlds.[46] Rather than "first person shooters" we might consider these to be "first person investigators" wherein the player is unwinding hidden histories and exploring affective and ethical relationships with other characters, rather than hunting down enemies.

Network Writing: Massively Multiauthored Online Fictions

Some of the most compelling digital fiction projects of the twenty-first century involve what I refer to as "network writing": electronic literature that is created for and published on the Internet. Network writing may interrogate the nature and materiality of the network itself, exploit the Internet's potential for collaborative writing, or explore the network as a site for performance. Core to this idea is that in addition to the text-processing affordances of computation, access to an expanded sensorium through multimodality, and interactivity with cybertexts, the network itself presents authors with both new forms of textual material and new ways of writing together.[47]

One type of networked writing that illustrates the collaborative potentialities of digital media is collective narrative: works that are written by groups of people working together, leveraging networked communication technologies to produce works that could not have been written by any single individual alone but are instead the product of a collective. Collective narratives have ranged from works by small groups of writers working together, such as the earlier-referenced *The Unknown*; attempts to develop novels written by large groups of people, such as *Invisible Seattle* (1983); database works that welcome and integrate input from readers, such as Judd Morrissey's *The Last Performance* (2007); and a number of "netprov" projects organized by Mark Marino, Rob Wittig, and others during the 2010s.[48]

Wittig and Marino have long been interested in the idea that with each new networked writing platform, the potential for a new style of writing, new audiences for fiction, and new cultural vernacular emerge. As far back as the early 1980s, Wittig was part of the group responsible for *Invisible Seattle*, a novel that was composed of recombined fragments of text written by anonymous contributors from the city of Seattle, gathered in part by means of a computer database. Wittig also experimented with fictions in the form of a hacked website in *The Fall of the Site of Marsha* (1999), a comic time travel novel written in the form of email messages written by an advertising copywriter who smuggled a laptop along with him on a trip to fourteenth-century Italy in *Blue Company* (2002), and other works.[49] Marino has authored fictions such as *The Los Wikiless Timespedia* (2009), a parodic collaborative writing project based on the premise that the *Los Angeles Times* had switched to a wiki-only publishing model, with all articles written by unpaid contributors, and *The Ballad of Work Study Seth* (2009), based on the premise that Marino's Twitter stream had been hijacked by a work-study student that the overcommitted professor hired to tweet for him.[50] Many of their works both simultaneously consider the materiality of the given writing platforms they are writing in and enact a comic critique of human social interactions mediated by the platforms.

During the 2010s, Wittig and Marino together developed a new genre, Netprov, which integrates their shared interest in the narrative styles and comic potential of network communication platforms with an interest in large-scale collective writing practices. Marino and Wittig define Netprov as "Netprov = networked improv literature. Netprov uses everyday social technology plus the ol' tricks of literature, graphic design, and theater to create stories that unfold in realtime within public mediascapes."[51] Netprovs most often unfold on social media such as Twitter, Facebook, YouTube,

Periscope, and Snapchat. They are typically structured around a given theme or cultural phenomenon. One of their earliest netprovs, *Occupy MLA* (2011), fictionally featured a group of adjunct faculty gathering on Twitter to protest their working conditions, and then organizing an Occupy-style protest at the Modern Language Association conference.[52] Not everyone was pleased when the project was revealed to be a fiction and a hoax. Michael Bérubé, then president of the MLA, weighed in against the project in a posting on an article in the *Prof. Hacker* blog in *The Chronicle of Higher Education*. Wittig and Marino's netprovs often comment satirically on the absurdity of our contemporary relationships with technology. *I Work for the Web* (2015), for example, focused the fact that the majority of contemporary web content is produced by users in social media (likes, posts, comments, and photos) for the financial benefit of large international corporations and proposed the formation of the Webbelies, an international union of web workers.[53] *#Behindyourbak* (2018) focused on the FOMO (Fear of Missing Out) syndrome that drives addiction to social networks.[54] Netprovs typically enlist dozens of writers and are often used pedagogically in creative writing courses.

Extending Digital Fiction to Critical Digital Media

Although I cannot comprehensively address all the forms of contemporary digital fiction in the space of this chapter, I will mention that beyond what I would consider to be the core genres of digital writing, there are many examples of works that are adapting some techniques from these genres and taking them into new directions with technologies such as tablet computers, AR/VR and CAVE environments, and other newer technologies. Samantha Gorman and Danny Cannizzaro's *Pry* (2015) is a novella in the form of an iPad app that integrates aspects of electronic literature, cinema, and games while working innovatively with the touch screen interface.[55] *Pry* is about a soldier, James, a demolitions expert, returned from the war in Iraq with PTSD and failing eyesight. The reader's interaction with *Pry* is primarily about reaching into the protagonist's mind to access his thoughts and emotions. Physical gestures serve as metaphors as well as ways to traverse the text. *Pry* is one of the few works to emerge from the artistic electronic literature community that could be described as an unqualified commercial success. It served as the foundation of the Tender Claws studio, which has now made several innovative and well-funded projects including the parodic VR project *Virtual Wobblies Reality* and the AR work *Tendar*. In each case, the Tender Claws projects represent substantial experiments with new narrative technologies, while retaining a commitment to storytelling, metaphor, and linguistic play.[56]

I'll conclude by mentioning the concept of "Critical Digital Media." I would describe a number of compelling digital fictions in this vein. Critical Digital Media involves both narrative storytelling and critical engagement with significant societal issues of our time. In some cases, this might involve the specificities and power relations embedded in our relationship with the major corporate actors who through technology now mediate fundamental aspects of our daily lives, such as Facebook, Google, and Amazon. Many of the Netprovs discussed above engage with the technical apparatus, and language artists such as John Cayley and Daniel Howe have made digital works that specifically critique the practices of Google, Facebook, and Amazon. Other author/artists are using digital media either to narrativize documentary materials or to mix fact and fiction in producing digital fictions that consider other types of major contemporary challenges ranging from fake news to climate change. The generative recombinatory film project that I produced with Roderick Coover, *Toxi*City: A Climate Change Narrative* (2016), for example, recombines two narrative layers – one a panoramic near-future story of the catastrophic impacts and societal effects of a series of fictional hurricanes and the other a series of death stories from actual victims of Hurricane Sandy.[57] The interactive CAVE virtual reality theater work *Hearts and Minds: The Interrogations Project* (2015) that Coover and I produced with Daria Tsoupikova and Arthur Nishimoto reconfigures segments of interviews that social scientist John Tsukayama conducted with American soldiers who had either witnessed acts of battlefield torture or themselves committed such war crimes in a surreal VR environment that mirrored the embodied affect of PTSD.[58] A number of Sharon Daniel's works, such as *Public Secrets* (2008) and *Inside the Distance* (2015) have employed hypertext and hypermedia, digital cinema, and interactivity in projects that communicate and model narratives of difficult situations, such as the mistreatment of women prisoners in American jails, or models of mediation between assault victims and the perpetrators of their crimes.[59] The use of interactive techniques arguably creates a different sort of affect and involvement in these narratives than would a simpler documentary style. Egyptian-American author Amira Hanafi's *A Dictionary of the Revolution*, winner of both the 2019 Public Library Prize for Electronic Literature and the 2019 New Media Writing Prize, is another compelling example of Critical Digital Media.[60] In this case, the author interviewed many people of different socioeconomic, religious, and ideological backgrounds, asking them for brief responses to concepts written as a single word on a note card. She then cross-referenced and visualized these responses into a lexicon and network visualization, allow the reader to move nonlinearly and conceptually between dramatic individual narratives and experiences of the 25th of July 2011 Egyptian Revolution in a work that both captures a panoramic impression of the chaos of a single revolution and perhaps reveals something conceptually about the nature of revolution as a concept itself.

Although it should be clear from this discussion that digital fiction already has a rich history that has resulted in a diverse body of work, as Bachman-Turner Overdrive sang in the 1970s, "You Ain't Seen Nothing Yet." Although electronic literature remains a marginal and fundamentally experimental literature in comparison to the mainstream, there is a significant body of creative work and a growing academic field dedicated to its production, history, analysis, preservation, and dissemination. Electronic literature faces some challenges – because it is produced and distributed on devices and software that are subject to much faster cycles of obsolescence than the printed book, researchers in the field are called upon to document and archive this work with some degree of urgency. At the same time, the technical creative affordances of the field are many and various. During a time when digital literacy is becoming more and more essential, and when digital environments frame our everyday lives, the types of reflective literary experience offered by digital fiction are (un)bound to become a more significant part of the American literary landscape. The digital turn has already changed our world substantially. Digital fictions present us with the specific opportunity to create and reflect on the changes that have taken place not only within our media environment but within our society both playfully and critically. Literary critics of the future will encounter literary objects that engage with different aspects of the sensorium, that are written as much by algorithms as they are by humans, that link together large-scale writing communities across borders, that are written for a global network rather than a regional tradition, that reframe our ideas of authorship and even the nature of the written text. Most of the story of twenty-first-century digital fiction is yet to be written.

NOTES

1 Nick Montfort et al., eds., *Electronic Literature Collection, Volume One* (College Park: Electronic Literature Organization, 2006), http://collection.eliterature.org/1/; Laura Borràs et al., eds., *Electronic Literature Collection, Volume Two* (Cambridge, MA: Electronic Literature Organization, 2011), http://collection .eliterature.org/2/; and Stephanie Boluk et al., eds., *Electronic Literature Collection, Volume Three* (Cambridge, MA: Electronic Literature Organization, 2016), http://collection.eliterature.org/3/.

2 Judy Malloy, *Uncle Roger* (1986), https://people.well.com/user/jmalloy/unclero ger/partytop.html; and Michael Joyce, *afternoon, a story* (Watertown: Eastgate Systems, 1987).

3 Stuart Moulthrop, *Victory Garden* (Watertown: Eastgate Systems, 1991).

4 Robert Coover, "The End of Books," *New York Times*, June 21, 1992, https://archive
  .nytimes.com/www.nytimes.com/books/98/09/27/specials/coover-end.html?scp=1&
  sq=robert%2520coover%2520the%2520end%25oof%2520books&st=cse.

5 Theodor Holm Nelson, "Complex Information Processing: A File Structure for
  the Complex, the Changing and the Indeterminate," in *ACM'65 Proceedings of
  the 1965 20th National Conference* (Cleveland: MIT Press, 1965), 84–100,
  https://dl.acm.org/citation.cfm?id=806036.

6 Vannevar Bush, "As We May Think," *The Atlantic*, July 1945, www.theatlantic
  .com/magazine/archive/1945/07/as-we-may-think/303881/.

7 Nelson, "Complex Information Processing," 96.

8 Theodor Holm Nelson, "Computer Lib / Dream Machines," in *The New Media
  Reader*, edited by Nick Montfort and Noah Wardrip-Fruin (Cambridge, MA:
  MIT Press, 1970), 313.

9 Tim Berners-Lee, "Information Management: A Proposal," March 1989, www
  .w3.org/History/1989/proposal.html.

10 For a more extensive discussion of hypertext in the context of postmodernism, see
   chapter 3 of *Electronic Literature*. Scott Rettberg, *Electronic Literature*
   (Cambridge: Polity, 2019).

11 James Joyce, *Ulysses* (Paris: Sylvia Beach, 1922).

12 Roland Barthes, "The Death of the Author," in *Image, Music, Text*, edited by
   Roland Barthes (New York: Hill and Wang, 1977), 142–148.

13 Shelley Jackson, *My Body & A Wunderkammer* (1997), www.altx.com/thebody;
   and Shelley Jackson, *Patchwork Girl* (Watertown: Eastgate Systems, 1995).

14 Mary Shelley, *Frankenstein* (London: Lackington, Hughes, Harding, Mavor &
   Jones, 1818).

15 Theodor Holms Nelson, *Literary Machines* (Sausalito: Mindful Press, 1981).

16 Kurt Vonnegut, *Breakfast of Champions* (New York: Delacorte Press, 1973);
   Kathy Acker, *Empire of the Senseless* (New York: Grove / Atlantic, 1988).

17 Jacques Derrida, *Dissemination* (Chicago: The University of Chicago Press,
   1983); Donna Haraway, "A Cyborg Manifesto: Science, Technology, and
   Socialist Feminism in the Late 20th Century," in *Simians, Cyborgs, and
   Women: The Reinvention of Nature* (New York: Routledge, 1991), 149–182;
   and Barbara Maria Stafford, *Body Criticism: Imagining the Unseen in
   Enlightenment Art and Medicine* (Cambridge, MA: MIT Press, 1991).

18 William Gillespie et al. *The Unknown* (1998), http://unknownhypertext.com/.

19 John Barth, "Frame Tale," in *Lost in the Funhouse* (New York: Doubleday,
   1968), 1–2.

20 Stuart Moulthrop, *Hegirascope, The New River* (1997), www.cddc.vt.edu/jour
   nals/newriver/moulthrop/HGS2/Hegirascope.html.

21 Stuart Moulthrop, "Reagan Library," in Montfort et al. *Electronic Literature
   Collection, Volume One*, http://collection.eliterature.org/1/works/moulthrop__
   reagan_library.html.

22 Stuart Moulthrop, *Pax: An Instrument* (2003), www.smoulthrop.com/lit/pax/.

23 Tom Philips, *A Humument*, 6th ed. (London: Thames & Hudson, 1966), www
   .tomphillips.co.uk/humument.

24 Robert Coover's *A Night at the Movies, or, You Must Remember This* (Normal:
   Dalkey Archive Press, 1992) or Curtis White's *Memories of My Father Watching
   TV* (Normal: Dalkey Archive Press, 1998).

25 N. Katherine Hayles, "Print Is Flat, Code Is Deep: The Importance of Media-Specific Analysis," *Poetics Today* 25, no. 1 (2004): 67–90.

26 Jay David Bolter and Richard Grusin, *Remediation: Understanding New Media* (Cambridge, MA: MIT Press, 1999).

27 Talan Memmott, "Lexia to Perplexia," in Montfort et al. *Electronic Literature Collection, Volume One,* http://collection.eliterature.org/1/works/memmott_lexia_to_perplexia.html; and Mark Amerika, *Grammatron* (1997), http://grammatron.com.

28 Julio Cortazar, *Hopscotch: A Novel,* 1st Pantheon paperback edited ed. (New York: Pantheon, 1987); or J. Cortazar, *Rayuela* (Buenos Aires: Editorial Sudamericana, 1963); Jorge Luis Borges, "The Garden of Forking Paths," in *Ficciones* (New York: Grove Press, 1962), 89–101.

29 Robert Arellano, *Sunshine '69* (1996), www.sunshine69.cesom/69_Start.html.

30 D. W. Gillespie et al. *The Unknown* (1998), http://unknownhypertext.com/.

31 Shelley Jackson and Pamela Jackson, *The Doll Games* (2001), www.ineradicablestain.com/dollgames/.

32 Shelley Jackson, *Riddance: Or: The Sybil Joines Vocational School for Ghost Speakers & Hearing-Mouth Children* (New York: Black Balloon Publishing, 2018).

33 Alan Bigelow, *When I Was President* (2007), www.webyarns.com/wheniwaspresident.html.

34 Alan Bigelow, *How to Rob a Bank* (2017), http://webyarns.com/howto/howto.html.

35 Nick Montfort, *Twisty Little Passages: An Approach to Interactive Fiction* (Cambridge, MA: MIT Press, 2005), 24.

36 Emily Short, *Galatea* (2000), http://ifdb.tads.org/viewgame?id=urxrv27t7qtu52lb.

37 Emily Short, *Savoir-Faire* (2002), http://ifdb.tads.org/viewgame?id=pocizeb3kiwzlm2p.

38 Emily Short, *Counterfeit Monkey* (2012), http://ifdb.tads.org/viewgame?id=aearuuxv83plclpl.

39 In 2017, for example, the Whitney Biennial included a seven-piece exhibit of Porpentine's works.

40 Porpentine Charity Heartscape, *Howling Dogs* (2012), http://slimedaughter.com/games/twine/howlingdogs/.

41 Porpentine Charity Heartscape and Emily Short, "Interview with Porpentine, Author of *Howling Dogs*," *Emily Short's Interactive Storytelling*, November 23, 2012, https://emshort.blog/2012/11/23/interview-with-porpentine-author-of-howling-dogs/.

42 Porpentine Charity Heartscape, *With Those We Love Alive* (2014), http://slimedaughter.com/games/twine/wtwla/.

43 Jason Nelson, *Game, Game, Game, and Again Game* (2007), www.secrettechnology.com/gamegame/gamegamebegin.html; Jason Nelson, *I Made This. You Play This. We Are Enemies* (2008), www.secrettechnology.com/madethis/enemy6.html; and Jason Nelson, *Nothing You Have Done Deserves Such Praise* (Turbulence, 2013) http://turbulence.org/project/nothing-you-have-done-deserves-such-praise/.

44 The Fullbright Company, Gone Home (video game) (Portland, 2013), https://fullbrig.ht.

45 Annapurna Interactive, What Remains of Edith Finch (video game) (Los Angeles, 2017), https://annapurna.pictures/interactive/what-remains-of-edith-finch/.

46 Camp Santo, Firewatch (video game) (San Francisco, 2016), www.camposanto
.com/about/.

47 Espen Aarseth, *Cybertext: Perspectives on Ergodic Literature* (Baltimore: Johns
Hopkins University Press, 1997).

48 Seattle, *Invisible Seattle: The Novel of Seattle* (Seattle: Function Industries Press,
1983); and Judd Morrissey, *The Last Performance* (2007), http://
thelastperformance.org/title.php.

49 Rob Wittig, "The Fall of the Site of Marsha," in Montfort et al. *The Electronic
Literature Collection, Volume One*, http://collection.eliterature.org/1/works/wit
tig__the_fall_of_the_site_of_marsha.html; and Rob Wittig, *Blue Company*
(2002), www.robwit.net/bluecompany2002/.

50 Mark C. Marino, *The Loss Wikiless Timespedia* (2009), https://web.archive.org/
web/20121110190808/http://bunkmagazine.com/mediawiki/index.php?title=Newy_
new_new_shiny_wiki_wow_Main_Page; and Mark C. Marino, *The Ballad of Work
Study Seth* (2009), www.springgunpress.com/markmarino/markmarino/seth/index_
2columns.html.

51 Mark C. Marino, "Netprov – Networked Improv Literature," *WRT: Writer
Response Theory* (2011), http://writerresponsetheory.org/wordpress/2011/05/
12/netprov-networked-improv-literature/.

52 Mark C. Marino, *Occupy MLA* (2011), http://markcmarino.com/wordpress/?
page_id=117.

53 Mark C. Marino and Rob Wittig, *I Work for the Web* (2015), http://robwit.net/
iwfw/.

54 Mark C. Marino and Rob Wittig, *#BehindYourBak* (2018), http://
behindyourbak.robwit.net/.

55 Danny Cannizzaro and Samantha Gorman, *Pry* (Los Angeles: Tender Claws,
2015), http://prynovella.com/.

56 Tender Claws, *Virtual Cyphertext Reality* (2016), https://tenderclaws.com/vvr;
and Tender Claws *Tendar* (2019), https://tenderclaws.com/tendar.

57 Roderick Coover and Scott Rettberg, *Toxi*City: A Climate Change Narrative*
(2016), www.crchange.net/toxicity/.

58 Roderick Coover et al. *Hearts and Minds: The Interrogations Project* (2015),
www.crchange.net/hearts-and-minds/.

59 Sharon Daniel and Erik Loyer, "Public Secrets," in Borràs et al., *Electronic
Literature Collection, Volume Two*, http://collection.eliterature.org/2/works/
daniel_public_secrets.html; and Sharon Daniel, *Inside the Distance* (2015),
www.sharondaniel.net/inside-the-distance.

60 Amira Hanafi, *A Dictionary of the Revolution* (2018), http://qamosalthawra
.com/en.

PART II
Approaches

6

CANDICE M. JENKINS

Afro-Futurism/Afro-Pessimism

Science fiction is not about the future; it uses the future as a narrative convention to present significant distortions of the present.

Samuel R. Delaney[1]

A simple enough term for withstanding the ugliness of the world – and learning from it – might be suffering and Afro-Pessimism is, among other things, an attempt to formulate an account of such suffering, to establish the rules of its grammar, "to think again about the position of the ex-slave ... [w]ithout recourse to the consolation of transcendence."

Jared Sexton[2]

In the twenty-first century, what has been described as the genre turn – bolstered by the increasing prominence of genre fiction and narrative in popular culture – plays a significant role in how African American literary fiction reckons with both history and temporality.[3] This turn to genre, which includes literary forays into science fiction (SF), fantasy, magical realism, and other speculative content, takes place in a historical moment, the early twenty-first century, which has rapidly shifted over the last decade from what we might call neoliberal optimism (or "cruel optimism," as Lauren Berlant has outlined it) to a widespread pessimism about both our present moment and what is to come.[4] This affective change has been precipitated by both formal and grassroots political shifts – perhaps the two most central being the emergence of the Black Lives Matter movement, founded by three black women in 2012 in response to increasingly visible extrajudicial killings of black people, and the historic election of reality television personality and businessman Donald Trump to the presidency of the United States in 2016, seemingly despite his hostile anti-immigrant, anti-woman, and antiblack rhetoric. And while there have been a number of black literary works that have appeared in, and engaged with, this dark contemporary moment in ways that do not fall under the rubric of the speculative – Claudia Rankine's *Citizen* (2014) and Ta-Nehisi Coates's *Between the World and Me* (2015), for instance, both works that respond directly to police violence against unarmed African Americans, come to mind – there does seem to be an increasing movement toward what I might call *speculative pessimism* in the field, an emergent trend that I will outline in what follows.

Black Speculative Fiction in the Black Lives Matter Era

A few definitions might help to clarify the parameters of, if not speculative pessimism, specifically, then at least the genre turn, broadly conceived. The term *Afro-Futurism* – coined by cultural critic Mark Dery in the mid-1990s – refers to a literary and cultural aesthetic that incorporates SF and fantasy, magical realism, and non-Western cosmology, appearing in creative works that challenge the racial homogeneity of conventional genre fiction and that explore questions of black identity and subjectivity in futuristic contexts.[5] While it is possible to use "Afro-Futurism" somewhat interchangeably with the terminology of the "black speculative," these terms are in fact more overlapping than synonymous. Given the relative expansiveness of the latter term, in fact, we might say that all Afro-Futurist work is a part of the black speculative, but not all black speculative work is Afro-Futurist. The black speculative, for instance, concerned with "what if, if only, and if this goes on," includes works stretching the boundaries of the real in ways that not only look toward the racial future, but that reimagine the past and its relationship to the here and now, or that distort and disrupt our understanding of the present and its limits.[6] For instance, while we might view something like 2017's blockbuster Disney/Marvel film (and cultural phenomenon) *Black Panther* as both Afro-Futurist and black speculative, another African American film from that year, Jordan Peele's social thriller *Get Out*, might easily be understood as a black speculative text – including, as it does, science fictional plot points like the surgical transfer of minds between bodies – without necessarily qualifying as Afro-Futurism.[7]

Although I have offered cinematic examples to distinguish between Afro-Futurism and the black speculative, this notion of the speculative, writ broadly, has recently gained increasing purchase in twenty-first-century black literature (and, although beyond the scope of this chapter, to the visual arts, music and other performance, and television).[8] While earlier, pre–Black Lives Matter iterations of this phenomenon might fall under what Ramón Saldívar calls "speculative realism," linked, for Saldivar, to a somewhat optimistic "post-racial" ethos that necessitated new narrative forms, as historical events of the twenty-first century have moved in an increasingly brutal direction, so has the presence of the speculative in African American literature begun to shift further in the direction of the dystopian and pessimistic.⁹ Of course, it seems important to acknowledge that the shift I gesture toward, here, like any other product of the emergent present, is as of yet both partial and incomplete. As such, these later contemporary texts still might be read as part of a longer aesthetic history – not only of narrative experimentation in the vein of earlier writers like Jean Toomer or Ralph Ellison, but also of speculative work across the field of black literary and cultural production.¹⁰ Yet as I will argue further below, such dystopian, pessimistic work, precisely in its refusal of long-cherished notions of black progress, also exemplifies a new direction, or new emphasis, in African American literature. This emergent shift might even be understood as the beginnings of a temporal and thematic break – one that grows out of what I would call the Black Lives Matter (#BLM) moment within the contemporary, and that uses a panoply of speculative elements to engage with the most painful figurative and literal aspects of black "reality."

While I place the beginning of the #BLM era at roughly 2012, it is possible to observe sporadic trends in this direction in Afro-Futurist and black speculative work even in earlier moments of the twenty-first century – works that stand out for their tendency toward a pessimism that has cohered and come to fuller fruition in recent years. Representative texts from the past nearly two decades include the late Octavia Butler's final published novel, a vampire text called *Fledgling* (2005); Mat Johnson's satirical racial fantasy *Pym* (2011); Jesmyn Ward's prison-centered ghost story, *Sing, Unburied, Sing* (2017); Colson Whitehead's fatalistic zombie novel *Zone One* (2011); as well as his Pulitzer Prize–winning speculative historical novel *The Underground Railroad* (2016), which imagines the titular railroad as an actual system of subterranean trains; Kiese Laymon's *Long Division* (2013), about two generations of kids in Mississippi who stumble into time travel; the nearly uncategorizable horror fiction of Victor LaValle, including 2009's *Big Machine*, 2012's *The Devil in Silver*, and most recently the modern-day fable *The Changeling* (2017); in addition to work by literary SF and fantasy writers Nnedi Okorafor (*Who Fears Death*, 2014) or N. K. Jemisin, whose *Broken Earth* trilogy has since 2016 garnered her three separate, consecutive Hugo Award wins.

In this chapter, part of my project is to consider a handful of these texts in concert with broader questions about the use of the speculative in contemporary African American fiction, particularly in light of the first epigraph, above, from black SF pioneer Samuel L. Delaney. In this line from Delaney's 1984 essay "Some Presumptuous Approaches to Science Fiction," Delaney points to "the future" as a narrative device that allows SF authors to speak to present-day questions about the social world. The project of SF, for Delaney, is one of *distortion*, and one of the things I ask in these pages is how we might consider the projects of these speculative twenty-first-century African American texts in concert – even when the speculative convention is not a narrative invocation of "the future," but in fact of "the past," broadly conceived, or of an alternative and disquieting near-present. How might such texts use "the past," or other iterations of "now," as narrative conventions to undertake "significant distortions of the present"? What new understandings of present, past, and future do such speculative moves enable?

The (Afro) Pessimist Imagination

As suggested by the second epigraph, above, my project here is also to engage with a contemporary school of thought that has generated significant controversy in the field of black studies: Afro-Pessimism. Founded by writer, dramatist, and scholar Frank Wilderson and drawing upon foundational critical texts by Hortense Spillers, Orlando Patterson, and Saidiya Hartman, Afro-Pessimists argue that the position of the black subject in Western society is synonymous with that of the Slave, a condition of nonbeing – absolute fungibility and subjection – based in the slave's status not as *worker*, but *commodity*. Further, the Afro-Pessimist position insists that the violent exclusion of black nonbeing creates the conditions for the existence of the Human, and indeed that civil society's structuring around anti-blackness, and the position of the black subject vis-à-vis that society, is one of *antagonism*: "an irreconcilable struggle between entities, or positions, the resolution of which is not dialectical but entails the obliteration of one of the positions."[11] For the Afro-Pessimist, total destruction of civil society is the only way to resolve – or dissolve – this antagonism. And yet, "[i]t is the extreme improbability of civil society mustering the desire for, or even willingness to recognize the parameters of, such a revolution that grounds the *pessimism* in Afro-Pessimism."[12]

If Afro-Pessimism is, by definition and self-ascription, a pessimistic project, we might also think of it as a *speculative* one. Sexton has made this claim directly, in response to those who accuse the school of thought of "a reductive and morbid fixation on the depredations of slavery that superimposes the figure of the slave as an anachronism onto ostensibly post-slavery societies."[13] What Sexton calls in the following quote the "rhetorical dimensions" of the Afro-Pessimist project, I understand as its pointedly speculative aspects:

> Astonishingly, all of this refuses to countenance the rhetorical dimensions of the discourse of Afro-Pessimism (despite the minor detail that its principal author [Wilderson] is a noted creative writer and its first major statement is found in an award-winning literary work of memoir) and the productive

theoretical effects of the fiction it creates, namely, a meditation on a poetics and politics of abjection wherein racial blackness operates as an asymptotic approximation of that which disturbs every claim or formation of identity and difference as such.[14]

In other words, Afro-Pessimism creates (or conjures) a *fiction* that dismisses the notion of slavery as an historical event that has ended, and instead acknowledges (or *imagines*, in the sense of "seeing with the mind's eye") its totalizing and perpetual relationship to the modern world: "a strange and maddening itinerary that would circumnavigate the entire coastline or maritime borders of the Atlantic world, enabling the fabrication and conquest of every interior – bodily, territorial, and conceptual."[15] Afro-Pessimism is a speculative project, too, in its conviction that revolutionary violence, and the destruction of civil society, is the only solution to global antiblackness and the black/Human antagonism – and not merely because civil society refuses to recognize or acknowledge this possibility. In fact, a genuinely revolutionary project is always a speculative project, in that it dares to imagine a radically different, indeed a completely new, world.

Thus, although they are not yet frequently considered together, Afro-Pessimism and the literary and cultural movement called Afro-Futurism – or black speculative fiction more broadly – might be said to have a similarly *imaginative* provenance. (This is not, to be clear, the same as arguing that Afro-Pessimism's claims are not real, or not true. Instead, I posit that to accept such claims requires seeing, or imagining, the world differently, in a manner that departs radically from liberal humanism's fictions of universality.)[16] Samuel Delaney has suggested, in a 2011 interview, that "Science fiction isn't just thinking about the world out there. It's also thinking about how that world might be – a particularly important exercise for those who are oppressed, because if they're going to change the world we live in, they – and all of us – have to be able to think about a world that works differently."[17] N. K. Jemisin expresses a similar sentiment when, in her 2018 Hugo Award acceptance speech, she describes writers of SF and fantasy as the "aspirational drive of the Zeitgeist: we creators are the engineers of possibility."[18] In that same speech, however, Jemisin also makes statements – in fact, she begins her remarks with those statements – that suggest that Afro-Futurism and the black speculative not only share a sense of imagination with Afro-Pessimism, but also, perhaps, a similar *pessimism*:

> This has been a hard year, hasn't it? A hard few years. A hard century. For some of us, things have always been hard. I wrote the *Broken Earth* trilogy to speak to that struggle, and what it takes just to live, let alone thrive, in a world that seems determined to break you.[19]

The feeling of weariness and even defeat in these lines is palpable. *For some of us, things have always been hard.* Perhaps it takes a sort of pessimism about the world, as it exists, to *want* to imagine that world differently.[20] Considering, and crafting, a radical departure from the present, such that an alternative future, present, or even another understanding of the past take shape on the page – may well speak to a fundamental cynicism, fatalism, or despair about the "real world." Especially as that world, like the civil society that Afro-Pessimism implicitly critiques, is structured upon "present institutions and logics" of antiblackness within which "a black future looks like no future at all."[21]

If Afro-Futurism and the speculative both can be understood as tending toward the pessimistic, either in inspiration – turning to the future in response to a "hard," dispiriting world – or in narrative outcome, wherein these speculative works depict dark, dystopian futures or dwell within the imaginary of an unbearable past, and if Afro-Pessimism has a speculative, ominously imaginative core, then what possibilities might thinking Afro-Pessimism and the black speculative together open up for the consideration of twenty-first-century African American literature? My use of the phrase "speculative pessimism" is meant to capture some of the potential of this pairing. I am not arguing, however, in favor of reading these projects as one and the same, nor even suggesting that they be understood as deliberate converses of one another. Rather my goal, here, is to suggest the interpretive fruitfulness of putting these seemingly disparate discourses in conversation. When read together, it is easier to see the ways that a pessimistic turn within the black speculative is indicative of more than simply despair, or capitulation to contemporary political circumstances.

Instead, we might say that Afro-Pessimism and Afro-Futurism have in common a certain radicalism – one inclined toward both building and destroying worlds. If the stated project of much of SF and fantasy is elaborate world-building, such that SF landscapes are frequently more "complex, active, and psychologically charged" than the characters who populate them, for Afro-Pessimism the building of a new world cannot begin until the old world, such as it is, is demolished.[22] As Wilderson puts it, "I do believe that there is a way out [of the foundational oppression of antiblackness]. But I believe that the way out is a kind of violence so magnificent and so comprehensive that it scares the hell out of even radical revolutionaries."[23] And although in the same interview Wilderson is deliberately vague about the specifics of the magnificent violence he envisions, to articulate this violence as a possibility is, itself, a speculative act that demands a very different sort of engagement with "the future" than is conventional for black writers and thinkers.

Indeed, there is a kind of fundamental lack of interest in traditional narratives of *progress* and (stated or assumed) hope for the future that happens in both Afro-Pessimist discourse and in the twenty-first-century African American speculative texts I consider here. The expected liberatory *telos* of the black literary project is set aside in these works, in favor of a much less programmatic relationship to the meaning of history and to the potentiality of black futurity. Such works bear the marks of what Erica Edwards has called "the new black novel as . . . devastated form," and point toward new methods of engaging with what has come before – both textually and temporally – and of dwelling within what is and what might be.[24] Indeed, we might usefully think the disruptive emergence of speculative pessimism in conversation with Afro-Pessimist methodologies that are similarly divorced from humanist metanarratives of progress: Christina Sharpe's *wake work*, for instance, which is a "method of encountering a past that is not past," and "a sitting with, a gathering, and a tracking of" antiblackness; or Calvin Warren's formulation of "build[ing] a way into an abyss – without recourse to the metaphysical finality-teleology of an answer."[25] The speculative becomes part and parcel of giving voice to this lack of interest in capital-P Progress, an affective position that we might understand as, if not *hopelessness*, then certainly a kind of matter of fact acceptance of the persistent and perpetual nature of history, a sense that this history and its wounds and violences continue to haunt us and to disrupt any sense that we have moved beyond the past, into another, safer and more productive temporal space. As Aliyyah Abdur-Rahman notes, "We are living in the future tense of abolition, decolonization, integration, first-, second-, and third-wave feminism, and black power, yet contemporary black life remains mired in regressive, recursive time."[26] If Afro-Pessimism speculates on a radical exit from this temporal recursivity, twenty-first-century black fiction engages the speculative in order to both dwell in and insist upon the past's continued presence, and to meditate upon the nature of (African) American superpowers, ghosts, monsters, and other fantastical possibilities across and through time.

The Implacable (Un)dead: *Zone One* and *Sing, Unburied, Sing*

Here, then, I want to turn to a representative selection of contemporary African American texts, placing them in conversation with Afro-Pessimist thought in order to consider in more detail how these works reinforce – but also play with, corrode, and disrupt – the regressive and recursive nature of black time, by re-visioning black present, past, and future via novel iterations of the speculative. Afro-Pessimism asks what it might mean to sit in a place of understanding, and acceptance, of blackness as enslavement, of a world that defines one's metaphoric and literal body as the marker of unfreedom and the end of the human. Colson Whitehead's 2011 novel *Zone One* (even more than his 2016 slavery novel, *The Underground Railroad*), seems to anticipate this query, its narrative offering a notably pessimistic approach to the acceptance of (social) death, using the speculative trope of the undead/zombie. *Zone One* tells the story of Mark Spitz, an unremarkable Everyman whose "aptitude lay in the well-executed muddle, never shining, never flunking, but gathering himself for what it took to progress past life's next random obstacle."[27] He credits this unwavering mediocrity – an uncanny ability to do only what is necessary, and no more, the "manifold survival strategies honed over a lifetime of avoiding all consequences" (177) – with his survival after a mysterious pandemic leads to a zombie apocalypse and the world is abruptly divided into the undead ("skels") and the human.

Mark Spitz, however, is remarkable in one way – he is a *black* Everyman, whose very name in the novel is a play on a racialized stereotype about the inability of black people to swim. Trapped, during a road-clearing mission, on a low bridge with an insurmountable mass of skels advancing, he chooses to fight rather than jump into the water and to safety, and when, afterwards, he reveals to his compatriots (all of whom had jumped from the bridge already) that he did not jump because he couldn't swim, "they laughed. It was perfect. From now on he was Mark Spitz" (182). Yet his refusal to jump is as much about his belief in the salvific power of his mediocrity as it is about any fear of the water:

> He was a mediocre man. He had led a mediocre life exceptional only in the magnitude of its unexceptionality. Now the world was mediocre, rendering him perfect. He asked himself: How can I die? I was always like this. Now I am more me. He had the ammo. He took them all down. (183)

Spitz's mediocrity is framed, here, as a gift that allows him to master this newly mediocre world, a world in which the old systems and structures no longer apply. By the end of the text, however, his willingness to fight the undead, and his sense of himself as differentiated from skels, is transformed into a countervailing willingness to become them, or at least to stop resisting their presence – to embrace, finally, the destructive mayhem they bring.

Mark Spitz observes, for instance, the zombies that move through the street after overtaking the barricade between Zone One (lower Manhattan) and the uncleared areas – another body of skels that he must find a way through in order to survive – and sees not the agent-less undead, but affective rage: "These were the angry dead, the ruthless chaos of existence made flesh.

These were the ones who would resettle the broken city. No one else" (321). This "ruthless chaos of existence made flesh" recalls Wilderson's analysis of the "radical incoherence" imposed by the black American subject onto the "assumptive logic" of civil society.[28] In fact, *Zone One* goes so far as to suggest that the skels taking over lower Manhattan are the coming of a new order, their undead march not simply portending this shift's arrival, but serving as proof that it was already here: "That was where they were now. The world wasn't ending: it had ended and now they were in the new place. They could not recognize it because they had never seen it before."[29] If this is the new world, a world in which the dead have destroyed what has come before, then we might read the ending of the novel as a kind of capitulation to what Wilderson calls the "incoherence of civil war":[30]

> On to the next human settlement, and the one after that, where the barrier holds until you don't need it anymore. He tightened the strap of his armadillo helmet. He strummed his vest pockets one last time and frowned at the density beyond the glass. They were really coming down out there. No, he didn't like his chances of making it to the terminal at all. The river was closer. Maybe he should swim for it. It was a funny notion, the most ridiculous idea, and he almost laughed aloud but for the creatures. He needed every second, regardless of his unrivaled mediocrity and the advantages this adaptation conferred in a mediocre world. Fuck it, he thought. You have to learn how to swim sometime. He opened the door and walked into the sea of the dead.[31]

How does one swim in the "sea of the dead," without dying oneself? Perhaps one does not – the question of suicide is raised, repeatedly, throughout the novel, and the death that zombies bring would seem to precipitate that "forbidden thought"[32] because zombie-hood itself can be understood as a kind of slavery, analogized to social death in its half-alive, half-dead, or living dead, status.[33] Suicide is a way to circumvent this fleshly subjugation – but it also isn't quite the same thing as what happens with Mark Spitz at the end of *Zone One*. Mark Spitz chooses to "learn to swim," rather than, say, to shoot himself with his gun, or, as another prominent character does, to "ja[m] a grenade into his mouth" (251).[34] Instead, "learn to swim" suggests a different sort of surrender, one that depends upon the protagonist's ability to blend in and accept, not to resist – to "swim" along in the "sea of the dead" rather than fighting his way out as he did in the scene on the bridge. Mark Spitz's walk into this sea suggests, in fact, a "desire to be embraced, and elaborated, by disorder and incoherence," to walk into the world's end, into the civil war that is that "Black specter waiting in the wings, an endless antagonism that cannot be satisfied (via reform or reparation), but must nonetheless be pursued to the death."[35] Mark Spitz, in other words, chooses dissolution amongst the (un)dead, entry into a "new place" that is only made possible via total human destruction.

Jesmyn Ward's 2017 *Sing, Unburied, Sing*, winner of the 2018 National Book Award for fiction, also tarries with death, in this case drawing upon the stories of the dead – ghosts – to dwell within the suffering that accompanies the social position of both the prisoner and the slave, bringing the past to literal and present-day voice in the text. Ward's text brings to life what Wilderson has called the "renaissance of slavery, i.e., the reconfiguration of the prison-industrial complex" a social system that, like slavery, "has, once again, as its structuring metaphor and primary target the Black body."[36] The novel is set, like much of Ward's other writing, in rural Mississippi. It follows thirteen-year-old Jojo, the young son of meth-head Leonie, as the latter drives with a friend and fellow junkie (Jojo and his toddler sister, Kayla, in tow) to pick up the children's white father, Michael, from the Mississippi State Penitentiary, Parchman. Given Michael's absence and Leonie's addiction, Jojo and Kayla have been raised, largely, by Leonie's parents, Pop (River) and Mam, a rootswoman who is dying of cancer.

The complications of Jojo's family narrative do not end there, however, as we learn early in the text that Michael's cousin was responsible for the death of Leonie's older brother, Given, when the two were in high school – the cousin having shot Given over a lost bet, in what is later called by Big Joseph (the local sheriff, who is also Michael's father and Jojo's other grandfather) a "hunting accident."[37] Notably, Leonie's relationship with Michael begins with his apology, a year after Given's murder, as he sits next to her in the grass outside of their high school and says, *"I'm sorry my cousin is a fucking idiot"* (53) – but also admits that his father *"believes in niggers"* (53). Leonie's ability to accept this admission, to see the similarities between Michael and his father and still to insist that *"the father was not the son"* (53) speaks to the depths of her hunger for what Michael does provide: "[H]e saw me. Saw past skin the color of unmilked coffee, eyes black, lips the color of plums, and *saw me*. Saw the walking wound that I was, and came to be my balm" (54).

As already noted, *Sing, Unburied, Sing* is also a ghost story; the central ghost in this text is Richie, who haunts not only Parchman, the plantation and work camp-turned-state prison where he had been sent, at twelve years old, for stealing food, but also the family of the man who killed him. Richie is called back from death – "pull[ed . . .] from the sky" (186) – by Parchman, the place tethering him to the earth and existing for him as "past, present, and future all at once" (186). There is another ghost in the novel as well: Given, Leonie's brother and Jojo and Kayla's uncle, who seemingly haunts only Leonie, and only when she is high (34). As readers, we might initially ask whether Given is a figment of her imagination, but once we are introduced to Richie, we recognize that Given, even if he is that, cannot *only* be that, because in this narrative universe, ghosts are real, present, and fully visible to characters, like JoJo, with the gift of second sight.

Richie gives voice to a different kind of haunting, however, than does Given – or rather, while both figures are products of violent deaths, the sort that create an unsettled, haunting spirit (236), only Richie can be understood as a ghost that makes particular demands on the living. If Given's presence in Leonie's drug-addled environment operates as a kind of silent reproach, a haunting that is also a critique either of her meth use or of her choice to be with a man so closely related to Given's killer, or both; Richie is a ghost with a story to tell, and needs to fulfill. He does this through JoJo, whom he recognizes immediately as Pop's descendant: "The boy is River's. I know it. I smelled him as soon as he entered the fields, as soon as the little red dented car swerved into the parking lot" (133). Jojo's second sight, the skill inherited from his maternal line, from Leonie and from Mam before her – which in his case includes the ability to see the dead – enables Richie to negotiate with the living world. And what Richie wants to negotiate are answers to the question that has haunted him about Pop/River: "You was the only daddy I ever knew ... I need to know why you left me" (222). Thus, Richie enters the car with Jojo at Parchman, follows the boy back to his grandfather, and insists that Jojo procure the answers Richie needs, by persuading Pop to tell "the end to that story ... about that boy, Richie" (249), a story that Pop has begun for Jojo many times before, but has never been able or willing to finish.

The answer Richie is seeking proves terrible beyond words – Pop reveals to Jojo the entirety of what he remembers, as Richie supplements Pop's telling. While Pop thinks Richie has run, tried to escape Parchman, with another brutal inmate, Blue, who beat and raped a female inmate and then fled, Richie clarifies:

> "I found them," Richie says. "He was climbing up off her. Big bloody hands. Was one of the strongest gunmen; he could outpick most everybody. He say to me: *You want a face like hers, boy?* I told him no. And he waved one of them big hands and said: *Come.* Part of me went because I didn't want him to turn my face red like hers. And part of me went because I was sick of that place. Because I wanted to go." (250–251)

Pop/River is the one tasked with tracking the pair, and once Blue attempts to attack a young white girl (252), his efforts thwarted by Richie, the search leads to a gruesome lynching for Blue, who is dismembered and skinned alive. Pop recounts his certainty that the same fate awaited Richie: "They was going to do the same to him …. They was going to come for that boy and cut him piece from piece till he was just some bloody, soft, screaming thing, and then they was going to string him up from a tree" (255). So, when he finds Richie first, he stabs him in his neck, "[i]n the big vein on his right side" (255), and holds him close until he dies.

This scene recasts the maternal filicide of Toni Morrison's *Beloved*, wherein Sethe "collected every bit of life she had made … and carried, pushed, dragged them … [o]ver there. Outside this place, where they would be safe."[38] Pop/River is not Richie's biological father, but he nonetheless fathers him, tries to protect him from the worst of the prison while they are together at Parchman. But Parchman is a place where suffering cannot be avoided – in Michael's words, "*this ain't no place for no man. Black or White. Don't make no difference. This is a place for the dead.*"[39] And escaping from Parchman, as Richie was forced to do by his encounter with Blue, has even more dire consequences. Thus Pop/River's decision to take Richie's life, to save him from the mob of "white men and boys gathering and swarming. Moving like one thing. To kill" (254) is, like Sethe's insistence upon putting "[her] babies where they'd be safe," an act of violence that is also an act of mercy.[40] Ultimately River's words, "*Yes, Richie, I'm a take you home*" suggest that death is the only *home* for a subject, the black prisoner, who is already socially dead.

The tree of ghosts at the end of the novel, where Richie eventually ends up, also recalls *Beloved* and the "people of the broken necks, of fire-cooked blood and black girls who had lost their ribbons," the "roaring" of the black dead who have suffered the violence of slavery.[41] In *Sing, Unburied, Sing*, these voices extend into the present, as the novel's depiction of a tree full of restless ghosts makes clear that (gratuitous, cf. Wilderson) violence against black bodies has no temporal end point, and indeed that such violence is indistinguishable and applies to black subjects indiscriminately across gender, age, and historical time:

> They speak with their eyes: *He raped me and suffocated me until I died I put my hands up and he shot me eight times she locked me in the shed and starved me to death while I listened to my babies playing with her in the yard they came in my cell in the middle of the night and they hung me they found I could read and they dragged me out to the barn and gouged my eyes before they beat me still I was sick and he said I was an abomination and Jesus say suffer little children so let her go and he put me under the water and I couldn't breathe.* Eyes blink as the sun blazes and winks below the forest line so that the ghosts catch the color, reflect the red. The sun making scarlet plumage of the clothes they wear: rags and breeches, T-shirts and tignons, fedoras and hoodies.[42]

If their deaths are indicative of consistently indiscriminate violence, a violence that endures across time, their clothing – from rags and tignons to hoodies – makes clear that they are temporally disparate, and that death, as a state of being and as a violent and recurrent series of events, collapses the distinctions of history. The novel, here, in its refusal of historiographical ordering, recalls Sexton's description, in another context, of "the slow time of captivity, the dilated time of the event horizon, the eternal time of the unconscious, the temporality of atomization."[43]

Antiblackness in The Stillness: *The Fifth Season*

If Ward's text insists upon the implacability of the past, and Whitehead's offers an alternative understanding of the "scandal" and "incoherence" of our present – a zombie-laden present in which the name Mark Spitz nonetheless still has historical salience in relation to swimming – then N. K. Jemisin's 2016 *The Fifth Season*, a speculative/fantasy novel and first volume in Jemisin's award-winning *Broken Earth* trilogy, transports readers into another timeline altogether. The world of *The Fifth Season*, a fantastical milieu that might be read as a long-distant future for Earth or simply as an entirely different universe, does have one thing in common with the "real" of the present day: it is a world structured upon enslavement. The novel depicts a continent called The Stillness, ironically named because it is constantly in motion, with recurrent earthquakes ("shakes") and volcanic activity that are kept in check in part by an elaborate and culture-wide system of preparation for the worst. The "fifth season" of the title is this world's name for the period after a catastrophic shake or other geological event that causes ash to cover the sun, plants to die, "the animals that depend on them . . . [to] starve, and the animals that eat those" to starve as well.[44] A Season might last two years or twenty, and "the people of the Stillness live in a perpetual state of disaster preparedness. They've built walls and dug wells and put away food, and they can easily last five, ten, even twenty-five years in a world without sun."[45]

This world, however, also controls the mercurial land they inhabit by harnessing the talents of a group of people with the inborn ability to manipulate the earth – *orogenes*, also known by the slur "roggas," who can draw kinetic power from their surroundings and quell a shake or move and reshape rock. Notably, orogenes are hated and feared by the people of the Stillness. In the continent's largest and most well-known city, Yumenes, young orogenes – either "ferals," cruelly exiled from their "still" (normal) families when their talents are discovered, or those born in captivity, to already-disciplined orogenes – are trained at an institution called the

Fulcrum to serve the society they live in, their abilities rigidly controlled. Fulcrum orogene behavior is regulated, not only by their years of training, but by a maroon-clad order called Guardians, who are fitted with implants that allow them to physically negate and numb orogene power when necessary, and to kill orogenes who step out of line.

Elana Gomel suggests that "In SF, space ceases to be the passive medium for the protagonist's actions in time. Instead, the subject is embedded in, and integrated with, the setting."[46] Thus, in reading *The Fifth Season* through Afro-Pessimist thought, we might consider not only the story of the central character of this text, Essun (formerly the Fulcrum-trained *Syenite*, and before that, prior to her family discovering her orogenic abilities and exiling her to the Fulcrum, *Damaya*), but also the significance of the world of the Stillness itself. It is striking, for instance, that the continent's central and most powerful city, the location of the Fulcrum, is named *Yumenes* – the homophonic link to *humans* suggesting the boundary outside of which the orogene (inverted, this word is remarkably similar to *Negro*) is positioned, just as we might understand the black subject, the Slave, in civil society to be situated, figuratively, beyond the boundary of the human, and constitutive of that boundary. This human-orogene opposition, or perhaps, following Wilderson, this antagonism, is more than just implied in Jemisin's text, however, as orogenes or *roggas* – and another homophonic connection, to *niggers/niggas*, is surely suggested by that slur – are repeatedly referred to in the novel as slaves. Essun/Syenite/Damaya realizes the extent to which this is true for even herself, someone relatively privileged, when she sees the extremes to which the Fulcrum takes the harnessing of orogene power.

When Syenite and her more powerful orogene mentor, Alabaster, travel from Yumenes to a remote coastal outpost to clear a blocked harbor using orogeny, their journey there is interrupted by a violent shake, which Alabaster determines originated at a rural node station, one of many such outposts where otherwise "untrainable" orogenes spend their days quelling small earthquakes in order to keep the Stillness somewhat stable for human inhabitants. Syenite believes that such "node maintainers" are simply low-level functionaries with boring jobs, akin to a clerk marking time in a backwater town, but what Alabaster, who knows the truth, shows her is far more sinister: "The body in the node maintainer's chair is small, and naked. Thin, its limbs atrophied. Hairless. There are things – tubes and pipes and *things*, she has no words for them – going into the stick arms, down the goggle-throat, across the narrow crotch."[47] In other words, the node maintainer, a child (since even "[a] newborn orogene can stop an earthshake" [141]) is kept alive, "immobile, unwilling, indefinite" (140), reduced by crude surgery to only the child's orogenic instinct. For Syenite, this scene of fleshly torture has implications for all orogenes:

> If the Fulcrum can do this, or the Guardians or the Yumenescene leadership or the geomests or whoever came up with this nightmare, then there's no point in dressing up what people like Syenite and Alabaster really are. Not people at all. Nor *orogenes*. Politeness is an insult in the face of what she's seen. *Rogga*: This is all they are. (144)

Given this realization, and what she has observed, it is perhaps not surprising that later in her story, Syenite (like *Sing, Unburied, Sing*'s River, and like *Beloved*'s Sethe before them both) murders her first child, Corundum, to protect him from being taken by the Fulcrum. And as she does it, the text's narrator proclaims in her voice, "She will keep him safe. She will not let them take him, enslave him, turn his body into a tool and his mind into a weapon and his life into a travesty of freedom" (441). Notably, this "travesty of freedom" would be Corundum's fate whether he is consigned to a half-life as node maintainer or whether he becomes a "respected," Fulcrum-trained orogene, precisely because in this text the life of a rogga, any rogga, is that of a slave: "all roggas are slaves, [and] the security and sense of self-worth the Fulcrum offers is wrapped in the chain of her right to live, and even the right to control her own body" (348).

There is far more in this vein to be found in a close reading of Jemisin's text, which depicts, ultimately, a group considered by their own society to be little more than "useful monster[s]" (143) and who are thus socially dead – treated as nominally human only when they are controlled. It is worth noting that Syenite and Alabaster are assigned to travel together on a mission in part so that they will produce a child together – forced breeding among Fulcrum orogenes another signal of their Othered status. This enslaved but gifted Other, the orogenes or roggas, possess an ability understood by those around them as a danger and a curse from "Father Earth" (not unlike, it would seem, the curse of Ham), a curse that links them to actual death, for others, for themselves, and for, if they are powerful enough, the entire world. Indeed, the novel – largely the recollections of Essun as she travels the Stillness, searching for her daughter and her former husband, who has murdered their toddler son after discovering his orogenic ability – is framed by Alabaster's decision to literally break the earth, snapping the Stillness in two at a major fault line, and causing an apocalyptic explosion and shake. His actions bring on a Season with the potential to last for thousands of years (8) effectively ending not just the rule of Yumenes, but the world of the Stillness as they know it. It is only in the final lines of the text that Essun/Syenite, reunited with Alabaster after many years, recognizes that he has done this deliberately, that instead of a madman who has lost control of his immense power, he is "not crazy at all, and he never has been" (449). She recognizes this only when Alabaster, now dying, asks her for help not to fix the catastrophic break he has engendered, but to "make it worse" (449). While Wilderson asserts that "[e]radication of the generative mechanisms of Black suffering would mean the end of the world," Jemisin's text seems to ask whether the obverse might also be true. Alabaster brings about the end of the world – and in doing so, he may create the only conditions under which rogga suffering might end.

Finally, then, these speculative texts, when read in concert with Afro-Pessimist thinking – itself a speculative critical gesture that, like a ghost story, relies upon an imaginative angle of vision, on our seeing a system that is commonly perceived as belonging to the past, slavery, as alive in and enabling of the present – suggest that the movement of twenty-first-century African American literature toward the sort of *speculative pessimism* I have outlined here is part of an emergent refusal to accept that famous truism from Martin Luther King, Jr., popularized in the twenty-first century by President Barack Obama, that "the arc of the moral universe is long, but it bends toward justice." This newer work instead speaks back to such optimistic cultural logics, challenging the metastructures, and metanarratives, of reality as we know it. Contemporary African American speculative *and* Afro-Pessimist work, refusing a straightforward *teleology* of progress, asks us to imagine possibilities that are not in any way guaranteed or even immediately knowable; it also asks us to perceive "reality" differently, and to consider the potentialities of not just change, but chaos.

NOTES

1 Samuel R. Delaney, "Some Presumptuous Approaches to Science Fiction," in *Starboard Wine: More Notes on the Language of Science Fiction*, rev. ed. (Middletown: Wesleyan University Press, 2012), 26.
2 Jared Sexton, "Afro-Pessimism: The Unclear Word," *Rhizomes: Cultural Studies in Emerging Knowledge* 29 (2016): paragraph 8, doi.org/10.20415/rhiz/029.e02.
3 See, for instance, James Dorson, "Cormac McCarthy and the Genre Turn in Contemporary Literary Fiction," *European Journal of American Studies* 12, no. 3 (2017): 1–16; Tim Lanzendörfer, ed. *The Poetics of Genre in the Contemporary Novel* (Lanham: Lexington Books, 2016); or Ramon Saldivar, "Historical Fantasy, Speculative Realism, and Postrace Aesthetics in Contemporary American Fiction," *American Literary History* 23, no. 3 (2011): 574–599.
4 Lauren Berlant, *Cruel Optimism* (Durham: Duke University Press, 2011).
5 See Mark Dery, "Black to the Future: Interviews with Samuel R. Delany, Greg Tate, and Tricia Rose," *SAQ: South Atlantic Quarterly* 92, no. 4 (1993): 735–778.

6 Gwendolyn D. Pough and Yolanda Hood, "Speculative Black Women: Magic, Fantasy, and the Supernatural," *Femspec* 6, no. 1 (2005): ix.

7 Arguing against the "sweeping inclusivity" (66) of the term *speculative fiction*, Kinitra D. Brooks suggests that black women authors frequently write what she calls "fluid fiction," a genre-bending "blend of horror/fantasy/science fiction that is specific to their themes and analytical needs." Kinitra D. Brooks, *Searching for Sycorax: Black Women's Hauntings of Contemporary Horror* (New Brunswick: Rutgers University Press, 2018), 56–57. In considering the genre turn in twenty-first century African American literature, however, I find "the black speculative" to be a productive term in discussions, like this one, of broad trends in the field that include but are not exclusive to black women authors.

8 I am thinking, for instance, of visual artist and filmmaker Wangechi Mutu; singer and actress Janelle Monae, whose investment in Afro-Futurism spans her entire musical oeuvre, including the recent "emotionpicture" *Dirty Computer*; as well as recent television series with premises ranging from the straightforward super-hero story (CW's *Black Lightning*), to various iterations of the black surreal (HBO's *Random Acts of Flyness*) – among many other examples.

9 Saldívar defines "speculative realism" as "revisions of realism and fantasy into speculative forms that are seeming to shape the invention of new narrative modes in contemporary fiction." Ramón Saldívar, "The Second Elevation of the Novel: Race, Form, and the Postrace Aesthetic in Contemporary Narrative," *Narrative* 21, no. 1 (2013): 3.

10 See, for instance, the works collected in Sheree R. Thomas, *Dark Matter: A Century of Speculative Fiction from the African Diaspora* (New York: Aspect-Warner Books, 2000), or speculative work by Pauline Hopkins (*Of One Blood*) and W. E. B. DuBois ("The Comet"), as well as later works by pioneering black authors working in SF such as Octavia Butler and Samuel Delaney.

11 Frank B. Wilderson III, *Red, White, and Black: Cinema and the Structure of U.S. Antagonisms* (Durham: Duke University Press, 2010), 5.

12 Sebastien Weier, "Consider Afro-Pessimism," *Amerikastudien/American Studies* 59, no. 3 (2014): 422, my emphasis.

13 Sexton, "Afro-Pessimism: The Unclear Word," paragraph 4.

14 Ibid., paragraph 6.

15 Jared Sexton, "The Social Life of Social Death: On Afro-Pessimism and Black Optimism," *InTensions Journal* 5 (Fall/Winter 2011): 30.

16 As Saidiya Hartman has argued in a text foundational to Afro-Pessimist thought, "[T]he universality or unencumbered individuality of liberalism relies on tacit exclusions and norms that preclude substantive equality; all do not equally partake of the resplendent, plenipotent, indivisible, and steely singularity that it proffers." Saidiya Hartman, *Scenes of Subjection: Terror, Slavery, and Self-Making in Nineteenth-Century America* (Oxford: Oxford University Press, 1997), 122.

17 Samuel R. Delaney, "Interview with Rachel Kaadzi Ghansah," *The Paris Review* 197 (Summer 2011), www.theparisreview.org/interviews/6088/samuel-r-delany-the-art-of-fiction-no-210-samuel-r-delany.

18 Transcript, N. K. Jemisin Hugo Award acceptance speech, reprinted on B&N Sci-Fi & Fantasy Blog, August 20, 2018, www.barnesandnoble.com/blog/sci-fi-fantasy/read-n-k-jemisins-historic-hugo-speech.

19 Ibid.

20 I am grateful to my sister and colleague Stefanie Dunning for pointing me to this line of questioning in one of our many conversations on this topic.

21 Kara Keeling "Looking for M – : Queer Temporality, Black Political Possibility, and Poetry from the Future," *GLQ: A Journal of Lesbian and Gay Studies* 15, no. 4 (2009): 578.

22 Elana Gomel, "The Zombie in the Mirror: Postmodernism and Subjectivity in Science Fiction," in *The Cambridge Companion to Postmodern American Fiction*, edited by Paula Geyh (New York: Cambridge University Press, 2017), 135.

23 Frank B. Wilderson III, Interview from "Against the Grain," KPFA Radio, Berkeley, California, March 4, 2015. Transcribed in "Afro-Pessimism: An Introduction," *Racked and Dispatched* (Minneapolis, 2017): 30, https:// rackedanddispatched.noblogs.org/files/2017/01/Afro-Pessimism2.pdf.

24 Erica Edwards, "The New Black Novel and the Long War on Terror," *American Literary History* 29, no. 4 (2017): 666.

25 Christina Sharpe, *In the Wake: On Blackness and Being* (Durham: Duke University Press, 2016), 13; Calvin Warren, *Ontological Terror: Blackness, Nihilism, and Emancipation* (Durham: Duke University Press, 2018), 14.

26 Aliyyah Abdur-Rahman, "Black Grotesquerie," *American Literary History* 29, no. 4 (2017): 685.

27 Colson Whitehead, *Zone One* (New York: Anchor Books, 2012), 11.

28 Frank B. Wilderson III , "The Prison Slave as Hegemony's Silent Scandal," in "Afro-Pessimism: An Introduction," *Racked and Dispatched* (Minneapolis, 2017): 71, https://rackedanddispatched.noblogs.org/files/2017/01/Afro-Pessimism2.pdf.

29 Whitehead, *Zone One*, 321.

30 Wilderson, "The Prison Slave as Hegemony's Silent Scandal," 79.

31 Whitehead, *Zone One*, 322.

32 Ibid., 318.

33 As Jessica Hurley points out, following Elizabeth McAlister, the Haitian origins of the zombie figure make this connection between zombie and slave explicit: "It was the racializing, dehumanizing effects of the Atlantic slave trade that gave rise to the figure of the zombie on Haitian sugar plantations." Jessica Hurley, "History Is What Bites: Zombies, Race, and the Limits of Biopower in Colson Whitehead's *Zone One*," *Extrapolation* 56, no. 3 (2015): 315. See also Elizabeth McAlister, "Slaves, Cannibals, and Infected Hyper-Whites: The Race and Religion of Zombies," *Anthropological Quarterly* 85, no. 2 (2012): 457–486.

34 The Lieutenant, head of the civilian band of "sweepers" of which Mark Spitz's team, Omega, is one part, takes this route; his suicide late in the text signals many kinds of collapse, but perhaps is best read as an indication that the fledgling "order" of the post-apocalyptic world cannot hold.

35 Wilderson, "The Prison Slave" 78.

36 Ibid., 73.

37 Jesmyn Ward, *Sing, Unburied, Sing* (New York: Scribner, 2017), 50.

38 Toni Morrison, *Beloved* (New York: Plume/New American Library, 1987), 163.

39 Ward, *Sing, Unburied, Sing*, 96.

40 Morrison, *Beloved*, 164.

41 Ibid., 181.

42 Ward, *Sing, Unburied, Sing*, 283.

43 Sexton, "The Social Life of Social Death," 5.
44 N. K. Jemisin, *The Fifth Season* (New York: Orbit, 2015), 7.
45 Ibid., 8.
46 Gomel, "The Zombie in the Mirror," 135.
47 Jemisin, *The Fifth Season*, 139.

7

JULIA H. LEE

Transpacific Diasporas

The transpacific. The Pacific turn. Rising Asia. The Asian century. These terms and phrases are not coeval or strictly equivalent, but their proliferation over the last several years in Asian American studies points to the increasing reorientation of the field toward the postnational with a specific focus on and across the Pacific toward Asia. It is important to note from the start that the transpacific means different things in different contexts and that the "transpacific" of Asian American studies is not the "transpacific" that one reads about in the newspaper, although they overlap and inflect each other in a variety of ways. While the term itself is not all that new, it has taken on a higher profile in the past decade due to the now-defunct Trans-Pacific Partnership (TPP), a trade consortium of twelve countries all bordering the Pacific Ocean that would have been the largest free trade deal in the world, covering about 40 percent of the global economy.[1] This "official" version of the transpacific – which the TPP exemplified – is actually part of a longer history that has conceived of the region as "a network of nation-states linked together by a highly militarized infrastructure through which economic and cultural capital can freely flow."[2] It fulfills long-held imperial "fantasies of economic expansion and domination,"[3] while also justifying military expansion and nuclearized violence into the region.[4]

Asian American studies, along with a number of other disciplines have taken up and reappropriated the "transpacific" as a means of resisting the imperial and colonizing narratives of the Pacific as propagated by the TPP and similar organizations such as the Asian Pacific Economic Cooperation (APEC) or the World Economic Forum.[5] Within Asian American studies, the term "transpacific" encompasses a constellation of concepts that emphasize the "contact, conflict, and exchange" between individuals, communities, and nations, suggesting how Asians living in diaspora across the Pacific have connected to each other in rhizomatic, multifaceted, and uneven ways.[6] While the transpacific is a fundamental "aspect of modern life in the twenty-first century," Janet Hoskins and Viet Nguyen go on to note that the transpacific is also "an intellectual and political project," one that "explore[s] ties between the ethnic homeland, the adopted home of present residence, and 'ethnoscapes' or geographically dispersed coalitions of coethnics."[7] It is, in other words, a space (or spaces) through which diasporans, travelers, and migrants can move, work, and go about their lives as well as an *imagined* site within which one can trace the "migration of cultural meanings."[8] The transpacific is an example of the "imagined world" that Arjun Appadurai writes about in *Modernity at Large*: the "multiple worlds that are constituted by the historically situated imaginations of persons and groups spread across the globe."[9]

The transpacific's emergence in an Asian American context is part of a "transnational turn"[10] within American studies more broadly, but as Sucheta Muzumdar and others have noted, these ideas of transnationalism have been a part of Asian American studies discourse for decades.[11] However, this most recent interest in the transpacific reflects a significant shift from previous theorizations of transnationalist frameworks. Earlier constructions of the region encompassing the transpacific – such as "Pacific Rim" and "Asia-Pacific" – tended to foreground those nations with trading power and global economic influence; they also "unif[ied] these vastly different categories [of class, ethnicity, nation] under a single racialized marker of 'Asianness.'"[12] Erin Suzuki argues that whereas "Asia-Pacific" and "Pacific Rim" were often presented as monolithic entities, the transpacific is defined by multiplicities that "conflict, intersect, and overlap," a conception of the transpacific that is echoed by other scholars.[13] It is this increasing sense that the transpacific is a transit zone for the movement and migration of people, culture, capital, and objects, combined with its history as the "Proving Ground" for American and Western empires eager to establish their "atomic modernity" upon the rest of the world, that makes it a compelling way to explore issues pertaining to Asian diasporic communities.[14]

The Transpacific Shift

It is important to note that the turn to the transpacific in Asian American fiction reflects shifts in how the field conceptualizes questions of representation, identity, community, globality, and its own constitution. These shifts are partly the result of the demographic changes brought on by the Immigration and Nationality Act of 1965, which ended immigration quotas based on country of origin. Changes to immigration law in the post-1965 era diversified the nation's Asian American population not only ethnically, but also in terms of socioeconomic status, educational attainment, religious affiliation, and immigration status. Post-1965 US immigration policy, which tends to privilege those immigrants who are highly skilled or have family already residing in the country, has resulted in what Sucheng Chang calls a "bimodal" Asian American population "with a large cluster of low-income earners and another large grouping of highly educated professionals and successful businesspeople."[15] Chan's point is to highlight the need to disaggregate the Asian American population into distinct Asian national groups in order to direct state and private resources toward those Asian American ethnic groups that most need them, but I would argue that this increasing bimodality has also contributed to Asian American literature's transpacific turn. An orientation toward the transpacific – whether because significant segments of the Asian American and Asian diasporic population have familial, financial, or affective ties to sites in Asia – defines both of these otherwise bifurcated groups.

Along with the increasing sense that immigration to the United States doesn't foreclose the possibilities of movement or affiliation across the national borders or oceanic spaces, Eleanor Ty also notes that the "improved technology and enhanced modes of transportation" of the last few decades have eased the flow of people, goods, and capital between locations that were once geographically remote and temporally distinct from each other.[16] Two brief examples here exemplify the ways in which bimodal factors and technology play an increasingly important role in maintaining transpacific identities and communities. In Mia Alvar's short story "The Kontrabida" (2015), which is the first story in her collection *In the Country*, Steve, a *balikbayan* working as a nurse and living permanently in the United States, returns to suburban Manila to say his final farewell to the dying father who beat him and Steve's mother Loretta for decades. When Loretta calls Steve to tell him that his father is sick, Steve dutifully "wires money into a Philippine National Bank account that I kept open for my family. Whenever someone needed rent or medicine or tuition back home, I sent what I could."[17] Steve's emotionally troubled relationship with his parents drives him to work overseas, but the instantaneous nature of international banking means that he can never truly disconnect himself from his parents or the family he left behind. The speed with which packages can be delivered overseas and financial transactions – both small and large – can be completed makes clear how entangled Steve's life is with his family's even though they are separated geographically, educationally, and in terms of class. Furthermore, as an overseas Filipino worker (OFW), Steve understands that his position is entangled in both financial and affective economies: upon his return to Manila, his extended family expects *pasalubong* or homecoming gifts from him; more important than these (expensive) material tokens of connection is the almost ritualistic conversation in which Steve feels compelled to engage, performing his affiliation with his Filipino upbringing even though he has completely abandoned it. "The Kontrabida" is part of a growing body of Filipinx writings in English that depict the Philippines as part of a transpacific and global circuit of labor. The title of Alvar's short story collection may be *In the Country*, but the experiences of the Filipinx workers that are its focus are anything but.

Likewise, in Ruth Ozeki's novel *A Tale for the Time Being* (2013), the ability for characters to be able to connect with each other instantaneously, despite the distance of time and space, crucially informs the lives of the protagonists, Naoko and Ruth, both of whom have personal ties and financial stakes in sites across the transpacific. Multiple plot points hinge on the ability of characters to text each other or search the Internet for information they need. That very technology that allows Naoko to text or chat with her beloved great-grandmother Jiko at any time can also heighten her sense of isolation and alienation. When Naoko leaves the United States as a teenager to return to Japan, she starts a blog "The Future is Nao!" in order to stay in touch with her American friends, classmates, and teachers. It is only after writing several posts that she realizes that the very small community that she treasured and left behind is disconnecting from her: the hit counter on her website eventually dwindles down to zero.

As these examples indicate, Asian American literary works – particularly novels – emphasize the geopolitical and imagined spaces of the transpacific as filled with "violent contact, exchange, and asymmetries," and they do so often in narratives that are formally innovative.[18] Given the historical association of the novel as a genre and the nation as a geopolitical formation, it is perhaps not surprising that literary works interested in transnational spaces like the transpacific, which call into question and/or supersede the boundaries of the nation, tend to engage in a certain amount of genre-bending. The plot of Don Lee's novel *Country of Origin* (2004) reads like that of a murder mystery: Lisa Countryman, a young, biracial African American woman who is in Japan ostensibly to do research for her PhD has disappeared after becoming involved in Tokyo's nightlife scene. Tom Hurley, a young half-Korean American diplomat stationed at the US embassy who claims to be "Hawaiian" in order to stave off questions regarding his racial identity, and Kenzo Ota, a socially awkward and professionally ostracized local Japanese police officer, are tasked with finding out what happened to her. Despite the presence of certain conventions associated with such novels – a mysterious victim with a past, plenty of suspicious characters who may have benefited from Lisa's death, an "exotic" foreign locale – the novel doesn't seem as interested in methodically narrowing down a list of suspects as it does in exploring Lisa's sense of alienation surrounding her black and Asian ancestry and her adoption as a child by an African American family. The novel also resists the conventions and unity of chronology and narration: each chapter alternates from the perspective of Lisa, Tom, and Kenzo, but they each occupy staggered or different temporal frames (Lisa's chapters, for example, although they are interspersed with Tom and Kenzo's, occurred earlier). The personal histories of Lisa, Tom, and Kenzo reflect the breadth of transpacific migration. As the reader attempts to piece together what happened to Lisa in the novel's present, he or she is simultaneously discovering the truth of Lisa's origins, namely, that she was the unwanted product of a romance between an American soldier and a *zainichi* (an ethnic Korean resident of Japan) woman.[19] Lisa's mother's shame at bearing a half-black child is heightened by her "stateless" status as a Korean living in Japan, a reminder that the militarized histories of the transpacific are not limited to the United States or Europe. The novel's transpacific orientation highlights the "complicated history of competition, conflict, and negotiation" between Asian and Western empires and reminds us that Asian countries are often "implicated in [the] problems of power" that cause the dispersal of excluded groups.

A fractured narrative structure and a geopolitical frame that tracks the movements of displaced and dispossessed populations across the expanse of the Pacific also characterizes Min Jin Lee's *Pachinko* (2017). The novel follows several members of a *zainchi* family across the span of the twentieth century, unspooling a narrative that is deeply rooted in the colonial histories and forced migrations of groups across East Asia. The United States is a shadowy presence in the novel, referenced passingly by the characters as they grapple with the everyday realities of war, hunger, violence, discrimination, and forced migration. Even when, at the end of the novel, a grandson of the family immigrates to the United States to receive an education and work for a multinational corporation – the foundations of many an Asian American immigrant narrative – *Pachinko*'s focus remains on the multilayered histories of movement that do not position the United States at the center, despite the outsized impact that US foreign policy and military interventions have had on the transpacific throughout the twentieth century.

Transpacific Trash

As novels like *Pachinko* and *Country of Origin* indicate, the movement of people in the transpacific is characterized by displacement and is often the result of transnational projects of empire and capital. Ozeki's *A Tale for the Time Being* also explores these issues but rather than focusing exclusively on the movement of humans across the transpacific, the novel takes an object-oriented approach to that space, one that challenges the notion that the Pacific region is "empty" of humanity. *A Tale for the Time Being* has two narrators: Naoko, a Japanese teenager who is being horrifically bullied by her classmates because she lived for a time in the United States, and Ruth, a biracial Japanese American writer who is living on Cortes Island, off the coast of British Columbia. One day, while walking along the beach, Ruth stumbles upon a sodden Hello Kitty lunchbox that contains Naoko's diary, a notebook written in French, letters written in formal Japanese, and a man's watch, all items pertaining to Naoko and her family's history. The chapters alternate between Naoko and Ruth: all of Naoko's chapters are from her diary, while Ruth's chapters narrate her experience of reading Naoko's diary. As she reads, Ruth becomes increasingly worried that Naoko may have been in the Sendai area visiting her beloved great-grandmother Jiko on March 11, 2011, the day that the Tohoku earthquake struck Japan, triggering a tsunami that leveled many communities on the eastern coast of the archipelago, which in turn caused the meltdown of the Fukushima Daiichi nuclear power plant, events that killed tens of thousands of people and displaced hundreds of thousands. Ruth's attempts to find out if Naoko or her family survived are stymied not only by Cortes Island's unreliable power grid (which tends to go down during storms) but also because there doesn't seem to be any digital trace of the family or Naoko herself, despite the fact that Jiko is purported to be a fairly famous feminist anarchist Buddhist nun and that Naoko's tech-savvy classmates enjoy adding to her torment by filming their violence toward her and putting the videos up on social media websites.

The uncertainty that characterizes Ruth's increasingly futile search for proof of Naoko's existence and survival pervades the entire novel, calling into question a number of axioms of modernity: the ascent of quantum physics, the nature of time and space, the permanence of text, the relationship between the "natural" and the "technological," and even the relationship between writer and reader. The novel's interrogation of these foundational structures manifest in a number of ways: through a fractured narrative structure that leaps back and forth in time and space; an obsessive interest in the book as a material object (Naoko writes her diary in a volume of Proust's *À la recherche du temps perdu* that has been "hacked," i.e., all of the novel's pages have been neatly cut out and new, blank pages have been seamlessly sewn in between the covers); and a fascination with textuality that manifests in a profusion of footnotes, appendices, and varying fonts.

The intercutting of genres and the emphasis on the relativity of time and its relation to space in *A Tale for the Time Being* suggests that the transpacific enables the exploration of different kinds of literary form, a not unexpected conclusion given the extent to which the novel as a genre is associated with the spaces and times of the nation-state as a political entity. If the novel is coterminous with the nation, then this novel aligns itself oceanically. That oceanic framework is an integral part of the novel's construction of identity and community. "Imagine the Pacific," says Oliver, the life partner of Ruth. Oliver explains to Ruth that the Pacific contains enormous gyres, which are circulating arcs of ocean current; each gyre "orbits at its own speed . . .. And the length of an orbit is called a tone. Isn't that beautiful? Like the music of the spheres . . .. The flotsam that rides the gyres is called drift. Drift that stays in the orbit of the gyre is considered to be part of the gyre memory."[20] The "beauty" of the gyre and of the Pacific lies in the ways that it incorporates movement, time, and objects into its ceaseless ebb and flow. The comparison between ocean and music also implies that there is a composed, aesthetic, or planned quality to the ocean's movements. Oliver's imagining of the Pacific as a space with its own uninterrupted flows of space, time, and matter is a contrast to how the Pacific is traditionally imagined by Western and Asian empires, as an area – an "isolated island" – whose lands and waters are empty and therefore are an ideal location for the testing of atomic weapons.[21] The inhabitants and histories of the Islands were effectively removed, rendering the spaces they had occupied for centuries empty and ahistorical – the perfect blank canvas upon which to paint a giant bull's-eye. Oliver's imagining of the Pacific, on the other hand, is based on it as an ecological system, in which waves, nonhuman animals, and inanimate objects (flotsam and jetsam) are interconnected or harmonize with each other.

The novel's particular construction of the transpacific isn't shared by other inhabitants of Cortes Island. Ruth describes the Island as being populated by "retired white people, who'd come to spend their twilight years on the island"; "summer people with yachts and vacation homes"; "happy hippie farmers raising organic veggies and bare-bottomed babies"; and "yoga teachers, body workers, and healers every modality, drummers, shamans and gurus galore."[22] At the post office, Ruth runs into a gaggle of these neighbors who have heard about the Hello Kitty lunchbox and fear that it and its contents have exposed the islanders to radiation from the Fukushima nuclear disaster. The neighbors want Ruth to turn the lunchbox over to the Royal Canadian Mounted Police, although how such an act would save anyone from radiation exposure is never really explained. The locals – an oyster farmer, a middle-aged math teacher, a young yoga instructor – seem to equate the diary and other items from Japan as contaminated and contagious; at one point, Purity, the yoga instructor, explains her fear of the objects by stating defiantly that she doesn't "want to get cancer and have deformed babies" (145) The characters' reliance upon a yellow peril discourse is not surprising – Asia has long been viewed as the source of physical illness and potential moral ruin. What is perhaps more novel is that they're expressing their anti-Asian sentiments through the rhetoric of "wellness" and environmental responsibility – Purity notes that the radiation from the nuclear meltdown is a part of the air they breathe, and from there it "gets into the aquifer, and like the whole, entire food chain, and then our bodies and stuff" (145). Even as Asian American authors look for different ways to conceptualize the communities of the transpacific, racist conventions continue to portray Asian people or objects as somehow unhealthful/ dangerous to the body, both politically and individually.

Ozeki's notion that the transpacific encompasses the narratives and every-day experiences of diasporic subjects is especially notable in the following passage, which I would suggest is crucial for understanding the novel as a whole, precisely because it links the historical erasures that nations perpet-rate with the perception that the objects that we use and consume are truly disposable. As Ruth tries to locate Naoko in the present (which is, of course, the future for the Naoko writing the diary), she reads about the tragic loss of life caused by the tsunami as well as the slowly unfolding environmental catastrophe in the aftermath of the Fukushima meltdown. As these various pieces of information swirl about in Ruth's mind, she wonders about the correlation between currents of information (like the Internet) and the currents of the ocean. If, as Oliver states, the "gyre memory" consists of all the flotsam – or drift – that remains in the gyre, then what does this mean for our conception of memory and its relation to identity, experience, and history? The implication of Oliver's statement about "gyre memory" is that memory can have a material rather than merely conceptual form, that trash can be a memory in the same way that a photograph is. What's more, materializing memory means that these memories can never be wasted, lost, or thrown away. This means that a wave, which comprises tiny particles, is made up of a million different stories or memories such as:

- a mobile phone, ringing deep inside a mountain of sludge and debris;
- a ring of soldiers, bowing to a body they've flagged;
- a medical worker clad in full radiation hazmat, wanding a bare-faced baby who is squirming in his mother's arms;
- a line of toddlers, waiting quietly for their turn to be tested (114).

The debris of contemporary life, which the tsunami dislodged and destroyed, "edd[ies] and grows old ... slowly breaking down into razor-sharp frag-ments" until they're sucked into the "garbage patch of history and time" (114). Rather than thinking of the debris the wave created as simply trash that vanishes once it's been damaged, destroyed, or no longer of use to us, the novel imbues those objects circling in the center of the Pacific with "memory." Although Oliver calls gyre memory – the objects floating in the gyre – "all the stuff we've forgotten," it might be more accurate to call it "all the stuff *we want to* forget." Another way of putting this might be: how do we measure our historical amnesia, our unwillingness to confront the violence and erasures that mark the relation between the Americas, the Pacific, and Asia? This passage suggests that the excluded, the victimized, the disappeared – the parts of history and experience that nations wish to forget or ignore – are never really gone, although they may not be visible. In that sense, the novel represents the Anthropocene as a social phenomenon as much as an ecological one. The trash of human history lingers. It never goes away.

This notion of remembrance in the face of violence returns when Ruth, in a dream-like state, seems to travel through time and space in order to prevent Naoko's father, Haruki #2, from killing himself. While she talks to him, she urges him to find his daughter, who is on the verge of suicide herself after the death of her beloved great-grandmother Jiko. Ruth's travel through time-space is triggered by her anxiety over the fact that entries at the end of Naoko's diary seem to be disappearing, leading her to believe that Naoko is dead. As Ruth rewrites the laws of quantum physics in order to save Naoko, the novel enumerates the physical and metaphoric manifestations of the spaces that divide people: "What does separation look like? A wall? A wave? A body of water? A ripple of light or a shimmer of subatomic particles, parting? What does it feel like to push through?" (346). The text questions these traditional symbols and markers of boundaries and borders in both the natural/lived world (a wall, a wave, a body of water) and on the subatomic level, both of which are supposed to define the limits of our bodies and experiences. That Ruth is able to "tear" through these axiomatic facts of quantum mechanics and modernity is explained by the fact that paper has a "fibrous memory" that enables it to retain some characteristics of the tree that it once was: "The tree was past and the paper is present, and yet paper still remembers holding itself upright and altogether. Like a dream, it remembers its sap" (346). That paper is capable of "memory" strains the fundamental binary that governs human life, that is, the divide between the animate and the inanimate, or what theorist Mel Chen has called "animacy."[23] *A Tale for the Time Being* follows the notion that matter mediates – rather than divides – humanity's understanding of itself.

The novel's emphasis on the "half-life" of the radioactive elements released by events like the atomic bombings of Hiroshima and Nagasaki or the meltdown of the Fukushima Daiichi nuclear power plant trouble the presumed dichotomy between what is alive and what is not alive.

Thus the polluted and polluting material objects that circulate in the trans-pacific – which has long been the preferred site for these types of detonations precisely because it is seen as empty of "human" life (Pacific Islander and Asian bodies notwithstanding) – not only remind us of the histories that empires tend to dismiss, they also reveal how "provisionally constituted, illusorily bounded, and falsely segregated" the human/nonhuman divide is.[24] Within *A Tale for the Time Being*, it is not people who cross the Pacific but rather nonhuman animals (like the Jungle Crow or oysters) and inanimate objects (the Hello Kitty lunchbox). While both protagonists have traveled across the ocean (Naoko spent the early years of her life in California before moving back to Japan with her family; Ruth, who is American, lived in Japan and now calls Canada home), their relative rootedness during the course of the novel dovetails this notion that the transpacific maps a space that is about more than the "human."

Unboxing Histories

While Ozeki's *A Tale for the Time Being* takes a seemingly more expansive view of the transpacific as a repository of that which cannot be forgotten, Thi Bui's graphic memoir *The Best We Could Do* (2017) imagines the transpacific as a series of interlocking spaces and histories through which the narrator and her family move constantly in an attempt to evade the violence of Western colonialism and American empire. *The Best We Could Do* is a graphic memoir that narrates the experiences of Bui's family in and between Vietnam and the United States, but it is also a textual cartography of the transpacific, mapping the Bui family's migration onto these spaces. As Harriet Earle notes, "Bui places family landmarks and [Vietnam] conflict landmarks in close contrast …. In closely juxtaposing births and conflict events … on the page – often in adjoining or overlapping panels – Bui maps her own history onto the wider history of the country."[25] The visual nature of graphic narratives makes the overlaying of the family's landmarks onto the historical landmarks associated with the Vietnam War more discernible, allowing the reader to switch registers, zooming out to describe important historical events before zooming back in to examine how those events inter-sected with the personal travails of the family. For example, the panel depicting the narrator's father Bố, rejecting once and for all his abusive father is juxta-posed with a panel depicting a mushroom cloud, which represents the atomic bombs that were dropped on Hiroshima and Nagasaki. The panel on the left shows Bố angry and defiant face dominating the lower portion of the vertical panel, with his father's face above his. His words ("You / are not my papa") are written in dialogue boxes that resemble billowing smoke, echoing and reflecting the image in the following panel. The parallel construction between these two temporally and spatially disjunctive panels reveals how events in Japan or elsewhere in the world – on the one hand, seemingly peripheral or irrelevant to the everyday lives of Bui's family, but, on the other hand, absolutely vital to it – have a complex and uneasy relationship with the family's own history. As in Lee's *Pachinko*, in which the militaristic and geopolitical machinations of great empires like Japan or the United States seem distanced from the everyday struggles of the novel's characters but are actually formative of them, the World War and Cold War battles that are nothing but newspaper headlines to Bui's family nevertheless impact every aspect of their lives, including their decisions about where to leave and where to live both in Vietnam and outside of it

National borders exist and their presence complicates the family's journey, but ultimately the transpacific is never completely contained or defined by these boundaries that are supposed to delimit the movement of people. Bui uses the visual nature of the graphic novel genre to drive home these points. Bui spends a great deal of time situating the family within the geography of the Vietnamese diaspora. Bui's grandparents and parents (Bố and Má) move throughout Vietnam before and during the war years in an attempt to escape the increasing violence and instability; they wind up crossing the South China Sea on a rickety boat before landing in Malaysia; from there, they are eventually sponsored by Bui's maternal aunt and travel to Chicago before heading to Hammond, Indiana, to be reunited with family; they make a final move to California in search of warmer weather and better opportunities. At times, Bui's narrative resembles traditional graphic novels, with panels – usually between four and six – set down in the traditional order of right-to-left and up-and-down. The passage of time or movement through space is conveyed by the movement across panels. However, Bui also makes strategic use of single-page panels, in which movement and time are blurred via a single image. All of the panels depict transitions, and most of them depict the characters in the water: Bui's son birth and emergence from the waters of the womb (11); Bố's face becomes the pond in which he taught himself to swim in Hải Phòng (93); Bố looking at Orion's belt as he tries to navigate the boat toward safety away from Vietnam (249–250); Bui's son swimming underwater into the ocean (329). Rather than attempting to sequence the events the novel depicts – the Vietnam War, the births, the deaths, the refugee movements – via a static progression of images that suggest cause and effect, Bui spatializes these experiences across the page nonsequentially.

The stories that Bui tells about her father Bố stand as examples of how Bui uses the medium of graphic narrative to highlight the complexity of refugee histories and movements through the transpacific. In a chapter titled "Blood and Rice," Bui narrates the traumatic and peripatetic childhood of her Bố. Bố's father abused his mother and eventually kicked her out of the house to starve; after years of neglect, Bố's father finally abandons his son and leaves him to be raised by his own formidable mother and chronically unfaithful father. Despite his status as the son of landowners, Bố's father joins the Viet Minh as a way of insuring his survival. In describing the silence that permeates her relationship with her father and the fear she often felt for him as a child, Bui poses a series of striking images. In the first series on the top of page 92, the top left panel depicts Bui as a child looking at her father as he smokes at a card table, which is followed immediately by a panel that depicts almost the exact same image, only in the second panel, Bố the father has been replaced with Bố the child. The bottom left panel contains an image of Thi sitting with her father at the same card table, the two of them the same age. This is followed and mirrored by a panel in which a now-teenage Bui sits with her father, who is now the appropriate age. Bui's text is broken up across the panels: "To understand how my father became the way he was, / I had to learn what happened to him as a boy. / It took a long time / to learn the right questions to ask."[26] In the second series of images, there are four narrow panels spread across two pages. In the first, Bố is standing in the foreground, and in front of him, we see his grandparents as they all flee Lôi Đông for the relative safety Hải Phòng. In the second panel, we see Bui in the foreground. Her back is to us as she faces her father, who is sitting at the same card table, smoking a cigarette, looking stern and rigid. The third panel is a full body view of Bui clutching her doll, a look of sadness and fear on her face. And the final image is a profile shot of her father, whose figure is framed in a window but cast in darkness, as his long shadow fills the rest of the panel.

The sequence of images constitutes what Scott McCloud calls scene-to-scene transitions, in which "significant distances of time and space" are covered between panels, and it is up to the viewer to fill in the gaps between the images. They highlight how graphic narrative can "fracture both time and space, offering a jagged, staccato rhythm of unconnected moments."[27] The narrator's overarching point in this series of panels is that in order to understand the man who raised her she needs to understand the childhood he endured. The disconcerting replacement of the small boy for the grown man – a substitution that repudiates the logics of space and chronology – speaks to the ways that transpacific migration can alter chronologies and temporalities to such an extent that a young girl can feel that her grown-up father is really no older or better equipped at handling the vagaries of daily

life than she is. Generally speaking, the visual vocabulary of graphic narrative – the construction of panels, the juxtaposition of frames in relation to
each other, and the visibility of the gutter in between images – relies upon the
reader to create a "deliberate, voluntary closure" of the story as a means of
simulating the passage of time and the rhythm of movement.[28] "Closure" in
this sense is a technical term; according to Scott McCloud, it describes a
"phenomenon of observing the parts but perceiving the whole."[29] The way
that graphic novel as a genre presumes an inductive form of narrative – that
the bits will eventually lead you to the whole – is one of the issues with which
Asian American literary studies of the twenty-first century negotiates. As
Viet Thanh Nguyen writes in "Masticating Adrian Tomine," "the problem
for an Asian American literature composed purely of the written word is
that there is no formal way for it to deal with race's visual dimension, only
its narratives dimension."[30] In reading Tomine's well-known graphic
work *Summer Blond* (2002), which depicts only one identifiable Asian
American character, Nguyen argues that the graphic narrative "has the
advantage over written literature" because it "not only writes and rewrites
the stories of race, but draws and redraws the look of race."[31] In the case of
The Best We Could Do, Bui never relies upon the assumption that the viewer
is a "collaborator" in closing the story; in fact, Bui finds ways to visually
arrest the viewer so that he or she does not or cannot arrive at an understanding of a "whole" based on the fragments observed. This is particularly
the case in the full-page panel that follows the first sequence of images
I described: rather than relying on gutters or panel positioning to fill in the
psychological gaps, the panel is a collage of two images: at the top, the head
and shoulders of Bui's father, which gradually morph into shapes that
suggest a pond and lily pads. Centered in the transition area of the panel
between Bố and the water are the floating words "anecdotes without shape, /
wounds beneath sounds."[32]

Via the trope of water, Bố's life is connected to the birth and life of his own
grandson, Bui's own son, in a way that is not reliant upon notions of blood
or biology. The image of Bố swimming as a child and then as an adult to flee
the violence of Vietnam is an apt metaphor for the kind of mobility that
transpacific Asian American novels explore. It is a movement that is based
on necessity, violence, and displacement. But the transpacific framework
also represents the opportunity for Asian American authors to explore
questions of cultural production outside of the frame of the nation. As my
reading of *A Tale for the Time Being* suggests, the transpacific is a central
concept in Asian American imaginings about the Anthropocene, climate
change, and ecocriticism. To write about the transpacific is an "act of
deterritorialization" as it enables the examination of different types of

epistemologies (as in the case of *A Tale for the Time Being*) or geographies (as in the case of *The Best We Could Do*).[33] Given its significance within the relatively young canon of twenty-first-century Asian American literature, it seems likely that the transpacific will play an increasingly important role in future literary productions.

NOTES

1 For a more expansive definition of the Trans-pacific Partnership and what it would have entailed, see the Council of Foreign Relations website, www.cfr .org/backgrounder/what-trans-pacific-partnership-tpp.
2 Erin Suzuki, "Transpacific," in *Routledge Companion to Asian American and Pacific Island Literatures*, edited by Rachel Lee (New York: Routledge, 2014), 353. The obvious exclusion of China from the US-led TPP reveals the extent to which the TPP manifests long-held anxieties about China's rising economic might and global influence.
3 Janet Hoskins and Viet Thanh Nguyen, "Introduction: Transpacific Studies: Critical Perspectives on an Emerging Field," in *Transpacific Studies: Framing an Emerging Field* (Honolulu: University of Hawai'i Press, 2014), 2.
4 Elizabeth DeLoughrey has argued that the "myth of the isolate" was instrumental in the emergence of "ecosystem ecologies" in the mid-twentieth century. This conception of the Pacific and its islands as a "closed system" was promulgated by both the American military (specifically the Atomic Energy Commission) and buttressed by the American environmentalist movement in order to justify the exposure of the region and its inhabitants to nuclear weapons and radiation. See Elizabeth DeLoughrey, "The Myth of Isolates: Ecosystem Ecologies in the Nuclear Pacific," *Cultural Geographies* 20, no. 2 (2013): 168.
5 See also Paul Lyons and Ty P. Kāwika Tengan, "Introduction: Pacific Currents," *American Quarterly* 67, no 3 (2015): 557.
6 Suzuki, "Transpacific," 352.
7 Hoskins and Nguyen, "Introduction," 12.
8 Yunte Huang, *Transpacific Displacement: Ethnography, Translation, and Intertextual Travel in Twentieth-Century American Literature* (Berkeley: University of California Press, 2002), 3.
9 Arjun Appadurai, *Modernity at Large: Cultural Dimensions of Globalization* (Minneapolis: University of Minnesota Press, 1996), 33.
10 Shelley Fisher-Fishkin, "Crossroads of Culture: The Transnational Turn in American Studies – Presidential Address to the American Studies Association, November 2004," *American Quarterly* 57, no. 1 (2004): 20.
11 Sucheta Mazumdar, "Asian American Studies and Asian Studies: Rethinking Roots," in *Asian Americans: Comparative and Global Perspectives*, edited by Shirley Hune, Stephen S. Fugita, Hyung-chan Kim, and Amy Ling (Pullman: Washington State University Press, 1991), 40.
12 Suzuki, "Transpacific," 352–353.
13 Ibid., 353.
14 DeLoughrey, "The Myth of Isolates," 1.

15 Sucheng Chan, "Asian American Economic and Labor History," in *The Oxford Handbook of Asian History*, edited by David K. Yoo and Eiichiro Azuma (New York: Oxford University Press, 2016), 320.

16 Eleanor Ty, *Unfastened: Globality and Asian North American Narratives* (Minneapolis: University of Minnesota Press, 2010), x.

17 Mia Alvar, "The Kontrabida," in *In the Country* (New York: Vintage Books, 2017), 6.

18 Lisa Yoneyama, "Toward a Decolonial Genealogy of the Transpacific," *American Quarterly* 69, no. 3 (2017): 472.

19 For more information on the *zainichi*, see John Lie, *Zainichi (Koreans in Japan): Diasporic Nationalism and Postcolonial Identity* (Berkeley: University of California Press, 2008), 8–9.

20 Ruth Ozeki, *A Tale for the Time Being* (New York: Viking Penguin, 2013), 13–14.

21 DeLoughrey, "The Myth of Isolates," 8.

22 Ozeki, *A Tale for the Time Being*, 141–142.

23 For her definition of animacy, see Mel Chen, *Animacies: Racial Mattering and Queer Affect* (Durham: Duke University Press, 2012), 10.

24 Ibid., 5.

25 Harriet E. H. Earle, "A New Face for an Old Fight: Reimagining Vietnam in Vietnamese American Graphic Memoirs," *Studies in Comics* 9, no. 1 (2018): 94.

26 Thi Bui, *The Best We Could Do* (New York: Abrams Books, 2017), 92.

27 Scott McCloud, *Understanding Comics: The Invisible Art* (New York: Harper Collins, 1993), 67.

28 Ibid., 69.

29 Ibid., 63. The example McCloud provides is film, in which the viewer's mind "aided by the persistence of vision, transform a series of still pictures into a story of continuous motion" (Ibid., 65).

30 Viet Thanh Nguyen, "Masticating Adrian Tomine," *American Book Review* 31, no. 1 (2009): 12.

31 Ibid.

32 Bui, *The Best*, 93.

33 Michelle N. Huang, "Ecologies of Entanglement in the Great Pacific Garbage Patch," *Journal of Asian American Studies* 20, no. 1 (2017): 97.

8

MARY PAT BRADY

Hemispheric Routes

As the catastrophic potentialities of a warming planet have been clarified, many students of literature have toggled their analysis toward scale in an effort to think beyond a traditional orientation toward the local and the regional, to think past the national and from thence to the hemispheric and planetary, in order to think the cataclysmic.[1] By changing the angles of vision and shifting away from a single or central defining locus (for example, New England), scholars have enlarged the scale of their analyses. Deploying the tricks of cartographers, they tell persuasive new stories about interlinked cultures in the hopes of thinking effectively about the impact of climate change and imagining new ways to ward off ecological disaster.

This recourse to a cosmic scalar imaginary follows scholarship produced at the end of the last century that turned toward the ways thinking about literature only in regional or national terms represses all sorts of relations and literary movements. Turning to the hemispheric and the oceanic scholars such as Paul Gilroy, Anna Brickhouse, and José David Saldívar revealed complex creative genealogies and underscored the importance of various forms of translation and interpretation as well as settler-colonialist and Indigenous intellectual, creative networks. Such attention to the hemispheric helped to denaturalize "simplistic conflations of English language, US territorial statehood, and American culture by showing the legacies of military violence, territorial claims, and multiple languages and cultures contending with the perceived space of national culture" according to Gretchen Murphy.[2] In other words, the hemispheric turn highlighted the problems with organizing literary study at the scale of the nation-state or empire while also providing greater visibility to works on the edges of dominant national cultures.

Yet if jumping the scale by which texts are studied has been fruitful and if contemporary ecocriticism finds it vital, this practice also underscores the logic of scale itself and reinforces scale as a naturalized heuristic. Scale thrives as the obvious and necessary means by which one orients oneself as a being in the world; concepts such as local, regional, and hemispheric depend on the cartographic process that rationalizes space (by making it everywhere the same and therefore abstractable, rendered visually on maps, made available for conquest and as property). In this manner, scale tells stories that seem integral to the representation of place and people. It functions as a translator, transposing particularity into generality, the fields and planes of being, of activity, into numerical authority, into the abstraction of a sameness that can be pictured and transferred, sold and conquered. To think in scalar terms is to presume that space can be abstracted and rationalized via a seemingly neutral process.

The Pluriversal Novels of the Twenty-First Century

While scale seems like a handy way to articulate relations across vast territorial stretches, it also abstracts those relations into a scaffold, orienting them into a vertical relationship from small to large. In other words, scale offers a hierarchical story about how places and people are related to each other, creating spaces bounded by their spatial relations to other spaces. By such means, scale became an effective imperial and colonial tool with profoundly homogenizing effects. Put another way, and following the work of geographer Sallie Marston and her colleagues, not only does scale orient people vertically and hierarchically, it also reinforces a "scaffold imaginary" that prefers the larger over the small, the higher over the lower, along with an understanding of space and sociality that depends on binaries (local and global) and the romance of a small-large imaginary.[3] This conceptualization of the world, which renders it singular, is a founding abstraction of the global and helped initiate the fetishization of separability[4] and thereby produced what Henri Lefebvre called a "phallic verticality" in which the local is inserted into this scaffold imaginary as a nodal point within a nested hierarchy; the local is stuck; the hemispheric, the transnational move with vibrancy and power; visible movement can only be elaborated at a grand scale in this schema.[5] Thus, to global or hemispheric studies does the glamor of cosmopolitanism adhere.

Since scale organizes mass into a single, scaled world, what it can't capture it tends to erase. Scalar logic insists that the world is only knowable as singular, advocating what John Law calls monoworldism.[6] The monoworld, as Arturo Escobar suggests, has "arrogated for itself the right to be 'the' world, subjecting all other worlds to its own terms or, worse, to nonexistence."[7] Escobar further argues that this monoworldism is an approach that crystalizes a subject-object dualism and inhibits an understanding of relationality. The problem then is not necessarily study at the scale of the hemisphere; the problem is scale itself.

From Dualism to the Multiversal

Anticipating this critique of monoworldism by nearly twenty years, many novelists began to write from the cracks within the scaffold imaginary. Their novels do not disregard scale altogether or hemispheric connections, rather they offer conceptions of relations that fold multiple worlds together and also shear them apart, seeking thresholds. They tend to disentangle the logic of temporal linearity from discourses of world development, offering narratives that play with recursive structures, spectacularity, disruption, and speculation. These texts could be read as responses to the end of the cold war, to the proliferation of structural adjustment programs, and perhaps to the failures of postmodernism to grasp the arrogance of one-world theories, to misunderstand that destinies are complexly bound together.

One can see this relational sensibility in novels such as Leslie Marmon Silko's *Almanac of the Dead* (1991), Sandra Cisnero's *Caramelo* (2002), Junot Díaz's *The Brief Wonderous Life of Oscar Wao* (2007), Patrick Chamoiseau's *Texaco* (1992), Gayl Jones's *Mosquito* (1999), Toni Morrison's *A Mercy* (2008), Francisco Goldman's *The Ordinary Seaman* (1997), Jamaica Kincaid's *Autobiography of My Mother* (1996), Rosario Ferré's *The House on the Lagoon* (1995), Miriam Chancy's *The Loneliness of Angels* (2010), and Nelly Rosario's *Song of the Water Saints* (2002). All of these texts undertake a refusal; that is to say, they each unbend their stories from straightforward geographical singularities that might more aptly characterize, for example, the European bildungsroman or picaresque traditions, in order to weave together stories of becomings in which multiple worlds constitute each other and knowledge is produced from relations rather than about them. These texts could all be characterized as hemispheric in the sense that they move across places and territories and fold together geopolitical sensibilities that are not nation-bound. Yet they could also be called anti-hemispheric or, more accurately, multiversal, because they imagine many worlds coexisting together. It is also possible to identify these texts temporally with the scourge that became NAFTA and within whose temporality they were written. To do so is to see then that a second, post-NAFTA wave of hemispheric writing has since emerged, orienting readers without scale altogether.

To write against scalar structures is to write past them. Such maneuvering can be found among many twenty-first-century novelists who seek, as José Rabassa urges, to "elude the imperialist impulse of the Greco-Abrahamic conceptual apparatuses that reduce the totality of the world to its own concepts."[8] These writers offer visions of multiple worlds no longer dependent on a singularizing perspectival force. To pursue their stories is to engage a different kind of literary imagination where abstractions don't speak first. Recent novels that refuse the "scaffold imaginary" tend to have porous plots featuring multiple entangled stories and characters with richly complex understandings of place, dense portraits of immediacy, of sites shot with multiple conceptualizations of relationality. They tend to undermine what Harsha Ram succinctly calls the "easy marriage of world-system analysis to the study of the novel."[9]

To read these twenty-first-century texts, novels that move apart from but also across the hemisphere disregarding scale's nested hierarchies, is to read not vertically across scales, but densely through texts that fold together multiple narrators, multiple forms, and multiple histories. These texts hold both long memories and new refusals and have emerged as peoples in many places collectively refute the one-world logic that scale narrates and that has resulted in intertwined crises around food, energy, climate, water, air, power, and knowledge.[10] In a post-NAFTA, global trade regime in which structural adjustment programs hatched by the United States and foisted on peoples across the hemisphere came home to roost in the United States, writers have sought to make these multiple worlds more visible and to undo the logic of a narrative power that subsumes all explanation into a rational notion of one world. These are writers who honor Indigenous knowledges, who remember the Middle Passage, who seek to continue and develop a black and brown radical aesthetic, who do not enshrine the delineation of property as the rubric for connectivity. Rather, these writers open multiple worlds; they think about movement and connection, drawing from the novel form, refusing a conventional linearity and singular plot structure while also suggesting more complex entanglements of beings, of coming together, of interconnections and thresholds, all of which can disappear when narrated through verticality, or the small-large imaginary of the monoworld.

Crossing Thresholds between Worlds

Recognizing a pluriverse, acknowledging complex mutuality and relations among beings, refusing a dualism that depends on the human and nature as structures of difference and categories of distinction, offers a way to consider the textures of connection without relying on spatial abstraction and rationalization. Consider, for example, the analytical turn poet and novelist Linda Hogan (Chicasaw) offers in *Dwellings*, a collection of meditations arguing that living beings dwell in their own conscious worlds, worlds that hold integrity and depth, but may not be recognized by other beings. This "spiritual history of the living world" refutes an ontology that depends upon understanding humanness as discontinuous with nonhuman forms and, through a series of meditations, explores connectivity and meshes of relation that can't be rationalized or reduced to abstracted dualisms:

> [I]t is the world-place bats occupy that allows them to be of help to people, not just because they live inside the passageways between earth and sunlight, but because they live in double worlds of many kinds. They are two animals merged into one, a milk-producing rodent that bears live young, and a flying bird. They are creatures of the dusk, which is the time between times, people of the threshold.[11]

Hogan here focuses on the texture of connection that, acknowledging multiple worlds, opens forward and inward; this texture is denser, nubby, and utterly incongruous with a sensibility that reduces the many to one. Hogan insists on pluritemporality and on thresholds and passageways that refute singularity because such singularity cannot conceptualize betweenness, nor perhaps can a singularizing perspective encounter grace:

> The water jar was a reminder of how water and earth love each other the way they do, meeting at night, at the shore, being friends together, dissolving in each other, in the give and take that is where grace comes from.[12]

The water jar serves as a teacher, or as she calls it, a "reminder." Hogan is here offering a different logic of connection, one that opens the possibility of generosity, on thinking together densely rather than hierarchically. Scale ceases to be the lynchpin that organizes relationality. Scale can't organize grace or the dissolution of earth and water into each other to enact a kind of loving with "the give and take" in the "time between times," across worlds.

Wor(l)ds Apart; Worlds Together

Jennine Capó Crucet punctures the structures that naturalize the assumption that the world is one and not many in her 2015 novel that brings together the stories of a young Latinx first generation college student, Lizette Ramirez, with a fictionalized Elián González, the five-year-old boy found in 1999, clinging to an inner tube, one of the only survivors of a small group who had left Cuba aboard an aluminum boat bound for the United States. At first glance, the two primary stories are linked to the titular claim, "make your home among strangers," but not to one another. Yet as Lizette struggles to feel her way forward in her first year of college at a fancy private northeastern university far from her public high school in the hard-working community of Hialeah, Florida, Elián González is swept into an almost mystical storm, entertaining political junkies, titillating tragedy-mongers, and enlarging the structures of territoriality. Even as his father at home in

Cuba demands his safe return, his Miami relatives insist that he remain with them, a claim welcomed, underscored, and heightened by a grassroots movement of anti-Castro Miami residents, including Lizette's mother.

The world of the university and the world of the activists do not admit each other and Lizette, as narrator, discovers that to move between one and the other entails developing a "double-vision" in which she comes in contact with the labor of shame and distance such a passage can produce. Her first sense of doubling hits her, not in the college dorms, where she encounters fellow students who spectacularize her and the media frenzy circulating around little Elián, but at the airport where her mother has come to welcome her home for Thanksgiving:

> I just wanted to be alone somewhere to catch my breath, to have a minute to sync up my idea of home with reality. I'd seen my mother in that moment as *not* my mother; I saw her as a tacky-looking woman, as the Cuban lady the girls on my floor would've seen, alone in an airport. And I did not like that I suddenly had this ability to see her that way, isolated from our shared history. I didn't know if she'd changed or if she'd always looked that way but now I could just see through my feelings somehow. I felt instantly cold, and then I panicked.[13]

Lizette later describes this moment as the one in which she had developed a "double vision" that she would always use "against myself."[14] This form of estrangement structures the work of making home among strange worlds, because Lizette finds herself struggling not just with a double vision of her mother but also with a double vision of her "shared history," a shared history that entails Elián and the activists but not "the girls on the floor." The novel underscores this moment and knowledge through scenes that turn on misunderstanding. For example, early in the story an earnest academic mistakenly accuses Lizette of plagiarism and in another instance she and her soon to be ex-boyfriend misunderstand each other:

> I was about to just hang up on him when he asked, So you hear yet?
>
> – Omar, I told you I've *been* here but I'm leaving.
> – No, I mean the thing at school. The investigation thing. What happened?
> – Oh *that*.[15]

The play on hear/here emphasizes connection and captures the struggle Lizette navigates between the here (campus/Little Havana – neither home), the *hear* (her struggle to feel understood by her family, her dorm-mates) and the *hearing* (the academic committee who hears her case). It is as if she needs a multivectored sensibility to accommodate the multiple forms of here/hear/ing. In playing with the difference between the words, Crucet captures the abrasive differences between worlds that befuddle an anxious Lizette, horrified at the emergence of this unwelcome fractal vision. Such a vision in some ways excludes both her and the fictional Elián because, as she negotiates the wealthy classmates who drink too much and quickly wall off their social class, her own mother, transformed into an activist seemingly more energized by her concern for the little boy than her own daughters and an academic structure with little sensibility about the knowledge it hones and takes for granted, the frenetic passage between worlds nearly obliterates Lizette's confidence. What Lizette finds as she shifts between worlds is that the textures of these spaces refuse to be rationalized and abstracted into one world and that ultimately she can find refuge only in moving between worlds including the maritime world of the ocean to which she subsequently devotes her life to studying and preserving far from both Miami and the Northeast.

Julia Alvarez similarly entangles disparate stories drawn from historical events to reveal competing structures of worlding. In *Saving the World* (2006) Alvarez tells two stories about epidemics – AIDS and small-pox – while also meditating on the processes by which people have sought cures and in so doing have variously helped and exploited others in more precarious positions. Focalized through two different narrators in alternating chapters, the novel follows Alma Huebner, a successful but procrastinating writer who becomes enchanted with the story of an 1803 small-pox inoculation effort, the Royal Expedition of the Vaccine, that left Spain for its colonies in a single boat containing a single woman. That woman, Isabel Senales y Gómez, a historical figure about whom not much is known, is the second narrator. Alma's husband is a global health advocate and is drawn into an effort to build an AIDS clinic in the Dominican Republic while Alma struggles to write a novel she doesn't actually like even as she seeks refuge in her imagined fantasy of Isabel's story. Pulling together the parallels between these pandemics and the coloniality of health care with their complex relations to funding (royalty or NGOs) and their reliance on vulnerable peoples willing to submit to radical testing (orphans of Spain and its colonies, the abandoned youth of the Dominican Republic), the novel at once seeks to tell a story about a little-known effort to obliterate a deadly disease, to question the messy politics of a contemporary effort to obliterate a deadly disease, and to examine whether storytelling is adequate to the task of articulating so much awful.

The juxtaposed stories relentlessly interrupt each other as Alma ostensibly writes the novel she is not supposed to write, that is to say, writes instead Isabel's story of the expedition. Alvarez cleverly, even viciously, refuses to portray Alma sympathetically: The contrast between Alma and Isabel highlights at once the novel's investment in storytelling as a necessary form of mediation (a "lifeline" or an "antibody" that "must survive beyond her grief")[16] while also underscoring the fragility of what stories can accomplish. This is the point Isabel makes toward the end of her own life as she notes:

> It was not so much that I was believing this story, as I was running as fast as I could from the doubts pursuing me. And as I ran, I realized that I, too, was a carrier, along with my boys, carrying this story, which would surely die, unless it took hold in a future life.[17]

It's not unusual for a writer to refer to the healing power of storytelling, but it is unusual to align stories with viruses and narrators with their carriers and unread stories with the dead or, more positively, with yet-to-germinate seeds. But as Isabel concludes her account, beset by doubts about whether the costs of the expedition, the losses, and grief, and intangible results merited the breadth of futility in the face of a loss of the vaccine, she locates her account, the story she "carries," and, more broadly, literature itself, in the service of futurity. *Saving the World* suggests that if stories can inoculate against or spread diseases, then reading, engaging with the worlds of the novel – Vermont in all its middle-class white activist preciousness, Colonial Mexico struggling on the edge of Revolution with and against an avaricious ruler, the broad ocean traversed by a boat with small pox as its cargo, peopled by risk – entails being "thrown ruthlessly," as Toni Morrison writes, "into an alien environment as the first step into a shared experience with the book's population."[18] Alvarez's novel requires a kind of tacking back and forth through the formal movement between narratives even as it enacts this movement at the level of plot. Such movement is only possible if the reader is willing to join the complicated plot that entails, on the one hand, watching the scaling of the world – from the many to the one – unfold through a circumnavigation that seeks to undo what has been done but also to continue to do the possessing through articulation – and, on the other hand, gulping as Alma unfolds the damage and ongoing violence such scaling unleashes even centuries later.

Between the Folds

Alvarez and Crucet, whose families hail from the Caribbean, fold together doubled stories of fictional worlds and historical figures while assembling plots that interrupt each other and force the reader to stay agile, to move temporally and spatially without scalar moorings. Two recent novels by Gabby Rivera, who similarly has a sense of the Caribbean as stretched out, raise the capacity to tack among worlds to the level of a super power.

America Chavez, the eponymous superhero of Rivera's twelve-installment, two-volume Marvel graphic novel, has a specific, significant talent: she can punch through one dimension and into another. Such a powerful punch is useful since she battles a range of proxies attempting to perpetrate evil on behalf of a very nasty trans-dimensional enemy. Superhero Chavez mounts this fight across multiple dimensions while studying at Sotomayor University. Yet she must also find a way to understand the various dimensions she encounters because, as one fellow fighter tells her, "You grew up on the parallel. You haven't been **taught** how to find us"[19] The concept of the parallel haunts one-worldism even as Rivera satirizes it.

Such punching is also necessary for Gabby Rivera's other protagonist, also a college student. In *Juliet Takes a Breath* (2016), Rivera offers a "fighter" who finds herself moving between dimensions, albeit ones less grand than planets across the multiverse. Juliet Palante, having completed a year of college and come out as queer to the shock of some members of her family and the bemusement of others, travels to Portland, Oregon from her home in the Bronx to spend a summer working for a "radical lesbian," the author of the fictional best-seller, *Raging Flower: Empowering Your Pussy by Empowering Your Mind*. What Juliet finds when she settles into her internship is that Portland and the largely white queer culture around her comprise something like another dimension, so unmapped and uninteresting to her Bronx family that they consistently misremember its geographic locale (Idaho? Montana? Washington?). This misremembering aggravates Juliet who feels the distance gravely, so much so that, forced to face the patronizing ignorance that can constitute white queer liberalism, she flees for relief to Miami, Florida and to the welcoming arms of a cousin. But there too she discovers that she has entered yet another dimension. The vibrant queer of color scene to which her cousin introduces her offers another site of meaning-making, another set of textures that encompasses different forms of connection, of belonging. The colliding worlds constitute a crisis for Juliet, which as her last name, Palante, a clever play on the movement slogan Pa'lante – *forward together*, suggests, must find a way to cross into and out of these worlds. Ultimately, she does so, as this satirical bildungsroman would predict anyway but, brilliantly, not through confronting the demons invading each dimension but by learning something of history, notably the anti-colonial activism of Lolita Lebrón, and by finding both metaphorically and physically the power of her own breath.

If novels such as Rivera's seem to suggest that movement is necessary for one to enter alternate worlds, whether by plane, boat, or a powerful fist, Karen Tei Yamashita offers instead an argument for staying put in order to enter multiple worlds. Her monumental, extraordinary novel, *I Hotel*

(2010), shows that entangled worlds do not have to be distinctly mapped or discretely located.[20] They can overlap and enfold each other, requiring not the flight of an eagle to discover or command but the diligence of a stationary voyager who can recognize distinctions, differentiation, and entanglement. The novel incorporates the story of the historical I Hotel, which became a crucial space for sociality and organizing among Filipino migrant workers not primarily beholden to or brokered by white respectability politics. They ultimately had to fight financiers seeking another San Francisco site for redevelopment. I Hotel insists on the primacy of migration, of movement, and on the occasion or event of connection. Inherent to a national logic of migration is the concept that people who migrate are dislocated, disconnected from other people, compared frequently to birds (suggesting thereby that they do not have a clear impact on the places to which they move or that their movements may be traced). I Hotel refutes such characterizations by following not one or two entangled histories of people on the move but by following dozens.

The novel congeals ten novellas into one and refuses to let the novel as site solidify the worlds it seeks to unfold. This form of refusal is articulated not simply through the novel's dismissal of linearity but also through its abundant gift of form: screenplays; songs; floods of quotations drawn from Diana Ross, Eldridge Cleaver, and Imelda Marcos, to name three; as well as poetry; myths; dance instructions; and even conventional narrative fiction. All of these forms are woven throughout and across the novellas in vivid and frequently hilarious prose that alternately pokes fun at stereotypes, traces the machinations of activists trying and struggling to find common ground even as, at various points, the narrator is quick to critique the stories it recounts while also, perhaps, nudging readers for engaging in those stereotypes and the various practices that render people deficient. Because it is long (612 pages), it seems at first glance to embrace scale, yet in its refusal to provide a through line, I Hotel undermines scale's claims to narrate and organize through an iterative logic that rationalizes space, deterritorializes cultures, and presumes separability while also underscoring the theoretical insight of the imagination. Or as one character explains, "Move over revolutionaries! Here come the artists!"[21]

Oceans without Scale

Both Rivera and Yamashita experiment with multiplicities, offering complicated narratives of collectivities that aren't reconciled, that don't coalesce into seamless wholes even as the novels sample dense intertextual references and draw from uneven histories. Yet if circulation is crucial to both, they are perhaps less interested in a principal medium of circulation than is Linda Hogan. In *People of the Whale* (2008), Hogan examines the complex relationship between cultures interrupted by the violence of empire building ennobled by scalar force and carefully explores the experiences of people trying to restore, or perhaps exploit, whaling culture and life as "paddlers." Without scale, the narrator of *People of the Whale* explains, mapping entails "story and event and the old names."[22] Stories open forward, "Like the water, the earth, the universe, a story is forever unfolding. It floods and erupts. It births new worlds."[23] Hogan examines the possibilities of worlds of living not through a scaffold imaginary of nested hierarchies but through a horizontality that sees density and multiplicity, of worlds bumping against one another, entangled together. To understand these entanglements, Hogan suggests that it is necessary to undo abstractions completely, and to imagine what Denise Ferreira da Silva calls "sociality without the abstract fixities" such as race, or human.[24]

As the novel teaches: "The ocean is a great being."[25] So too the whale: "It was beautiful in its way, gray barnacles on it, sea lice, as if it supported an entire planet."[26] And the whale "was a planet. When they killed it he thinks perhaps they killed a planet in its universe of water."[27] None of these entangled worlds can be subsumed into abstraction. The whale is an apt creature (or planet) from which to begin such a consideration of multiplicity since it moves between air and water – living as if they are separate worlds to which it belongs, between which it can shuffle and shift. Joni Adamson suggests that the novel provides a "multi-species ethnography," an approach she argues helps to understand a kind of worlding that is less amenable to the abstraction of category (i.e., human, not human) and therefore, as I have been arguing, scale.[28] This vision of worlding is less interested or conducive to the scalar structure of contemporary literary studies with its reliance on hemispheric, transnational, diasporic, global, and world logics that implicitly and sometimes explicitly critique the local, regional, parochial, and especially national, because these all rely on the immanence of one world, not many.

Is the ocean a being as Linda Hogan writes or an archive as Omise'eke Natasha Tinsley suggests, "literary texts turn to ocean waters themselves as an archive, an ever-present, ever reformulating record of the unimaginable."[29] Ana-Maurine Lara invokes the ocean as both archive and being in *Erzulie's Skirt* (2006). A novel tracking across the long island encompassing Haiti and the Dominican Republic, and narrated by the spirit of the ocean, Erzulie, to her lover, Agwe, *Erzulie's Skirt* offers a broader potential reading of the ocean than its common conceptions allow. While its narrative structure is complex as it moves between the deaths, births, pasts, and presents of its main characters, the novel also focuses on Miriam and Macaela, one Dominican and the other a Dominican-born daughter of Haitian parents who have survived the Trujillo-led massacre; both women draw on their various spiritual heritages, as they love each other, survive brutal exploitation, and finally find peace in the folds of Erzulie's skirts in death.

The novel overlays the known maps of world history onto the less well-known worlds charted through spiritual knowledge. Perhaps most striking is the connection the novel makes between the Middle Passage and the treacherous Canal de las Monas, where people in tiny fishing boats, *yolas*, try to travel from the Dominican Republic to Puerto Rico seeking to escape hunger and violence, and – in the case of the novel, anti-Haitian violence especially. As Josune Urbistondo notes, this striking invocation means that "the middle passage becomes not only the women's past but the reader's as well."[30] Asking readers to enter the characters' worlds does not happen easily as the slave hold is made unflinchingly visceral in Lara's prose:

> She was surrounded by bloody bodies. Women's menstrual blood stained the floor around her, puss crusting at the edges of the shackle wounds. The sizzle of singed skin soaked the air with the acrid and sweet aroma of flesh .... She felt her body rise in a wave of urine and blood, the stench so wretched as to make her choke on her own breath.[31]

The upsurge of recollection, the way the Middle Passage crests and breaks into the novel, cutting the contemporary narrative of forced migration of people seeking to escape the exploitation immobility enables, presses readers to dwell on the smell and temperature and panoply of fluids crowding the ship hold, swirling around people dead and living. Lara brings slavery to bear on the contemporary scene of forced migration with sweeping deaths bloodying the ocean once again and thereby producing a new continuity. This continuity is neither magical nor nonmaterial, and it is not visible through a straightforward rationalism. In its use of such flexible temporality for a tale told across realms and by the very being of the ocean formed here as Erzulie, the novel suggests a far more complex interconnection across experiences, expanses, centuries, people, than the rigid definitions and abstract fixities that scale articulates. The ocean is being and archive of belonging.

Carceral Scale

By offering such a rich, not to say enigmatic, conceptualization of the seas, Hogan and Lara unbundle habits of categorization thereby undoing "abstract fixities" held in place by scale. Making live the continuities across centuries, undoing the way linear temporality appears to produce only vague forms of connection, is another way to deter scale's claims to formal neutrality. Yet another way, however, is to open these continuities as they emerge at the nodal points of scale's nested hierarchies. Evelina Zuni Lucero's *Night Sky, Morning Star* (2000) draws out such continuities almost as if they are reprimands aligning penitentiaries, reservations, boarding schools, Indian art markets, movement organizing, all junctures in a carceral system justified through recourse to the beauties of rational normativity. These sites, Lucero (Isleta Pueblo/Ohkay Owingeh) suggests, help scale function smoothly, locking in movement and regulating connections and thus knowledge.

Night Sky, Morning Star, like *I Hotel*, follows multiple narrators but moves across the United States from California to Arizona and back to New Mexico, as intertwining stories mime the fluidity of the fancy dances bringing people together in powwows and in memory. At its heart is the disappearance of a father, a man concealed from his son, but also destroyed by a "justice system" that wrongly convicted him and even twenty years later continues to refuse him parole. Told through different points of view, with a plot that converges and dissipates around strained and resilient connections, the novel weaves in and out of lives. This structure mirrors the novel's larger dismissal of normative scale: "That's the way it worked all over Indian country. Someone always knew someone else by either blood, association, or notoriety."[32] While this sentiment suggests how intertwined relations can be and illustrates how such connections weave between different forms of collectivity, it also indicates, more significantly, that the scalar logics organizing belonging according to nation, region, globe do not cohere in a meaningful way for everyone. "Indian country" refuses the scaled narrative of place as well as the logic of nation.

The novel also insists on underscoring the scalar logic that produces categories, abstract fixities, such as "Indian" and through which people renegotiate their implied meanings. Celia reflects on this logic while describing an exhibition of Indigenous artists' meditation on incarceration:

> It took me a few seconds to realize that the stark enclosure I was looking at was a prison cell in which Barbie dolls of various skin tones were situated. Naked, with blood-red paint streaked on their bodies, including their private areas, they were posed in various positions, lying down, sitting, standing in a corner, the hands and legs of some bound with string or handcuffs fashioned from string stiffened by glue. The title of the piece, "Inmate Barbie," shocked me in its play on Mattel's packaging slogans.[33]

The art work opens the relationship between branding and the structures of confinement (including stereotypes and state force). Celia's encounter with the piece also echoes the plot's own looping together of the art market, mass production, mass incarceration as each and all inform larger discursive questions involving sovereignty, blood quantum, gentrification, and authenticity. For Celia, the questions of belonging are easily tied to the very processes that incarcerate people of color (including her own lover) without recourse, that try to brand authenticity and thereby steal away crucial singularities leading to the loss of intimacies pushing people into "the melting pot ... the real colonial agenda,"[34] or ongoing homogenization through disappearance.

Scale is a tool to demarcate spatialized possession and therefore also a tool to establish boundaries and borders, to capture and contain. *Bright Night Sky, Morning Star* makes the daring connection between forms of containment and scalar boundary devices – not just those that are specifically structured by the state (prisons, reservations) but also those that capital more broadly enacts (art markets). Yet it is not just the productive work of nested hierarchies that structure relations, it is also their negative work. The forces of keeping out, of removal, deportation, and extraction also articulate scalar relations, as Daniel Peña's *Bang* (2018) illustrates in a novel that follows the movements of a family inadvertently caught in the clash between the narcotics economy and the US immigration economy. Their precarious ties to each other cannot withstand either the brutalities of the two economies nor those economies' dependence on violence, isolation, and disappearance as technologies of control and marketing. Peña traces the absurdity of the mechanisms people deploy to move between these economies even as he traces the ways cultural forms fail to provide sustained alternate imaginaries.

On the one hand, the novel provides portraits of resilience that require individuals to be aware of the logics of scale while they seek to exploit its frayed edges, by taking advantage of the tools necessary for the contemporary logistical regime that is the full realization of the scalar imaginary. It is here that Peña brings the heft of lyricism to bear on portraits of a mother and son working separately on plane and truck engines. If the pair seek to survive (albeit separately, lost to one another), they must slip into the interstices between or within scalar hierarchies, to use the nested structure of scale against itself. For this reason, among many, the text draws readers' attention to *transit*, to the poetry of mechanism, the artistry of flying a derelict plane:

> Cuauhtémoc rides the pocket of air until the plane violently shakes .... *Whap-whap-whap* go the blades cutting air. And then silence. That split second when everything swims in sync and the thing is airborne, ready to stall and yet still climbing skyward, another silver pin among the stars.[35]

Obversely descriptive, the novel's many passages such as this one draw attention to the connections between air, action, and mechanics so necessary for the gift of flight. The text moves, the plane moves, people move levers and bodies in flight seeking both refuge in the pocket-bubble and the lift only turbulence can offer. Far from romantic, the account of the plane's taxi and lift is cut by the italicized "whap" reinforcing the beating the air endures from the engine blades before lift, the six-hundred-year-old word "whap" seemingly dug out to accessorize the language of sync, spiral, turbulence. *Bang!* refuses a celebratory account of movement or migration. In its harrowing story of a violence so ruthless it's quotidian, the banalities of terror become the stuff of jokes; this nearly devoted poetry of flight and the technologies of movement is almost rudely juxtaposed against narco/US violence so as to highlight the costs of scalar logic.

Formal Folds

At the edge of what many think of as this Modern Age, Hernán Cortés's confessor, Francisco López de Gómara proclaimed in 1552 that "the world is only one and not many"[36] helping initiate a new form of agency, one established by universalizing regimes of law and representation, one that catalyzed an imperial imaginary framed through the solidification of a scalar architecture. Novelists such as Hogan, Lucero, Yamashita, Crucet, Alvarez, Peña, and Rivera unfix these colonial scalar structures, stretching them so that the hemispheric bundles composite worlds and can be disentangled from the ongoing logic of a globalization process that insists that the world is "only one and not many." Rather than solidify abstractions, their writing unfixes them, unmoors them from explanatory hierarchies. They write in the context of a massing critique of the devastation that the logic of "one world" unleashed and against the ongoing crises a damaged earth withstands. Stretching the hemispheric acts as a means to build a different imaginary, one that engenders mutuality without forced rationalization and homogeneity. This elastic hemisphere doesn't contain or possess, but signals temporal relations, historical continuities instead of geospatial relations of nested hierarchies. Perhaps for this reason these writers fold their narratives within multiple strands of history, form, and voice, creating fields of difference that cannot be separated into abstract fixities. These twenty-first-century hemispheric novels thereby dramatically animate less visible, even fugitive, assemblages welcoming the ocean as a being, a being who might be Erzulie, and telling stories that might well serve as antibodies or viruses.

NOTES

1 Ursula Heise, *Sense of Place and Sense of Planet: The Environmental Imagination of the Global* (New York: Oxford University Press, 2008).

2 Gretchen Murphy, "The Hemispheric Novel in the Post-Revolutionary Era," in *The Cambridge History of the American Novel*, edited by Leonard Cassuto, Clare Virginia Eby, and Benjamin Reiss (New York: Cambridge University Press, 2011), 565.

3 Sallie Marston, John Paul Jones, and Keith Woodward, "Human Geography without Scale," *Transactions of the Institute of British Geographers* 30, no. 4 (2005): 416–432.

4 See Denise Ferreira da Silva. "On Difference without Separability," in 32 *Bienal de São Paulo – Incerteza Viva*, edited by Jochen Volz and Júlia Rebouças (São Paulo: Fundacaçã o Bienal de São Paulo, 2016); and also Nahum Chandler, *Toward an African Future – of the Limit of the World* (Irvine: Living Commons Collective, 2013).

5 Henri Lefebvre, *The Production of Space* (Oxford: Blackwell, 1974), 36.

6 John Law, "What's Wrong with a One-World World," *Heterogeneities*, September 25, 2011. www.heterogeneities.net/publications/Law2011WhatsWrongWithAOneWorldWorld.pdf.

7 Arturo Escobar, "Thinking-Feeling with the Earth: Territorial Struggles and the Ontological Dimension of the Epistemologies of the South," *Revista de Antropología Iberoamericana* 11, no. 1 (2016): 15.

8 José Rabasa, *Tell Me the Story of How I Conquered You: Elsewheres and Ethnosuicide in the Colonial Mesoamerican World* (Austin: University of Texas Press, 2011), 194.

9 Harsha Ram, "The Scale of Global Modernisms: Imperial, National, Regional, Local," *Publications of the Modern Language Association of America* 131, no. 5 (October 2016): 1373.

10 Escobar, "Thinking-Feeling with the Earth," 15.

11 Linda Hogan, *Dwellings* (New York: W. W. Norton, 1995), 27.

12 Ibid., 46.

13 Jennine Capó Crucet, *Make Your Home among Strangers* (New York: St. Martin's Press, 2015), 139.

14 Ibid., 345.

15 Ibid., 72.

16 Julia Alvarez, *Saving the World* (Chapel Hill: Algonquin Book, 2006), 326.

17 Ibid., 353.

18 Toni Morrison, *Beloved* (New York: Vintage, 2004), xiii.

19 Gabby Rivera, *The Life and Times of America Chavez*, vol. 6, illus. Joe Quinones, Joe Rivera, and Ramon Villalobos (New York: Marvel, 2017).

20 Karen Tei Yamashita, *I Hotel* (Minneapolis: Coffee House Press, 2012).

21 Ibid., 288.

22 Linda Hogan, *People of the Whale* (New York: W. W. Norton, 2008), 299.

23 Ibid., 288.

24 Denise Ferreira da Silva, "On Difference without Separability," in Volz and Rebouças, 32 *Bienal de São Paulo Incerteza Viva*, 58.

25 Hogan, *People of the Whale*, 9.

26 Ibid., 112.

27 Ibid., 267.

28 Joni Adamson, "Whale as Cosmos: Multi-Species Ethnography and Contemporary Indigenous Cosmoplitics," *Revista Canaria de Esudios Ingleses* 64 (2012): 29–45.

29 Omise'eke Natasha Tinsley, "Black Atlantic, Queer Atlantic: Queer Imaginings of the Middle Passage," *GLQ: A Journal of Lesbian and Gay Studies* 14 no. 2–3 (April 2008): 194.

30 Josune Urbistondo, "Caribbean Bodyscapes: The Politics of Sacred Citizenship and the Transpersonal Body," PhD dissertation, University of Miami, 2012, 135.

31 Ana-Maurine Lara, *Erzulie's Skirt* (Washington, DC: Redbone Press, 2006), 173.

32 Evelina Zuni Lucero, *Night Sky, Morning Star* (Tucson, University of Arizona Press, 2000), 70.

33 Ibid., 200.

34 Ibid., 210.

35 Daniel Peña, *Bang* (Houston: Arte Publico Press, 2018), 114.

36 Francisco López de Gómara, *Historia General de las Indias 1552* (Madrid: Calpe, 1922), 8.

9

TRISH SALAH

Transgender and Transgenre Writing

This chapter is an attempt to think about the appearance of trans genre literatures in the early twenty-first century and about tensions between the minor and the minoritarian within this emergent body of work. In it I suggest that to understand how trans genre writing has come into visibility we may need to look to an earlier period of development, spanning from at least the early 1990s. Arguably, the visibility afforded trans literature's emergence post-2010 obscures a longer history of trans genre writing and occludes the ways in which trans genre literatures are overdetermined by gendered, racial, classist, and whorephobic economies of taste and cultural capital in ways that strongly impact their visibility and legibility. These in turn affect our affective and analytic capacity to classify and interpret trans genre writing. In thinking trans genre literature in terms of its emergence, I want to ask what are the historical conditions for the appearance of this new minor literature, its normative conventions, and its constitutive exclusions. And centrally, I also want to argue that genre and the literary can be extended to understand writing's role in constituting new ways of being gendered, racial, human subjects. In this way, I hope to afford some tools toward a future trans literary criticism, one that is already much belated and both needed and in play today.

Since around 2010, the topic of trans literature has been raised with increased frequency in a variety of literary, activist, scholarly, and pop-cultural forums. Aside from the ubiquitous listicle – seven trans authors you need to have already read and "hearted" on Facebook – trans literature has most often been discussed in the form of a question that perhaps echoes other problematics.[1] Certainly, it is difficult to ignore the last ten years' proliferation of avowedly trans literary texts: Topside's *Meanwhile,*

This chapter has benefited greatly from comments and feedback from the editor, Joshua Miller, and his research assistant Emily Na, as well as from Beau Molnar. All its faults are of course my own. A version of this chapter was first delivered as a talk at the Writing Trans Genres Conference at the University of Winnipeg in 2014.

Elsewhere: Science Fiction and Fantasy from Transgender Writers; Jamie Berrout's *Nameless Women: Fiction by Trans Women of Colour*; journals such as *Vetch, Plenitude, Them*; novels and short story collections by Jamie Berrout, Imogen Binnie, Elliot Deline, Tom Cho, Casey Plett, Jia Qing Wilson-Yang, Alec Butler, Sybil Lamb, Jeanne Thornton, Kai Cheng Thom, Torrey Peters, Roz Kavaney, Vivek Shraya, Ryka Aoki, Lady Dane Figuroa Edidi, and Rae Spoon; creative nonfiction and memoir by S. Bear Bergman, Janet Mock, T. Clutch Fleischmann, and Ceyenne Doroshow; mixed and intergenre books by Nathanaël, Ryka Aoki, Jai Arun Ravine, and Ariel Goldberg; poetry collections by Joy Ladin, TC Tolbert, Julian T. Brolaski, Samuel Ace, Trish Salah, Cameron Awkward-Rich, Oliver Baez Bendorf, Manuel Arturo Abreu, Kay Ulanday Barrett, Andrea Jenkins, Ari Banias, Kokomo, Joshua Jennifer Espinosa, Jos Charles, Nat Raha, Ching-In Chen, Lilith Latini, Trace Peterson, Ely Shipley, jayy dodd, Kay Gabriel, Gwen Benaway, Charles Theonia, Lucas Crawford, Amir Rabiyah, Andrea Abi-Karam, and Cat Fitzpatrick; and more.

More than three quarters of these writers' books were published in or after 2012,[2] the year Topside Press's groundbreaking anthology, *The Collection: Short Fiction from the Transgender Vanguard* came out, followed by the equally groundbreaking *Troubling the Line: Trans and Genderqueer Poetry and Poetics* from Nightboat in 2013. And it is unsurprising that this burgeoning of transgender literatures appeared to form a movement, one that broke radically from a past in which trans people were the objects of representation rather than its authors. These years saw an explosion in the number of community and academic panels on trans literature, aesthetics, and criticism, to say nothing of 2013's unprecedented symposium on Trans and Genderqueer Poetry and Poetics in Tucson, Arizona, and international conferences on trans literatures, politics, and cultural production in Winnipeg, Manitoba, in 2014 and 2015.[3] However, it is not adequate to think emergence merely in terms of the volume or venue of publications, though these may be part of the necessary precondition for the elaboration of a trans literature that comprises primarily trans people writing with trans people in mind.

Though there are long and contested histories of LGBTQ identity language, for the purposes of this chapter I am using trans as an umbrella term to refer to transgender, transsexual, crossdresser, genderqueer and gender-fluid people, communities, texts, and histories. I use transsexual (and other specific language) for those who self-identify as such, particularly if they disidentify with umbrella language and/or for contexts in which a lack of specificity is misleading. (For example, the transition memoir is [largely] a transsexual genre.) I use "trans-" as a modifier to suggest the activity or attribute of "trans-ing" phenomena (that is of demarking it as "crossing").

Rhetorically, this chapter asks if "trans" can ever not signify the partiality, belatedness, and precarity of subjectivities contingently afforded "being" in dependent relation, not only, as is often noted, to medical and juridical discourses of sex, but also to feminist and social scientific de/constructions of gender, and lesbian/gay/queer reformist as well as radical politics of sexuality. I suggest that "trans" is too easily able to appear in these relations, very often enveloped within the coloniality of white being. How do such dependencies ramify if the subject is trans literature? Arguably, trans genre literature is haunted by and working through these difficult histories and their contouring influence on the parameters of what can be written as trans in the present.

The Late Twentieth Century

The late twentieth century may not have had a tipping point,[4] but it saw rich and varied trans cultural and literary production, particularly in its last two decades, though little of that production reached the general public. Transsexual autobiographies and transition memoirs became a genre unto themselves during the latter half of the twentieth century, taking off after Christine Jorgenson's celebrated serialized life story published in *American Weekly* magazine in 1953.[5] In the 1950s and 1960s, trans women worked in cabaret alongside cis women as well as in "drag" revues, contributing to the creation a trans-specific showgirl culture.[6] Crossdressers and transgenderists created social networks in part through the creation and circulation of community periodicals, newsletters, and other publications.[7] In the 1970s and 1980s, authors such as Jan Morris and Rachel Pollack were acclaimed not for transsexuality but for their writerly talent, though Morris did author a noteworthy transition memoir, *Conundrum* (1974); and in 1993, Pollack introduced perhaps the first transsexual superhero to mainstream comics for DC's *Doom Patrol*, Kate Godwin aka Coagula, a transsexual lesbian. The early 1990s also saw the publication of Kate Bornstein's *Gender Outlaw* (1994) and Leslie Fienberg's *Stone Butch Blues* (1993), two books that moved beyond memoir to further nudge open the door to commercial and literary publication of trans-authored writing. Simultaneously, a new wave of politically radical transsexual and transgender zines began being published, such as *Gendertrash, In Your Face, TNT: Transsexual News Telegraph, TransSisters,* and *Willyboy*; though these circulated largely within trans communities, they also participated in the zine explosions of that decade.

Much of this happened shortly after the publication in 1991 of Sandy Stone's field-generating essay, "The Empire Strikes Back: A Posttranssexual Manifesto." Stone's essay boldly suggested "constituting transsexuals not as a class or problematic 'third gender,' but rather as a genre – a set of embodied texts whose potential for productive disruption of structured sexualities and spectra of desire has yet to be explored."[8] Often cited as the inaugural text of the field of transgender studies, the publication of Stone's essay functions as the originary moment for trans authored critique of transphobic institutional and social movement discourses on transsexuality.[9]

Stone's essay would be followed by a body of work produced by trans-sexual and transgender people, rather than about us. While some writers warned against the limitations of what Henry Rubin describes as "queer paradigmed" transgenderism, (i.e., transgender theory elaborated on the model of, and promoted within, queer theories and politics),[10] Susan Stryker describes the new transgender studies as performing an insubordination of knowledges previously obscured and negated by governmental discourses.[11] Arguably for Stryker, after Stone, trans studies emerged through collective labor and struggle for trans-subjective epistemologies and analytics and contested the dominance of cis-normative scholarship on transgender, transsexual, genderqueer, and intersex people and phenomena. While this is in itself remarkable and valuable, it falls short of the decolonizing possibility of new trans genres of human desiring and becoming.

The question of decolonization directs us necessarily to necropolitical[12] economies of sexuality and gender subtending the (re)vitalization of normativities, homo-, hetero-, cis- and even trans-.[13] It returns to us as we embark upon thinking trans's relationship to the "profitable brutalities"[14] of coloniality and anti-Blackness and their dense interpenetration and interanimation of the Human, and its generic Man.[15] In this thicket of struggle over the material possibilities for living, it may seem strange to tarry over the question of trans literature and its emergence.

While the emergence of trans studies from under the shadow of studies of transgender is being elaborated upon with greater and greater complexity, our understanding of trans genre literary writing remains largely under-articulated. Discussions of trans genre literary writing often stall between habitual condemnation, or at best critical exploration,[16] of the generic normativities of a "typical" transition narrative of movement from wrong embodiment toward a new bodily home, and recapitulation of Namaste's critique of the autobiographical imperative as a coerced performance of trans being for the cis gaze.[17] There are of course, salutary exceptions.

kari edwards's new narrative writing theorized identity performance as a commodity form[18] and Nathanaël has for nearly two decades offered an interlingual writing across sex that is not predicated on positivities or attributes, a contention with languages' lack.[19] T. Clutch Fleischmann[20] and micha cárdenas[21] each raise questions about genre, its multiplicity and traversal, while Petra Kuppers and Marty Fink work to crip trans reading practices.[22] Trace

Peterson,[23] C. Riley Snorton,[24] and Alexander Eastwood[25] variously press on matters of method, querying respectively the assumed opposition between biographical criticism and close reading, racial histories of trans inscription, and historiography as affective method. Cameron Awkward-Rich elaborates a depressive trans and feminist reading practice predicated on a lack of integration between trans and feminism, while Joy Ladin argues for a trans poetics unrestricted to and irreducible to questions of identity or representation.[26] The Topside Workshop[27] went the Bechdel test one better, theorizing trans literatures for and about trans people, imagining the formal and representational effects of writing a world in which trans people are not isolated or mediated primarily by their relationships to cis people. In short, there is no shortage of aesthetic and critical innovation and potentially generative dissensus on what we might call trans genre literary norms, poetics, and politics.

Conditions of Emergence

So, what are the shifting terrains and terms of transsexual, transgender, and gender nonconforming people's creative practices of inscription? Addressing the question of writing within the field of the written, we might begin with constitutive tensions between the minor and minoritarian, thus positing trans genre writing as disruption and interference as well as a practice of self-inscription that is constitutively slant to the conditions of subjectivation. In other words, thinking trans genres in a minor key means thinking such writing as simultaneously making an entry into the human and disrupting and reordering that genre of being.

That said, there is the question of the object of study. Which processes of selecting, presenting, reviewing, and theorizing trans literary production function to generate a trans canon as an archive of the present? How might they constitute evaluative and historicizing horizons for how an "emergent" body of literature, and the subjects it purports to represent, will be read? These questions concern political, rhetorical, and aesthetic economies in which an archive or canon might be constituted. Processes of emergence take place through publicity, selective (institutional) legitimation, and collective/identitarian engagement on the model of minority literature, and they possess a capacity to organize and determine aesthetic and political representation, if in asymmetrical fashion.

César Domínguez suggests common sense understandings of emergent literature as "nascent or breaking the surface" are predicated upon the idea of an "evolutionary phase of a national literature" as well as upon ideas of "all non-national and non-canonical literature, whether it be ethnic, regional or minority."[28] Certain hazards attend the thinking of emergent literature, for instance, a naturalization or essentializing of historical and political literary trends, codifying national literature as a minimal unit within a larger system of *weltliterature*, as well a failure to theorize complex processes of literary emergence (Domínguez 2006). The thinking of emergence then consequently risks a presentist, dehistoricizing rendering of the past as well as a certain telos for the future.

So, what does it mean to frame trans literatures as "emergent"? Domínguez argues new trends "either offer a new selective tradition parallel to the hegemonic (alternative literary emergence) or look for a total reconfiguration of the selective hegemonic tradition (oppositional literary emergence)." For our purposes, if the former significantly form themselves in the image of hegemonic models, making themselves available for incorporation within existing literary canons on the model of minority literature, then the latter refuse the dominant and attempt to fashion their own (counter-) hegemonic system.

I suggest that we understand trans genre writing as minor literature, rather than as an emergent, minority literature, to mitigate against these features of the emergent enumerated by Domínguez and against the fantasy of multicultural literature. This fantasy of representation or incorporation of the minoritarian into the universal implies the reinscription of a pluralist humanism.

I would argue, instead, that as a minor literature trans genres deterritorialize the terms of inscription, acting as a mode of interference against homologizing equivalences with the national or hegemonic. However, even this dichotomization obscures the work of *the minor* in minority writing: recall Sylvia Wynter's argument for the demonic grounding of the minority outside "the consolidated field of meanings of our present analogic ... for new objects of knowledge."[29] Wynter's program is to disenchant our romance with humanism, to refuse to produce a new true discourse of the minority group, and to attend critically and carefully to disenchantments of hegemonic desire. Still, with Wynter and with Deleuze might we not theorize trans genres as performing the work of the minor, even in the case of literatures that acquire a representative function as minoritarian as they are more widely read and acknowledged?

In this view, we might look to the writing of sex workers and racialized trans women for particular examples of the ways in which hegemonic desire produces occlusions at the level of the genre of the Human. While in the contemporary moment at least some trans political discourses recognize the importance of sex workers in the cultural life and political struggles of trans people (usually this is signaled by harking back to the long obscured but crucial contributions of Marsha P. Johnson and Sylvia Riviera in the early 1970s), there is less engagement with the ongoing cultural and aesthetic production by trans sex workers between the 1970s and the present moment. Why might that be? Or rather, how might we understand the literary production of sex workers and racialized trans women as persistently inassimilable to trans normative discourses in the moving present, even as they may be deployed within narratives of transcended, if fraught, origin?

Consider the relative paucity of critical attention to the one woman theatrical production, *Yapping Outloud: Contagious Thoughts of an Unrepentant Whore*, by Mirha-Soleil Ross a transsexual sex worker and activist of Quebecois and Indigenous mixed heritage, which was presented by the Mayworks Festival of Working People and the Arts in 2001, and which was renewed for a second run at Buddies in Bad Times Theatre in 2004, after going on to the National Transgender Theatre Festival in New York in 2003. Ross's play is a fundamental challenge to necropolitical economies of trans representation, offering an extended diagnosis of the interconnections between feminist, state, and far-right discourse on sex work and transsexuality, and a powerful refusal of the violence inflicted upon trans and gender variant and/or sex working women by social workers, rescue feminists, and serial killers (*Yapping Outloud*, 2002).[30] Thus, Ross performs militant satire and aggressive disidentification as a cultural pedagogy deterritorializing coercively inclusive modes of identity politics. Even her identity, metonymically given as its reductive textualization, in the generic form of the performer/film-maker/contributor/activist bio is implicated as Ross contemplates the damning contents of her hard drive: the first movement of the monologue comes to a head with the repeated utterance,

> "Mirha-Soleil Ross is a transsexual video maker, performance artist, activist and prostitute.": "Mirha-Soleil Ross is a transsexual videomaker, performer, and PROSTITUTE!"

> "We're looking for a PROSTITUTE to speak at our next event and who better than YOU, Mirha-Soleil Ross-videomaker-performer-and-PROSTITUTE!"

Through this mantra-like repetition, and the play of her voice, which descends and distends each syllable in a snorting sneer as she enunciates the word "prostitute," Ross affectively conveys the disgust and censure associated with the disclosure that one works in the sex industry. That affect is both achieved and lightened by the vocal effect in a way that is comic, clownish, and slightly grotesque; this kind of sneering "yap" is one of the common gestures in Ross's repertoire when she is conveying difficult information. Arguably what this yap does, linking Ross's speech to the inhuman speech of coyote, is figure the prostitute as infrahuman and outside of the possible ambit of liberal humanist reform projects. This important work has however generated little press or scholarly critical engagement even among those who often write on these topics.

Likewise, there has been little in the way of press or critical attention to the extraordinary intergenre memoir-cookbook by Black trans woman sex worker, Ceyenne Doroshow, *Cooking in Heels*. Published by Red Umbrella Productions in 2012, this is a book that, in addition to its gorgeous recipes, tells stories of Doroshow's encounters with mentors, family, and lovers, the police and the prison system.

> It turned out that my next door cell-mate was the nephew of my old friend Bernie, the man who had once been my drug dealer, whose son I had looked after. His name was Drew …. Bernie found out I was there and word got around and Drew said, "Everyone here knows you're special to Bernie and he won't let anyone mess with you."
>
> And then he said, kind of shyly… "Um, you know the food in here is horrible. What can we do to fix up jail food?"[31]

Food in Doroshow's text is a way of marking out and making relations, of creating kinship and care worlds in contexts that are stigmatized and marked as inhuman and unlivable: Black, trans, sex working, imprisoned, drug using. Like Ross's play, Doroshow's memoir cookbook enacts a trans genre pedagogy that does not sit easily within generic, literary, or identitarian classifications and value systems. Nor do either of these texts circulate as representatives of the new wave of trans genre writing.

What then is emerging in a minor key? If trans genre writing is a minor literature, it is not a trans minority literature, or not simply. If some trans writers aspire to inclusion, the structural position of Black, Indigenous, and sex working trans women as not human, as well as the formal constraints on trans inscription mitigate against that possibility. Nor is trans genre writing simply a subclass of either queer or various national literatures. Or writing toward queer inclusion and participation within national literature involves both dependency and deformation. The language we are hidden in is not imagining an "us." If trans genre texts are subalterned, they cannot simply ask for inclusion but rather need to rearticulate the human through the literary. Language itself is transformed where the literary reconstitutes or refuses the terms of the human. However zones of exclusion and liberation are virtually distinguishable in thought, how do they actualize in the social world?

The title of Kai Cheng Thom's novel, *Fierce Femmes and Notorious Liars: A Dangerous Trans Girl's Confabulous Memoir* (2016), offers a clue with its irreverent citation of the imperative that transsexuals only speak our autobiographies. Though fictionalized autobiography is not a new genre, Thom's use of memoir in her title is not only a parodic citation of trans normative convention but also points to the reclaiming and processing of experience that fiction may fabulously perform.

A second point, on the side of keeping what is emerging as "minor," from what Deleuze and Guattari say in *Kafka: Toward a Minor Literature*: "its cramped space forces each individual intrigue to connect immediately to politics. The individual concern thus becomes all the more necessary, indispensable, magnified, because a whole other story is vibrating in it."[32] In Thom's novelesque fabula, we see this in the production of a fantastical tribe of trans girl revolutionaries, lovers, friends, rivals, and enemies and their collective armed struggle against gentrification, whorephobia, transphobia, and racism, within which questions of individual striving, scarcity, community, love, and lateral violence are at play. Riven by conflict and scarcity, the collective subject is only tenuously and fractiously possible, neither representative, nor totalizable. Likewise, Lady Dane Figueroa Edidi's Afro-Futurist parable, *Yemaya's Daughters* (2013), enacts a collective subject that telescopes time and space to tell the stories of many Black women, centrally including a Black trans woman, as part of a singular story. Again, in Edidi's work Black women's collectivities are characterized as both necessary conditions of existence, and as riven by rivalry, fragility, and colonial societal violence. Representing a contested multiplicity of trans subjects at the level of the terms of enunciation, these texts disturb the conditions necessary for respectability or representativeness, that is, they write their subaltern status and divided subjects as interference with established genres of the human and the canonical, even the counter canonical.

This also suggests that if trans genre writing is a minor literature, then it works to both problematize and collectivize enunciation, which is not to say that the literature is homogenous, but rather that it works "to express another possible community and to forge the means for another consciousness and another sensibility."[33] Thom, Edidi, and Doroshow's thematic and performative invocations of possible communities might remind as well here of the interlangue inscription of Gloria Anzaldua's La Facultad within *BorderLands/La Frontera* (1987), not only writing between English and Spanish, but rather writing Pachuco, TexMex, Chicana, Mexican Standard, and other "Spanishes" within and upon the globalizing horizon of English linguistic domination. While legible as resistant, such writing is also of internecine demarcation. The opacity of trans as umbrella and analytic shields conversations that both divide and circulate between genderqueer, transgender, two spirit, intersex, non-binary, ftm, and mtf transsexual communities. Beyond this opacity, a fractious and impossible collectivity/nonrepresentativeness marks the work of the minor against minoritarian becoming.

"Trans genre," which is both a pun and a neologism, associates cross genre writing with writing that interferes with or intervenes in the classification of gender. This might be seen as a reductive legacy of Sandy Stone's

"Post transsexual manifesto"; that is, queerly-inflected trans genre writing can be seen to highlight and perform linguistic innovation and generic code switching as both a formal and a social intervention into the classificatory norms of gender. In this it articulates through and interferes with other modes of rewriting gender (for example, écriture feminine and queering language). But Sandy Stone's thinking on the subjects of "genre" and "genres" can mean more than this, if put into conversation with Sylvia Wynter's engagement with those terms:

> To foreground the practices of inscription and reading which are part of this deliberate invocation of dissonance, I suggest constituting transsexuals not as a class or problematic "third gender," but rather as a genre – a set of embodied texts whose potential for productive disruption of structured sexualities and spectra of desire has yet to be explored.

> In order to effect this, the genre of visible transsexuals must grow by recruiting members from the class of invisible ones, from those who have disappeared into their "plausible histories."[34]

Stone's imperative to wrestle with genre, rather than class or gender or identity, asks transsexuals to forego what is, as she suggests, our raison d'être, to pass. Invoking "posttranssexuality," or transgender, Stone suggests deconstruction and genre crossing might be methods of living as well as of textual production. How might we set this proposal for being in the face of social negation, alongside Wynter's analysis of the overvaluation and overgeneralization of one genre of being human, which Wynter designates as MAN? As Wynter argues MAN hegemonically stands in for the Human as such.

> This issue is that of the genre of the human, the issue whose target of abolition is the ongoing collective production of our present ethnoclass mode of being human, Man: above all, its overrepresentation of its well-being as that of the human species as a whole, rather than as it is veridically: that of the Western and westernized (or conversely) global middle classes.[35]

If Black, Indigenous, Trans subjects are symbolically and institutionally cast as exemplary abjects, necropolitical markers of the performative force animating privileged genres of Cis, White, Settler, Masculinity; if racialization occurs as the delineation of species of infrahuman nonbelonging in Man, how do we understand Stone's invitation to read oneself out of the gender binary, to write oneself within a set of texts of refusal? Arguably, this is again an invitation to those that pass, from the vantage of those who don't. In the context of the ubiquity of annihilating violence we come to Wynter's call to unmake Man, which is so say the genre of exclusive and race/class/gender privileged Human being.

Viviane Namaste's *Invisible Lives*, which documents extensive, even pervasive institutional and symbolic exclusion and violent trans erasure, nonetheless begins from the presumption that trans lives are lived, and hence livable.[36] Similarly, trans genre writing must insist upon and for, Black, Indigenous, and Trans lives, without flattening their differences, alongside the imperative to disassemble or deterritorialize genres.

Stone's imperative insistently diagnoses a form of what we might call trans normativity, and in a certain radical lexicon, this corresponds with bolstering racial and settler hierarchies. And yet does identification as trans *rather* than as a man or a woman entail a minoritarian rather than minor form of belonging? Or at least privilege those trans people most easily embraced by queer communities, that is, those who are gay and lesbian and/or stage a sexual minority identity on the model of ethno-racial identity. Arguably, doing so risks erasing multiple ways of being trans; occluding heterosexual relationships, politics grounded in Black or Indigenous community struggles, those who make community around sex work or drugs, and those who are poor.

This seems like a double bind. To negotiate it could require giving more weight to Stone's recognition that in asking transsexuals "to forgo passing" she proposed the "inconceivable" (168). For what does passing entail if not the fashioning of a relationship toward new possible genres of the Human? As Riley Snorton argues in his own deeply engaging response to Stone, "for transsexuals like me, passing is a hopeful stance that sustains an ability to articulate a transsexual identity in the face of discourses of clinicization and social misreading."[37] In this vein, we might also read differently Stone's deconstruction of the genre of trans autobiography and her rejection of its naïve gestures toward fashioning a life story not defined by rupture, coercion, and ontological unbelonging. What would it mean to reconceive Stone's imperative, understood as aspirational and invested with resources Wynter provides?

Engaging the Eurocentric, global production of humanity and not humanity, for Wynter genre also indexes the literary, what for Frantz Fanon is the space of invention: "I should constantly remind myself that the real leap consists of introducing invention into existence."[38] That is, the literary is a space of self-creation. Bringing the literary to the scientific, Wynter's science of the word[39] allows her to theorize our hybrid humanity and deploy the poetic to intervene against anti-Black knowledge formations. Is there a way in which we might find in trans genre creative writing more than a politics of representation (reparative or paranoid) or an identitarian description, more than a transition into normativity? Might this something *more* allow for new modes of transformation and invention of ways of being human?

Trans Genre Constraints?

Though it might seem unlikely, we can alternately think this problem in terms of the minor in literature as circumscribed by a "poetics of constraint." Now to speak of a poetics of constraint, what typically comes to mind is writing "generated according to rule-governed procedures"[40] such as Georges Perec's novel *A Void* (1969), written without the letter E, or NourbeSe Philip's *Zong!* (2008) working off the source discourse of a one-page legal document, *Gregson* v. *Gilbert,* the court decision in the contested insurance claim over the slave ship's human cargo. As this pairing illustrates, while some constraint-based writing may seem to essay a purely formal project, one hermetically sealed off from narrative content or social or political contexts, this is not necessarily the case. Consider, for instance, that the normative character of grammar and syntax, particularly the designation of subject and object, link the linguistic orders to the generic production of Man and the human.

Some of trans genre literature's normative constraints then might thus be understood in relation to binary organizations of gender, pronominally given. These in turn mask the naturalization of race and whiteness as racelessness. Trans genres necessarily contend with differing species of trans erasure. Where non-trans embodiments are naturalized and homo/hetero desiring itineraries are the affective norm trans genres are constructed as deficit. For the writer, there is the phenomenological problematic of writing from the body when the body is not one's sex or gender of identification, or of writing from the body in its always partial and incomplete becoming in relation to one's sex or gender of identification. We might also consider here the hyperbolization of memoir as a paradigmatic conventional form for telling non-trans subjects about trans difference, which may respond to the longer histories of rhetorical vilification of transgender figures in clinical, queer, feminist, left, and anti-colonial writing[41]

Stone's imperative is, simply put, that trans subjects' becoming birth new modes of inscription. Again, the question may be, how do trans negotiations with the normative constraints arising from a cisnormatively worlded existence and our naturalized erasure conjure possibilities both within the genre of MAN and his occluded, yet still emergent racial others.

The idea of emergent literature then, is a troubled one, troubled by the minor, with the matter of social erasure, with trans as one genre of infrahumanity, with trans's normative constraints and occlusions; after this trouble we are left again with the question of what is emerging and obscured under the aegis of trans. To what extent does our writing of this moment, of the emergence of trans literature or literatures enact the relations of

dependence, desires for canonical incorporation, essentialization of difference, and presentist dehistoricization of its own itinerary highlighted by
César Domínguez in his reading of literary emergence?

Untimely Genres

To get at these questions, I'd like to present some particular problematics
that seem to be contouring our production of our literary present, past, and
future:

(1) Since the beginning of the queer moment (c. 1991), we hate our autobiography.[42] From Sandy Stone's discussion of transsexual memoir as
collusion with the medicalization of transsexuality and the production of
heteronormative genders, we can look backwards to Janice Raymond's
hostility toward our narratives of becoming and to the skepticism of
medical doctors toward transsexual patients' self-presentation, and we
can look forward as well to our disdain for contemporary memoir (seen
as always privileging the non-transsexual reader, and as boring and
hackneyed to boot). I suspect an ambivalence to life writing, creative
nonfiction, and anecdotal theory are also fallout of the moment we're in.

(2) We have arrived. Now that we have a literary discourse, we never had
one before. If, on the one hand, the second decade of the twenty-first
century has seen an explosion of trans literary production and the
emergence of a self-declared literary avant garde in the spheres of both
poetry and fiction, it may have also invested this moment with some of
the dynamic prejudices of literary modernism. The disavowal of tradition, and/or the overly vigilant rendering of its parameters as our
tradition, may disdain more than memoir. Thus, we write literary histories that exclude our folk forms, our obscene, erotic, and illicit forms,
our woodworked and transsexual writers, non–Anglo European and/or
non–university educated writers, and/or nominate only worthy, canonical progenitors for the current moment of flourishing. Do we catalog
our work in terms that reify national traditions, period, or generic
boundaries?

(3) Positive representation: even as we dismiss the memoir as pandering to a
non-trans readership, how are values of authenticity, whiteness, and
respectability, which are predicated upon legibility, implicit frames for
the work we center as we produce our emergence as a literary and
political event?[43]

As the problematics I've just articulated suggest, there is a political economy to what is emerging. At the same time, there is the economy of a certain

becoming, a resistance to the already constituted terms of the human, and in places, we might see within that resistance a productive destruction. What kinds of historical violence might it risk in making itself appear, and what are its implications in forms of trans subjectivity in the process of becoming habitable?

So, we might ask, what is receding from view as the new emerges? As I've mentioned, from the 1950s to the1990s, there were successive waves of intense cultural production by transsexual, transvestite, and transgender peoples. The last two decades of the twentieth century saw theater, perform-ance art, and video work by Aiyyana Maracle, Imani Henry, and Mirha-Soleil Ross; the collection and editing of an unpublished collection of international trans poetry by Rupert Raj; poetic work and short fiction by Christine Beatty, Xanthra Phillipa, and numerous others published in com-munity magazines and newsletters; even multiple award-winning science fiction novels by Rachel Pollack; to name just a few examples that predate, disappear under, and/or uneasily coexist alongside the second decade of the new millennium's boom in transsexual and transgender literature. Similarly, circa millennial novels, such as Kate Bornstein and Caitlin Sullivan's *Nearly Roadkill* (1996), Billy Martin (aka Poppy Z. Brite)'s *Lost Souls* (1992), T. Cooper's *Some of the Parts* (2002), Charlie Anders's *Choirboy* 2005, and Alicia Goranson's *Supervillainz* (2007), seem to disappear from view in the shadow of the outpouring of publishing during the second decade of this century. While much of the earlier writing, performance, and video work coincided with the first wave of the new queer literature and new queer cinema, as Mirha-Soleil Ross suggests in an interview with Viviane Namaste; after queer, that work has been largely displaced and erased.[44] Arguably, it is nonetheless also this earlier work, which is a secret sharer in the precondi-tions for what later emerges as trans literature.

How then are trans literatures appearing in our time and place? If they appear as newly fashioned things, how are they made from what has disap-peared from view? How might we think about emergence without producing either a national or a minority canon? What and how do trans somatech-nics,[45] transsexual critique, which I would also describe as trans sex worker critique,[46] and trans of color poetics[47] speak to or through one another, engage or refuse minority discourse, contest or subvert the trans normative? Finally, if, as Viviane Namaste argued some twenty years ago, (white) queer theory's theoretical program rested upon the transgender (or crossdressing) figure, while offering no political space to actual living and dying transsexual people, how has trans figuration shifted since we transgender signaled, in Marjorie Garber's terms, a "Crisis of elsewhere?"[48] Contemporary trans literature is both haunted by and working through these difficult histories.

We have yet to fully know how this work exerts a contouring influence on what can be written as trans in the (contested) present.

Nevada, in a Minor Key

Imogen Binnie's novel *Nevada* (2013) is not the first novel written about transsexuality nor the first by a transsexual author, though it is among the first to assume a transsexual audience with all that implies. Of course, constituting such a "we" is a fraught task. Generically postpunk literary fiction, the novel is split; the first half centers on Maria Griffiths, a young, white, trans woman living in New York, working at the Strand bookstore and trying to figure out her life, which is to say, her desire. Eventually, Maria borrow/steals her ex's car and leaves the city intending to just drive west.

The second half is set in Star City, Nevada, and centers on James, a twenty-year-old working at Walmart, who is trying to figure out his life, that is, his desire. Aroused and frightened by the thought of becoming a woman, he has a dress in his closet that he bought online. He thinks he might be an autogynophile. When Maria walks into the Star City Walmart, he can't take his eyes off of her, feeling both terrified and interpellated by her. Maria believes she recognizes herself in him: sure he is transsexual, if desperate not to be. What this explicitly imperfect mirroring allows is a precise inversion of the temporality of the traditional transition narrative with a pointed elision of those scenes of transition that vouchsafe transsexuality as spectacle for cis audiences. Binnie's narration mostly stays very close to Maria's consciousness until James is on the scene and then alternates between them in dialectical fashion. The narrative form gives Maria the platform to meditate and pontificate on all things trans political and queer theoretical, though at times in a mode close to satire:

> Eventually you can't help but figure out that, while gender is a construct, so is a traffic light, and if you ignore either of them, you get hit by cars. Which, also, are constructs.

It also allows for radical intimacy.

> I was thinking about being a girl while I jacked off, she says, Like, as soon as I started jacking off. For years I thought it was because I was a pervert, that I had this kink I must never, ever tell anyone about, right? Which was sad. There weren't really any misogynist or otherwise fucked up connotations to the specifics of what I was thinking about – I just wanted to be a woman, which gets framed as *a priori* quote unquote *perverted*. Right?[49]

What is powerful about Maria's discourse is that in her conversation with James, and earlier in her internal monologues and well-rehearsed conversations with other trans people, she gives voice to both trans people's political discourse and to our uncertainties, antagonisms, and ambivalent desires. This is of course a partial enterprise, one that reflects Maria's and Binnie's own demographic: younger, white, postpunk, queer, negotiating between US metropole and more rural/small town belongings. In ways this is capacious space, inclusive of disability, and to a degree class difference. And yet.

Binnie's *Nevada*, cognizant of the ways in which the conventional self-making enacted by trans autobiography may be doubled in the shame-inflected eroticism of both transgender internet porn and medical diagnosis, destabilizes all three genres, while also creating space for their uneasy, contradictory coexistences. Inscribing these narrative and affectively signifying repertoires as dubious reifications that are nonetheless possible constituents of mtf subjectification, Binnie's text suggests ways in which they may work to commute the traumas of everyday trans erasure, both cleaving to and putting into question the logic of diagnosis, while inscribing an open ended if not unproblematic hope for self-making and community making. Binnie not only allows for the hopeful possibility of personal and also collective transformation but also for the desiring identifications and disappointments that share in that process. At the novel's conclusion, James and Maria accidentally lose one another, and the possibility of relationship is derailed. Their encounter unresolved, the novel ends with uncertainty as to what is to come next. In *Nevada*, community and self-making are both unpredictable affairs, inflected by both aggressive and wishful fantasies. Writing the novel as an affectively laden and open-ended fragment, sampling one woman's post-transition ordinary unhappiness, and another person's pre-transition cocooning, Binnie refuses the autobiographical convention – a narrative about transition – engaging in a minor key the problem of how we shape and are shaped by narrative, while refusing either the reassurance of closure or the foreclosure of transsexuality. *Nevada* takes us a certain distance in understanding the elaboration of new genres of transsexuality that refuse the pathologizing taxonomy of autogynophilia, while also refusing the shame ascribed to that diagnosis, as well as memoir's normative temporality.

Within this troubling of sex and the human, whiteness stays intact, even as ability, gender, and subjectivity are put into productive trouble. This is a delicate point – that the delimitation of the human may be troubled, and racial grounds may remain settled. In a broader context, Topside Press, Eoagh, Trans Genres Press, Metonymy, and other trans-forwarding presses actively pursue a proliferation of racialized trans representation, beyond the bounds of representativeness and respectability, that is, beyond incorporation in a counter canon. One is nonetheless emerging.⁵⁰ The predict-ability of my citation of *Nevada*, an excellent and important text, is evidence of this. To counter this process requires more than proliferation and more than readership that passively consumes the fiction of a new transgender avant garde however oppositional or multiracial; it requires the political activation of histories of trans cultural and literary production that vex the presentist mood and challenge the dynamic subalterning of transsexual discourses and subjects under queer. It requires the lifting up of Indigenous, Black, racialized, sex working and otherwise criminalized people's writing, not only as literary product but as insurrectionary intervention into the terms of the civil, the social, and the human. It needs to foster conversations between and across forms, refute national and generic distinctions, temporal periodization, and disciplinary distinctions, such as those between the study of poetry, nonfiction, and fiction. That is, between life and literature.

The Subject of Trans Poetics

How does trans genre writing account for these appearances under erasure, their strange temporalities, minor belongings, and generic deconstructions? If trans poetics mark the becoming of the body, perhaps its impossible narration, or its recitation of codes and norms per forms of being otherwise, how does it contend with what is anterior to body? In the words of Hortense Spillers, "before the 'body' there is the 'flesh' that zero degree of social conceptualiza-tion." Ungendered, by torture and colonial violence, that distinction is "the central one between captive and liberated subject-positions."⁵¹ Thus trans genres are written between individual being and species being in the space of race, or as Fanon puts it, sociogeny, a structural ordering mandating the persistent fleshly status of Black and Indigenous subjects.

To conclude with a work that draws on many of the trends I've outlined, I turn to a prose poem by Cam Awkward-Rich:

> The little girl sits in the center of the poem, like the poem is a room we share. The little girl swallows everything that catches light. I offer my hand & she takes it. I offer my tongue but she has one of her own. She moves beside me in the poem. She wants a story. She wants to be held, not like a little girl, but like a little lake. Sometimes I don't want to walk around carrying a lake. Sometimes she spoils the party. Sometimes I ruin the floors. Sometimes I leave the poem & she tells the stories. She says she grew a new furred body. She says she hung from the rafters, a girl with glass wings … & she waits & she doesn't say anything after that.⁵²

Is Awkward-Rich's prose poem actually made of bodies or of flesh as Hortense Spillers (1987) might say? How does a Black American trans man become, and when he becomes, is it the human through which he becomes, in the genre of Man? Does he? While there is undeniably a becoming masculine being in this text, he is also haunted by the shadow of a girl, a mouth, feathers, the trans-species as the infrahuman. In "Now that you're a white man ..." Max Wolf Valerio critically discusses how his transition seemed, for some, to move him from category woman of color to white man, assumed to hold all the privilege that might entail.[53] This misreading of Valerio effected a violent erasure, an impossible position. For Awkward-Rich's text, there are other erasures and impossibilities at play. Reading across Awkward-Rich's prose poem, its shifts in tense and subject, we see how the abject, the in-between and the haunt trouble any straightforward temporality or achievement of human embodiment. Do such gestures not teach us something about the impossibility of writing outside of our histories of inscription and erasure? Other questions remain. For example, might we say that queer literature, as opposed to trans genre writing, is positioned as homologous to national literature, that is, allowing it to appear as minority literature?

Awkward-Rich's little girl "moves beside me in the poem. She wants a story." Differences are not arbitrary or without consequence; after all, what is the "the," but the definite article and hence the categorical body. And so the question of poesis, of making, returns us to the question of genres, writing, invention, and livability. On the one hand, trans genre writing, writing in a minor key, interferes with and innovates against the normative status of the genre of Man, among the varieties of occluded and refused humanities. Mobilizing the resources of prose, poetry, embodied perform-ance, and of writing between and beyond genres, this writing inscribes presences and absented existences outside of Man's regime.

This is, as C. Riley Snorton might say, a "hopeful" sign. A vitalizing literary innovation putting a *minor* pressure on the available genres of the Human. Still, racial subjection, colonial subjugation, gender unintelligibility, whorephobia, and poverty persist and reiterate as forms of in/humanity that are not only delimited around trans subjectivity. It remains a contested question: How does writing in between or across genres of humanity actual-ize our subjective and collective being?

NOTES

1 Here are some examples: Gabrielle Bellot, "What Counts As Transgender Literature?," *Lit Hub*, December 9, 2016, https://lithub.com/what-counts-as-trans gender-literature; Judi Tichacek, "Can Trans Literature Stand on Its Own?," *GLBT Reviews*, 2016, www.glbtrt.ala.org/reviews/can-trans-literature-stand-on-its-own; Hans Rollmann, "How Do You Define the Genre of Trans Literature?," *Pop*

Matters, September 27, 2015, www.popmatters.com/how-do-you-define-the-genre-of-trans-literature-2495490457.html; Zoe Tuck, "What Is Trans Literature?," *Michigan Quarterly Review*, June 17, 2014, https://sites.lsa.umich.edu/mqr/2014/06/what-is-trans-literature; and the piece that perhaps first raised the question in a popular context, Cheryl Morgan, "Is There, or Should There Be, Such a Thing as 'Trans Lit?,'" *Lambda Literary*, February 25, 2010, www.lambdaliterary.org/features/02/25/is-there-or-should-there-be-such-a-thing-as-trans-lit.

2 Though numerous anthologies of trans *and* queer writing were published in the previous fifteen years, few were trans specific (the exception being trans erotica). However, the publication of these two literary anthologies brought attention to the number of trans people writing and seemed to galvanize trans publishing. For examples of early aught trans genre writing, see kari edwards, *A Day in the Life of P* (s.l.: Subpress Collective, 2002); Trish Salah, *Wanting in Arabic* (Toronto: TSAR Books, 2002); T. Cooper, *Some of the Parts* (Brooklyn: Akashic Books, 2002).

3 "Troubling Tucson: Trans and Genderqueer Poetry Symposium," Tucson, Arizona, May 9–12, 2013; "Writing Trans Genres: Emergent Literatures and Criticism," University of Winnipeg, May 22–24, 2014; "Decolonizing and Decriminalizing Trans Genres," University of Winnipeg, February 28, 2015.

4 The phrase "transgender tipping point" comes from the May 28, 2014 *Time Magazine* story by Katy Steinmetz, which featured actress Laverne Cox on the magazine cover, and quickly became shorthand for premature and overly celebratory discourses of progress in the arenas of trans media representation and civil rights. Celebratory talk of a "transgender tipping point" in popular representation persists alongside justifiably anxious responses to a flurry of anti-trans legal measures that operate under the aegis of "bathroom bills," as well as with the ongoing and intensifying fact of murderous violence directed at sex working, drug using, poor, Black, Indigenous, and brown trans women.

5 Joanne Meyerowitz, *How Sex Changed: A History of Transsexuality in the United States* (Cambridge, MA: Harvard University Press, 2004), 64–66.

6 Viviane Namaste, *C'était du spectacle: L'histoire des artistes transsexuelles à Montréal, 1955–1985* (Montreal: McGill-Queen's University Press, 2005).

7 Meyerowitz, How Sex Changed, 181–182.

8 Sandy Stone, "The Empire Strikes Back: A Posttranssexual Manifesto," in *Body Guards: The Cultural Politics of Sexual Ambiguity*, edited by Kristina Straub and Julia Epstein (New York: Routledge 1991), 296.

9 I discuss Stone's paper later in this chapter, and in greater length in Patricia Salah, "Writing Trans Genres: An Inquiry into Transsexual and Transgender Rhetorics, Affects and Politics," PhD diss., York University, 2009, 302–312.

10 Henry Rubin, "Phenomenology as Method in Trans Studies," *GLQ: A Journal of Lesbian and Gay Studies* 4, no. 2 (1998): 276.

11 Susan Stryker, "(De)Subjugated Knowledges: An Introduction to Transgender Studies," in *The Transgender Studies Reader*, edited by Susan Stryker and Stephen Whittle (New York: Routledge, 2006), 12–13.

12 C. Riley Snorton and Jin Haritaworn, "Trans Necropolitics: A Transnational Reflection on Violence, Death and the Trans of Color Afterlife," in *The Transgender Studies Reader 2*, edited by Aren Aizura and Susan Stryker (New York: Routledge, 2013), 68–76.

13 Homonormativity has been defined in relationship to a dual gesture that confirms gay respectability through both mimicking forms of heteronormative social reproduction within racial capital and the settler state (celebrating the gay consumer, campaigns for equal marriage, participation in the military and policing) and distances itself from practices and subjects who vex respectability (racialized and poor queers, transsexuals and transgender people, cruising, militant, and transformative movement politics, kink, sex work) (Lisa Duggan, "The New Homonormativity: The Sexual Politics of Neoliberalism" in *Materializing Democracy*, edited by Russ Castronovo and Dana Nelson [Durham: Duke University Press, 2002], 175–194.). Cisnormativitiy, like heteronormativitiy, trades in its invisibility and naturalized status; however, what is meant by trans-normativity remains contested. The operation of a presumptive whiteness, English language monolingualism, and uncritical participation in capitalist and state forms subtend such normative pursuits. See Dean Spade, *Normal Life: Administrative Violence, Critical Trans Politics and the Limits of Law* (Boston: South End Press, 2011); and Vivian K. Namaste, *Sex Change, Social Change: Reflections on Identity, Institutions, and Imperialism* (Toronto: Women's Press, 2005).

14 Katherine McKittrick, ed., *Sylvia Wynter: On Being Human as Praxis*, (Durham: Duke University Press: 2015), 7.

15 Sylvia Wynter, "Unsettling the Coloniality of Being/Power/Truth/Freedom: Towards the Human, After Man, Its Overrepresentation – An Argument," *CR: The New Centennial Review* 3, no. 3 (2003): 257–337.

16 Nael Bhanji, "Trans/scriptions: Homing Desires, (Trans) Sexual Citizenship and Racialized Bodies," in *Transgender Migrations: The Bodies, Borders, and Politics of Transition*, edited by Trystan Cotton (New York: Routledge, 2012): 160–178.

17 Namaste, *Sex Change, Social Change*, 61.

18 kari edwards, "I belong to the regulated," in *iduna* (Oakland: O-Books, 2003).

19 Nathanaël, "Want: L'Intraduisible" in *At Alberta* (Toronto: Bookthug, 2008): 9–35.

20 T. Clutch Fleischmann, "A Ninja Turtle Theory of a Trans Essay," *Essay Daily*, May 23, 2016, www.essaydaily.org/2016/05/t-clutch-fleischmann-ninja-turtle.html.

21 micha cárdenas, "Trans of Color Poetics: Stitching Bodies, Concepts, and Algorithms," *The Scholar & Feminist Online* 13, no. 1 (2016), https://sfonline.barnard.edu/traversing-technologies/micha-cardenas-trans-of-color-poetics-stitching-bodies-concepts-and-algorithms.

22 Marty Fink, "It Will Feel Really Bad Unromantically Soon: Cripping Insomnia through Imogen *Binnie's Nevada*," *TSQ: Transgender Studies Quarterly* 6, no. 1 (2019): 4–19.

23 Trace Peterson, "Becoming a Trans Poet: Samuel Ace, Max Wolf Valerio, and kari edwards," *TSQ: Transgender Studies Quarterly* 1, no. 4 (2014): 523–538.

24 C. Riley Snorton, *Black on Both Sides: A Racial History of Trans Identity* (Minneapolis: University of Minnesota Press, 2017).

25 Alexander Eastwood, "How, Then, Might the Transsexual Read?: Notes toward a Trans Literary History," *TSQ: Transgender Studies Quarterly* 1, no. 4 (2014): 590–604.

26 See Joy Ladin, "Ours for the Making: Trans Lit Trans Poetics," *Lambda Literary*, December 6, 2011, www.lambdaliterary.org/features/oped/12/06/ours-for-the-making-trans-lit-trans-poetics; and Cameron Awkward-Rich, "Trans, Feminism: Or, Reading like a Depressed Transsexual," *Signs: Journal of Women in Culture and Society* 42, no. 4 (2017): 819–841.

27 "Is There a Transgender Text in This Classroom?" *Topside Press*, November 7, 2013, https://topsidepress.tumblr.com/post/66341897663/zine-is-there-a-trans gender-text-in-this-class.

28 César Domínguez, "Literary Emergence as a Case Study of Theory in Comparative Literature," *CLCWeb: Comparative Literature and Culture* 8, no. 2 (2006), doi.org/10.7771/1481-4374.1304.

29 Sylvia Wynter, "On Disenchanting Discourse: 'Minority' Literary Criticism and Beyond," *Cultural Critique* no. 7 (Autumn 1987): 207–244.

30 This paragraph condenses elements of my discussion in Trish Salah, "What's All the Yap? Reading Mirha-Soleil Ross' Performance of Activist Pedagogy," *Canadian Theatre Review* 130, no. 1 (Spring 2007): 64–71.

31 Ceyenne Doroshow and Audacia Ray, *Cooking in Heels* (New York: Red Umbrella Project, 2012), 19–20.

32 Gilles Deleuze and Felix Guatarri, *Kafka: Toward a Minor Literature* (Minneapolis: University of Minnesota Press, 1986), 17.

33 Ibid.

34 Stone, "The Empire Strikes Back," paragraph 44.

35 Wynter, "Unsettling the Coloniality of Being/Power/Truth/Freedom," 313.

36 Viviane Namaste, *Invisible Lives: The Erasure of Transsexual and Transgender People* (Chicago: The University of Chicago Press, 2000).

37 C. Riley Snorton, "'A New Hope': The Psychic Life of Passing," *Hypatia* 24, no. 3 (July 2009): 68.

38 Frantz Fanon, *Black Skin, White Masks* (New York: Grove, 1967), 229.

39 The science of the word entails both understanding the human as "bio-mythoi," cultured of narrative and nature, as well as describing a method of interdisciplinary movement, inquiring in the poesis of knowing, for instance. See Katherine McKittrick, Frances H. O'Shaughnessy, and Kendall Witaszek, "Rhythm, or On Sylvia Wynter's Science of the Word," *American Quarterly* 70, no. 4 (December 2018): 867–874.

40 Watkin, William. "Systemic Rule Governed Violations of Convention," *Contemporary Literature* 48, no. 4 (2007): 499.

41 These latter representations are almost invariably also anti-prostitute representations. E.g., Abject Transvestites in Mafouz's *Midaq Alley*, Joanna Russ's *The Female Man*, Angela Carter's *Passion of the New Eve*. Given that, one might argue trans sex workers are rendered the most abject of subjects in much feminist utopian, rescue and swerf/terf discourses, in which they are radically confined to infra/nonhumanity. How surprising then is it that we persistently fail to register let along read their literary and cultural production? And conversely how disruptive are the interferences they might unleash within dominant discourses on and of transgender? For more on this, see T. L. Cowan, "Transfeminist Kill/Joys: Love, Rage and Reparative Performance," *TSQ: Transgender Studies Quarterly* 1, no. 4 (2014): 501–516.

42 Periodizing queer is not a simple or straightforward endeavor. However, for my purposes here, I will follow the conventional attribution of queer theory's inception to writing of the early 1990s (Butler, Sedgwick, etc.), coinciding with the time of the "new" queer cinema and the emergent activist "queer nation." Saying this, I recognize the fictive and political dimension of periodization and also the queer writers who predate this period, such as Anzaldua and Genet.

43 Bobby Noble's invocation of Baldwin's "price of the ticket" signals the stakes here, where authenticity and respectability both trade in aspirational white supremacy, class ascendency, and for Noble, masculinism and gender normativity. Certainly, the demand that trans subjects become known in terms that confirm cis-normative expectations, as well as implicitly white and Euro-American centrisms, works to affirm those categories as natural and real. Jean Bobby Noble, "Sons of the Movement: Feminism, Female Masculinity and Female To Male (FTM) Transsexual Men," *Atlantis* 29, no. 1 (2004): 26.

44 Namaste, *Sex Change, Social Change*, 89.

45 Nikki Sullivan "Somatechnics," *TSQ: Transgender Studies Quarterly* 1, nos. 1–2 (2014): 187–190.

46 Ross in Namaste, *Sex Change, Social Change*.

47 cárdenas, "Trans of Color Poetics."

48 This argument, made in her *Vested Interests*, has drawn much criticism in trans communities, as it seems to make the point of trans people our appearance as signifiers of phenomena unrelated to our lives (Namaste, *Invisible Lives*, 90–93). That said, I would argue that Garber's argument can be read against its grain.

49 Imogen Binnie, *Nevada* (New York: Topside Press, 2013), 214.

50 Here it is important to highlight the work of Jamie Berrout, an anthologist, translator, and publisher who consistently centers and where possible pays for the work of economically and linguistically marginalized, Indigenous, Black, and racialized trans writers. See, for example, her translation of the Venezuelan transgender writer, Esdras Parra, *The Collected Poems of Esdras Parra*, trans. Jamie Berrout (s.l.:Create Space Independent Publishing Forum, 2018).

51 Hortense Spillers, "Mama's Baby, Papa's Maybe: An American Grammar Book," *Diacritics* 17, no. 2 (Summer 1987): 67.

52 Cameron Awkward-Rich, "The Little Girl Will Never Tire of Confession," *Cream City Review* 3, no. 1 (2015): 105.

53 Max Wolf Valerio, "'Now That You're a White Man': Changing Sex in a Postmodern World – Being, Becoming, and Borders," in *This Bridge We Call Home: Radical Visions for Transformation*, edited by Gloria Anzaldúa and AnaLouise Keating (New York: Routledge, 2002), 239–254.

IO

HEATHER HOUSER

Climate Fiction

Sands could move like seas. Evolution could run in reverse and human procreation become anomalous. Gated communities could become fortifications against the unchosen. Bioengineered birds, bears, foxes, and humans could form kinships and bloody antagonisms in cities ravaged by scarcity. These are the scenarios for a climate-changed world offered by Claire Vaye Watkins, Louise Erdrich, Chang-rae Lee, and Jeff VanderMeer, respectively. Even when the contours of this world are less extreme – for example, in Barbara Kingsolver's *Flight Behavior* (2012) – readers enter an uncanny valley of familiarity and radical alteration when they enter climate fiction. Though similar in this respect, the narratives this chapter examines do not tell *one* story of planetary disturbance. As the fiction on global climate change (GCC) spins varied climate scenarios, it also highlights difference. The experiences of the white male hedge fund manager in Manhattan, the pregnant Ojibwe woman in Minneapolis, and the young Chinese-American laborer in an erstwhile Baltimore will not conform to their neighbors' experiences when sea levels rise, bodies mutate, and arable land disappears.

We can approach climate narratives through the field most closely aligned with this literature's themes: ecocriticism or environmental literary studies.[1] In general, few climate-focused studies of recent fiction exist, a paucity that contrasts the robustness of climate cultural theory. Adam Trexler has most extensively surveyed the state of "cli-fi"[2] and criticism in *Anthropocene Fictions* (2015).[3] His study proves that, while veins of climate representation proliferate in twenty-first-century fiction, there is currently a dearth of monographs and path-breaking articles tackling these plots. Trexler explains why "ecocriticism was slow to engage with climate change" and asserts the tide is turning.[4] As one contribution to that shift, Trexler's book argues that cli-fi contains multitudes; that is, it incorporates a plethora of material objects and the relations among them and thereby models non-anthropocentric forms of agency.

Anthropocene Fictions aside, ecocritical studies have approached recent climate cultural production in three dominant modes. The most often repeated refrain within the scholarship is that planetary disturbance stretches the novel's capacities, in terms of scope, time, setting, subjectivity ... name your narrative feature. Two of the most germinal twenty-first-century ecocritical studies sing this refrain. Concluding *Sense of Place and Sense of Planet* (2008), Ursula Heise places GCC among other "global systemic transformation[s]" that "pos[e] a challenge for narrative and lyrical forms that have conventionally focused above all on individuals, families, or nations, since it requires the articulation of connections between events at vastly different scales."[5] Rob Nixon also makes climate the closing gesture of *Slow Violence and the Environmentalism of the Poor* (2011) with an epilogue that places climate injustice under the umbrella of slow violence, that is, "a violence that occurs gradually and out of sight, a violence of delayed destruction that is dispersed across time and space."[6] Violences such as the displacement of island nation peoples due to inundation and the damages of fossil fuel extraction raise the question of the "drama deficit of climate change"[7] and how to combat the traditionally short-term time scales of narrativization and policymaking.

Literary scholars acknowledge the narrative challenges Heise, Nixon, and many others identify yet refuse to capitulate and instead investigate creative and critical frameworks for innovation. In "new novels of a newly self-aware geological epoch," Kate Marshall finds temporal forays that do not stop at the individual, national, or even imperial scales but go geological.[8] These works "locate forms of sentience within the material stratum [currently] under production" and "embed ... nonhuman viewpoints within the most human of geological formations."[9] The nonhuman or posthuman framework also compels Mark McGurl for its ability "to draw together a number of modern literary works in which scientific knowledge of the spatiotemporal vastness and numerousness of the nonhuman world becomes visible as a formal, representational, and finally existential problem."[10] McGurl's sights are not exclusively on GCC, but his musings on genre certainly encompass it. Narratives push post- the human when their time scales expand out to the thousands of millions of years. At these fringes, weird fiction relates a posthuman comedy. This is comedy as the absurdity of human endeavors and institutions in the face of forces that "enclose, infiltrate, and humiliate human designs," comedy that leads to outbursts of horror as easily as guffaws.[11]

Julie Sze and Mike Ziser echo the mantra that "[t]he underlying problem [of GCC] is one of scale," but they pinpoint the injustices that geophysical alterations create and augment. In addition to exemplifying climate ecocriticism directly addressing social justice, their work also highlights a second key mode of this scholarship: advancing popular film and nonfiction as crucial – if not always successful – avenues for public engagement on climate. Sze and Ziser read the 2007 documentary *Up the Yangtze* as "mov[ing] successfully between the multiple scales of the individual, national, and global in ways that escape" xenophobia, nativism, racism, classism, and a myopic focus on science at the expense of culture and race.[12] Go looking for literary criticism on twenty-first-century *fiction*, however, and the truth of Amitav Ghosh's point that "novels and short stories are very rarely to be glimpsed within this horizon [of 'serious' literary journals]" rings somewhat true.[13] While the fiction is irrefutably robust, as we'll soon see, documentaries, advertisements, disaster films, policy documents, activist performances, and popular science writing have collectively attracted more ecocritical attention than their fictional brethren.[14]

The final approach to GCC ecocritics have favored thus far is to include it as an amplifier or cause of another environmental crisis that their projects analyze. Heise's *Imagining Extinction* (2016), which studies the cultural meanings of anthropogenic extinction, detours through climate discourse to cogitate on "what being a 'species' means, from a biological and ecological as well as a social perspective" and closes with climate advertisements and documentaries.[15] Heise recovers species as a relevant social category for climate action in refutation of Dipesh Chakrabarty's "skepticism toward species thinking"[16] in his germinal statement on the Anthropocene, "The Climate of History."[17] Heise's *Imagining Extinction* is just one example of an ecocritical study situating the phenomenon it examines in terms of GCC; others include those on the fate of the oceans,[18] the materiality of technology,[19] and the enduring economic and sociocultural dominance of fossil fuels.[20]

As droughts ravaging the West and Southwest and unprecedented hurricanes striking U.S. coasts and islands (Katrina in 2005, Sandy in 2012, Harvey and Maria in 2017) render climate change spectacular, authors stand at the ready to weave these conditions into their realist or speculative worlds. They may do so in ways that utterly define the narrative from the outset as in Watkins's novel of a desiccated California or that enter belatedly or implicitly, as in Jesmyn Ward's *Salvage the Bones* (2011) and Ben Lerner's *10:04* (2014). Given the prevalence of these devastating events and the climate fiction they spur, twenty-first-century ecocriticism is bound to contribute even more to climate change studies.

This chapter sketches unfolding literary trends that inspire, dovetail with, or fan out from inquiries within the environmental humanities. In a long tradition of dialogue between creative writing on the environment and social and scientific approaches to it, climate fiction fits hand in glove with other strains of environmental discourse today, including socioeconomic analysis, multispecies studies, environmental medicine, indigenous rights, new materialism, and biotechnological studies. Contributing to these strains of environmental thought, the novels to which I turn shortly typically share Roy Scranton's attitude that "the concern is not ... how we might prevent [global warming], but how we are going to adapt to life in the hot, volatile world we've created."[21] In this respect, the fiction shores up what have become vital keywords for climate planning, policy, and equity in the 2010s: adaptation and resilience. Twenty-first-century climate novels specifically speculate on social, urban, architectural, and ecological adaptations forming in the crucible of GCC. I suggest that in addition to these adaptations, three preoccupations define this area of literary creativity and complement the environmental discourses mentioned above: economic, racial, and geographical inequalities; the potential for new or revived collectivities; and alterations to the body and creaturely relations. By no means a comprehensive survey of the past two decades of cli-fi in US letters, this chapter elaborates on these literary preoccupations and the experiments with wordplay, tone, narrative perspective, and suspended endings that they afford. It thus expands on Marshall's, McGurl's, and others' studies of literary responses to the challenges of representing an altered planet in all its scalar and species multiplicity. Novelistic takes on the inequalities, collectivities, and creaturely relations that are instigated by GCC also engender interpretive possibilities within ecocriticism only partially fulfilled by the extant criticism. Acting on these possibilities promises to keep ecocriticism and kindred fields within the environmental humanities central to understanding and responding to a planet in anthropogenic flux.

Great Divergences

In 2014, Rob Nixon remarked, "the most influential Anthropocene intellectuals have sidestepped the question of unequal human agency, unequal human impacts, and unequal human vulnerabilities. If, by contrast, we take an environmental justice approach to Anthropocene storytelling, we can better acknowledge the way the geomorphic powers of human beings have involved unequal exposure to risk and unequal access to resources."[22] The Anthropocene concept designates a new epoch in which human activities such as the burning of fossil fuels and use of plastics register in the geological record and alter planetary processes.[23] These alterations include increased carbon dioxide and methane concentrations in the atmosphere as well as ocean acidification, land use changes, soil exhaustion, the sixth mass extinction, and the toxification of air, water, and soil. Nixon calls for

Anthropocene researchers to study and decry not only the "geomorphic powers" that humans have accrued since the "Great Acceleration" of post–World War II industrialization, but also the rampant "divergence" that those powers fuel. If we include creative writers among "the most influential Anthropocene intellectuals," however, the oversight Nixon identifies is not so vast. In fact, aligning these two perniciously "Great" phenomena of the past fifty years, Nixon puts his finger on the pulse of a thriving body of climate stories. The "widening chasm of inequality between the superrich and the ultrapoor" and how it "articulates" with the Great Acceleration are at the heart of climate storyworlds.[24] Recent authors imagine environmental disruption intensifying inequalities that came into glaring light with the Great Recession of 2008 and its aftermath. The confluence of climate collapse and financial crisis arguably inspires writers to tell stories of how the burdens of environmental instability fall especially on poor, minoritized, and invisibilized populations in the United States. These writers also draw out new or less obvious divergences that occur as people move, cities reconfigure, and ecosystems morph under climate pressures.

Chang-rae Lee's *On Such a Full Sea* (2014) harbors dual desires to underscore disparity and to universalize vulnerability. The novel immediately signals the latter with its use of the third-person plural narrative voice. Functioning like a chorus, the "we" hails readers into the story of Fan, a Chinese-American teenager who dives to tend fish, a precious food source, in the labor colony of B-Mor. The narrator bucks tradition by proclaiming that Fan's adventures are in fact "no grand tragedy, no apocalypse of the soul or of our times."[25] Along with the "we," demoting her travels functions as a leveling technique. "C-illness" is another great leveler: "Nobody goes C-free – nobody," the narrator declares (117).[26] "C," which is never called cancer but might as well be, operates as Lee's "central world-building principle."[27] It cuts down everyone by later middle age, whether one is ensconced in elite "Charters," works in colonies, or roves in the barbarous "open counties" (2).

Such universalizing elements chafe against the extreme class stratifications expressed by these spatialized distinctions. Controlled by a nebulous "directorate" (11), the output of laborers like Fan travels up the class chain, feeding those in walled-off Charters who enjoy privatized privileges such as nutritious vegetables, advanced medical technologies, and protection from the sun on high-UV days. Disparity defines space despite a shared sense of bodily vulnerability. B-Mor is a "production settlement" of refugees from China (148), which experienced the worst ravages of toxic pollution coupled with GCC. Though the labor colony is largely inhabited by the Chinese diaspora and a Black minority, racial and ethnic differences do not strictly demarcate Charter, B-Mor, and the open counties beyond. The extreme privatization of opportunity produces the greatest disparities under the directorate. Privatization manifests at the experiential level in "fierce competition for whatever one might do, at every level"; competition for spots on "Power Lists" turn the advantages of being a member of the 1 percent into "malaise ... that empty lunged feeling that can come from being measured, unceasingly" (134).

Competition becomes even fiercer and cross-class community even scarcer in the dry and depleted environment of Paolo Bacigalupi's *The Water Knife* (2015). For this novel, the author's customary science-fiction scenarios of android sex slaves and mercenaries give way to more realistic if gory representations of corporate capture of water. *The Water Knife*, like *On Such a Full Sea*, reconfigures the categories of privilege and depravation in ways that, to return to Nixon, "remold the Anthropocene as a shared story about unshared resources."[28] The novel contributes to a burst of narratives about endless drought in the West, Southwest, and Texas that have appeared in the 2010s.[29] Desertification clearly occupies the fear centers of literary minds, and Bacigalupi's book underscores the long history of battles over who controls water flow and access in the face of this threat. *The Water Knife* relegates Texas to a state of hopelessness in which water conservation and climate action were sacrificed to Governor Rick Perry's climate denialism and faith that prayer would bring rain. The narrative dubs migrants from the vilified state "those Merry Perry fools."[30] Phoenix is creeping toward Texas's fate and competes with Nevada for the Colorado River water that Caroline Case, "Queen of the Colorado" (55), kills to control. Water knives are Case's hired henchmen who, in return for hunting water and torturing the competition, have prospects of entering the gated "arcologies" built by Chinese "biotects" linked to Case (4). Arcologies appear to be fantasias of water waste. Angel Velasquez, the top water knife in Las Vegas, approaches an arcology and focalizes the scene: "Huge-ass fountain, spraying water straight up into the air. Dancing water spouts. Water like diamonds in the sun" (42). Yet they're also eco-architectural marvels, "big living machine[s]" in which engineers "[f]igure out how to balance all the plants and animals, how to clean up the waste and turn it into fertilizer they can use in their greenhouses, how to clean the water, too" (91).

Lee and Bacigalupi both envision divergence in terms of built space and privileged access to precious goods like quality water and food for the superrich. As I noted above, both twenty-first-century novelists express the distinction between haves and have-nots along multiple vectors but primarily through the partitioning of space that attempts to defy the meandering flows of water and goods and vulnerability to disease. Great divergences also manifest geographically in Claire Vaye Watkins's *Gold Fame Citrus* (2015). The narrative shares Bacigalupi's Western and Southwestern focus, but the reviled group here are long-term inhabitants of California rather than Perry's Texans. Known as the "Mojavs" for the desert sprawling across their state and Nevada, Californians are denied rights to resettle in other parts of the United States and are abandoned to the ravages of desertification because "'[t]hey were feckless, yeah? Schemers. That's why no one wants them now.'"[31] This discrimination echoes the history of race-based exclusion in the United States through signs pronouncing, "MOJAVS NOT WELCOME. NO WORK FOR MOJAVS. MOJAVS KEEP OUT," and songs declaring the people unhygienic.[32]

Climate fiction that tilts generically toward realism and geographically toward the rural also employs GCC as a lens onto startling stratifications, especially as they present geographically and economically after the 2008 financial crisis. Kingsolver's *Flight Behavior* (2012), for example, narrates how the politics of climate action plays out differently depending on gender, regional, socioeconomic, and occupational positions. The novel intersects with a body of research, exemplified by Candis Callison and Kari Marie Norgaard, on "how climate change comes to matter" to diverse social groups.[33] In this respect, the novel, like others in the cli-fi corpus, incorporates and responds to popular discourse on climate change as well as expert analyses. It ventriloquizes behavioral psychologists, right-wing radio personalities, and tree-hugging activists alike.

Catastrophe has three trajectories in Kingsolver's Appalachian novel set in the winter of 2010–2011: domestic, economic, and ecological. Dellarobia Turnbow's marriage is falling apart as financial strains increase during the Recession. Crossing this path is an errant migration of monarch butterflies whose proximate cause is global warming. As the un- and underemployed Turnbows come to terms with the consequences of the butterfly visitation, ideological and economic disparities within the United States jump out. Dellarobia's values and experience of GCC as a rural stay-at-home mom without a college education and with significant family obligations clash with those of the scientists and activists who alight following the monarchs. The novel demonstrates how the rural working class become "ecological others," Sarah Jaquette Ray's term for those who are "perceived by dominant environmental thought as a threat to the environment, but whose tenuous relationship vis-à-vis nature is *blamed* for environmental crisis, even as it is more a *symptom* of broader power relations."[34] While *Flight Behavior* doesn't give rural laborers a pass for their contributions to climate change, it questions one-size-fits-all approaches to motivating climate politics. An L. L. Bean–clad eco-activist urges Dellarobia to sign a "Sustainability Pledge" whose commitments – foregoing bottled water and disposable takeout containers, buying used goods through Craigslist – are irrelevant to those at the Turnbows's level of poverty. Realist rather than speculative, *Flight Behavior* underscores how the ongoing "great acceleration" of planetary disturbance goads plots of divergence that remind readers of the injustices with which we already contend and the ones that arise or become more volatile with systemic collapses.

Hacking Crisis

Might a great sundering such as climate change lead to a great suturing? Novels by Kim Stanley Robinson and Louise Erdrich pursue this question through stories of financial capital's nadir-apotheosis and controlled reproduction, respectively. Their books share a focus on stratification examined in the preceding section, but their plots glimmer with utopian possibility, particularly for marginalized groups.

Robinson's *New York 2140* (2017) drops readers into the heart of affluence and seems to have eavesdropped on Nixon's 2014 remarks in *Profession*. The novel stands with a crop of scholarly texts examining the economic order that has unleashed unprecedented greenhouse gas emissions. Donna Haraway, Andreas Malm, and Jason Moore contest the dominant Anthropocene narrative through the lens of political economy.[35] All three theorists question "the story of Species Man as the agent of the Anthropocene,"[36] and dismantle this monolithic story by specifying ecological and climatological transformations that accompany the plantation economy, steam power, and rampant accumulation of capital, respectively. Robinson's narrative shares some of their insights about capitalist accumulation but with a tighter focus on the financial mechanisms that, on the one hand, augment disparities and, on the other hand, could promote communalism.

In Robinson's version of a capitalist America, Lower Manhattan is "flooded like a super-Venice, majestic, watery, superb."[37] Inundation, however, has not drowned the prospects for real estate speculation, financial capitalization, and the overall "whitmanwonder" of the city (7). In this respect, *New York 2140* shares features with another climate fiction about a flooded NYC, Nathaniel Rich's *Odds against Tomorrow* (2013). It too has a cast of technological and investing wizards who wend their way through the devastation of sea-level rise and super-hurricanes. In both novels, cooperative forms of living are at times in competition with neoliberal market forces and at other times complementary to them. Robinson shows the tug between competition and cooperation in the context of GCC through a city divided between the flooded and not.

Uptown, land is dry and habitable, and its value exceeds even the exorbitant prices plaguing New Yorkers today. "Superscrapers looming ... in all their gehryglory" shelter the superrich of these "Cloisters" (17). The midtown intertidal zone vacillates between dry and wet according to the tides and displays innovations in sustainable and aqueous architecture that make New York a leading "aquatropolis" (285). Meanwhile, Chelsea swims, but its destitution also spurs creativity and queerness: "the city regarded as a giant collaborative artwork; blue greens, amphibiguity, heterogeneticity, horizontalization, deoligarchification" (209).

The descriptions cited above spotlight one of Robinson's stylistic innovations for GCC: when the city goes brackish, portmanteaux and neologisms proliferate. In addition to inspiring wordplay, climate change also inspires play with narrative perspective and tone in *New York 2140*, a feature it shares with Lee's *On Such a Full Sea*. The role of narrative focalizer rotates among a Pynchonian cast of eight oddball characters, and genres spanning comedy, romance, thriller, history, economics textbook, and technological manual interweave in Robinson's novel. Comedy is of note here from a novelist known for his technologically dense science fiction. *New York 2140* deserves the attention of ecocritics, among them, Michael Branch, Allison Carruth, and Nicole Seymour, exploring the humor and cunning threading through environmental culture.[38] As Seymour reminds us, "seriousness is not the only affective trajectory possible" for eco-culture or -criticism; these also "deman[d] 'unserious' affective modes such as irony, self-parody, and playfulness."[39] *New York 2140* traffics in these modes, as do *On Such a Full Sea* through its ironic chorus and generic parodies and *Gold Fame Citrus* through its hapless protagonist Luz Cortez Dunn. Robinson's novel announces its playfulness through the concluding section titles – "The More the Merrier" and "The Comedy of the Commons" – and the evolving epithets it assigns one of the chapter narrators – "that citizen," "the citizen redux," and "the city smartass again." The extradiegetic "citizen" narrator demonstrates the voracious intellect of Robinson himself, but he also peddles in puerile puns – "If you don't care about such an antiquarian sailor's fact [about Hudson Bay], bight me" (32) – and wry addresses to an assumed cynical reader – Manhattan as "capital of capital" and "capital of hype too, ya think?" (35).

The citizen offers invaluable perspective on the waves of boom, crash, and recovery – known as the First Pulse and the Second Pulse – that New Yorkers have stalwartly endured into the twenty-second century. This voice explains resilience through economic logics, specifically "the tyranny of sunk costs" (33). Out of stubbornness, a utopia just might emerge. And emerge, ironically, from the same logics that produced catastrophe and stratification.

Robinson's novel ends with an unexpected alliance between characters – rich and poor, young and old, hedge fund manager and social worker, cop and criminal – who use financial instruments to hack capitalism. This financial hack joins others in transportation, architecture, and communal living that show the ingenuity that collectivized individuals – and not just "disaster capitalists"[40] – can exercise in calamity. We can debate just how utopian Robinson's text is given the citizen's caution that "there was no guarantee of permanence to anything they did, and the pushback was ferocious as always, because people are crazy and history never ends" (604). In this respect, the novel ends in a state of suspension common to other climate fictions I treat here – notably, *On Such a Full Sea*, *The Water Knife*, and *Flight Behavior* – in which some plot lines come to a tight closure yet questions of survival and thriving on an altered planet remain unresolved due to plot twists, reversals, or narrative asides. Even as *New York 2140* wavers between utopia and business-as-usual, the novel is undoubtedly a record of the opportunities for equalization – not to mention aquatecture – that are at our fingertips if people collectivize across difference.

A globally changed world also affords possibilities for indigenous groups in Louise Erdrich's *Future Home of the Living God* (2017). The first-person narrator, Cedar Songmaker, is an Ojibwe woman who was "adopted" into a deep-green white family as an infant. (*Adopted* in scare quotes not only because of the questionable legality and ethics of indigenous adoption in the United States but also because of revelations in the plot.) The narrator situates readers in GCC through descriptions of a future Minneapolis – "This is an unusually cool day for August, which means it is only ninety degrees" – and through recollections of cold and snow – "That was the year we lost winter. Lost our cold heaven."[41] Super-hot summers and once-in-a-lifetime snows are hardly the world's dominant concern, however. Evolution seems to be reversing itself, and the future of the title may hold very few, or no, human babies. Twenty-six and pregnant, Cedar is facing not only the uncertainties of birthing a child but also "this great uncertainty that life itself has suddenly become" (5). Unknown viruses and bacteria are blooming, perhaps from the melting permafrost or from an evolutionary wrinkle, and prehistoric megafauna are taking up residence in suburban landscaping. Uncertainty and ignorance are the troubling refrains in Erdrich's version of a "sterility apocalypse."[42]

De-evolution sends scientists, world leaders, and everyday people into a panic and leads to the forced detention of pregnant women and those who have birthed "originals" rather than evolutionarily ambiguous babies (142). These conditions open opportunities for Cedar's Ojibwe relations. As in *New York 2140*, resilience to crisis offers detours on the apocalyptic trajectories of the novel's speculative scenarios. The husband of Cedar's birth mother, Eddy, reminds her that "Indians have been adapting since before 1492 so I guess we'll keep adapting" (28). "[B]iological apocalypse" (139) opens a pathway to regaining the lands that the United States stole from the Ojibwe through treaties and the Dawes Act of 1887, which intensified white settlement and indigenous dispossession. Eddy leads the tribal council to its rightful occupation of stolen lands. White flight makes "compassionate removal of non-tribal people" unnecessary and provides space for those who live "off res" to return and rebuild tribal society (214).

   Kyle Powys Whyte's analysis of indigenous responses to climate change accords with Erdrich's narrative. Whyte lays crucial foundations for addressing climate-exacerbated inequalities through the lens of "indigenous climate change studies." He locates indigenous groups' resilience in "long histories of having to be well-organized to adapt to seasonal and inter-annual environmental changes" as well as in the perpetual need to "reckon with the disruptions of historic and ongoing practices of colonialism, capitalism, and industrialization."[43] Adapting to the rapid changes of global warming is akin to adapting to rapacious colonialism in that the consequences of GCC are enormous and injurious and its causes are anthropogenic and imposed from outside. Erdrich imagines ways that indigenous groups can regain self-determination despite the colonial policies and capitalist practices that would limit adaptability to crisis. *Future Home*'s plot of territorial sovereignty, however, unfolds alongside worsening persecution of women. Women's sovereignty over their bodies has utterly deteriorated. Cedar must escape her imprisonment or either face permanent detainment as a successful "breeder" or the murder of her non-"original" baby. As in *New York 2140*, utopian, communalist hacks in the context of GCC coexist with enduring or threatened counterforces of oppression.

Creaturely Interventions

Future Home of the Living God carries us back to *On Such a Full Sea* insofar as both books insist that the makeup of beings' bodies mutate when geophysical forces shift. In this respect, these novels coincide with two fruitful paths for climate fiction studies: ecosickness and biotechnology studies. I coined the former term to capture the entanglements of environmental disruption and bodily dysfunction in eco-cultural texts.[44] Erdrich and Lee provocatively explore how ecosickness expands under such a global-scale disturbance. GCC stresses bodies to their limits due to disease, starvation, desiccation, inundation, and toxification, and novels depict these stresses as well as concerted interventions into the substance of human and other-than-human beings. These representations of creaturely intervention, whether for pleasure, surveillance, violence, or ecosystem design, appear in Bacigalupi's *The Windup Girl* (2009), Ruth Ozeki's *A Tale for the Time Being* (2013), and Jeff VanderMeer's *Borne* (2017) and its companion novella, *The Strange Bird* (2017).

This selection of novels, diverse as it is, stages encounters among a variety of animate beings, some biotechnological, some animal, some vegetal. Their plots about weird interactions between animate beings position them in a thriving discourse in the environmental humanities on multispecies and material relations. For Bacigalupi and VanderMeer, these relations emerge from bioengineering projects that weaponize life-forms in battles for survival and dominance. Emiko, Bacigalupi's titular windup girl, is a "collection of cells and manipulated DNA" that was reared in a Japanese crèche to serve as a geisha, but her status has fallen and she now serves the sexually violent and humiliating fantasies of clients at a Thai brothel.[45] She is one of many biotech inventions that populate the novel; others include engineered viruses used for corporate bioterrorism, "generipped versions of U-Tex rice[, and] vermilion-variant poultry."[46]

In both *Windup Girl* and *Borne*, designed life-forms thrust humans into the uncanny valley of similarity and difference, of attachment and repulsion. VanderMeer's Borne begins as an amorphous blob that the first-person narrator, Rachel, scavenges. It (soon, "he") is clearly a product of the biotech "Company";[47] however, his constitution and purpose become unclear and increasingly frightening when he osmotically learns to talk, think, and relate to his human mother-surrogate. Rachel and her companion survivor, Wick, discover that Borne's development is attributable to his "sampling" other beings, that is, absorbing them into his ever-expanding body and consciousness.[48] Borne's connection to an engineered bear-weapon named Mord spurs Wick's suspicion that Borne is also part of the enemy's arsenal.

Bacigalupi's and VanderMeer's novels demonstrate science fiction's interest in the nebulous boundaries between humans and lively biotech inventions. Placing these entities in a climate-changed world prompts a series of speculations that are ripe for ecocritical analysis. First, this strain of cli-fi delves into the consequences of technological fixes and whether they have a role in addressing climate impacts. Entangling a variety of beings – the organic, the mechanical, the bioengineered – in encounters that can be as violent as they are salutary, these novels also extend studies of multispecies interactions and other-than-human agencies from a range of eco-scholars.[49]

Finally, as new animacies supplant notions of a pristine "nature" in biotech cli-fi, the literature investigates the nature of desire and affective attachment when life itself is so fundamentally altered. In this respect, this literature represents ongoing conversations about radical ecologies, those that emerge from damage but still manage to thrive on their own terms. As Anna Tsing asserts, "Ruins are now our gardens. Degraded ('blasted') landscapes produce our livelihoods. And even the most promising oasis of natural plenty requires massive interventions."[50] The question is, what will grow and how will life function in these "post-wild" gardens?[51] Love, sexualities, and modes of parenting may sprout. Art and novel foods may sprout. New subjectivities or no subjectivity at all.

Though it doesn't feature bioengineered creatures per se, Ozeki's *A Tale for the Time Being* provides a blueprint for such an unruly garden. The narrative alternates between the diary of a Japanese teenager on the cusp of suicide that "Ruth" discovers on a British Columbia beach following the 2011 tsunami and Fukushima nuclear disaster and "Ruth"'s first-person account of failing to write a novel as the diary absorbs her attention. Meanwhile, the "NeoEocene" project by Ruth's husband Oliver adds deeper strata to the already layered temporalities of the dual narratives: "Anticipating the effects of global warming on the native trees, [Oliver] was working to create a climate-change forest on a hundred acres of clear-cut …. He planted groves of ancient natives – metasequoia, giant sequoia, coast redwoods, *Juglans*, *Ulmus*, and ginkgo – species that had been indigenous to the area during the Eocene Thermal Maximum, some 55 million years ago," when Earth's temperatures exceeded even the worst projections for the coming centuries.[52] In this forest "blasted" by clear-cutting, Oliver launches an art-science experiment that, as Allison Carruth notes, carries the scent of "a deep ecology nostalgia for primordial wildness" because he retains a baseline of the Eocene and idea of nativeness, but it also "improvise[s] climate change adaptation … attuned to pasts and futures outside the Anthropocene."[53]

*

"Outside the Anthropocene." Few novels venture into this beyond, and Ozeki's only anticipates it through a forest rewilded according to human design. The sampling of twenty-first-century climate fiction in this chapter dwells within rather than outside. At the same time, the literature anticipates who will become the outsiders and what collectivities and animacies might form when a crisis that ramifies so widely also registers so intimately. In this respect, VanderMeer's *The Strange Bird* scores an apt song for climate change and its fictions. This is a song of loss and recapture for an unfolding crisis in which we may just be the living dead but remain alive and creative nonetheless: "So much was leaving her, but of the winnowing, the Strange Bird sang for joy . . .. Not because she had not suffered or been reduced. But because she was finally free and the world could not be saved, but nor would it be destroyed . . .. [A]nd the two birds sang one to the other, the dead communicating to the dead in that intimate language."[54]

NOTES

1 A trove of introductions to ecocriticism and the environmental humanities more broadly has recently appeared. Notable among them are Robert S. Emmett and David E. Nye, eds., *The Environmental Humanities: A Critical Introduction* (Cambridge, MA: MIT Press, 2017); Greg Garrard, ed., *The Oxford Handbook of Ecocriticism* (New York: Oxford University Press, 2014); Ursula K. Heise, Jon Christensen, and Michelle Niemann, eds., *The Routledge Companion to the Environmental Humanities* (New York: Routledge, 2017); Serenella Iovino and Serpil Oppermann, eds., *Environmental Humanities: Voices from the Anthropocene* (London: Rowman & Littlefield, 2017).

2 Dan Bloom coined this abbreviation for climate fiction that has taken hold in the field.

3 Adam Trexler, *Anthropocene Fictions: The Novel in a Time of Climate Change* (Charlottesville: University of Virginia Press, 2015).

4 Ibid., 17.

5 Ursula K. Heise, *Sense of Place and Sense of Planet: The Environmental Imagination of the Global* (New York: Oxford University Press, 2008), 205.

6 Rob Nixon, *Slow Violence and the Environmentalism of the Poor* (Cambridge, MA: Harvard University Press, 2011), 2.

7 Ibid., 264.

8 Kate Marshall, "What Are the Novels of the Anthropocene? American Fiction in Geological Time," *American Literary History* 27, no. 3 (2015): 524.

9 Ibid., 533–534.

10 Mark McGurl, "The Posthuman Comedy," *Critical Inquiry* 38, no. 3 (2012): 537.

11 Ibid., 550.

12 Michael Ziser and Julie Sze, "Climate Change, Environmental Aesthetics, and Global Environmental Justice Cultural Studies," *Discourse* 29, nos. 2–3 (Spring–Fall 2007): 384, 387.

13 Amitav Ghosh, *The Great Derangement: Climate Change and the Unthinkable* (Chicago: The University of Chicago Press, 2016), 7.

14 An unexhaustive list of this scholarship includes Greg Garrard, "Worlds without Us: Some Types of Disanthropy," *SubStance* 41, no. 1 (2012): 40–60; Nicole Seymour, *Bad Environmentalism: Irony and Irreverence in the Ecological Age* (Minneapolis: University of Minnesota Press, 2018); Julie Sze, "Environmental Justice Anthropocene Narratives: Sweet Art, Recognition, and Representation," *Resilience* 2, no. 2 (2015); Alexa Weik von Mossner, *Affective Ecologies: Empathy, Emotion, and Environmental Narrative* (Columbus: The Ohio State

University Press, 2017); Lee Zimmerman, "The Importance of Rescuing the Frog: What We Don't Talk about When We Talk about the Climate Crisis," *Post45*, October 14, 2012, http://post45.research.yale.edu/2012/10/the-importance-of-rescuing-the-frog-what-we-don't-talk-about-when-we-talk-about-the-climate-crisis.

15 Ursula K. Heise, *Imagining Extinction: The Cultural Meanings of Endangered Species* (Chicago: The University of Chicago Press, 2016), 225.
16 Ibid., 224.
17 Dipesh Chakrabarty, "The Climate of History: Four Theses," *Critical Inquiry* 35, no. 2 (Winter 2009): 197–222.
18 Stacy Alaimo, *Exposed: Environmental Politics and Pleasures in Posthuman Times* (Minneapolis: University of Minnesota Press, 2016); Elspeth Probyn, *Eating the Ocean* (Durham: Duke University Press, 2016).
19 Sean Cubitt, *Finite Media: Environmental Implications of Digital Technologies* (Durham: Duke University Press, 2017); Jennifer Gabrys, *Program Earth: Environmental Sensing Technology and the Making of a Computational Planet* (Minneapolis: University of Minnesota Press, 2016).
20 Stephanie LeMenager, *Living Oil: Petroleum Culture in the American Century* (New York: Oxford University Press, 2014).
21 Roy Scranton, *Learning to Die in the Anthropocene: Reflections on the End of a Civilization* (San Francisco: City Lights, 2015), 17.
22 Rob Nixon, "The Great Acceleration and the Great Divergence: Vulnerability in the Anthropocene," *Profession*, March 19, 2014, https://profession.mla.org/the-great-acceleration-and-the-great-divergence-vulnerability-in-the-anthropocene.
23 For a useful overview of the concept, see Will Steffen et al., "The Anthropocene: Conceptual and Historical Perspectives," *Philosophical Transactions of the Royal Society, A* 369 (March 2011): 824–867.
24 Nixon, "The Great Acceleration and the Great Divergence."
25 Chang-rae Lee, *On Such a Full Sea* (New York: Riverhead, 2014), 3.
26 Fan's quest for Reg, her lover and the father of the fetus she carries, hinges on him being an exception to this axiom.
27 Christopher Fan, "Animacy at the End of History in Changrae Lee's *On Such a Full Sea*," *American Quarterly* 69, no. 3 (2017): 680.
28 Nixon, "The Great Acceleration and the Great Divergence."
29 Surveying Young Adult fiction alone, we find *The Water Wars* (Cameron Stracher, Naperville: Sourcebooks Fire, 2011); *Not a Drop to Drink* (Mindy McGinnis, New York: HarperCollins, 2013); and *Memory of Water* (Emmi Itäranta, New York: Harper Voyager, 2014).
30 Paolo Bacigalupi, *The Water Knife* (New York: Knopf, 2015), 26.
31 Claire Vaye Watkins, *Gold Fame Citrus* (New York: Riverhead, 2015), 23.
32 Ibid.
33 Candis Callison, *How Climate Change Comes to Matter: The Communal Life of Facts* (Durham: Duke University Press, 2014); Kari Marie Norgaard, *Living in Denial: Climate Change, Emotions, and Everyday Life* (Cambridge, MA: MIT Press, 2011).
34 Sarah Jaquette Ray, *The Ecological Other: Environmental Exclusion in American Culture* (Tucson: University of Arizona Press, 2013), 179–180.
35 Donna Haraway, *Staying with the Trouble: Making Kin in the Chthulucene* (Durham: Duke University Press, 2016); Andreas Malm, *Fossil Capital:*

The Rise of Steam Power and the Roots of Global Warming (Brooklyn: Verso, 2016); Jason Moore, *Capitalism in the Web of Life: Ecology and the Accumulation of Capital* (Brooklyn: Verso, 2015).

36 Haraway, *Staying with the Trouble*, 47.

37 Kim Stanley Robinson, *New York 2140* (New York: Orbit, 2017), 6.

38 See Michael P. Branch, *Raising Wild: Dispatches from a Home in the Wilderness* (Boulder: Roost, 2017); Allison Carruth, "Wily Ecologies: Comic Futures for American Environmentalism," *American Literary History* 30, no. 1 (2017): 108–133; Seymour, *Bad Environmentalism*.

39 Nicole Seymour, "Irony and Contemporary Ecocinema: Theorizing a New Affective Paradigm," in *Moving Environments: Affect, Emotion, Ecology, and Film*, edited by Alexa Weik von Mossner (Waterloo: Wilfrid Laurier University Press, 2014), 61.

40 See Naomi Klein, *The Shock Doctrine: The Rise of Disaster Capitalism* (New York: Picador, 2007).

41 Louise Erdrich, *Future Home of the Living God* (New York: HarperCollins, 2017), 266.

42 Rebekah Sheldon, *The Child to Come: Life after the Human Catastrophe* (Minneapolis: University of Minnesota Press, 2016), 151.

43 Kyle Whyte, "Indigenous Climate Change Studies: Indigenizing Futures, Decolonizing the Anthropocene," *ELN: English Language Notes* 55, nos. 1–2 (2017): 153–154.

44 Heather Houser, *Ecosickness in Contemporary U.S. Fiction: Environment and Affect* (New York: Columbia University Press, 2014).

45 Paolo Bacigalupi, *The Windup Girl* (San Francisco: Night Shade Books, 2009), 34.

46 Ibid., 3.

47 Jeff VanderMeer, *Borne* (New York: Farrar, Straus and Giroux, 2017), 4.

48 Ibid., 184.

49 See, for example, Stacy Alaimo, *Bodily Natures: Science, Environment, and the Material Self* (Bloomington: Indiana University Press, 2010); Karen Barad, *Meeting the Universe Halfway: Quantum Physics and the Entanglement of Matter and Meaning* (Durham: Duke University Press, 2007); Jane Bennett, *Vibrant Matter: A Political Ecology of Things* (Durham: Duke University Press, 2010); Mel Y. Chen, *Animacies: Biopolitics, Racial Mattering, and Queer Affect* (Durham: Duke University Press, 2012); Jeffrey Jerome Cohen and Lowell Duckert, eds., *Elemental Ecocriticism: Thinking with Earth, Air, Water, and Fire* (Minneapolis: University of Minnesota Press, 2015); Serenella Iovino and Serpil Oppermann, eds., *Material Ecocriticism* (Bloomington: Indiana University Press, 2014); Michael Marder, *Plant-Thinking: A Philosophy of Vegetal Life* (New York: Columbia University Press, 2013).

50 Anna Lowenhaupt Tsing, "Blasted Landscapes (and the Gentle Arts of Mushroom Picking)," in *The Multispecies Salon*, edited by Eben Kirksey (Durham: Duke University Press, 2014), 87.

51 See Emma Marris, *Rambunctious Garden: Saving Nature in a Post-Wild World* (New York: Bloomsbury, 2011).

52 Ruth Ozeki, *A Tale for the Time Being* (New York: Penguin, 2013), 60–61.

53 Carruth, "Wily Ecologies," 16.

54 Jeff VanderMeer, *The Strange Bird* (New York: Farrar, Straus and Giroux, 2017), 109.

PART III

Themes

II

MARK GOBLE

Convergence

It is hard to know exactly when the story starts in Richard McGuire's remarkable 2014 graphic novel *Here*, but easy enough to know where everything takes place. Expanding on a six-page comic strip from 1989, McGuire tries to capture more than three billion years of history at a single site, near his childhood home in Perth Amboy, New Jersey, which is not much larger than a living room. We discover that *Here* is happening *here* because a crucial sequence in the book shows us characters who are properly historical, with Ben Franklin featuring briefly as a visitor to a house across the way from *Here*'s main setting. There, about halfway through *Here*, is where we see Franklin arriving for a tense reunion with William Franklin, his illegitimate son who served as colonial governor of New Jersey until the outbreak of the Revolution, and who remained a Loyalist throughout the war and after. "Life has a flair for rhyming events," says Franklin on an unnumbered page that is dated 1775. This fleeting moment of Americana gives the reader something to hang onto amidst the more than 400 panels in *Here*, which are beautiful and uninformative about the various individuals – from sixteenth-century Native Americans to twenty-fourth century survivors of some ambiguous apocalypse – that pass through or occupy this space. With just a little digging or a look at *Wikipedia*, Franklin's cameo provides a way of orienting ourselves in time and space, while also – and more importantly, I would argue – teaching us how to understand the baroque complexity of incidents and episodes we're asked to trace for centuries and millennia and epochs that literally go nowhere. There will be floods (in 2011, 1,000,000 BCE, 2126, and 1307). There will be costumes (in 1931, 1990, and 1975). There will be dancing (in 1932, 2014, and 1993); name-calling (in 1949, 1957, 1955, 1950, 1960, 1968, 1963, 1967, 1965, 1961, and 1984); and games of Twister (in 1971, 1966, and 2015). There will be kids (in 1956, 1957, 1911, 2017, 1949, 1924, 1988, and 1945). Things will be lost: a dog (in 1937); eyesight (in 1951 and 2014), hearing (in 1962), an earring (in 1994); and a to-do list (in 1972). All these "events" lend pattern and a sense of place to a past so remote that it is hard for human beings to even grasp and to a future that looks, again, like a world without us. The last sign of human beings is a towel or sheet drifting through an inset panel in 2314. Something like a hairless cat with the feet of a strange primate has evolved by 101,075. By 22,175, all that's left are lilies, hummingbirds, and a creature about the size of a goat with a long flexible neck and the splayed toes of a bird. The planet for the billions of years before humanity – a trivial flickering of furniture styles and technologies, genocides and revolutions – rhymes with whatever planet will endure forever after, or at least until, according to a TV program a family watches in 1999, the sun becomes "a red giant ... engulfing the orbits of Mercury, Venus, and our Earth." This moment slyly introduces another story about deep time to frame the graphic novel. The 1999 documentary that McGuire imagines is off by about four or five billion years for this particular end of the world, though for all of us long dead and utterly forgotten, what's a billion "here" or there.

Here, *Here*, and Now

Though *Here* unfolds along a timeline spanning over three billion years, it pictures very little of this outrageous sweep of history. If McGuire evenly distributed his 400 or so individual panels across this range, for instance, there would be 7.5 million invisible years between each picture in the book, which would make it likely that we'd never even see a human being. Indeed, only 62 panels show us something happening before 1800, and fewer still – just 24 – depict an image from "our" future. The remaining 334 drawings are minimally structured for plot and narrative, but they are, by any real measure, densely clustered to suggest that modernity may represent the merest fraction of the whole of time but, nonetheless, is where the action is. "Toward the end of the eighteenth century," writes Reinhart Koselleck, "voices proliferated that came to see all of history from the perspective of increasing acceleration."[1] His point is not simply that various technologies we associate with the Industrial Revolution – driven always by the imperatives of capitalism – speed up systems of production, transportation, and communication in Europe and beyond. Koselleck argues more broadly that "there is a peculiar form of acceleration which characterizes modernity," and that any reckoning with its empirical effects must also understand how the sheer rapidity of progress "abbreviated the spaces of experience, robbed them of their constancy, and continually brought into play new, unknown factions, so that even the actuality or complexity of these unknown quantities could not be ascertained."[2] For many contemporary writers interested in both the formal possibilities and political imperatives that come from thinking about some of history's longer durations and slower speeds, the present figures as a period of remarkable convergence: where even the smallest increments of time can suddenly open onto epochs of almost imperceptible size and scale. Writing of slowness as a signature aesthetic of twenty-first-century life, Katja Kwastek and Erin La Cour argue that for many figures, ideas of relational speed – and its relative absence – can help "address the complexities of contemporary society's production and reception processes with a heightened sensibility to multilayered temporalities and time scales."[3] It is not just a matter of finding narrative techniques that can match the velocities of twenty-first-century life, nor of retreating to the more established rhythms of prior novelistic modes. Some of the most compelling writers of our time are trying to tell stories that can simultaneously move at all the speeds that come together to make our experiences living now feel so historically embedded, and yet so fleeting at the same time.

From this perspective, *Here* slows down when history goes faster. To keep up with an increased flow of information, the sampling rate diminishes so that we won't feel like we're losing too much of what's meaningful. Of course, this makes the artifice of human temporality itself more visible since, as Koselleck reminds us, "the acceleration of time" in the modern era is conceptualized as "a human task" (12). Eschatology and apocalypse are transposed from figures in a language of religious prophecy and Christian metaphysics and into a discourse of "prognosis" and "calculability" within the "dimensions of the political situation" (18–19). When these ideas about history emerge at the end of the eighteenth century, the perception of a somehow "self-accelerating temporality" that "robs the present of possibility" expresses intellectual anxieties about potentially interminable cycles of revolution and reaction (22–23). But this is not how the world will end in our most compelling fictions of the present. The world in *Here* ends with rising temperatures and sea levels, mysterious readings on Geiger counters and people in hazmat suits in 2313, and then, just one year later, no signs of life except some fluttering fabric until a mutant cat comes back to New Jersey eight millennia later.

Here, alas, is not the occasion for all there is in *Here*. Let me briefly explain instead what makes McGuire's project so powerfully emblematic for a strain of contemporary US fiction that, informed by an awareness of climate change and other long-term ecological disasters, conceives the present as a weird convergence of past and future temporalities. Put differently, *Here* is one of several recent texts that offers us some answers – however tentative or partial – to some questions put to us by Fredric Jameson near the end of *The Antinomies of Realism* (2013): "in light of present-day enfeeblement of historical consciousness," he asks, "is [the historical novel] still possible?"; or, later, "What kind of History can the contemporary historical novel then be expected to 'make appear?'"[4] For Jameson it must be history with an "H" to remind us that he's finally tracking – as he always has been – a particular set of economic and political transformations whose cultural effects and consequences provided Western Marxism with its most important narrative, if not its entire rationale.

The genre of the historical novel, as codified by György Lukács, not only lends shape and resonance to this account of what modernity under capitalism means; the very form itself comes to represent an object lesson that teaches us how to read the work of art for its mode of production.[5] Perhaps anxious about the limits of the historical terrain this maps, Jameson admits that it is "tempting" to define the historical novel "as the intersection between individual existence and History, the lightning bolt of wars and revolutions that suddenly strikes a peaceful village or an urban daily life."[6] Or a patch of countryside that will become a suburb in New Jersey where, for a few pages anyway, we trace a private drama between a father and son that just happens to take place on the margins of the American Revolution. But McGuire and Jameson are each aware that this type of "History" might not be the history we need now. Jameson goes on to propose that "the historical novel of the future (which is to say of our own present) will necessarily be Science-Fictional inasmuch as it will have to include questions about the fate of our social system, which has become a second nature."[7] It is not just that the familiar trappings of bygone periods and their respective characters feel somehow less capable of registering the forces that demand description in the twenty-first century. The present is a convergence of so many crises – economic, ecological, political – that its contours cannot be mapped, nor its pasts and futures dreamed, in just a single "chronotope," to invoke Bakhtin's famous term for the "intrinsic connectedness" of space and time in literature.[8] "The historical novel today," Jameson continues, "must be seen as an immense elevator that moves us up and down in time, its sickening lifts and dips corresponding to the euphoric or dystopian mood in which we wait for the doors to open."[9] This sounds like quite an elevator, and it labors metaphorically to do what McGuire achieves in *Here* with stunning elegance. Still, there is a larger impulse that Jameson and McGuire share, and we'll see it in the works of other writers in what follows. The histories that make our present are too many and too numerous, and an "acute consciousness" of what Jameson calls "the historicality of our historical situations" requires "a temporal span far exceeding the biological limits of the individual human organism."[10] With billions of years of history – both in the past and in the future – now bearing on the present, writers like

Convergence

Richard McGuire, Ruth Ozeki, Richard Powers, and William Gibson are finding ways to make their novels go fast and slow at the same time, which is how so many of us experience a modern world that feels like it is accelerating and going nowhere all at once.

Fictions of Duration

From Wordworth's "Lines Written a Few Miles above Tintern Abbey" to Matthew Arnold's "Dover Beach," the juxtaposition of different scales of time and history are a familiar, if not founding motif in English and American literature since 1800. As is fitting for the century that popularizes the idea that modernity might be just a passing instant against unfathomable archaeological and geological durations, Romantic and Victorian writers regularly invoked visions of what, following John McPhee's *Basin and Range* (1982), we now call "deep time."[11] High Modernist authors such as Joyce (*Finnegans Wake* [1939] famously begins with the image of "riverrun, past Eve and Adam's") and Faulkner ("the big woods" of "The Bear" in *Go Down, Moses* [1942], "bigger and older than any recorded document") used grander, more mythic timelines to frame their narratives of modern change, decay, and transformation. Virginia Woolf's experiments with both accelerations and dilations of narrative time are particularly striking and influential, from the several centuries (and genders) lived by the title character in *Orlando* (1928), to the radically diverse temporalities of novels such as *To the Lighthouse* (1927) and *Mrs. Dalloway* (1925), each of which describes a thickly detailed and slowly experienced social present that simultaneously contains a dizzying array of other times that can come at us with surprising velocity. Thus Peter Walsh, whose brief encounters with Clarissa Dalloway are narrated almost in real time, leaves Clarissa at one point and then hears another woman's voice, "a frail quivering sound ... with an absence of all human meaning" that still somehow echoes "through all ages – when the pavement was grass, when it was swamp, through the age of tusk and mammoth."[12] These references to longer, slower periods of time are, it should be said, largely devoted to broadening the symbolic sweep of the modernist novel as opposed to extending its narrative reach as such. In Gérard Genette's helpful terminology, passing mentions of inhuman time scales or epochs of deep time like those in *Mrs. Dalloway* do not really count toward what we would call the "duration" of "story time" that is parceled out and paced in the "narrative time" that marks our experience as readers.[13] Or to borrow from the equally familiar narratological language of Russian formalism, the *fabula* of a novel like *Orlando* does, in fact, span several centuries of chronological events that are then related to us, with all sorts of time dilations, ellipses, and manipulations, in the *sujet* that is the novelistic discourse that we find on the page.[14] But adding several millions years to the *fabula* of *Mrs. Dalloway* seems like a category error since, however powerfully they are rendered, they contain actions or events within a plot that obviously begins before she buys the flowers herself – with World War I? with Clarissa's adolescent kiss of Sally Seton? – but hardly spans the Cenozoic. For modernist novels that don't just thematize but try to narrate something like deep time, critics such as Mark McGurl and Charles Tung would have us look at works of science fiction such as H. G. Wells's *The Time Machine* (1895), Olaf Stapledon's *Last and First Men* (1930), or the weird tales of ancient, eldritch forces that H. P. Lovecraft mastered.[15]

For the writers I'm examining here, however, two mid-century figures provide a better way of tracking how contemporary historical fiction tries to place itself within an expanded field of temporalities and time scales. While Woolf and other modernists remain important landmarks for writers trying to reckon with relations between the lived present and the aeons that might inform it, the twenty-first-century authors we will turn to shortly are perhaps better understood as the conceptual heirs to various mid-century efforts to think differently – and more expansively – about the very nature of what counts as an event in either the historical past or present. Perversely enough, the works that distinguish Isaac Asimov and Fernand Braudel as central figures in crafting narratives of great historical duration are published just two years apart, a virtual simultaneity in deep time: Asimov's *Foundation* comes out in 1951, collecting and novelizing stories that had been appearing since 1942 in *Astounding Magazine*; and Braudel's *La Méditerranée et le Monde Méditerranéen à l'Epoque de Phillippe II*, which he began in 1942 while still a German prisoner of war, comes out in 1949. I am definitely not suggesting any influence, nor think it likely that the preeminent historian of the *Annales* school had even the slightest interest in Asimov who was himself the author of several popular histories and timelines, but probably not among the English-language readers waiting for the translation of Braudel's signal work as *The Mediterranean and The Mediterranean World in the Age of Philip II* in 1972–1973. Rather, Asimov and Braudel might be considered in parallel as writers whose preference for narratives of what Braudel termed the *longue durée*. The 20,000 years of space opera that Asimov chronicles in his first *Foundation* trilogy exceed by several millennia the span that Braudel explores in *The Mediterranean*, but for both, history proceeds as a patterned network of interactions between people and technologies, geographies and economic systems, mentalities and environments – all of which move and change far slower than the speed of man.

My point, however, is not that Asimov and Braudel are secret sharers in a single project, but rather to observe that a fascination with longer, less eventful forms of historical analysis and representation transposes some familiar motifs of modernist literature – motifs themselves derived from nineteenth-century figures in geology and evolutionary biology – and works across a range of post–World War II languages and narrative techniques, converging in a kind of slow-motion storytelling that makes history out of the observation of small changes over large domains of time. Neither Lewis Mumford nor Siegfried Giedeon, for example, were associated with Braudel's *Annales* school, but their individual approaches to the history of technology reflect a similar emphasis on anonymous innovations that become important over centuries and epochs.[16] Immanuel Wallerstein and Giovanni Arrighi, on the other hand, were colleagues at Binghamton University's Fernand Braudel Center, and world-systems theory derives quite closely from *Annales* school methodologies and time scales. As Joshua Clover notes, Arrighi's *The Long Twentieth Century* (1994) "has the grandeur of a sprawling epic."[17] Clover further reminds us that Nobel Laureate and *New York Times* contributor Paul Krugman was drawn to economics because he so admired the figure Seldon cut in Asimov's *Foundation* novels, a looming minor character who preserves civilization's future with bar charts and regression analyses. Long durations, in short, have something of a generic appeal from history to economics and science fiction in the decades after World War II. In a few thousand years, give or take, we'll know which genre came closest to getting it right.

But these are not durations in which most works of fiction can operate for very long, and even Asimov's *Foundation* novels feature dramatic swerves and oscillations of what Friedrich Kittler once called "time axis manipulation," or the "different arrangement of a stream of temporal data" in a particular medium.[18] Writing, for Kittler, represents "the first such time manipulation technology," and literary critics and narratologists have developed especially rich vocabularies for discussing how this works in practice.[19] In the service of, well, time, Genette's terms will more than do: he identifies four narrative "movements" that include two extreme techniques for either speeding fiction up (ellipsis) or slowing fiction down (pause); and two less radical narrative modes that go relatively faster (summary) or slower (scene) to produce conventional novelistic discourse as we know it.[20] Curiously enough, Genette insists that even within the "variable tempo[s]" of summaries and scenes, it is impossible in most novels for there to be "a sort of scene in slow motion" where a duration of narrative time is dilated or stretched so that it takes longer to read the resulting scene that it would to experience the fictional events in their real time.[21] He invokes the many, many long scenes in Proust that are tests of readerly endurance, but "not exactly slowed down" as accounts of action or exchanges of dialogue because they are actually extended by "extranarrative elements or interrupted by descriptive pauses."[22]

Few would accuse Asimov of indulging in very much that's "extranarrative" in the *Foundation* trilogy, which is propelled almost entirely by summary and can only cover its millennia of narrative time, like McGuire's *Here*, with ample and continuous ellipsis. Still, it's worth recalling that the success of Seldon's plan is salvaged from an unforeseen contingency in a scene of epic slowness. Using his power to unconsciously direct and permanently reorient the will of people in his presence, the Mule constitutes a true singularity – an aberration of both genetics and historical causality – that the planners of Seldon's Second Foundation must defeat after the Mule conquers the First Foundation, whose rise from the ruins of empire we track across the first two novels in the series. An agent of the Second Foundation, which has developed a range of learned mental practices that can match the Mule's innate abilities, finds himself, as one does in space operas, "[staring] into the muzzle of a blaster" with only "about one-fifth of a second" to preserve the course that history has been following for centuries.[23] Asimov devotes three pages to this micro-interval of time as the agent slowly – but actually in a brief instant – bends the Mule to his will instead. "It was a tableau," writes Asimov, "that endured far less than the significance adhering to it should require from a dramatic standpoint."[24] But even here in space, thousands of years into a future that will unfold according to a logic of systemic planning and tactical delay, the merest fraction of a moment can be mined for interstitial drama that feels not so much like experimental fiction, but like the realist novel as we have always known it. A galactic empire of impossible technologies and superhuman intelligence comes down to an exchange that Asimov could have lifted from Edith Wharton: "Only a word or two passed between Channis and the Mule – only a word or two and that utterly revealing stream of emotional consciousness that remains forever the true interplay of understanding between such as they."[25]

Saving Time

I want to turn now to a survey of some contemporary US novels that play games with time and temporality that follow in the spirit of Asimov and McGuire, though of course to different ends. One of these novels will look a lot like science fiction, and the other two will function well within the generic limits of literary fiction in the twenty-first century. All three examine the shape of our present as it has been made – and maybe ruined for perpetuity – by longer histories of "slow violence," to borrow Rob Nixon's helpful phrase that tries to capture the damage that capitalism is doing, and has already done, beneath the thresholds of our accelerated everyday perceptions.[26] These are fictions that explore the limits of both speed and of the slowness that would seem to represent a stark and possibly redemptive set of alternatives. It is this anxious, often melancholic sense that time is running out that most distinguishes these works from other twentieth-century Anglo-American fictions that experiment with the logic of chronology (Martin Amis's backwards-running *Time's Arrow* [1991], for example) or with the conventions of narrative speed (Nicholson Baker's hyper-detailed temporal realism in *The Mezzanine* [1988]). Or put differently, these contemporary fictions are less interested in breaking the forms that novelists have used to narrate time out of any sense that history has ended or is exhausted. These are novels that want – desperately and critically – to represent ongoing histories of the present that might, at the same time, leave us wondering what (if any?) future we have left.

These fictions can also help us learn again a lesson that Braudel inspired. In a discussion of Braudel and the *Annales* school in *Time and Narrative*, Paul Ricoeur ventures a somewhat enigmatic observation that "absolutely speaking, speed does not apply to intervals of time but to movements traversing them."[27] Ricoeur casually summons up a philosophical tradition spanning back to Augustine and Aristotle with this remark, whose implications would take a world of time to consider. At the very least, though, we can better understand how some especially ambitious works of twenty-first-century fiction reckon with questions of space and time together with an awareness – and not always in despair – that we have already used up a future's share of both.

Ruth Ozeki's *A Tale for the Time Being* (2013) and Richard Powers's *The Overstory* (2018) are novels set among the trees. This is not only a reflection of each author's preoccupation with climate change and the specter of ecological collapse, though these contexts are made particularly prominent for both. It is more the case that trees embody – indeed, that trees are synecdoches for – a feeling of radically expanded temporality that various characters in the novels come to appreciate for its utter lack of human scale. So, while these are abundantly historical novels in at least one generic sense – with everyday individuals involved in personal dramas operating in the shadow of world-shaping events from World War II through 9/11 and the 2008 financial crisis – there are just as many moments in each text that render even this version of a long twentieth century virtually ephemeral. Ozeki's elegantly double-plotted novel, for example, sets her autofictional narrator, Ruth, on a mission to discover the fate of a young Japanese girl whose diary washes up in British Columbia, where it has been carried by the currents and aftershocks of the 2011 tsunami that also caused the Fukushima meltdown. The diary's author, Nao, relates a narrative of her traumatic bullying at the hands of classmates after her family re-emigrates to Japan after her father loses his job in Silicon Valley. But her narrative also includes the nested stories of both her great-grandmother, a Taishō-era intellectual turned Buddhist nun and now a centenarian, and that of her son, Nao's great-uncle, who died at the end of World War II by crashing his plane into the sea instead of completing a kamikaze mission.

As even this breathless summary should indicate, the novel has a lot of "nows" for readers to keep track of, and Ozeki almost never misses an opportunity to turn the pun that makes Nao – as a "time being" according to the tenets of Zen Buddhism – into a figure for the "now" that is only ever a past present until the narrative shifts into Ruth's contemporary timeline. Early in the novel, Nao discovers that her name itself can invoke the specious present. She recalls that when she was six or seven, she would whisper "*Now!* ... *Now!* ... *Now!* ..." while riding in the backseat of the family car.[28] It seems quite deliberate for Ozeki to treat this revelation as an epiphany one might have in elementary school, for the novel has much more to say on the experience of time's passing than the simple, useless fact that "in the time it takes to say *now*, now is already over. It's already *then*" (99). But as the book proceeds through plots nested in plots and more events that come to rhyme with more events, Ozeki lets Ruth's husband, an environmental artist named Oliver, make a very telling joke when he realizes that he's blown a publication deadline from the Friends of the Pleistocene. "That's the trouble with the Pleistocene," he says, "It's always rush rush rush. They want everything yesterday" (355). What makes this deep-time dad joke work so well is that Oliver's "latest artwork" is a "botanical intervention ... called the Neo-Eocene," which he imagines as a "climate-change forest" featuring formerly indigenous species that flourished in the Canadian Pacific over fifty-five million years ago – and likely will again (60). His role throughout the novel, in other words, is to "[take] the long view" and "[accept] his lot as a short-lived mammal, scurrying in and out amid the roots of the giants" (61). Ruth, we are soon told, "was neither patient nor accepting," which is why we have double protagonists in the present to trace the double stories of multiple protagonists in the other "presents" of the past (61).

Powers's *The Overstory* is somewhat more conventionally multiplotted, with its many characters literally and metaphorically connected by way of trees. The novel's sections, for example, proceed from "Roots" to "Trunk" and "Crown" and "Seeds," and at one point later in its expansive plot several characters find themselves up the same giant redwood tree. At once a chronotope and proto-character, "Mimas" has been targeted for lumber harvesting, which is why its highest reaches have been occupied by two of Powers's protagonists – environmental activists of interest to another figure in the novel who wants to study them as part of his dissertation research into the psychology of extreme political beliefs. All to say that Powers's novel seems very self-conscious about the use of "tree" structures to represent a kind of postmodern or contemporary fiction (also known, after Jorge Luis Borges, as "forking path" narratives) that involves densely networked patterns of character interaction, both direct and highly mediated, as well as plots that turn on contingencies and chance events that could just as readily, along another "branch," unfold some other way.

However, Powers's narrative logic is almost relentlessly convergent in the novel, and he is interested in "trees" as symbols for – and living systems of – connection and dependence, which makes his novel feel less like an experiment in multiplying possibilities and more a reckoning with an ethics of responsibility and care. In *The Overstory*, every character is introduced to us by early, formative encounters with trees; every character in the novel will become devoted to some sort of ecological radicalism; and every character in the novel will finally pursue, to variously self-destructive or restorative ends, a version of what Adam, the psychology student who will later join several of the novel's characters in a band of ecoterrorists, as "a position that any reasonable person in our society thinks is crazy."[29] When his dissertation advisor presses him for something more concrete, he answers that he wants to study people who are willing to risk their lives for "plant rights" or "plant personhood" at a time when "claims are being made for a moral authority that lies beyond the human" (237). In this and other moments in the novel, we can see Powers aspiring toward a model of the passionate "sincerity" that Lee Konstantinou identifies as one of twenty-first-century fiction's most distinguishing features, as it becomes less postmodern and, for the time being at least, still "contemporary."[30]

Powers does not include in *The Overstory*'s more than five hundred pages any excerpts of this fictional dissertation. But there are several moments in the novel where, like Ozeki, he explores the potential power of other forms and other media to push at literary fiction's spatial and temporal limits. If Oliver's project of conceptualist forestry is the most ostentatious way Ozeki gestures toward the slower speeds of ecological time, the fact that Nao's diary appears beneath a cover reading "*À la recherche du temps perdu* Par Marcel Proust" is another way Ozeki shows that she is interested in a longer "now" that links her characters across world wars, atomic devastation, 9/11, and the effects of environmental ruin in the Pacific.[31] Powers begins *The Overstory* with an equally audacious reference as a woman sitting underneath a tree enters into communion with the world of plants. "*The air is raining messages,*" according to the narrator, and "*Signals rain down around her like seeds.*"[32] Since one of the novel's characters is a botanist who discovers that trees do, in fact, communicate, this probably is a reference to the scientific work of Suzanne Simard, a forest ecology professor at the University of British Columbia, or perhaps to conservationist Peter Wohlleben's best seller, *The Hidden Life of Trees*. On the other hand, Powers's botanist hears these messages and signals only when "her ears tune down to the lowest frequencies – which sounds very much like an echo of Ellison's *Invisible Man*.

Making trees into the figures of a racial allegory is a natural extension of *The Overstory*'s politics and literalism on the subjectivity and even legal "personhood" of plants. This opening allusion to the "lower frequencies" of Ellison casts into even starker light a later passage concerning Neelay, a young boy who will go on to become a computer pioneer whose AI "learners" seem poised by the novel's last pages to replace humanity should we fail to change our ways. Like Powers himself, Neelay is an avid reader of science fiction. One night he reads a story about aliens who land on Earth but are invisible to humans because "they zip around like swarms of gnats, too fast to see – so fast the Earth seconds seem to them like years" (97). But this is no story about a peaceable kingdom of alternative temporalities, and since humans fail to answer when the aliens try to communicate – and since, because they move so slowly, humans appear as "nothing but sculptures of immobile meat" – the aliens "tuck into the frozen statues and start curing them like so much jerky" (97). Living things that do not seem alive enough – that live too slowly, we might say, on the "lower" temporalities – are so much raw material for consumption in the form of genocide, or vice versa.

These allusions to other stories do not distend the novel's timeline, nor do they depart from the conventions of literary reference very dramatically. But elsewhere in *The Overstory* Powers does suggest that we must venture beyond the novel to operate on the vast temporal scales that count as history for the present. The first major character we meet in the text is Nicholas Hoel, an artist later drawn into violent environmental activism and then returned to a much different kind of artistic practice by the novel's end. An American Chestnut tree on the Hoel family farm in Iowa becomes the first major tree to which Powers introduces us, and multiple generations of Hoel men – in fulfillment of a patriarchal charge passed down from father to son – take monthly pictures of the tree as it grows and, more importantly, survives the spread of chestnut blight that decimates the species in the early twentieth century. Using first a No. 2 Brownie and then an Instamatic, the photographs are assembled into a flip-book that eventually takes five seconds to run as what the narrator calls, "the oldest, shortest, slowest, most ambitious silent movie ever shot in Iowa" (13).

This project of arboreal-compulsion disorder – "growing at the speed of wood" – patterns the shape of Nick's subsequent career as an artist and pushes him into a relationship with Olivia Vandergriff, who will become the focal figure in the novel's examination of environmental activism and the politics of ELF-style direct action (16). Long after an attempted arson leads to Olivia's death and the group's disbanding, Nick continues at the end of the novel to make environmental art at scale: Working both alone and with some strangers taken by his project's strangeness, Nick arranges pieces of downed wood "into letters compete with tendril flourishes" that "spell-out a gigantic word legible from space: STILL" (502). As a monumental last word in a novel trying to capture both the recent past and its deeper "roots," this is an ambivalent gesture at best. To the aliens living and dying at a high velocity in the science fiction Neelay reads as a child, humans look "still" indeed – which is why they are cut down and processed for a species that might not be evil, but just going by too fast. That this final message – a giant "still" amidst the novel's cinematic sprawl of characters and events – gets delivered to the AIs that Neelay has already released into the wilds of the Internet further implies that Powers is looking forward, and perhaps not apocalyptically, to future readers who will be more receptive to this work of art because they are not human. "The learners will puzzle of the message that springs up there," Powers writes, pulling back in space and flashing forward into time. "Two centuries more, and these five living letters, too, will fade back into the swirling patterns, the changing rain and air and light. And yet – but *still* – they'll spell out, for a while, the word life has been saying, since the beginning" (502). Not every reader will find consolation in a future that might be populated by sentient computer programs and trees we have avoided killing only by sheer accident; but Powers ends *The Overstory* on a rhapsody that leads us, like McGuire, to precisely "here" and to a future that endures extravagantly without us.

The End of the End of Everything

Despite all the apocalyptic ambience of works like *Here, A Tale for the Time Being,* and *The Overstory* – each in different ways shadowed by fears of climate change and the inevitability of human destruction in its wake – they end with signs pointing in the direction of survival too, and for Ozeki and Powers, I think, this might well be a way of enlisting the form of the contemporary novel on behalf of arguments for ecological resilience.

In much the same way that David Mitchell's *Cloud Atlas* (2004) conceives its interlocking stories as describing a larger arc that bends toward justice – in fantasy of liberal politics that feels, after Obama, even more improbable than reincarnation letting a wronged soul win out after all – Ozeki and Powers want to hold on to futurity as a natural resource that literary fiction can help us recognize and actively preserve. Nowhere is this more visible than in Ruth's staggering intervention into the past of Nao's story in the novel and that literally gives her, and us, more "now" to live. Having decided to kill herself, Nao's diary comes to a sudden stop. "This is what now feels like," Ruth reads, and there is no more for the time being. But that night she dreams herself into Nao's narrative, imagining that she travels back in time – and to Japan – to give her father back the World War II diaries of his own uncle, which Ruth finds bundled with Nao's Proustian notebook when it washes up on shore. Within the novel's baffling games with time and reverse-causality, it is Ruth's retrospective return of these earlier diaries that puts them there for Nao to find earlier and then read before committing suicide, inspired by her great-uncle's suffering in the last days of the war to change her mind so that there is now more of Nao's "now" to narrate. Reading in the present not only makes for "time regained," to follow on the novel's grandest allusion since Ruth gets to experience a past she never knew; reading in Nao's future, Ruth's desire for more of Nao's own story seems indeed to bring her back to life.

Powers also suspends a character's life within a loop of indeterminacy and readerly desire. Called to give a speech after a life spent trying to understand and fight for trees, the botanist Patricia Westerford, whose writings we've seen other characters discuss throughout the novel, decides that words are not enough. Westerford frames her fictional talk around the question of what is the "single best thing a person can do for tomorrow's world," and, on the evidence of the poison she has prepared for the occasion, it appears that suicide is the answer she is about to very publicly perform (464). And then she does and doesn't kill herself, as Powers instead gives us two versions of how her story ends: "The speaker raises her glass, and the world splits. Down one branch, she lifts the glass to her lips, toasts the room – *To Tachigali versicolor* – and drink. Down another branch, this one, she shouts, 'Here's to unsuicide,' and flights the cup of swirling green over the gasping audience" (466). It's a bravura gesture that turns away from utter desolation, insofar as Powers continues with the novel down the "branch" where she ends up surviving. And it spares at least one version of the audience – and the readers that they represent – from facing the implications of such a commitment to self-negation. We get off easy in our timeline. Westerford's stunt does nothing more than leave us all wet.

Again, the nod to Borges here aligns *A Tale for the Time Being* and *The Overstory* with a particular style of postmodern fiction that, as Catherine Gallagher writes, "[crosses] with scientific thought to produce a subcategory of science fiction" where narrative divergences within a limited set of events produces alternate histories or appropriations of the "many-worlds" theory developed in the 1960s and 1970s by quantum physicists.[33] Even a book like *Here*, which situates a single sequence of events along an incredibly long timeline, could be considered a variation on this form since its visual layout of floating, overlapping windows lets us witness a multiplicity of coexisting times happening in a shared location. But many of the works that draw most explicitly on these ideas – works that, as Gallagher points out, make "very superficial use" of ideas that "quantum physicists and analytical philosophers have been debating for decades" – flourish in genres far more popular than literary fiction. From classic science fiction novels such as Philip K. Dick's *The Man in the High Castle* (1962) to episodes of *Star Trek* (in the original series and all its sequels) to films such as *Run Lola Run* (1998) and *Sliding Doors* (1998) and TV shows like *Community* (2011's "Remedial Chaos Theory") and Amazon's *The Man in the High Castle* (the more things change, I guess ...) we all know the contours of these narrative structures and the pleasures of thinking in this particular counterfactual mode that "helps satisfy our desire to quicken and vivify historical entities, to make them seem not only solid and substantial, but also suspenseful and unsettled."[34] In the "darkest timeline," I have a sinister goatee; along a happier branch, I'm writing about something else since anthropogenic climate change was slowed and ultimately reversed after the revolution. In reality, the books I've been discussing are so fascinated by the possibility of spatial and temporal convergences over long historical durations because the horizons of a great many futures we might conceivably imagine feel foreshortened and determined in advance by events, technologies, and economic systems that have already done their damage.

Which is why I want to end with a brief look at a final work of contemporary fiction that experiments not only with narrative structures of duration and chronotopes of nonhuman time, but also makes a case for thinking harder about the limits of futurity as a political temporality. William Gibson's *The Peripheral* (2014) features the sort of plot that readers of his fiction, from his seminal cyberpunk novels of the 1980s through his post-9/11 realism of the "Blue Ant" series, will recognize immediately: shadowy conspirators play games of power by putting individuals with particular talents (hacking, trendspotting, public relations) in search of some rare, mysterious MacGuffin that provides the predicate for elaborate worldbuilding and stylish anthropologies of temporalities we may or may not be inhabiting already. *The Peripheral*, technically speaking, marks a return to science fiction. Unfolding across two future timelines (twenty-five and ninety-five years ahead respectively), its story of twenty-second century oligarchs competing for dominance by way of quantum computers capable of exchanging information with the past would be hard to summarize even if I could go as slowly as the job demands. But it is not the plot that interests me about *The Peripheral*, nor even the genuinely moving ways the novel tries to capture the uncanny feelings we might have for other times and histories. It is instead how Gibson exploits the logic of apocalypse as a narrative horizon – as the constant background noise of all the texts I have considered, and many more I could have – that makes *The Peripheral* strike me as so, in a word, central to some of the most highly imaginative fictions of time and space today.

In the novel's twenty-second century, past timelines are called "continua," and they are accessed by what Gibson describes as "a device that sends and receives information, to and from the past."[35] Such connections are at once difficult, expensive, and, weirdly enough, inconsequential, since every intervention from the future itself "generates" a now distinctly different past that is, from that point forward, no longer the history of the present that just reached back in time. People from the future can, in theory, try to kill as many butterflies, great-great grandparents or baby Hitlers as possible using their limited means of action; nothing will change their present, even as their interference makes a new version (a "continuum") that becomes another future for the altered past to have instead. But most of the "enthusiasts" who enter into communication with the past don't have nearly such dramatic motivations; they are instead, for the most part, "romantic[s]" with a "distaste for the present rooted in the sense of a fall from grace. That some prior order, or perhaps the lack of one, afforded a more authentic existence."[36] They are misguided "antiquarians," as Nietzsche would call them, and though they definitely are committing an abuse of history, they are doing it for love.[37]

But not every relationship between the past and future over centuries is quite so harmless, and perhaps the most arresting moment in *The Peripheral* has nothing to do with high technologies (twenty-second century clones controlled by VR headsets in the past; 3D printed bodies; weaponized, flesh-eating nanobots), but with an oddly mediated but still straightforward bit of historical narration when Wilf Netherton, a PR professional from the far future, tells Flynne Fisher, a semi-professional online gamer in the near future, about the past that may not be her future any longer. From Wilf's perspective, on the other side of the apocalypse that the survivors come to call "The Jackpot," the times had never been better: after everything gets

worse and worse for almost everybody, and "seriously bad shit … killed
80 percent of every last person alive," new technologies come online too late
to help the masses, but with such belated ingenuity that "the richest had
gotten richer, there being fewer to own whatever there was."[38] This is not
the future liberals want, as one of 2017's most charged memes would put it,
but it's definitely a future that seems plausible and, even within the generic
constraints of science fiction, almost prosaically real.[39] The other futures we
have glimpsed in McGuire, Ozeki, and Powers also imagine death and
devastation at catastrophic scales, but they also harbor, however marginal,
the possibility that there are still times that can be changed. Even the AI's
that might replace us in *The Overstory* are "learners," after all, and so who
is to say that humans won't learn too? But Gibson reminds us that many of
the terms on which we'll face the future are already set, and that unless we're
willing not just to change our minds, but continue struggling against the
same forces we've seemingly been at war with for the duration – the "oligarchs, corporations, neomonarchists" that Netherton describes to Flynne,
with no discernible irony, as the "majority of empowered survivors" – all
our histories will end up in the same place. The future might remain technically unknowable, but for Gibson, at least, it is perhaps already too imaginable as the convergence of eighteenth-century economics destroying the
world with nineteenth-century technologies that show precious few signs
of slowing down as the twenty-first century goes on. Here we go again,
or else.

NOTES

1 Reinhart Koselleck, *Sediments of Time: On Possible Histories*, trans. Sean Franzel
   and Stefan-Ludwig Hoffmann (Stanford: Stanford University Press, 2018), 96.
2 Reinhart Koselleck, *Futures Past: On the Semantics of Historical Time*, trans.
   Keith Tribe (New York: Columbia University Press, 2004), 22.
3 Katja Kwastek and Erin La Cour, "Introduction: As Slowly As Possible," *ASAP/
   Journal* 4, no. 3 (2019): 457–466. Many of the pieces in this special issue on
   slowness resonate with the texts and authors I am considering, though in a
   different and powerfully global context.
4 Fredric Jameson, *The Antinomies of Realism* (New York: Verso, 2013), 259, 263.
   Subsequent citations internal. For a fascinating discussion of another set of postmodern and contemporary fictions as variations on the classic "historical novel,"
   see Mitchum Huehls, "Historical Fiction and the End of History," in *American
   Literature in Transition, 2000–2010*, edited by Rachel Greenwald Smith
   (Cambridge: Cambridge University Press, 2017), 138–151. The writers I am discussing here could also be considered as examples as what Huehls insightfully
   characterizes as the "concerted literary attempt to produce a historical sense free
   from the compromises that a more postmodern worldview requires" (140).

5 Georg Lukás, *The Historical Novel*, trans. Hannah Mitchell and Stanley Mitchell (Lincoln: University of Nebraska Press, 1962). See especially Fredric Jameson's "Introduction" in this edition.

6 Jameson, *Antinomies of Realism*, 262.

7 Ibid., 298.

8 Mikhail Bakhtin, *The Dialogic Imagination: Four Essays*, trans. Caryl Emerson and Michael Holquist (Austin: University of Texas Press, 1981), 84.

9 Jameson, *Antinomies of Realism*, 301. This very specific metaphorical language is derived from a discussion of Christopher Nolan's *Inception* (2010).

10 Ibid.

11 For more on the idea of deep time, see John McPhee, *Annals of the Former World* (New York: Farrar, Straus and Giroux, 1998); and Martin J. S. Rudwick, *Bursting the Limits of Time: The Reconstruction of Geohistory in the Age of Revolution* (Chicago: The University of Chicago Press, 2005); Stephen Jay Gould, *Time's Arrow, Time's Cycle: Myth and Metaphor in the Discovery of Geological Time* (New York: Penguin, 1988). For discussions of how ideas of deep time might shape literary-critical thinking, see Wai-Chee Dimock, *Through Other Continents: American Literature Across Deep Time* (Princeton: Princeton University Press, 2008); and Mark McGurl, "The Posthuman Comedy," *Critical Inquiry* 38 (Spring 2012): 533–553.

12 Virginia Woolf, *Mrs. Dalloway* (New York: Harcourt Brace & Company, 1925), 81.

13 Gérard Genette, *Narrative Discourse: An Essay in Method*, trans. Jane E. Lewin (Ithaca: Cornell University Press, 1980), 87.

14 Viktor Shklovsky, *Theory of Prose*, trans. Benjamin Sher (Champaign: The Dalkey Archive, 1990), 170.

15 In addition to McGurl's "The Posthuman Comedy," see Charles M. Tung, "Baddest Modernism: The Scales and Lines of Inhuman Time," *Modernism/Modernity* 23, no. 3 (September 2016): 515–539.

16 I am thinking in particular of Lewis Mumford's long-duration histories of technology (*Technics and Civilization* [New York: Harcourt, Brace, and Company, 1934] and *The Myth of the Machine*, 2 vols. [New York: Harcourt, Brace, and Company, 1967 and 1970]), as well as Siegfried Giedeon's *Mechanization Takes Command* (New York: Oxford University Press, 1948) and *Space, Time, and Architecture* (Cambridge, MA: Harvard University Press, 1941).

17 Joshua Clover, "Autumn of the Empire," *Los Angeles Review of Books*, July 18, 2011, https://lareviewofbooks.org/article/autumn-of-the-empire.

18 Friedrich Kittler, "Real Time Analysis, Time Axis Manipulation," trans. Geoffrey Winthrop-Young, *Cultural Politics* 13, no. 1 (March 2017): 1–18.

19 Ibid., 6.

20 Genette, *Narrative Discourse*, 94–95.

21 Ibid., 95.

22 Ibid.

23 Isaac Asimov, *Second Foundation* in *The Foundation Trilogy: Three Science Fiction Classics* (New York: Doubleday, 1951), 60.

24 Ibid., 61.

25 Ibid.

26 See Rob Nixon, *Slow Violence and the Environmentalism of the Poor* (Cambridge, MA: Harvard University Press, 2013).

27 Paul Ricoeur, *Time and Narrative*, vol. 1, trans. Kathleen McLaughlin and David Pellauer (Chicago: The University of Chicago Press, 1983), 104.

28 Ruth Ozeki, *A Tale for the Time Being* (New York: Penguin, 2013), 98.

29 Richard Powers, *The Overstory* (New York: W. W. Norton & Company, 2018), 237.

30 See Lee Konstantinou, *Cool Characters: Irony and American Fiction* (Cambridge, MA: Harvard University Press, 2016); and also Amy Hungerford, "On the Period Formerly Known As the Contemporary," *American Literary History* 20, nos. 1–2 (Spring/Summer 2008): 410–419.

31 Ozeki, *A Tale for the Time Being*, 11.

32 Powers, *The Overstory*, 3.

33 Catherine Gallagher, *Telling It Like It Wasn't: The Counterfactual Imagination in History and Fiction* (Chicago: The University of Chicago Press, 2018), 71

34 Ibid., 11.

35 William Gibson, *The Peripheral* (New York: G. P. Putnam's Sons, 2014), 189.

36 Ibid., 281.

37 Friedrich Nitezsche, *On the Advantage and Disadvantage of History for Life* (1874), trans. Peter Preuss (Indianapolis: Hackett Publishing, 1980), 14.

38 Gibson, *The Peripheral*, 322.

39 "This is the future liberals want" first emerged as an attack on the left's perceived fixation on issues surrounding diversity (and more) after a picture taken on the New York subway of a woman wearing a hijab next to a man in drag was posted to Twitter by a right-wing user. But the phrase was almost immediately embraced by thousands of "liberals" to express support for what the image showed; what the original poster saw as a sign of virtual apocalypse, in other words, was seized on for its utopian potential. For more, see https://knowyourmeme.com/memes/this-is-the-future-that-liberals-want.

12

CRYSTAL PARIKH

Dissolution

The novelist and essayist Valeria Luiselli concludes her 2017 book, *Tell Me How It Ends: An Essay in Forty Questions*, with a series of shadowy photographs of one of the Central American children and adolescents she interviewed when serving as a translator for the legal advocates of young asylum-seekers in 2014. In the final of the three shots, as Manu López turns a somersault on a trampoline, the camera catches him in the air, upside down, appearing to hang by his knees from the electrical wires behind him. Luiselli prefaces the image with a short update on her prior account of his case, which, as she observes earlier, is one that has obsessed her, "It lives with me now, grows in me, all its details clear in my mind and constantly revisited. It's a story I know well and follow closely, but for which I still cannot see a possible ending":[1]

> Manu has SIJ status now. He has found a church where he feels welcome, and he has mentors at S.T.R.O.N.G. who have helped him pull through. He's also learning English with the TIIAS, and comes to play soccer on campus sometimes. He told me he wanted his real name to be disclosed in this book, so he could send it to family and friends back in Honduras. But, because he has yet to apply for a green card, and times are dire and volatile, immigration lawyers we consulted thought it best to maintain his anonymity. When I told him this, he said, Okay, fine, no pasa nada. In the meantime, he said, he'll be practicing the art of flight in his front yard in Hempstead.[2]

Classified as a "special immigrant juvenile" (SIJ), Manu is permitted to seek lawful permanent residence in the United States. Organizations such as S.T.R.O.N.G. (a nonprofit working to keep youth away from gang activity) and TIIAS (a group organized by Luiselli's own students at Hofstra University in Long Island), along with his church, provide him some moorings in his new home. But the anecdote is nevertheless unquestionably also

I am very grateful to Joshua L. Miller and Catherine Romagnolo for their helpful comments as I developed this chapter.

one of irresolution. "The art of flight" that the camera momentarily captures could indicate hopefulness in regard to Manu's future, but just as easily signal an urgent need once again to flee an untenable situation with little notion of what will come next.

Structured around themes derived from the intake questionnaire used to determine the status of child migrants – "border," "court," "home," and "community" – *Tell Me How It Ends* reflects on the plight of those children and youth who arrived across the US-Mexico border by the tens of thousands in 2014. As Luiselli – an award-winning novelist originally from Mexico City – and her family await their own green cards that would secure their place as permanent alien residents in the United States, she charts the ambiguities in identity and legal status she shares with the children she interviews, while also recognizing the profound differences in legal, social, and class status that separates her from them. The text's title comes from the question her daughter, fascinated with the plight of the migrant children, repeatedly asks her, "tell me how it ends." While Luiselli can offer no definitive conclusions about the outcomes of each case, nor as to what kind of "persons" the children will be in the "end," she seeks to honor the many possibilities of becoming in the partial and affecting accounts she does provide. As such, she embeds the children's stories as fragments, snapshots of them in their flight away from the precarious social and political conditions that make life intolerable, and perhaps even impossible, in their home nations. But Luiselli also seeks to avoid the logic of detention and interrogation that the state imposes upon them, classifying them strictly as innocent victims or as security threats to the nation, by elaborating the risks, injuries, and suffering the children have faced, but also the tenacity and resilience they exhibit in having arrived in the United States.

Fragmented Narratives of Interruption, Isolation, Suspense, and Precarity

I begin this chapter on dissolution and fragmentation in twenty-first-century American fiction with a work of *non*fiction to underscore the urgency and stakes involved in the production of formal narrative modes that represent the financial instability, social isolation, globalized labor, violence, and precarity facing the world's "99%."[3] Lee Gutkind, the ostensible "Godfather behind creative nonfiction," harkens to the "basic rules of good citizenship" when he delineates guidelines for practicing this literary form, which he summarizes as: "Do not recreate incidents and characters who never existed; do not write to do harm to innocent victims …. Over and above the creation of a seamless narrative, you are seeking to touch and affect someone else's life – which is the goal creative nonfiction writers share with novelists and poets. We all want to connect with another human being – or as many people as possible."[4] But if creative nonfiction means to convey a *"larger truth* than is possible through a mere compilation of verifiable facts, the use of direct quotation and the adherence to the rigid organizational style of [traditional journalism]," this chapter considers the challenges that both fiction *and* nonfiction encounter in capturing the "larger truth" about citizenship (and other forms of legal status) and other human beings in the twenty-first century.[5]

Fragmented narrative forms hardly originated in the twenty-first century, and postcolonial, multiethnic, and diasporic writers have for at least several decades now adopted such forms to represent social inequalities, political struggle and unrest, and the relations of power and violence whose scale escapes both perception and transformative agency at the individual level. And yet, as progressive ideological narratives of development, security, and autonomy become increasingly more difficult to sustain – when, that is, such narratives become increasingly visible as ideological *fictions*, and further-more as perhaps unappealing fictions, for broad swaths of the world – the production of such alternative forms demand careful attention from us as readers of the contemporary moment. This chapter considers how narratives of suspense, interruption, isolation, and scarcity adopt dissolution and the fragment as vital aesthetic and stylistic forms to convey the splintering effect that global modernity in the twenty-first century induces.

Vulnerability, Security, Precarity

For mainstream American politics and culture, the terrorist attacks of September 11, 2001 seemed to pose a kind of decisive break in a national narrative of American progress, ascendance, and indomitability. At the end of the twentieth century, some observers ventured so far as to deem the US triumph over the Soviet-led Communist world "the end of history," with the nation seemingly poised to govern over a "new world order" as the world's sole superpower. The 9/11 attacks ruptured such assumptions regarding the United States as an uncontested global hegemon and its capacity to protect and provide for its own citizenry at home. The "war on terror," which followed 9/11, has been conceived as a kind of "forever war" that to date has had its most devastating fronts in Afghanistan, Iraq, Pakistan, and subsequently Syria. An estimated two million civilians have been killed and millions more displaced, and the crusade against "terrorism," a notoriously slippery label that can be (and has been) applied quite indiscriminately, has had indelible implications across the world.[6]

While numerically, the losses suffered on 9/11 pale in comparison to other wars, civil violence, and natural disasters that occurred around the same time, as well as those that the war on terror brought about, the spectacular and unforeseen character of the attacks engendered a sense of unprecedented vulnerability and risk, that in turn, elected officials and policymakers insisted, called for exceptional countermeasures.[7] Such representations of American loss correspond to an American exceptionalism that continually posits both the United States as the home of exceptional freedom and prosperity and American lives and the American way of life as superior and more worthy of protection than those of others across the globe. But 9/11 and its aftermath, as well as the "Great Recession" of 2008 (which saw the most significant economic downturn in the United States since the Great Depression), can also make visible the way in which constructions of vulnerability, security, and emergency had long been naturalized in political and cultural discourses.

Political theorists and cultural critics from various disciplines have hence begun investigating forms of vulnerability, replacing the autonomous, self-knowing subject that liberalism (and neoliberalism) has presumed to be the natural unit of social life, political agency, and intellectual inquiry with the embodied human subject, whose exposure in and to the world requires social and institutional forms of reciprocity, care, and protection. Unlike liberalism's epistemological approach that defines its normative subject as one in possession of particular capacities – for example, the capacity to reason or the capacity to labor – the "vulnerability thesis" posits that in the human body's openness to harm, injury, suffering, and pain, vulnerability constitutes a "universal, inevitable, enduring aspect of the human condition that must be at the heart of our concept of social and state responsibility."[8] The fact of human vulnerability entails a "dependency on infrastructure for a livable life," the many material, social, and cultural institutions, practices, and arrangements that shelter and sustain human beings.[9] If humans mostly lack in the "instincts" by which other animals survive in their environments, the material cultures and societies humans create serve at least partially to offset that deficit.

Encounters with suffering and violence might sometimes occur randomly, but for the most part there is little that is wholly arbitrary and unpredictable about how and why only some people routinely come to experience such shared vulnerability as extremely precarious life. In the United States, modern biopolitics has organized with astounding precision a social order along hierarchical divisions of race, nation, and class – and these in turn are shaped by and organize norms of gender and sexuality – with the aim of protecting and cultivating *white* life, and even then, only some segments of that population. As cultural critic Dylan Rodriguez thus argued in the aftermath of Hurricane Katrina (which provided an example early in the new century of how intense vulnerability quickly leads to suffering and death):

> [W]hite America occupies a category of social existence that is without global parallel. It lives within a historical structure of life wherein it is capable of *presuming entitlement* to things like bodily integrity, communal (read: racial) security, and militarized state responsiveness in a manner that no other human category can allege to share in this moment. Imagine, then, the sheer accumulation of racially organized death, vulnerability, and bodily disintegration that must accrue in order to render these white life entitlements so massively that they can, in fact, be taken for granted by whites *and* their racial others.[10]

Rodriguez points to how white Americans generally enjoy a safe distance from precariousness (while also putting under erasure), the kinds of "natural" disasters, large-scale atrocities, and social and political violence with which racialized peoples in the United States and across the Global South are all too familiar. But even further, he contends, that sense of security *depends upon and requires* the bodily suffering and violence visited upon abjected others.

To the extent that US national culture heralds an impenetrable sense of security, it requires a corresponding vision of bodies that are themselves self-contained, readily legible and managed by power. Neoliberalism extends the promise of freedom and flexibility to those who inhabit their bodies properly, whose bodies are located in their proper places, carrying out their proper function, and it admits a very few people of color and others who have been previously marginalized into that social contract. But the cultivation of the good life of those privileged few – who, in the lexicon of popular social protest in the new millennium, have been designated the "1 percent" – depends upon, even as it occludes the existence of, vast numbers whose lives and labor are considered interchangeable and disposable, that is the 99 percent. If vulnerability therefore refers to a shared feature of all human life, "precarity" registers conditions of existence bereft of predictability or security, due to the systemic and remarkably unequal distribution of risk and protection afforded to individuals and groups. Furthermore, contemporary governance has only intensified the routinized experience of insecurity as it withdraws social provisions, protections, and care, such that precarity comes to seem normal and to be expected on the heels of sweeping changes across the globe in the decades following World War II, and especially after the Cold War. The globalization of capitalism has transformed the function of national states, which increasingly serve to protect the corporate interests of market agents.

238

On a landscape where most of the world's people have no access to stable jobs or income, and are subject to volatile economic, environmental, and social conditions, even those who do enjoy some modicum of security feel themselves at considerable risk for poverty, homelessness, and isolation. As political theorist Isabell Lorey observes: "There is virtually no longer any reliable protection against what can be foreseen, planned ... contingent. Through the removal and remodeling of collective assurance systems, every form of independence disappears in the face of the dangers of precariousness and precarization."[11] Thus, while vulnerability proves a constant, ineradicable feature of human existence, it is simultaneously "particular, varied, and unique on the individual level," given both the differences of embodiment across individuals, as well as the differences that arise in relation to social and institutional relationships that are themselves changing under the tremendous pressure of market forces.[12]

Undoing the Fictions of Security and Development

The fact of vulnerability can evoke a range of possible responses. Most spectacularly, the security state – girded by the technologies of mechanized surveillance and warfare – reproduces the fantasy that we might transcend our collective vulnerability. "Securitization" calls for walling off borders, launching military interventions, and locking down those deemed to be security threats, whether they are citizens in US prisons, "unlawful enemy combatants" in military detention centers such as the one at Guantánamo Bay, Cuba, or undocumented migrants held by Immigration and Customs Enforcement (ICE), including the children about whom Luiselli writes, and entire families who are being detained along the US southern border at the time this chapter is being written. As feminist critic Inderpal Grewal argues: "Security has become the rationale for militarized cultures of surveillance and protection that lead to insecurities, threats and fears, which work at material, affective and embodied levels."[13] As Grewal further explains, "security" has been used (not unlike "terrorism") to refer to "heterogeneous and unstable state, social, and economic powers," blurring "distinctions between individuals, corporations, the state, public entities, and private entities": "[Security] can also refer to the demands made on the state for safety and protection that it cannot ensure, and which it often refuses to ensure. Security works affectively through the promise of the safety of home and of nation, but also enables the powers of protection claimed by patriarchies, fraternities, and nationalisms that work through violence."[14]

How in turn, then, does vulnerability operate in the arena of literary narrative and prose fiction? Social theorist Judith Butler has posited that our vulnerability extends to language itself, to the speech acts and, I would add, the narrative forms, to which we are subject and that provide the names by which we come to recognize (or misrecognize) ourselves as social agents and political subjects:

> [W]ho we are, even our ability to survive, depends on the language that sustains us .... We do not only act through the speech act; speech acts also act on us. There is a distinct performative effect of having been named as this gender or another gender, as part of one nationality or a minority, or to find out that how you are regarded in any of these respects is summed up by a name that you yourself did not know and never chose.[15]

Our susceptibility to "name-calling" activates the promise of security that language enacts or, conversely, withholds.

Vulnerability need not, however, call for only exceptionalist fantasies that affix us to names and identities through vertical arrangements of police power and forceful securitization. Instead, vulnerability might also give rise to nascent forms of solidarity that build upon the crucial interdependency of human life. Indeed, many of the social movements that have emerged in the United States since 2001 – the Occupy Movement and Black Lives Matter have been two of the most exemplary and coalitional in their perspectives – have embraced such a broad-based vision of collective change. The dynamic character of language, which shapes us as speaking and acting beings, also provides the very grounds for the enterprises of literary creation, translation, and interpretation. The iteration of new or alternate names, narratives, and forms hence generates other imaginative possibilities for human relations of protection, care, security, and solidarity.

In particular, narratives of fragmentation and dissolution by contemporary writers counter the stranglehold that those of progressive and linear development, especially the bildungsroman, have had in constructing the ideal subject of liberal humanism. The "novel of education" or "formation," has been typically regarded as a nineteenth-century phenomenon that was upended by modernist movements in art and literature by the beginning of the twentieth century, at least amongst Anglo-American and European writers. Yet the genre continued to prove essential throughout the twentieth century in the literature of postcolonial, multiethnic, and diasporic writers.[16] As those groups who had long been relegated to an "imaginary waiting room of history" – because they were considered undeveloped, uncivilized, and thus unable to govern themselves – were newly offered the prospect of integration into liberal personhood, such authors adopted the bildungsroman to probe the possibilities, challenges, and limits that notions of the "universal human" posed for embodying their own histories, experiences, and aspirations.[17]

As literary theorist Franco Moretti observed at the beginning of the twenty-first century about the genre: "wide cultural formation, professional mobility, full social freedom – for a long time, the west European middle-class man held a virtual monopoly on these, which made him a sort of structural *sine qua non* of the genre."[18] Indeed, Moretti describes the generic function of the bildungsroman, in its European heyday during the previous *fin de siécle*, as a transition and *compromise* between two distinct regimes, the new bourgeois class (whose emergence was rooted in the rise of capitalism, the democratic revolutions of the eighteenth century, and new modes of liberal humanism) and the gentry of the older European aristocracy. Novels of education and development, he avers, "were not trying to shape consistent worldviews, but rather *compromises among distinct worldviews.*"[19] The later introduction of racialized and formerly colonized subjects into that compromise had the effect of troubling the uneasy peace the bildungsroman achieves (to the extent that it does): "Whereas traditional novels of formation figure society as a normative construct, the novel of *trans*formation portrays a dialogical process. The hero no longer merely changes with the world; instead, the world also changes with and through him."[20]

Conventional approaches in literary studies have moreover tended to cast multiethnic American literatures (often against what were regarded as more theoretically sophisticated postcolonial literatures, as well as more mainline contemporary fiction by white writers) in the late twentieth century as the last stronghold of a "peripheral realism" that had waned dramatically elsewhere. Under closer investigation, though, such distinctions hardly seem to hold up, as these American writers have approached the novel of development through experimental modernist and postmodernist aesthetic strategies, on the one hand, and as the meaning and aims of "realism" as a literary practice have also been conceptually rethought, on the other. If realism is defined by its attempt to capture a "totality" through the positivist rendering of "reality," literary critics have observed that "a realistic mode of representation is not meant to reproduce reality but to interrupt the quasi-natural perception of reality as a mere given" by spotlighting "the interrelations and interactions between disparate phenomena."[21] In such a case, even while literature maintains its "referential function," it nonetheless requires "extraordinarily flexible and active ways of reconceiving and transcoding social referents."[22]

Returning to the origins of the bildungsroman, literary critic Tobias Boes has remarked upon how, despite a close relationship between the novel in its earliest instantiations and the practices of history writing, a conceptual shift in the eighteenth century came to distinguish the two as separate narrative forms. Where realism "aims for the typical and the true ... in an age in which history is regarded as merely an accumulation of individual stories" as it was in the early 1800s, "a novel that transcends contingencies in order to present the general laws uniting everyday experiences provides a valuable skeleton key to historical meaning."[23] However, over the course of the eighteenth century, philosophers came to see history as itself having, and being, a story, thus giving rise to a distinction between the individual subject and the subject of history – identified with the nation – even as the individual and the nation were to share a corresponding plot of "development." Together, the individual protagonist of the bildungsroman and the national protagonist of history journey from fragmented existence into an integrated self, the former serving as synecdoche and analogue for the latter through the chronotope of "national-historical time."[24] But, as Boes observes, the bildungsroman also requires the arrest of the forward movement of history through a "happy resolution." Drawing on the long tradition of utopian narratives, but plotting the arrival at the good or ideal destination in temporal rather than spatial terms, the bildungsroman depicts a protagonist who "at the endpoint of his or her development, eventually crosses an ontological barrier where historical contingency yields to something altogether different and the narrated subject makes way for a narrating subject."[25] The nineteenth-century bildungsroman enacts historical progress but also always brings "a sense of closure and a logical endpoint" to the "forward motion" of history.[26]

Boes's account sheds a helpful light on the "transnational" or "diasporic" turn in American literature that by the beginning of the new millennium made visible the fissures and contradictions in a narrative of development meant to cement the individual citizen in a unity with the American nation as it moved toward its own "end of history." Indeed, as the subjects of literature and literary analysis migrated across the borders of nations and national literatures – usually under the very conditions of precarity I describe above – the construction of such borders themselves became a central object of the literary imagination and critical inquiry. Many contemporary American writers have hence morphed the bildungsroman (when not forgoing it altogether for other narrative forms and genres) and its formulations regarding the development and arrival of the autonomous, integrated self in order to give expression to a precarious present that remains very much saturated by contingency. A considerable range of twenty-first-century fiction has taken up this effort; these include works such as Paul Beatty's *The Sellout* (2015), Junot Díaz's *The Brief Wondrous Life of Oscar Wao* (2007), Zinzi Clemmons's *What We Lose* (2017), Jennifer Egan's *A Visit from the Goon Squad* (2011), Louise Erdrich's *Round House* (2012), Tayari Jones's *An American Marriage* (2018), Jhumpa Lahiri's *Unaccustomed*

Earth (2008), Viet Thanh Nguyen's *The Refugees* (2017), Ruth Ozeki's *A Tale for the Time Being* (2013), Danzy Senna's *New People* (2017), Angie Thomas's *The Hate You Give* (2017), Amy Waldman's *The Submission* (2011), Jesmyn Ward's *Sing, Unburied, Sing* (2017), Colson Whitehead's *The Underground Railroad* (2016), and numerous others. Representing contemporary conditions of vulnerability, insecurity, and precariousness does not then necessarily entail pitting "realism" against experimental forms, so much as querying how our expectations of reality are themselves *fantasies of narrative structure*. In their fragmented fictions of suspense and interruption, short stories and novels such as the one to which I turn next, Celeste Ng's *Everything I Never Told You* (2014), articulate the vulnerabilities and insecurities that pervade and characterize the twenty-first century.

The Lost Child

Celeste Ng's debut novel, *Everything I Never Told You*, begins with the startling declaration: "Lydia is dead. But they don't know this yet."[27] This certain eventuality – by the end of the first chapter, the police have located Lydia's drowned body in a town lake – thus opens what can be described as a novel of suspense, organized around the "missing child," a phenomenon that has become in the twenty-first century an almost histrionic obsession for American media and commercial culture. The stories of missing girls like JonBenet Ramsey and Elizabeth Smart and the advent of policing mechanisms such as Amber Alerts and sex offender registries speak to a deep anxiety that the white American child might be clutched from the safety of the nuclear family home by the lone predatory sexual deviant. Ng's novel, however, insists on construing the missing child through quite different forms and terms. If the loss of the child seems almost always to signify the dissolution of the future, this literature compels us to think the conditions of precarity that convert vulnerable subjects, a characteristic that all human beings share, into missing persons, devastated hopes, and grieved lives.

The stories of the mixed-race Lee family – the "they" of the novel's second sentence, which also includes Lydia's Chinese American father James, her white mother Marilyn, as well as her older brother Nath and younger sister Hannah – follow upon her funeral and the reckoning with the past that her death demands. Tellingly, one of the first extended descriptions that Ng offers involves the autopsy report, which James reads later the same day that Lydia is buried:

> He learns the color and size of each of her organs, the weight of her brain. That a white foam had bubbled up through her trachea and covered her nostrils and

mouth like a lace handkerchief. That her alveoli held a thin layer of silt as fine as sugar. That her lungs had marbled dark red and yellow-gray as they starved for air; that like dough, they took the impression of a fingertip; that when they were sectioned with a scalpel, water flowed out. That in her stomach were snippets of lake-bottom weeds, sand, and six ounces of lake water she'd swallowed as she sank. That the right side of her heart had swollen, as if it had had too much to hold. That from floating head down in the water, the skin of her head and neck had reddened to her shoulders. That due to the low temperature of the water, she had not yet decomposed, but that the skin of her fingertips was just beginning to peel off, like a glove .... He can't imagine telling Marilyn that these things could happen to a body they loved.   (70)

The detailed account provides a ground zero for the ontological condition of exposedness to their environment that constitutes all human bodies. But in the forensic portrait, the vulnerable body becomes unrecognizable as human, much less as a familiar to her loved ones. Dissolving the singular body into sectioned data points, it can offer only very general, biotic clues as to who Lydia was.

To locate Lydia as a human *person* then entails telling the story of her place in her family. But that narrative is as much about silences, isolation, and fragmentation ("everything I never told you") as it is about secure social bonds. In the process of its telling, it hence devises new, distinctive relations between its subjects. The novel must bring to the surface gendered and racial arrangements of labor, care, love, and power to make sense of Lydia's life and death. James's repression of memories of racism impedes any empathy he might offer when Nath undergoes similar experiences. At the same time, after her mother's solitary death, Marilyn despairs about the medical education and career as a physician that she decided not to pursue, in order to raise her children and tend to their home; she briefly abandons James and her children in an attempt to resume her undergraduate schooling. In the spell of Marilyn's absence, the family's life is suffused with uncertainty, depicted poignantly through a young Nath and Lydia's confusion by the "mother-shaped hole" (135) in their world, but also in James's misunderstanding of what Marilyn means in the recovered shreds of an unfinished letter of explanation, "*I always had one kind of life in mind and things have turned out very differently*" (125). He assumes that it is their interracial marriage that Marilyn regrets, as he is unable to fathom her longing to have excelled in a career of her own. In any case, upon discovering that she is pregnant with her third child (Hannah, who eventually becomes a quiet observer of her family that mostly overlooks the youngest child's presence altogether), Marilyn returns to her family and begins to project her own ambitions for independence onto Lydia, which in turn fixes everyone else's attention upon the seemingly favorite middle child.

As a suspenseful narrative, the stories hinge upon the central question of how and why Lydia drowned, who was to blame, and the reasons for her death. Here too, all the characters are misguided in their speculations. Marilyn is convinced that a stranger had abducted Lydia; Nath that a neighbor boy with whom Lydia had grown friendly (and who unbeknownst to Nath, has long harbored feelings for him) had seduced her and was somehow responsible; the police that Lydia's "*strangeness*" – as an "Oriental girl" and a loner at school – had led her to commit suicide (112). James is certain that the "mistake was much earlier, deeper, more fundamental," rooted in his interracial romance and marriage: "A million little chances to change the future. They should never have married. He should never have touched [Marilyn] . . .. He sees with utter clarity: none of this was supposed to happen. A mistake" (203). But Lydia's own reflections, and her determination to become her own person, just prior to her death, reveal it ultimately to be an accidental drowning: "From now on, she will do what *she* wants. Feet planted firmly on nothing, Lydia – so long enthralled by the dreams of others – could not yet imagine what that might be, but suddenly the universe glittered with possibilities. She will change everything" (275).

Lydia's parents place their hopes for progressive change in her. James hopes that she will escape from the subtle but unmistakable anti-Asian racism he feels pervade every day of his life. Marilyn aspires for Lydia to achieve as a professional and intellectual all that motherhood made impossible for the older woman. But Lydia's death poignantly stages the impossibility of fully controlling the direction in which our individual choices and actions lead us, as well how they will affect those others upon whom our lives are interdependent. Even as Ng's third-person narrator begins Lydia's story with those of her parents, she acknowledges that this particular frame could stretch much further back, as James and Marilyn's stories depend upon those of their parents, and so on:

> How had it begun? Like everything: with mothers and fathers. Because of Lydia's mother and father, because of her mother's and father's mothers and fathers. Because long ago, her mother had gone missing, and her father had brought her home. Because more than anything, her mother had wanted to stand out; because more than anything, her father had wanted to blend in. Because those things had been impossible. (24)

In this series of sentence fragments, the conjunction "because" does not join two parts of a sentence in a relation of strict causality, but rather serves to link the different sentences contingently, but concretely, to one another.

If Lydia feels "how hard it would be to inherit their parents' dreams. How suffocating to be so loved," it is because she inherits not only their own personal hopes but the impersonal, and often imperceptible, structures of difference and power that have freighted those dreams. Lydia thus at the same time grasps the intractable uncertainties that constitute family life: "Ever since that summer without her mother, their family had felt *precarious*, as if they were teetering on a cliff. Before that she hadn't realized how fragile happiness was, how if you were careless, you could knock it over and shatter it" (272–273, emphasis added). In elaborating the bonds between her characters, Ng maps what one literary critic has described as a "field of anticipation" that "addresses itself to an imminent yet indefinite future – a fragile future – which may arrive quite suddenly or be delayed, which may emerge from constructive or destructive processes, which may be reversible or irreversible."[28] From this perspective, human existence is essentially defined by its susceptibility to gradual or sudden change, change that is always a possibility, if not necessarily a given.

Writing Intimacies

What should we make of a novel like Ng's, authored in the twenty-first century but set in 1977, thus as much concerned with looking back as forward to the future? And furthermore, what might a narrative focused on the very singular troubles of a family caused by rather particular factors and circumstances tell us about structural conditions of vulnerability and precarity in the new millennium? In order to make connections across different decades, across the divisions of fiction and "reality," and across the specific and the general, we should read "suspense" as operating in multiple keys. *Everything I Never Told You* is, as I have been explaining, of course suspenseful in the sense of a mystery; Lydia's death spurs its drive toward uncovering what happened, how and why she drowned, and "who done it," that opens out onto an ever-receding horizon of other subjects and stories. But the death also interrupts a liberal narrative that centers on middle-class families in "middle America" (e.g., the novel is set in Middlewood, Ohio) in which all sorts of subjects (women, racial minorities, immigrants, queer folks) are supposed to progressively integrate as full and equal citizens, assimilating to the norms of a possessive, autonomous individualism. By unearthing how the racial and gendered histories that organize labor, family, and security persist as embodied social difference, the novel questions a liberal faith that the present is safely cordoned off from the past, and that the future portends a predictable extension of the current social order.

Indeed, the decade that passes between Marilyn's disappearance and Lydia's death is marked as one of turbulence and transformation, as both

246

social movements in the United States and the exigencies of the late Cold War and decolonization across the planet gave way to a new national and international order:

> Years passed. Boys went to war; men went to the moon; presidents arrived and resigned and departed. All over the country, in Detroit and Washington and New York, crowds roiled in the streets, angry about everything. All over the world, nations splintered and cracked: North Vietnam, East Berlin, Bangladesh. Everywhere things came undone.[29]

In other words, the 1970s marks the beginning of the end of postwar liberalism's promise of progressive integration at home and around the world. The break in the expected social order hence calls attention to another meaning of "suspense." Here suspension connotes stoppage or withdrawal, where conventional forms of authority are challenged, and states begin dramatically scaling back their provisions of rights, protections, and resources for their citizenries under the pressures of global economic restructuring.

To be clear, *Everything I Never Told You* does not treat this aspect of suspense directly. In fact, the political turmoil and social unrest of the period is only ever indexed as a backdrop that never seems to affect the Lees directly. But, as Butler contends, the routinized disavowal of vulnerability in liberal philosophy and neoliberal political economies conceives a masculinist national body that is expected to weather precarity unscathed, even as it is the subject of state securitization. Against the fantasy of invulnerability, Ng's novel situates Lydia's vulnerable body in the world by treating it at the scale of the intimate and the ephemeral. As feminist scholars have elaborated, "intimacies" offer a heuristic for examining the "distribution of sentiment and desire" through which categories of difference and identity congeal and are made sensible in quotidian life.[30] Interactions in the "domain of the intimate," for example, "who slept with whom, who lived with whom, and who acknowledged doing so; who was recognized as one's child and by whom one was nursed, reared, educated; who was one's spiritual light and by whom one was abandoned" – produce the very racial and national boundaries that organize national states and colonial administrations, and through which these larger-scale structures exercise their power.[31] In Ng's novel, the strictures of heteronormative, bourgeois family life fail to protect and foster the child's ascendance into autonomous, fully self-realized personhood. In order to grapple with that failure, the family drama must dredge up all that is forgotten, excluded, or left unsaid, and by extension, what has been forgotten, excluded, and left unsaid in the constitution of the securely free subject of modernity.

If the figure of the child in American culture represents both vulnerability in need of protection and the face of the future the nation desires, Ng's meditation on the lost child insists that the ideological frames, narrative forms, and conceptions of the body that we bring to bear will determine *which* children's lives and *which* futures will be cherished and which will be cut short or discarded. It is this point Luiselli takes to heart for the children about whom she writes in *Tell Me How It Ends*. The questionnaire Luiselli administers renders children's lives according to the very narrow and hardened distinctions of citizen, alien, asylum seeker, authorized resident, and undocumented migrant. Luiselli, in contrast, not only translates from Spanish to English, and from the language of the child to that of the law. She recovers intimate dimensions of embodied subjectivity through the devices of the literary imagination. Indeed, literary techniques prove crucial – for example, she must fictionalize Manu's name – to represent children whose lives remain precarious even upon their arrival.

"Children," Luiselli writes, "do what their stomachs tell them to do. They don't think twice when they have to chase a moving train. They run along with it, reach for any metal bar at hand, and fling themselves toward whichever half-stable surface they may land on …. They have an instinct for survival, perhaps, that allows them to endure almost anything."[32] The reconstructed narratives of children's lives mean to provide them a provisional shelter, while also striving to do justice to the tenacious, instinctual will that propels them across all sorts of borders and into the future. Serving as a bridge between her own daughter, her readers, and the migrant children, unable to meet with any certainty the imperative to "tell me how it ends," Luiselli nevertheless insists that there *are* modes by which to tell the story of the child in flight. The essential task of contemporary American fiction is to supply both the literary means and the critical literacy by which to perceive the vulnerable human in and against the conditions of interruption, isolation, suspense, and precarity that produce her.

NOTES

1 Valeria Luiselli, *Tell Me How It Ends: An Essay in Forty Questions* (Minneapolis: Coffee House Press, 2017), 70.
2 Ibid., 106. Published just after the 2016 presidential election and in the face of the sweeping racist and anti-immigrant sentiments that fueled its outcome (the "dire and volatile" times to which Luiselli refers), *Tell Me How It Ends* was described by the *Texas Observer* as "the First Must-Read Book of the Trump Era." See "Mexican Writer Valeria Luiselli on Child Refugees & Rethinking the Language Around Immigration," *Democracy Now*, April 18, 2017, www.democracynow .org/2017/4/18/mexican_writer_valeria_luiselli_on_child.
3 "We are the 99%" was the slogan coined and disseminated by Occupy Wall Street, a progressive protest movement that arose in 2011 to draw attention to worldwide economic inequality.

4 Lee Gutkind, "Creative Nonfiction: A Movement, Not a Moment," *Creative Nonfiction* no. 29 (2006): 9, 18.

5 Gay Talese quoted in Gutkind, "Creative Nonfiction," 6.

6 Because the US government refuses to tally civilian casualties with any accuracy (if at all), it has been left to news organizations and NGOs to provide estimates. While the numbers are certainly disputed, it is clear that the loss of life – as well as infrastructure, livelihoods, and property – has been immense.

7 Jasbir K. Puar, *Terrorist Assemblages: Homonationalism in Queer Times* (Durham: Duke University Press, 2007), 7.

8 Martha Albertson Fineman, "The Vulnerable Subject: Anchoring Equality in the Human Condition," *Yale Journal of Law and Feminism* 20, no. 1 (2008), 8.

9 Judith Butler, "Rethinking Vulnerability and Resistance," in *Vulnerability in Resistance*, edited by Judith Butler, Leticia Sabsay, and Zeynep Gambetti (Durham: Duke University Press, 2016), 12.

10 Dylan Rodriguez, "The Meaning of 'Disaster' under the Dominance of White Life," in *What Lies Beneath: Katrina, Race, and the State of the Nation*, edited by South End Press Collective (Cambridge, MA: South End Press, 2007), 136.

11 Isabell Lorey, "Governmental Precaritization," trans. Aileen Dereig, *Inventions*, January, 2011, http://transversal.at/transversal/0811/lorey/en.

12 Martha Albertson Fineman, "Equality, Autonomy, and the Vulnerable Subject in Law and Politics," in *Vulnerability: Reflections on a New Ethical Foundation for Law and Politics*, edited by Martha Albertson Fineman and Anna Grear (Abingdon: Routledge, 2013), 21–22.

13 Inderpal Grewal, *Saving the Security State: Exceptional Citizens in Twenty-First-Century America* (Durham: Duke University Press, 2017), 2.

14 Ibid., 12–13.

15 Butler, "Rethinking Vulnerability and Resistance," 16–17.

16 Tobias Boes, "Modernist Studies and *Bildungsroman*: A Historical Survey of Critical Trends," *Literature Compass* 3, no. 2 (2006): 239.

17 Dipesh Chakrabarty, *Provincializing Europe: Postcolonial Thought and Historical Difference* (Princeton, Princeton University Press, 2000; 2008), 8.

18 Franco Moretti, *The Way of the World: The Bildungsroman in European Culture*, trans. Albert Sbragia, (London: Verso, 1987; 2000), ix.

19 Ibid., xii.

20 Boes, "Modernist Studies and the Bildungsroman," 240.

21 Jed Esty and Colleen Lye, "Peripheral Realisms Now," *Modern Language Quarterly* 73, no. 3 (September 2012): 277. See also Ulka Anjaria, "Twenty-First-Century Realism," in *Oxford Research Encyclopedia of Literature*, edited by Paula Rabinowitz (Oxford: Oxford University Press, 2016), n.p.

22 Esty and Lye, "Peripheral Realisms Now," 278.

23 Tobias Boes, "Apprenticeship of the Novel: The *Bildungsroman* and the Invention of History, ca. 1770–1820," *Comparative Literature Studies* 45, no. 3 (2008): 272.

24 Ibid., 276–277, 278.

25 Ibid., 282.

26 Ibid.

27 Celeste Ng, *Everything I Never Told You* (New York: Penguin, 2014), 3.

28 Mark Botha, "Precarious Present, Fragile Futures: Literature and Uncertainty in the Early Twenty-First Century," *English Academy Review* 31, no. 2 (2014), 3.
29 Ng, *Everything I Never Told You*, 158.
30 Ann Laura Stoler, "Intimidations of Empire: Predicaments of the Tactile and Unseen," in *Haunted by Empire: Geographies of Intimacy in North American History*, edited by Ann Laura Stoler (Durham: Duke University Press, 2006), 2.
31 Ibid., 3.
32 Luiselli, *Tell Me How It Ends*, 19–20.

13

DENNIS CHILDS

Immobility

At the outset of his 2016 Grammy Awards show performance, Compton-raised hip-hop artist Kendrick Lamar walks toward center stage dressed in a blue prison uniform, striding in lockstep formation with four other Black men, chained to one another by the wrists and ankles. The five members of this modernized chain gang are surrounded by prison cages filled with more Black men, including members of the onstage band supplying sonic back-drop for Lamar's live medley of "The Blacker the Berry," "Alright," and "Untitled 3." Taking as its thematic cue the unspeakable circumstances of Black teenager Trayvon Martin's 2012 murder at the hands of a White vigilante – and the subsequent court verdict that exonerated the youth's killer under the time-honored racist legal guise of *justifiable homicide* – "Untitled 3" represents a gothic rendering of the ways in which police/vigilante terrorism, racial profiling, and incarceration function as quotidian realities of Black life and death under contemporary US empire. However, while expressing the degree to which he experiences Martin's murder as personally endured physical and psychic injury, Lamar also underlines how the horrors of the twenty-first-century present are intimately bound to the chattel slavery past:

> On February 26th I lost my life too / It's like I'm here in a dream / Nightmare, hear screams recorded …. That was me yelling for help when he drowned in his own blood …. And for our community do you know what this does? / Add to a trail of hatred / 2012 was taped for the world to see / Set us back 400 years / This is modern slavery.[1]

Lamar's "Untitled 3" expresses in sonic form what Hortense Spillers describes as the "timeless," or gallingly repetitive, nature of white suprema-cist state violence in the United States.[2] As such, it deploys a critically important trope within the narrative and sonic tradition of hip-hop from its inception in the late 1970s – a moment that not coincidentally also represented the birth of today's prison industrial complex (PIC).[3] Indeed, since the moment of hip-hop's inception, many of those who comprise what is often described as the "hip-hop generation" have in fact been an *incarcerated generation*, subject to the "War on Drugs," mandatory minimum sentences, the criminalization of youth as adults, the treatment of youth gangs as domestic "terrorist" organizations, the school to prison pipeline, racial profiling, and police/vigilante terrorism. For Lamar, however, Trayvon Martin's murder is symbolic not only of the unlivable predicaments faced by Black communities under the modern US police/prison state, but how these realities of racial state terror are inseparable from patterns of social death, dispossession, and familial rupture that constituted the organizing logics of the Middle Passage and plantation slavery. Indeed, his work, and others I discuss in this chapter, represents a collective response to the horrors that have prevailed against Black people and other historically repressed communities since the very legislative act that was to have resulted in collective emancipation – the Thirteenth Amendment to the US Constitution (1865) – began to reenslave Black people under the pretext of penal sanction, or, in the words of the amendment itself, as "punishment for a crime."[4]

That Lamar performs his Grammy Awards medley in a prison uniform, surrounded by cages, represents how the almost daily murder of Black men, women, and children by police and vigilantes on the streets of the United States is joined by the machine-like operation of another kind of "murder" – yet on a much larger scale. That is, his sonic prison narrative expresses what I have described elsewhere as the collectivized situation of "living death"[5] faced by Black, Brown, Indigenous, migrant, Muslim, and poor captives under today's updated system of slavery – the PIC – a system that currently encages over 2.3 million human beings. This number includes an alarmingly high number of Black and Latina women; a large number of trans- and gender nonconforming persons of color; those branded as "enemy combatant" in zones of US imperialist warfare; an ever-increasing number of migrant subjects hailing from points south of the US border with Mexico; and, as of 2009, an astounding one out of every nine Black men between the ages of twenty and thirty.[6]

In fact, while not the centerpiece of this essay, the connection between the imprisonment of Black, Brown, Indigenous, and poor "citizen" subjects and the encagement and deportation of migrants from countries such as Mexico, Honduras, El Salvador, Haiti, and Guatemala represents a critically important repressive nexus of US empire – one that is emblematic of how the PIC operates as a system of warehousing collectivities marked as disposable under a globalized, neoliberal, and neocolonial order.[7] Novelists such as Reyna Grande (*Across a Hundred Mountains*, 2006) and Ann Jaramillo

(*La Línea: A Novel*, 2016) have begun to chronicle in narrative form the horrific lived experiences of familial severance, economic devastation, and legalized terror endured by migrants to/in the United States – situations of racial capitalist precarity that connect the Obama/Trump-era war against undocumented peoples directly to the daily injustices faced by Black "citizens" as expressed so poignantly in Lamar's performance.[8]

"The Past Is Present": Anti-Carceral Hip-Hop and Black Neoabolitionist Narratives

As a lyrical expression of the centrality of anti-Blackness to the US carceral state – and how present-day manifestations of legal terror are intimately connected to ostensibly "past" moments of US white supremacist history – "Untitled 3" and other narratives of police terrorism and racialized incarceration found within the hip-hop lyrics (and sound) of those such as Dead Prez, Jayo Felony, Askari X, KRS-One, Main Source, Sister Souljah, and Public Enemy stand in conversation with a long tradition of Black prison/slave narratives stretching back to the putative abolition of America's original system of "mass incarceration" better known as chattel slavery. This narrative and sonic tradition is inclusive of conventionally "literary" works of fiction by writers such as Chester Himes (*Yesterday Will Make You Cry*, 1999 [1952]), Donald Goines (*White Man's Law, Black Man's Injustice*, 1973), James Baldwin (*If Beale Street Could Talk*, 1974), Toni Morrison (*Beloved*, 1987), and Monifa Love (*Freedom in the Dismal*, 1998); the autobiographies and prison letters of Black radical political prisoners such as Angelo Herndon (*Let Me Live*, 1937), George Jackson (*Soledad Brother*, 1970), Angela Davis (*Autobiography*, 1974), and Assata Shakur (*Autobiography*, 1981); along with a seemingly limitless assortment of sonic narrations of neoslavery found within prison blues, work songs, and field hollers beginning in the late nineteenth to early twentieth century. Central to each of these examples of what, in *Slaves of the State*, I describe as Black *narratives of neoslavery*,[9] is an adamant refusal of models of history that describe slavery as a relic of an embalmed, or historically eclipsed "past": for Jackson, Shakur, Davis, and the many Black radical hip-hop voices that have followed, "law and order" has represented a kind of time-warping instrument whereby forms of state-sanctioned terror, kidnapping, and incarceration that have laid siege to Black communities since the birth of the PIC in the late 1970s have borne striking resemblance to putatively bygone horrors of chattel slavery and Jim Crow apartheid.

In framing this essay with a discussion of the centrality of hip-hop as what can be called a "long twenty-first century" (late 1970s to the present) narrative modality essential to our engagement with police terrorism and incarceration, I am intentionally beginning with what for some readers may appear to be a curious provocation. However, by opening with a work such as "Untitled 3" which some scholars might deem *unliterary* – and most definitely would not be considered within the pantheon of "great works" that would normally merit inclusion within an anthology of US literature – I am arguing that no serious cultural-historical encounter with social atrocities such as the PIC can operate with a normative conception of the literary.

In what follows, I organize my discussion of narratives of racial capitalist state violence through analyses of key examples of anti-carceral hip-hop to signal how this aesthetic practice represents the quintessential storytelling method for those most commonly targeted for police killing and imprisonment. In the same manner that prison blues, chain gang songs, and work songs of the immediate postbellum period bore the most visceral aesthetic imprints of slavery's legal rebirth, sonically rendered oral literature – or *orature*[10] – produced in segregated, "post-industrial" cities such as New York, Los Angeles, Oakland, Chicago, Philadelphia, Detroit, and Atlanta from the late 1970s to the present, has functioned as a means by which hyper-policed, dispossessed, and incarcerated Black and Brown youth have developed counter-narratives to hegemonic discourses of racialized criminalization and social demonization.[11] Insofar as they represent a collective reframing of "law and order" as state criminality, the works I discuss in this chapter take part in what Kenyan writer and theorist Ngugi wa Thiong'o describes as the important communal role of orature for oppressed peoples throughout Africa and the rest of the colonized world: "The oral aesthetic has social functions arising from its intimate relationship and involvement with society .... In the anti-colonial resistance, song and dance played a pivotal role in recruiting, rallying, and coding the social vision. The colonial authorities feared orature more than they did literature."[12]

Ngugi's conceptualization of politically resistive (and fear-inducing) orature can be seen as a contemporary rephrasing of what Black radical anticolonial theorist Frantz Fanon described as a "literature of combat"[13] – and this is exactly what rap duo Dead Prez's debut album, *Let's Get Free*, represented upon its release in February of 2000. Created at a moment when the corporate seizure of hip-hop had rendered the sonic orature of "conscious" rap artists such as Public Enemy, Paris, Queen Latifah, Poor Righteous Teachers, Medusa, KRS-One, Askari X, Goodie Mob, and the Coup, ostensibly passé – *Lets Get Free* suggests how powerful vestiges of social justice consciousness survived in the wake of a well-organized corporate co-option process that profited from the medium's misogynist, homophobic, and hyper-consumerist tendencies. Specifically, Mutulu "M-1" Olugbala and Khnum Muata "stic.man" Ibomu present a series of songs that amount to a Black radical concept album, whereby the constant frame of reference for their poetics of combat is the real-world system of racial capitalist *domestic warfare*,[14] which, by the time of the album's release, had landed approximately two million people in US prisons, jails, and immigrant detention centers. As in the case of Kendrick Lamar's above-referenced work, Dead Prez define the system of "law and order" as a modernized replay of putatively "past" formations of white supremacist state violence – namely, chattel slavery. In the album's first song, for instance, a piece entitled "I'm a African," M-1 (whose name clearly signifies the militant propensities of the group's work) begins the second verse by claiming the positionality of a twenty-first-century fugitive rebel slave: "My life is like *Roots* / It's a true story … I'm a runaway slave watching the North Star / shackles on my forearm, runnin' with a gun in my palm / I'm a African, never was an African American." stic.man reiterates this disavowal of civil belonging for Black people in the next verse: "I'm not an American … Democrat or Republican …. My mama worked all her life and still strugglin' / I blame it on the government."[15]

While functioning as a clear assertion of the duo's connection to the political thought of socialist thinker and organizer Omali Ishatela – whose voice opens the album in the form of a recorded speech – "I'm a African," and subsequent tracks appearing on *Lets Get Free*, present a well-studied Black radical citational practice connecting the work of Dead Prez to a broad cross-section of Black leftist, nationalist, and Pan-Africanist organizations and political philosophies. Interspersed between many of the album's tracks are recorded speeches and citations of important revolutionary thinkers, including Fred Hampton, Assata Shakur, Steven Biko, and Malcolm X – the last of whom spoke in words strikingly similar to those of M-1 and stic. man in his "Ballot or the Bullet" speech in 1964: "I'm not a Republican, nor a Democrat, nor an American – and got sense enough to know it. I'm one of the 22 million Black victims of the Democrats, one of the 22 million Black victims of the Republicans, and one of the 22 million Black victims of Americanism."[16]

Like Malcolm X in his Detroit speech, Dead Prez consider the experience of imprisonment to be the clearest indication of the collectively unfree (and thereby un-"American") status of Black people in the United States. This point is made repeatedly throughout the album, and most explicitly in "Police State," "Behind Enemy Lines," and "We Want Freedom," the first of which features a "hook" (or chorus) spelling out the uniquely targeted positionality of Black men under the PIC: "The average Black male / spends a third of his life in a jail cell / 'cuz the world is controlled by the white male / and the people don't never get justice ... can you relate? / We're livin' in a police state." Here the fact that Black men in the United States represent one of the most incarcerated collectivities in the world is presented not only as a problem of racial and class violence, but one that can be described in terms of gendered, racial violence – *genocidal engenderment*.[17] However, in "Behind Enemy Lines" and "We Want Freedom," Dead Prez articulate their understanding of the degree to which Black women and girls also represent main targets of the US program of internal warfare via imprisonment.[18] They frame this horrifying reality by expressing the ways in which the incarceration of their male partners and family members contributes to the dispossessive aspects of social incarceration for Black women and children in the "free world," and by referencing the direct targeting of Black women for captivity in the prison world.

M-1 reveals how the harmful effects of racialized penal law are experienced by families outside the official prison. In M-1's piece specifically, he connects the modern imprisonment of Chicago-based activist Fred Hampton Jr., to the murder of his father, Black Panther leader, Fred Hampton Sr., by the FBI and Chicago Police Department as a part of J. Edgar Hoover's notorious domestic warfare campaign known as COINTELPRO (Counterintelligence Program). Then, he suggests how the burden of racialized state terror is inherited by Fred Hampton's granddaughter who must contend with the protracted absence of her own imprisoned father – a Black radical activist who was indeed encaged upon the composition of *Let's Get Free*. This brings to mind "Trap Doors" (2011), a poetic rendering of state-inflicted familial severance offered by Samiya Hameeda Abdullah, aka "Goldii," the recently deceased daughter of Black radical political prisoner, and former Black Panther Party leader, Mumia Abu-Jamal, in which she speaks directly to how the prolonged encagement of her father represents a predicament of living death for her entire family and Black people in general.[19]

In direct conversation with Mumia, Assata, Goldii, and countless (often nameless) others, Dead Prez's portrayal of intergenerational harm experienced by the Hampton family in "Behind Enemy Lines" exposes the modern carceral state's redeployment of the chattel slavery management technique of *natal alienation* – the systematic severance of the slave from familial and communal bonds.[20] This dynamic is further illuminated during a skit that appears in the middle of Dead Prez's piece wherein a male prisoner makes a collect call to his partner outside of the prison walls to ask her to put money in his commissary account. The melancholic voice on the other end of the phone can only say "Where are you? ... Have you been alright? ... I feel lonely, lonely, lonely ..." As Cheryl Keyes points out in her comparison of Black women hip-hop artists and classic blues singers, this aspect of natal alienation has also been expressed in the work of Black women rappers such as Eve Jihan Jeffers-Cooper (aka "Eve"), who in her song, "Gotta Man," writes of a woman's separation from an encaged lover, "wounds from your war ... I'm the getaway driver so my n***a can escape ... [he's] spending nights in jail / Drawing hearts on the wall with our names around the cell."[21]

However, whereas "Gotta Man," and "Behind Enemy Lines" portray the devastating effects of Black male imprisonment on women and children outside of the prison, Dead Prez's "We Want Freedom," considers the horrific commonality of Black women's captivity *inside* carceral spaces. After reasserting the connection between imprisonment and chattel slavery – "Yo, this world is so cold, I think about my ancestors / being sold" – stic. man describes conditions inside the modernized slave plantation: "Locked up you get three hot meals and one cot / Then you sit and rot, never even got a fair shot / That's where a whole lot of n****s end up / My man's moms even got sent up / tryin' to keep the rent up." Not to be lost in stic.man's staccato rhyme technique here is the fact that the last line indicates that a young friend of the speaker in the piece – referred to affectionately as "my man" – has had his mother disappeared to prison for the "crime" of simply trying to survive. This recalls Assata Shakur's observation in her Black radical prison autobiography that most of the women with whom she was incarcerated while held as a political prisoner in the 1970s – nearly all of whom were Black or Puerto Rican – were encaged for petty crimes having to do with structural dispossession in zones of de facto racial apartheid.[22]

While not as prominent as the examples offered by their cis-gendered, Black male counterparts in terms of sheer volume, women, trans, and gender nonconforming MC's have followed Assata's lead by responding to the carceral state's ever-increasing targeting of Black, Brown, Indigenous, and poor women with critically important neoabolitionist works such as "The Door," by Detroit-based artist Invincible (aka Ill Weaver). Released as a part of *The We That Sets Us Free: Building a World Without Prisons* (2004) – a CD compilation produced by the Oakland-based human rights organization Justice Now, "The Door" speaks directly to the specificity of Black, Brown, Indigenous, and poor women's predicaments of social incarceration that often lead to official incarceration. Specifically, it underlines how their attempts at self-defense in situations of domestic violence are criminalized even as their pleas for protection from violence are often ignored by the state. While outlining the specificity of women of color's carceral experience, Invincible also touches on how the PIC represents the encroachment of chattel slavery into the time frame of precarious freedom for all prisoners:

"2 million filling their prisons now they claim we're safe? / Prison bars looking like bar codes / freedom was sold, case closed / by arm in a dark robe bangin' a gavel to send you travelin' in carloads / down gravel on stark roads like cargo ..." Here, like Assata, Dead Prez, and others I have discussed above, Invincible expresses what can be called a radical, anti-white supremacist temporality – one that connects the disappearance of more than two million Black, Brown, Indigenous, migrant, Muslim, and poor bodies directly to the Middle Passage and plantation slavery. For them, like the prisoners of slave ships, today's prisoners represent the "cargo" of *land-based slave ships*. In this sense, Invincible articulates how *the door* of the prison represents a haunting double for *the door of no return* – the entryway into slave fortress/prisons like El Mina and Cape Coast Castle in Ghana through which millions of Africans were kidnapped and transmuted into breathing commodities.

Imprisoned Intellectual Hip-Hop's Black Radical (Re)sound

As in the case of Black Liberation Era political prisoners such as Shakur, George Jackson, Angela Davis, Mutulu Shakur, Mumia Abu-Jamal, and James Yaki Sayles, many of the most important (anti)prison narratives in hip-hop have derived from those who have actually experienced incarceration. Furthermore, as in the case of their Movement Era predecessors, the act of rappin' about the experience of racialized captivity is often as much a process of *theory-making* as it is an act of storytelling. Oakland-based MC and producer Askari X (aka: Ansar El Muhammad) represents a clear-cut example of what prison studies scholar Joy James describes as the "imprisoned intellectual."[23] And, as in the case of many of his incarcerated Black radical predecessors, the main element of Askari X's writerly and theoretical voice has to do with his enumeration of the vexing interconnections between chattel and penal servitude. Released in 1995, while he was between terms at the notorious California Youth Authority (CYA) and Folsom State Prison, the song "Gotta Go" stands as one of the most important "neo-slave narratives" ever produced in any medium (even as it has never been mentioned in a literary reference volume such as this).[24] Except, while the more commonly acknowledged version of the neo-slave narrative offers modern meditations on slavery as a legally concluded formation of racial terrorism, X's version considers the ways in which the unspeakable past constantly invades the lives of present-day Black people in the forms of police terrorism and imprisonment:

> When I was locked down I studied they history ... and I can correctly / sum up
> the role of a punk ass pig / that's strollin', patrollin', my ghetto / lookin' for a

brotha like me / the shit started off back in slavery / when a Black man would run for freedom / the pigs would hunt him down / they'd catch him, and beat him / maybe shoot him, maim him, hang him / But if they don't, they'd bring him back to the motherfuckin' plantation / its known today as a police station.[25]

For Askari X, history is no mere artifact. It is what Antiguan writer Jamaica Kincaid describes as an *open wound* that reopens *again and again* with every arrest, beating, "justifiable homicide," and inhuman encagement.[26] Like other artists I have discussed above, X deploys a Black radical temporality: a form of aestheticized thought that loosens the realities of racialized experience from the grips of the capitalist-colonial mythos of social progress. In this sense, the past serves as much more than prologue to the now. It is the interminable main act – a deadly, transhistorical presence that landed Askari X in a police car and CYA cage as a child. It is the everlasting menace that murders Black people every day, up to the very minute of this writing, under the Orwellian police state banner of "to protect and serve." After issuing an incisive breakdown of the way in which the nearly infinite procession of television "cop shows" in the 1970s, '80s and '90s conditioned society into hegemonic acceptance of police terrorism, X describes the de facto white supremacist role of law enforcement in the lives of Black people in general, and that of his family in particular, having witnessed his father's wrongful arrest and imprisonment as a child, and then offering an assessment of the devastating effects on his entire family of what amounted to his father's legal kidnapping:

What about my sisters and my brothers? / I was only 12 and had to be they father figure / My mama lookin' for a job / but they wouldn't let her get one / so you know what I done? / stood on the corner played the white man's game / sold the cocaine . . . the odds was against me / I found that out when the police hit me / and slammed me to the concrete / put the slave chains on me / and threw me in the backseat / of the mothafuckin' slave ship / say we goin' to a plantation / WE NEED LIBERATION!

Askari X's neoabolitionist call for liberation from conditions of neoslavery that terrorized his family, and that continue to lay siege Black communities throughout the United States, represents a critical contextualization of the militant chorus in "Gotta Go." "A pig is a pig that's what I said / the only good pig is a pig that's dead . . .. Piggy wiggy, oooo weee, I said, you got go now, oink oink, bang bang, dead pig." This passage represents a key example of a large collection of anti-police sonic phrasings produced by groups such as NWA ("Fuck the Police"), KRS ("Sound of Da Police"), Public Enemy ("Black Steel in the Hour of Chaos"), and Main Source ("A

Friendly Game of Baseball") – resistance "anthems," as Shana Redmond would define them, that police departments and national political figures attempted to cast as evidence of the pathologically violent tendencies of hip-hop music in the late 1980s to mid-1990s.[27] However, what these diatribes against young Black rap artists conveniently obfuscated was the fact that hip-hop's sonic combat with police, courts, and prison guards represents nothing if not a completely rational desire on the part of the Black community for a mechanism of self-defense – whether real or fantastical – against a system of legal terror that has tortured, lynched, and imprisoned millions of its people since the passage of the Thirteenth Amendment to the US Constitution in 1865. From this perspective, the desire for retaliatory response on the part of contemporary Black victims of police violence and racialized imprisonment is no less reasonable than similar resistive longings expressed by African captives with respect to the daily horror they experienced at the hands of overseers and masters on the slave plantation. Indeed, this connection is presented in clearest possible terms in the lyrics of the hip-hop classic, "Sound of Da Police," by KRS-One: "Overseer, overseer, overseer, overseer-officer, officer, officer, officer / Yeah officer from overseer / You need a little clarity? / Check the similarity."[28]

In this light, it is important that we recognize the fact that Askari X's anti-police chorus in "Gotta Go" is no raving, sociopathic rant by an untutored street "thug." The gallows humor line, "Piggy wiggy ... you gotta go now! Oink oink, bang bang, dead pig," actually represents a verbatim, political recitation of a common chant employed at Black Panther rallies in the 1970s in protest against the political imprisonment and "justifiable homicide" of leaders such as Huey P. Newton, Ericka and John Huggins, Lil' Bobby Hutton, Alprentice "Bunchy" Carter, and Fred Hampton, all of whom were members of the Black Panther Party for Self-Defense (BPP).[29] The combative spirit of "Gotta Go" also connects Askari X to a long list of poetic and musical voices deriving from the Black Arts Movement – important figures such as Gil Scott-Heron ("No Knock" and "Gun") and June Jordan, whose "Poem about Police Violence" represents a thematic and aesthetic blueprint for hip-hop's wailings against legal lynching and imprisonment from the late 1970s through today's Black Lives Matter movement: "Tell me something! / What you think would happen if every time they kill a Black boy / then we kill a cop? / Every time they kill a Black man / then we kill a cop? / You think the 'accident' rate would lower subsequently?"[30]

Whereas Askari X's "Gotta Go" expresses the tradition of Black self-defense militancy through what can be called testimonial form, Main Source's "Just a Friendly Game of Baseball" (1992), articulates the banality of Black injury at the hands of police through poetic allegory. Accompanied by a bass-heavy sample from Lou Donaldson's Jazz classic, "Pot Belly," Main Source's lead MC, William Mitchell (aka "Large Professor"), uses the metaphor of a baseball game to express the degree to which the killing of Black life can also be viewed as "America's favorite pastime." At the outset of the piece, the speaker describes how he must prepare to defend himself against the police, who in his community amount to what in Black Panther parlance is an *occupying army*: "Aww shit, another young brother hit / I better go over to my man's crib and get the pump / 'Cause to the cops, shootin' brothas is like playin' baseball / and they're never in a slump. I guess when they shoot a crew, it a grand slam / and when it's one, it's a home run."[31] Here, Large Professor intervenes against the common portrayal of baseball as a symbol of US national innocence, repurposing the sport's terminology to reflect the way in which Black lives have been devalued to such an extent that police murder victims have been turned into notches on a racist national scorecard, the equivalent of hunting game. Consequently, for the socially incarcerated speaker, the prospect of being sent to "jail for a century" after receiving what he refers to later in the piece as "Three Strikes,"[32] is the experiential equivalent of being gunned down in the streets and buried "underground."

Recognizing the way in which his body amounts to an object of legalized human target practice, the speaker decides to resort to militant self-defense. "My life is valuable and I protect it like a gem / Instead of cops shootin' me, I'm goin' out shootin' them …. It's grim, but dead is my antonym." Large Professor's later depiction of a single "savage" White cop who reaps financial reward for harming Black youth actually is representative of a larger structure of *public profiteering* that has been endemic to the PIC from our present moment back to its genealogical beginnings in the convict lease camps, chain gangs, and prison plantations of the late nineteenth to mid-twentieth century.[33]

For Large Professor, the chilling fact that the daily procession of Black bodies legally murdered and encaged in the United States can be compared to "a friendly game of baseball," represents how Black injury serves as a perverse brand of social entertainment within a national social structure predicated on white supremacy. When not mobilized for the purpose of on-the-ground social justice movement building to the ends of depolicing and deincarceration, the seemingly infinite public display of racial violence in the form of cell phone and dash cam videos can, as in the case of lynching photography of the early twentieth century, perform a kind of porno-graphic labor whereby the "scene of subjection" is transmuted into a commodity of spectatorial consumption – this even when the production and reception of such imagery are wrapped in liberal veneers of "tragedy" or "complaint."

Specters of *Beale Street*: (Im)possible Love under US Prison Slavery

As stated above, the abjection of state-inflicted familial rupture within spaces of neoslavery links the hip-hop voices of those such as Askari X, Dead Prez, and Goldii to a long history of Black literature from the slave narrative to the contemporary prison narrative. While it has not garnered nearly the critical attention it deserves, Monifa Love's novel, *Freedom in the Dismal* (1998), represents an important nexus point connecting the twentieth-century prison/slavery narratives of Toni Morrison (*Beloved*), James Baldwin (*If Beale Street Could Talk*), and George Jackson (*Soledad Brother*) to the modern predicament of neoslavery experienced by members of today's "hip-hop generation." As such, her work represents a perfect link between prison "literature," in the narrow sense of the word, and the anti-prison orature of hip-hop, insofar as it represents a lyrical pastiche, a technical "remix" of form, ranging from the epistolary, to the poetic, to the racialized Gothic[34] – the last of which appears throughout her text in the form of a seemingly interminable list of slave names. Acting as a kind of living, apparitional chorus, this procession of (un)dead enslaved Africans serve as "witnesses" to the horrific intimacies of their own experience of chattelized captivity to that endured by one of the novel's protagonists, David, who, at the outset of the novel, receives a thirty-year sentence to a maximum-security prison in Richmond, Virginia.

David's incarceration subjects him to death simulation in the form of natal alienation, except in Love's text, familial severance is signaled most poignantly through the Black prisoner's forced separation from his lover, Royce, a Black "free" woman who suffers under David's capture in a manner that underlines the aforementioned predicament of social imprisonment as experienced by loved ones of the incarcerated. Constructed around a series of letters between the couple, the novel's action centers on their desperate attempt at salvaging something of a life out of conditions of living death. For them, words on the page become charged revenants of the absent lover's body. This is expressed early in the text in a letter from Royce, dated March 25, 1983: "Letters from you are real close to sex. I get aroused, no matter what news there is to tell. I can hear your voice as I read your words. You know its always been your voice that's turned me on …. I sat in your closet for a while just smelling your smell."[35] The work of intimate synecdoche – with the writerly part of the encaged lover standing in for the whole person – gives the couple the momentary feeling that "love is possible." However, for David, in a manner similar to Paul D in Toni Morrison's *Beloved*, whose chain gang experience forces him to contain his emotions within a self-protective "tobacco-tin" inside his chest, the attempt at romantic attachment from within the zone of prison slavery is the equivalent of a fool's errand. David expresses in poetic form the degree to which love, sexual pleasure, and life itself are impossible for one who has been murdered by way of encagement, solitary confinement, and sexual deprivation:

> Do I tell you of this coffin space? Do I need to? / When you closet-sit smelling me are you already here / in this closeness . . . . There is no place to weep or grieve / No room for penance . . . . There is nothing between my legs / All around me / Brothers work nonexistent dicks / Trying to extract life . . . .[36]

The incarcerated partnership of David and Royce bears a close connection to that of Fonny and Tish, James Baldwin's protagonists in his prison novel, *If Beale Street Could Talk*. Both pairs fall in love just after surviving childhood fights with one another; both couples' plans for getting married are forcibly interrupted by the male partner's legalized kidnapping; and both David and Fonny realize that their partners are pregnant after being placed in a prison cage. However, whereas the unborn baby in Baldwin's novel represents a symbol of possible redemption for Fonny, who, by the end of the text, feels he must sustain himself "for an appointment he must keep" with his soon-to-be-born child, Royce and David are disallowed any such redemptive sign.[37] This is represented in most tragic terms by Royce's miscarriage, which occurs early in David's imprisonment. Moreover, unlike Baldwin's characters, Royce and David are never able to see one another by way of carceral visitation – a grueling aspect of the novel that reaches a peak when Royce is subjected to what amounts to sexual assault by a group of prison guards as she makes an unsuccessful attempt at passing through the prison's security area. And finally, while Baldwin's imprisoned Black male protagonist is portrayed as one wrongly accused of rape, Love chooses to position David as definitively guilty of the charge of armed robbery. In this respect, Love's novel refuses readers the liberal comfort of individual innocence, an ideological construct that relegates the most common victims of racialized incarceration to the position of "deserving" penal enslavement.

For Love, as for imprisoned intellectual writers such as Assata Shakur and George Jackson, the ideological construct of individual guilt obfuscates the social and historical forces that make acts legally defined as "crime" nothing if not the predicable outcomes of racialized wealth, power, and privilege.[38] When read as a part of the historical continuum of legal terror in the United States, David's imprisonment is revealed to be as much about the social and ontological crime of being born Black in a white supremacist nation as it is about the official crime for which he has been convicted. By connecting David's imprisonment to the aforementioned procession of slave plantation, slave ship, and barracoon captives, including "62. Luke, a slave / 63.

Charlotte, a slave / 64. Cherry, a slave / 65. Ben, a slave / 66. Archer, a slave / 67. Shadrach, a slave"[39] – and over two million more of today's prison captives – Love exposes the radical asymmetry between David's individual "guilt" and the historical culpability of the racial capitalist system that landed him in prison in the first place. In this sense, what David says about his maximum security "coffin" in the early 1980s is applicable to today's entire structure of prison slavery: "in here the past is present."[40]

In our present moment of racial capitalist catastrophe, it is critically important that we engage contemporary texts such as Monifa Love's *Freedom in the Dismal* in connection with the relatively more well-known earlier prison narratives of writers such as James Baldwin, Malcolm X, Assata Shakur, and George Jackson. Furthermore, it is equally vital that in approaching this long tradition of Black (anti)prison narratives we take into account how no branch of "literature" is more pertinent to the crises of police terror and racialized imprisonment than the sonic poetics of those such as Kendrick Lamar, Dead Prez, Askari X, Large Professor, and many other hip-hop artists who rarely appear on literature department course syllabi. When brought into conversation with one another, all of these works express how we can rightfully invoke a riff with W. E. B. Du Bois in stating that *one of the greatest problems of the twenty-first century is the problem of the prison cage.*[41] And, given this harrowing reality, this collection of works also express how our contemporary carceral disaster cannot be fully engaged without recognition of the fact that modern imprisonment represents a horrifying remix of the first system of "mass incarceration" in US history – chattel slavery. Received in this light, the combative literature and orature that I have discussed in this chapter call for much more than mere inclusion on university course syllabi. Indeed, they demand at least as much of the twenty-first century reader (and hearer) as the autobiographies of rebel slaves such as Harriet Jacobs and Frederick Douglass did of their mid-nineteenth-century reading public. Notwithstanding their ultimate attainment of individual freedom in their classic texts, both Jacobs and Douglass demand in strongest possible terms that their readers become much more than interested spectators of the slavery experience – that they live according to the radical abolitionist tenet of Fannie Lou Hamer that *nobody's free until everybody's free.*[42]

NOTES

1 *Untitled 3*, by Kendrick Lamar, 58th Grammy Awards, Staples Center, Los Angeles, February 15, 2016.
2 Hortense Spillers, "Mama's Baby, Papa's Maybe: An American Grammar Book," *Diacritics* 17, no. 2 (1987): 68.

3 The term "prison industrial complex" refers to the consortium of political and economic interests that since the late 1970s have led to the greatest increase in imprisonment in US history – a rise of approximately 500 percent. This collection of interests has worked in the ideological arena to create a social consensus that imprisonment and policing represent the primary remedies for social problems stemming from racism, colonialism, sexism, and capitalism, such as drug addiction, alcoholism, unemployment, and homelessness. See Angela Davis, *Are Prisons Obsolete* (New York: Seven Stories Press, 2003).

4 "Neither slavery nor involuntary servitude, *except as punishment for a crime whereof the party shall have been duly convicted*, shall exist within the United States, or any place subject to their jurisdiction," Thirteenth Amendment to the US Constitution, passed January 31, 1865. For analysis of how the punitive exception within the "emancipation" amendment has subjected millions of people to conditions of prison slavery, see Dennis Childs, *Slaves of the State: Black Incarceration from the Chain Gang to the Penitentiary* (Minneapolis: University of Minnesota Press, 2015). See also Barbara Esposito and Lee Wood, *Prison Slavery* (Silver Spring: Joel Lithographic, 1982); Angela Davis, "From the Prison of Slavery to the Slavery of Prison," in *The Angela Y. Davis Reader*, edited by Joy James (Malden: Blackwell, 1998), 78; Colin (aka Joan) Dayan, "Legal Slaves and Civil Bodies," in *Materializing Democracy*, edited by Russ Castronovo and Dana Nelson (Durham: Duke University Press, 2002), 70; Alex Lichtenstein, *Twice the Work of Free Labor: The Political Economy of Convict Labor in the New South* (London: Verso, 1996) 17, 187; Dylan Rodríguez, *Forced Passages: Imprisoned Radical Intellectuals and the U.S. Prison Regime* (Minneapolis: University of Minnesota Press, 2006), 17, 36. See also the documentary film, *13th*, by Ava DuVernay, Netflix, September, 2016.

5 Childs, *Slaves of the State*, 5.

6 The total prison and jail population in the United States by year-end, 2015, was 2,173,800. Bureau of Justice Statistics, 2015, "Correctional Populations in the United States, 2015," December 29, 2016, www.bjs.gov. When including juvenile facilities and immigrant detention centers, this numbers reaches above 2.3 million. Prison Policy Initiative, "Mass Incarceration: The Whole Pie, 2017," March 14, 2017, www.prisonpolicy.org/reports/pie2017.html. The cited statistic on Black male incarceration derives from Pew Charitable Trusts, "One in 100: Behind Bars in America 2008," February 28, 2008, www.pewtrusts.org/en/research-and-analysis/reports/2008/02/28/one-in-100-behind-bars-in-america-2008. Between 1980 and 2014, the incarceration for women increased by more than 700 percent, with the incarceration of Black women being the largest element of that increase. For an excellent report on the specific attack against transgender and gender nonconforming people under the PIC, and specifically how this attack is largely focused on trans and intersex, Black and Brown people, see the Sylvia Rivera Law Project, "Its War in Here: A Report on the Treatment of Transgender and Intersex People in New York State Men's Prisons," 2007, https://srlp.org/its-war-in-here. For a discussion of the horrors of the current system of US immigrant detention with respect to sexual violence against migrant women, see Alice Speri, "Detained Then Violated: 1,224 Complaints Reveal a Staggering Pattern of Sexual Abuse in Immigrant Detention," *The Intercept*, April 11, 2018, http://the intercept.com.

7 For an important discussion of the PIC as a modality of Black expendability, see Barbara Ransby, "The Black Poor and the Politics of Expendability," *Race & Class* 38, no. 2 (1996): 1–12. For the way in which US prisons represent reservoirs for "surplus populations" of Black, Brown, and poor people more generally, see Ruth Wilson Gilmore, *Golden Gulag: Prisons, Surplus, Crisis, and Opposition in Globalizing California* (Berkeley: University of California Press, 2007), 70–185. For discussion of the state infliction of disposability onto migrant and Indigenous collectivities in Mexico through murder and disappearance, see Melissa Wright, "Epistemological Ignorances and Fighting for the Disappeared: Lessons from Mexico," *Antipode* 49, no. 1 (2017): 249–269; and Mariana Mora, "Ayotzinapa and the Criminalization of Racialized Poverty in La Montaña, Guerrero, Mexico," *Political and Legal Anthropology Review* (May 2017): 67–85.

8 My use of the term "Obama/Trump era" in reference to the mass imprisonment, deportation, and familial separation of migrant subjects cuts against the grain of the current treatment of Trump's anti-migrant policy as exceptionally horrific. Granting the unspeakable nature of the Trump administration's attack on migrant families, including children, the actual record of the Obama administration reflects that the current US anti-immigrant practice is in fact unexceptional with respect to warfare against undocumented people. In fact, more than 2.5 million people were deported during Obama's presidential tenure, a total that is more than all US presidencies combined excluding Bush II and Clinton – a statistic that caused migrant activists to refer to Obama as "Deporter-in-Chief." And while much attention has rightfully been given to the deaths of migrants (especially children) in US custody during the Trump presidency, seventy-four migrants are known to have died while imprisoned during the Obama presidency due to dehydration and other treatable illnesses. Roberto Lovato, "Stacey Abrams' Talk About Obama's 'Compassionate' Immigration Legacy Isn't Just Wrong: It's Dangerous Too," *Latino Rebels*, February 6, 2019, www.latinorebels.com/2019/02/06/staceyabrams. One of the most important policies that enabled the massive legalized disappearance of migrants during the Obama administration was that which was passed by Congress in 2010 (during a Democratic majority in both houses of Congress), which placed a quota of 34,000 on the number of undocumented people that were (and are) mandated to be encaged in US private and public prisons and jails on every single day of every calendar year. This policy has represented a boon to private prison companies that are paid $2 billion per year in tax dollars to incarcerate migrants. Livia Luan, "Profiting from Enforcement: The Role of Private Prisons in U.S. Immigration Detention," Migration Information Source, Migration Policy Institute, May 2, 2018, www.migrationpolicy.org/article/profiting-enforcement-role-private-prisons-us-immigration-detention.

9 This term represents a riff with a difference on the more familiar term "neo-slave narrative" – a genre of African Diasporic writing produced by writers such as Octavia Butler, Ishmael Reed, Toni Morrison, M. NourbeSe Philip, and Marlon James that represents a retrospective reimagining of chattel slavery by writers situated within what is often believed to be the "post" slavery moments. My term challenges the assumption that slavery actually ended. For an important assessment of the centrality of prison writing as an of the "neo-slave narrative," see Joy James, "Introduction" to *The New Abolitionists: (Neo)Slave Narratives and Contemporary Prison Writings* (New York: SUNY Press, 2005), xxii.

10 Coined by Ugandan linguist and literary theorist, Pio Zirimu, the term "orature" describes forms of oral and aural storytelling that are not dependent upon the written word, undercutting what theorists saw as a form of cultural imperialism in the Western academy that treated written "literature" as having greater cultural and intellectual value than forms of oral and sonic communication. For my knowledge of the term, I am indebted to the great African Diaspora studies scholar, VéVé Clark.

11 For an important consideration of the connection between modern Black women hip-hop and classic blues artists, see Cheryl Keyes, *Rap Music and Street Consciousness* (Urbana: University of Illinois Press, 2002), 186–209. I wish to be clear that this essay is not intended as a wholesale cultural anthropological explanation of "what hip-hop is." For important treatments of hip-hop from a cultural anthropological and sociological perspective, see Tricia Rose, *Black Noise: Rap Music and Black Culture in Contemporary America* (Hanover: University of New England, 1994); and Jeff Chang, *Can't Stop, Won't Stop: A History of the Hip-Hop Generation* (New York: St. Martin's, 2005). For analysis of how hip-hop has offered important deconstructions of racialized criminalization, see Bakari Kitwana, *The Hip-Hop Generation: Young Blacks and the Crisis in African-American Culture* (New York: BasicCivitas, 2002); and Donald Tibbs, "Hip Hop and the New Jim Crow: Rap Music's Insight on Mass Incarceration," *University of Maryland Law Journal of Race, Religion, Gender & Class* 15, no. 2 (2015): 209–228.

12 Ngugi wa Thiong'o, *Globalectics: Theory and the Politics of Knowing* (New York: Columbia University Press, 2014), 81. Importantly, Ngugi cites hip-hop as among the most important forms of modern orature, ibid., 83.

13 Frantz Fanon, *The Wretched of the Earth* (New York: Grove/Atlantic, 2007), 159. For my knowledge of this Fanonian term, I am indebted to Rodríguez, *Forced Passages*, 119.

14 Ruth Wilson Gilmore, *Golden Gulag: Prisons, Surplus, Crisis, and Opposition in Globalizing California* (Berkeley: University of California Press, 2007); and Rodríguez, *Forced Passages*. This mode of theorization goes at least as far back as the Black Panther Party's commentaries on how police in cities across the country amount to "occupying armies," and the "Double V" campaign of Black activists during the World War II era who argued that if Black soldiers would work for victory against fascism abroad then there needed to be a defeat of fascism at home in the forms of lynching, racist policing, and structural poverty. The term "racial capitalism" derives from the late Cedric Robinson's classic study, *Black Marxism: The Making of the Black Radical Tradition* (Chapel Hill: University of North Carolina Press, 2000).

15 Dead Prez, "I'm a African," track 2 on *Let's Get Free*, Loud Records, February 2000.

16 Malcolm X, "The Ballot or the Bullet," Detroit, Michigan, April 12, 1964.

17 Angela Davis, "Racialized Punishment and Prison Abolition," in James *An Angela Y. Davis Reader*, 105.

18 At the time of the release of *Let's Get Free*, Black women represented the demographic experiencing the greatest percentage increase in imprisonment in the entire country. However, the experience of Black women as targets of US racialized incarceration and penal torture goes all the way back to the birth of the

convict lease system, the chain gang, and the prison plantation. For excellent studies of this history, see Talitha LeFlouria, *Chained in Silence: Black Women and Convict Labor in the New South* (Chapel Hill: University of North Carolina Press, 2015); and Sarah Haley, *No Mercy Here: Gender, Punishment, and the Making of Jim Crow Modernity* (Chapel Hill: University of North Carolina Press, 2016).

19 Samiya Hameeda Abdullah, "Trap Doors," live performance at "All Out for Mumia" event, Philadelphia, Pennsylvania, December 9, 2011. Goldii's untimely death due to breast cancer and the barring of Mumia Abu-Jamal from proper mourning as he was trapped in his prison cell during her funeral expose the terrorist aspects of racialized incarceration as it lays siege to familial bonds both inside and outside prisons and jails. Goldii's lyrics resonate in carceral-blues fashion with those of her imprisoned father years earlier, in Mumia Abu-Jamal's "The Visit," in *Live from Death Row* (New York: Avon, 1995), 22.

20 Orlando Patterson, *Slavery and Social Death* (Cambridge, MA: Harvard University Press, 1982).

21 Eve, "Gotta Man," track 3 on *Let There be Eve ... Ruff Ryders' First Lady*, Ruff Ryders Entertainment, 1999. Keyes, *Rap Music and Street Consciousness*, 204.

22 Assata Shakur, *Assata: An Autobiography* (Chicago: L. Hill Books, 2001), 54. As Shakur reveals through her own experiences of gendered white supremacist incarceration, conditions inside US prisons for those Black and Brown women removed from their communities in this manner include an array of torture tactics indicative of chattelized captivity from unredressable rape by guards, to shackled childbirth, to often having children permanently taken away through "social service" systems of foster care and adoption.

23 Joy James, "Democracy and Captivity," introduction to *The New Abolitionists: (Neo)Slave Narratives and Contemporary Prison Writings* (New York: SUNY, 2005), xxi–xlii.

24 This branch of literature typically is represented as the contemporary narrative reimagining of pre-1865 slavery by modern authors. Commonly understood examples of the genre include Toni Morrison, *Beloved* (New York: Plume, 1987); Gayl Jones, *Corregidora* (New York: Random House, 1975); Octavia Butler, *Kindred* (Boston: Beacon Press, 2003); and Marlon James, *The Book of Night Women* (New York: Riverhead, 2009). However, prison studies scholars have challenged this definition arguing that the writings and music of the incarcerated represent a neglected branch of the form.

25 The Delinquents (feat. Askari X), "Gotta Go," track 2 on *Outta Control* (EP), Dank or Die Records, 1995. As in the case of Dead Prez, Askari X has been influenced by the political philosophy of the International People's Democratic Uhuru Movement, led by Omali Yeshitela. X has also been a long-time member of the Nation of Islam under the teachings of Ansar El Muhamad in Oakland, California.

26 Jamaica Kincaid, "In History," *Callaloo* 20, no. 1 (1997): 1–7.

27 Shana Redmond, *Anthem: Social Movements and the Sound of Solidarity in the African Diaspora* (New York: New York University Press, 2013). For discussion of the US political establishment's demonization of self-defensive hip-hop as violent pathology, see Chang, *Can't Stop Won't Stop*, 576–754.

28 Lawrence "Kris" Parker (KRS-One), "Sound of Da Police," track 7 on *Return of the Boom Bap*, Jive Records, September 28, 1993.
29 To hear this BPP, anti-police terror chant, see Howard Alk's important documentary, "The Murder of Fred Hampton," Facets Multi-Media, 1971. The BPP was started by Newton and Bobby Seale in 1966, in Askari X's hometown of Oakland, California, largely in order to stem the tide of "legal lynchings." This term refers to the way in which, by at least as early as the Depression Era, forms of white supremacist state violence such as capital punishment, police terror, and imprisonment superseded formations of white supremacist violence as enacted by private individuals and organizations such as such as the KKK. For more on this, see Dennis Childs, "'An Insinuating Voice': Angelo Herndon and the 'Invisible Genesis of the Radical Prison Slave's Neo-Slave Narrative,' in 'Unchaining Selves: The Power of the Neo-Slave Narrative Genre,'" *Callaloo* 40, no. 4, special issue (Fall 2019): 30–56; and James Clarke, "Without Fear or Shame: Lynching, Capital Punishment and the Subculture of Violence in the American South," *British Journal of Political Science*, 28, no. 2 (April 1998): 269–289.
30 June Jordan, "Poem about Police Violence," in *Passion: New Poems, 1977–1980* (Boston: Beacon Press, 1980), 34. However, this Black radical tradition of sounding the necessity of armed self-defense in the face of legally unredressable state violence also stretches back to the Panthers' political forerunners, including Malcolm X; Robert and Mabel Williams; the Deacons for Defense; rebel slave leaders such as Nat Turner, Gabriel Prosser, and Harriet Tubman; and the untold number of rebel slaves who created maroon – or *cimarrone* – communities from Florida, to Mexico, to Haiti, to Jamaica, to Columbia, to Brazil.
31 Main Source, "Just a Friendly Game of Baseball," track 5 on *Breaking Atoms*, Wild Pitch Records, July 23, 1991.
32 "Three Strikes" refers to a set of laws passed in states throughout the United States from the 1970s to the 2000s that instituted mandatory minimum sentencing, thereby drastically contributing to the boom in imprisonment under the PIC. California's infamous "Three Strikes Law" (1994), which invoked the very baseball metaphor that Large Professor inverts in "A Friendly Game of Baseball," was touted as an effort to curtail violent crime. See Brian Starks and Alana Van Gundy, "Race and the Three Strikes Law," in *Color Behind Bars: Racism in the U.S. Prison System*, edited by Scott Bowman (Santa Barbara: Praeger, 2014), 413–434.
33 Furthermore, as Michelle Alexander points out, today's highly militarized police departments have reaped huge financial rewards since the Reagan administration's pronouncement of the "War on Drugs" – a de facto war on Black, Brown, and poor people that Bill Clinton took to an unprecedented level during his two terms in office, a time that saw the greatest increase in prison and jail populations in US history. Michelle Alexander, *The New Jim Crow* (New York: New Press, 2012), 56–57.
34 On the racial underpinnings of the Gothic as a literary form, see Teresa Goddu, *Gothic America: Narrative, History, and Nation* (New York: Columbia University Press, 1997). See also L. Paravisini-Gebert, "Colonial Gothic: The Caribbean," in *The Cambridge Companion to Gothic Fiction*, edited by Jerold Hogle (New York: Cambridge University Press, 2002), 229–258; and Avery

Gordon, *Ghostly Matters: Haunting and the Sociological Imagination* (Minneapolis: University of Minnesota Press, 1997).

35 Monifa Love, *Freedom in the Dismal* (Kaneohe: Plover Press, 1998), 30.

36 Ibid., 56, 69.

37 James Baldwin, *If Beale Street Could Talk* (New York: Vintage, 2006), 192.

38 Notwithstanding the vitally important role of campaigns such as the Innocence Project – a legal aid effort that has led to the exoneration of 364 prisoners through the use of DNA evidence that has proven their innocence – the continued focus on locating the "wrongly convicted" among the millions of people who are, or who have been, encaged as a result of a racist, capitalist, misogynist, colonial social structure reifies the "properly convicted" position of society's most vulnerable peoples. For more on the problematics of culpability (and its manufacture) with respect to the US carceral state, see Saidiya Hartman, *Scenes of Subjection: Race Terror and Self-Making in Nineteenth Century America* (New York: Oxford University Press, 1997), 1–132. For my conception of the need for demystifying the liberal, legal ideology of guilt, I am also indebted to Ruth Wilson Gilmore.

39 Love, *Freedom in the Dismal*, 26.

40 Ibid., 56.

41 "the problem of the Twentieth Century is the problem of the color line." W. E. B. Du Bois, *The Souls of Black Folk* (Chicago: A. C. McClurg and Co., 1903), vii.

42 Fannie Lou Hamer, speech delivered at the founding of the National Women's Political Caucus, Washington, DC, July 10, 1971.

14

HAMILTON CARROLL

Insecurity

Fiction published since September 11, 2001, has born the burden of attempting to represent the event and its many repercussions, including both the so-called War on Terror and transformations in national identity as the result of what was widely understood to be the first foreign attack on American soil since Pearl Harbor. At the same time, in the almost two decades since the 9/11 attacks and the inauguration of the War on Terror by the Bush administration, those events have ceased to be "current" and have begun the slow retreat into history – so much so that for many readers of the novels that I discuss in this chapter, they will be either a distant memory or historical events from the lives of the previous generation. Nevertheless, both geopolitically and in terms of domestic politics, the legacies of those events, such as the racialization of everyday life and the attendant rise in Islamophobia around the globe, have been far reaching and continue to vex historians, politicians, and authors alike. Terror and insecurity are ubiquitous features in the lives of many, both within the United States and throughout the world, and authors such as Susan Choi, Mohsin Hamid, Joseph O'Neill, and Jess Walter have written novels that represent and work through those conditions of threat and precarity. Taken both individually and together, the novels written by these authors and others evidence the significant role that novel-length narrative fiction has had working through not only the events of 9/11 and their aftermath but also the rapidly changing world of the early twenty-first century, a world in which regional conflict, nuclear proliferation, refugee crises, and rampant ethno-nationalism across the West have all radically destabilized the post–Cold War consensus. History has returned with a vengeance, and fiction has been a principal site of reckoning with a transformed world.

As 9/11 has become more historically distant, its relationship to the broader history of the United States' relationship to the world, and of its cultural representations to their own antecedents, has become clear. Rather than the break with the past it was commonly understood to have produced, or the representational crisis it was believed to have inaugurated, 9/11 and its literary representations instead must be seen to fit within a broader trajectory of political change and representational anxiety that precede them. While it was foreshadowed by the 1993 bombing of the World Trade Center and preceded by the first Persian Gulf War, a transformed political and military relationship between the United States and the world was produced after 9/11. As I show in this chapter, much literature written in the aftermath of 9/11 and under the sociopolitical conditions of the new global order of the first decades of the twenty-first century has attempted to produce new representations of the present grounded in the epistemological uncertainties of what Timothy Melley calls the "covert sphere"[1] and the ontological insecurities borne of the conditions of precarity under which much of the world's population now live.

Citizenship and Terror in the Post-9/11 Novel

Immediately after 9/11, fiction appeared to undergo a crisis of relevance. Many authors, critics, and scholars wrote about the impossibility of representing an event that was, in its shocking immediacy and putative singularity, an overwhelmingly visual one. As the novelist Jay McInerney observed in 2005, "for a while, quite a while, fiction did seem inadequate to the moment."[2] Moreover, for many, the visual nature of the attacks already placed them in very specific cultural registers. As philosopher Slajov Žižek observed, "for the great majority of the public, the WTC explosions were events on the TV screen, and when we watched the oft-repeated shot of frightened people running towards the camera ahead of the giant cloud of dust from the collapsing tower, was not the framing of the shot itself reminiscent of spectacular shots in catastrophe movies?"[3] Likewise, for intellectual historian Susan Buck-Morss, "whether intended or not, images of the attack on New York mirrored the aesthetic experience of computer games, disaster movies."[4] W. J. T. Mitchell has observed that while, "images have always played a key role in politics, warfare, and collective perceptions about the shape of history ... there is something new in the emergence of public imagery" after 9/11: the exponentially greater number of images and the rapid increase in the speed of their circulation.[5] In the face of an overwhelmingly visual event seemingly long anticipated in popular visual culture, authors were confronted with what appeared at the time to be profound questions about the value of the written word. While the problems that 9/11 created for the written word found their most popular cultural expression in Jonathan Safran Foer's best-selling novel *Extremely Loud and Incredibly Close* (2005), major writers debated the value of literature in essays and opinion pieces published in some of the English-speaking world's most renowned newspapers and magazines. Writing less than two weeks after the attacks in *The New York Times*, for example, the novelist Richard Powers echoing Theodore Adorno's famous maxim about the Holocaust – "to write poetry after Auschwitz is barbaric"[6] – stated,

> there are no words. But there are only words . . .. No comparison can say what happened to us. But we can start with the ruins of our similes, and let "like" move us toward something larger, some understanding of what "is."[7]

In an essay published first in *Harper's* and then in *The Guardian*, Don DeLillo took on this impasse, claiming "the event itself has no purchase on the mercies of analogy or simile."[8] For Powers and DeLillo alike, simile stands as a synecdoche of figurative language, a part standing for a whole; but it is a specific part – one that refuses any ground for comparison, thereby confirming or securing the singularity of the event. Nevertheless, as they sought to find a way into the events, writers soon turned to a range of common tropes and linguistic registers, the most ubiquitous of which were trauma and domesticity.

It is undoubtedly the case that trauma has been the most common frame through which the events of 9/11 have been understood – by politicians, social commentators, the general public, critics, and writers alike – and that that trauma registered most acutely in the intimate spaces of home and family. For example, literary critic Kristiaan Versluys makes of 9/11 a traumatic event but one that can be overcome, in part, through literary representation. "Narrativizing the event amounts to an uncoiling of the trauma," he argues, "an undoing of its never-ending circularity: springing the time trap."[9]

However, as literary critic Donald E. Pease observes, casting the events of 9/11 as traumatic performs complex ideological work. For Pease, "traumatic events precipitate states of emergency that become the inaugural moments in a different symbolic order and take place on a scale that exceeds the grasp of the available representations from the national mythology."[10] Speaking in a similar vein, critic David Simpson suggested, "mourning and melancholia have both been made secondary to the initiation of a new state of emergency."[11] Taken together, the comments of Pease and Simpson suggest that, as the central means through which the events of 9/11 have been understood, trauma helped to inaugurate a set of codified responses to those events – the USA Patriot Act, the War on Terror, the subsequent ground wars in Afghanistan and Iraq – that used what historian Richard Slotkin has called regenerative violence to "heal" the psychic trauma of a great and innocent nation brought to its knees. In the words of theorists Ella Shohat and Randy

Martin, "An orderly and peaceful world has been subjected to arbitrary and irrational attack, and our own regenerative violence will restore the everyday order of the world 'before the fall,' a prelapsarian order for which the 'American Nation' is already nostalgic."[12]

One significant aspect of this restoration was the silencing of alternative or dissenting voices and the immediate codification of the language and linguistic techniques through which the events could be described, discussed, and represented. As theorist Susan Willis points out, in the wake of the 9/11 attacks "gone were satire, the mainstay of left and liberal criticism; and irony, commonplace of the postmodern condition; even sarcasm, bitter pill of the post-punk generation," both of which were replaced by trauma and fundamentalism; and, as Willis continues, "patriotism became the cure for trauma and the demonstration of fundamentalism."[13] With this turn came a return of cultural modes and tropes that had been partially dismantled or reformulated in the 1990s, not least the retrenchment of strict binary divisions of gender. In historian Elaine Tyler May's formulation, "as in the Cold War, the time had arrived for an image of reinvigorated manhood. Powerful men appeared as the major players on both sides of the 'good' and 'evil' equation, while women and children seemed vulnerable, in need of protection."[14] These reinvigorated figures of masculine authority would protect the nation from further harm and avenge the losses of 9/11, thereby returning the nation to the prelapsarian order it enjoyed before the attacks unsettled the security of so many. Or, as theorist Fredric Jameson succinctly put it, "all Americans are now receiving therapy, and it is called war."[15] In the decade and more since the commencement of the therapeutic "war on terror" Jameson describes, the effects of the United States' national trauma have played out globally, accelerating some preexisting conditions and inaugurating others. While the events of 9/11 have receded into history, the aftermath of the United States' response to them continues to affect the lives of many people around the world: the humanitarian crisis of the civil war in Syria, the European immigration crisis, the radical destabilization of the Middle East, and the proliferation of "soft target" terror attacks all evidence the global effects of the Bush administration's chosen response to a "national trauma."

If trauma was the primary psychological register through which the attacks of 9/11 were understood, the intimate spaces of the home and the family were the locations in which that trauma was understood most commonly to register, with the plots of many post-9/11 novels revolving around families that had been affected by the attacks. In novels such as Jay McInerney's *The Good Life* (2006), Claire Messud's *The Emperor's Children* (2006), Don DeLillo's *Falling Man* (2007), Helen Schulman's

A Day at the Beach (2007), and Amy Waldman's *The Submission* (2011) – not to mention Foer's *Extremely Loud and Incredibly Close*, the domestic becomes the principal location through which the effects of 9/11 are worked through. The "turn to the domestic" that accompanied the representation of trauma became the subject of a significant critical debate that took place after the publication of the first wave of novels that took 9/11 as their subject matter. In a well-known exchange, critics Richard Gray and Michael Rothberg debated what Rothberg called a "failure of the imagination" in US novels published after 9/11 – that both critics found wanting because of their inability to move beyond domestic national concerns or to place the events in a larger sociopolitical context.[16] For Gray, this failure was most clear in what he diagnosed as a "retreat" into the home, the family, and the domestic that stifled more meaningful intervention.[17] As Gray claimed, "many of the texts that try to bear witness to contemporary events vacillate ... between large rhetorical gestures acknowledging trauma and retreat into domestic detail. The link between the two is tenuous, reducing a turning point in national and international history to little more than a stage in a sentimental education."[18] However, in direct response to Gray and Rothberg, Catherine Morley has argued that, rather than a failure of – or particular to – post-9/11 fiction, such a turn is "one of the enduring and inevitable aspects of all literary fiction."[19] In each novel that I discuss in this chapter, the geopolitical and social transformations of the post-9/11 decades are refracted through the domestic, which is shown not to be a disconnected arena of "sentimental education" (as Gray would have it) but a vital location for the working through of the effects of those transformations of the individual subject.

In what follows, I argue that the novel was one of the primary locations in which the contested terrain of meaning and value that arose after 9/11 was addressed, and that the analysis of novel-length literary fiction is essential to any understanding of post-9/11 American culture. I make this argument through readings of a number of significant novels that, while varied in their styles, subjects, and genres, all work through the events of the post-9/11 decades in relation to common questions of citizenship, racial and gender identity, and national belonging. I show how these novels represent various perspectives on citizenship as it has been transformed by the events if 9/11 and the increasingly global and interconnected world. Whether representing protagonists who are attempting to hold on to previously privileged positions of power and authority, or those who have seen their opportunities merely to survive dwindle to almost nothing, all of the novels analyzed in this chapter represent a world of radical upheaval and stark global inequality. In their representations of the omnipresence of surveillance technologies in daily life; the pressures placed on individuals, families, and communities by civil war and the "collateral damage" of US military actions; the precarious states of being produced by enforced migration and political upheaval; and the forms of terror – state-sponsored or otherwise – that have become ubiquitous feature of daily life across much of the globe, these novels represent a world transformed by the 9/11 attacks and their aftermath in which the early decades of the twenty-first century have seen an amplification or acceleration of conditions that were previously merely nascent. Through its readings of these novels, the chapter sets out some of the particular thematic and formal features of the post-9/11 novel: it will consider the limits of the novel as a genre suited to the representation of contemporary conditions, and how authors have overcome them, and will make a case for the unique capacity of literary fiction to perform valuable sociopolitical work in precarious times.

The Minority Citizen as Other

After 9/11, new logics of citizen and terrorist held sway and were represented across a range of literary fictions. As legal theorist Leti Volpp put it, "there is a new national imagining as to what bodies are assumed to stand in for 'the citizen' and its new opposite, 'the terrorist.'"[20] While a number of authors attempted to "get inside the mind" of the terrorist by writing novels in which Muslim fundamentalists featured as central protagonists, others chose to think more critically about the post-9/11 racial logics in which the position of terrorist was seemingly the only one available to nonwhite subjects. In this section, I read three novels, Mohsin Hamid's *The Reluctant Fundamentalist* (2007) and *Exit West* (2017) and Susan Choi's *A Person of Interest* (2008), in which nonwhite protagonists are the subject of surveillance, suspicion, and distrust.[21] What these novels interrogate is the post-9/11 logics of ethnic and national identity in what Volpp calls the "consolidation of a new identity category that grouped together persons who appeared to be 'Middle Eastern, Arab, or Muslim.'" A new racialization took place "wherein members of this group [were] identified as terrorists and disidentified as citizens."[22] The three novels that I discuss here each refuse those arbitrary categorizations, based as they are on the reading (or misreading) of skin color and physiognomy, and return the concept of interiority to subjects that have been transformed into mere bodies – and in some cases into what philosopher Georgio Agamben has famously called "bare life" – by post-9/11 racial logics.[23]

Mohsin Hamid's *The Reluctant Fundamentalist* (2007) tells the story of Changez, a young Pakistani man educated in the United States, where he was a resident at the time of the September 11 terrorist attacks. As his name suggests, Changez's story is one of transformation and, growing increasingly disillusioned with the United States, and facing increasingly frequent instances of racial harassment, Changez leaves New York and returns to Pakistan. The novel is told in the first person in the form of an account of Changez's years living in New York, given to an unnamed American interlocutor in a Lahore market. What it describes is an end to the cosmopolitan global world that Changez – a graduate of Princeton and an employee of Underwood Sampson, a fictional elite financial institution – had previously believed himself to be a citizen (and a beneficiary) of. Through its first-person narration, the novel offers a representation of the post-9/11 national scene from the perspective of a character who, once a fully fledged believer in the neoliberal version of the American myth of self-making, believes that dream to have become a nightmare for those who do not fit into the narrowly conceived boundaries of racialized citizenship that were constructed after 9/11. Hamid, who is of Pakistani origin but was raised in the United States, has described the novel as "a look at America with a gaze reflecting the part of myself that remained stubbornly Pakistani."[24]

The narrator describes himself as a "lover of America" and goes on to describe the opportunity afforded him as an international student at an elite US institution: "We . . . were given visas and scholarships, complete financial aid, mind you, and invited into the ranks of the meritocracy. In return, we were expected to contribute our talents to your society, the society we were joining."[25]

"Yes, it was exhilarating," he states, "Princeton made everything possible for me" (15). As a recipient of the honors and privileges bestowed on him by his elite education, Changez is also able to cast off the shackles of national identity and to enter the flows of global capital; he is able, in short, to become a citizen of the neoliberal globalized world. As Changez describes, "I was, in four and a half years, never an American; I was *immediately* a New Yorker" (33). But Hamid's narrator is not only a citizen of New York, but also a corporate citizen. "I did not think of myself as a Pakistani," Changez claims, "but as an Underwood Sampson trainee" (34). This is a form of belonging in which the global city and the corporation have superseded the nation.

This is not to say that racial or ethnic differences cease to matter but that, before 9/11, Changez is able to employ them to his benefit; he is able to blend in by standing out in acceptable and nonthreatening ways. In the global meritocracy in which Changez moves, ethnic difference is employable as a marker of interest and is not yet – as it will become after the 9/11 attacks – a source of threat or discomfort. "In a subway car," he describes, "my skin would typically fall in the middle of the color spectrum" (33). At a slightly later point, unsure what to wear to an important dinner at the home of Erica, his soon-to-be girlfriend, the narrator decides to take advantage of what he calls the "ethnic exception clause that is written into every code of etiquette" and to wear a kurta (the traditional loose shirt worn by men on the Indian subcontinent). He feels "completely comfortable" on the subway in this attire – which also pleases Erica, who tells him "you look great" as she touches the embroidered hem with her fingers upon his arrival (48). The transformation of New York after 9/11 is a source of great distress to the narrator and is cast as the infiltration of the global city by the parochial nation. "Your country's flag invaded New York after the attacks," Changez tells his American interlocutor, "it was everywhere" (79). No longer a place of freedom, possibility, and comfort, New York becomes America for Hamid's narrator, with all of its racial and ethnic tensions and its increasingly intolerant Islamophobia; the city's position as one node in a network of global cities is displaced by its reclamation as part of a more parochial and inward-looking American nation. As the narrator describes it, "more than once, traveling on the subway – where I had always had the feeling of seamless blending in – I was subjected to verbal abuse by complete strangers" (130). After 9/11, the privileged cosmopolitanism the novel's narrator celebrates in its early pages gives way to retrenched forms of nativist nationalism that strengthened in the decade since its publication, and that appeared to reach their apotheosis a decade later in the "Make American Great Again" rhetoric of Donald Trump.

In *A Person of Interest* (2008), Susan Choi similarly imagines the life of a nonwhite American subject caught up in the aftermath of a terrorist attack. Unlike Hamid, however, Choi does not situate her novel in direct relationship to the events of 9/11 but makes a set of implicit – but highly significant – links between the highly racist security state that arose after 9/11 and longer-standing forms of racism and racialization in the United States. Choi's protagonist, an Asian-born professor of mathematics at a small regional college becomes the eponymous "person of interest" when a young colleague is killed by a letter bomb. *A Person of Interest* uses real-life examples of Asian American subjects caught up in domestic terrorism to explore the fraught relationship between minority subjectivity and national privilege. In Choi's novels, Asian-American characters are the subjects of the sorts of racial profiling and the abuse of state power that will be experienced by Muslim and Arab subjects after 9/11. While *A Person of Interest* is set in the 1990s and draws not only on the case of the Unabomber Ted Kaczynski but also of Wen Ho Lee, the Taiwanese-American scientist targeted by Federal authorities, Choi's novel nevertheless reflects on the sorts of racial and ethnic profiling that arose after 9/11 and situates them in a longer history of state violence and institutional racism.[26]

While in *The Reluctant Fundamentalist*, Changez is able to draw on the "ethnic exception" and to propel himself into the upper ranks of the neoliberal global meritocracy, Choi's Professor Lee hews to the different expectations for Asian minority subjects of an earlier era of US citizenship formation, that of the "model minority."[27] For example, as a PhD student at an elite US educational institution, Lee immediately feels himself to be separate from his classmates, who are "all men, all white and American-born except Lee."[28] Lee's classmates are described as fitting a certain mold of white male privilege: "All were goldenly handsome and brooding in the Byronic vein; all wore their hair distractedly untrimmed, their tweed jackets unmended, their ancient leather loafers unrepaired. All of them were young, well-bred, unapologetic introverts whose lack of cordiality and warmth was admired by professors and women alike as evidence of their genius."[29] In the face of this white privilege, Lee can muster only resentment and jealousy, emotions that he carries with him and that "had stained much of [his] life."[30] This is a far cry from the putatively color-blind meritocracy described by Hamid. What Choi's novel recounts is how easily stereotype and suspicion fuse to transform a citizen into a suspect. While Choi's novel is not about 9/11 explicitly, it inhabits a post-9/11 world of ethnic stereotypes, good and evil, citizens and terrorists. While these categories gain particular valences after 9/11, *A Person of Interest* intervenes in the dehistoricized understanding of citizenship and terrorism that pertained after the attacks by situating such profiling in a longer history of US racial categorizations.

Mohsin Hamid's later novel *Exit West* (2017) is concerned also with the categories of migrant and citizen that develop in the aftermath of the upheavals that result from the global War on Terror inaugurated by the United States after 9/11. Its representation of a world marked by surveillance and the hyper securitization of everyday life in the West (as it is called in the novel), which is contrasted with the perilous living conditions that pertain in much of the rest of the world, asks the reader to consider the costs of the global reach of the American homeland state. The novel's language – simple, hard, and direct in most places – opens up a space for the representation of the paranoia that increasingly subtends the hyper surveillance of contemporary daily life. In the novel, which mixes magical realism with a realist account of the perils of global migration and displacement, a series of magical portals are discovered that link the cities of the globe and allow near instantaneous movement between them. Saeed and Nadia, the novel's central protagonists, are a young Muslim couple whose unnamed city and country is being torn apart in a violent and bloody civil war. Making the decision to leave behind friends and family, the young couple pay a people smuggler who guides them to one of the newly discovered portals, through which they emerge on a beach on the Greek island of Mykonos. From there, the couple travel to London and eventually to San Francisco, where they settle in the "new city of Marin,"[31] and their relationship comes to an end.

The novel develops many of the same themes as *The Reluctant Fundamentalist*: the local effects of neoliberal globalization, the increasingly polarized relationship between the West and Islam, the psychic tolls of displacement and migration, the promise versus the realities of the United States. However, while Hamid's earlier novel casts these themes in direct relationship to the terrorist attacks, the later situates them in relation to the longer-term, global repercussions of the Western response to those attacks. If *The Reluctant Fundamentalist* portrays a world in which the United States is transformed by terror, *Exit West* portrays the catastrophic effect – rendered globally – of the nation's response to those transformations: the rise of fundamentalism following the Arab Spring of 2010, civil war in Syria, the global refugee crisis. As such, *Exit West* provides further opportunity to think about the profound interconnections between the different layers of privilege and possibility that stratify a globally interconnected but still radically uneven world. In *Exit West*, the cities of the world are connected still – as they are in *The Reluctant Fundamentalist* – but the manner of those connections has changed.

By suffusing its realism with magical or fantastical elements, *Exit West* is able to develop an analysis of the transformative effects of the global War on Terror and the increasingly securitized states that enable it. In London, for example, the sky is "drone-crossed" and an "invisible network of surveillance ... radiated out from their phones."[32] In another moment, surveillance becomes the lens through which the narrative is framed. Describing the plight of another family that has sought to escape Saaed and Nadia's homeland, the narrator describes how, having exited one of the magical portals in Dubai,

> the family was picked up again by a second security camera, traversing a hallway and pushing the horizontal bars that secured a heavy set of double fire-resistant doors, and as these doors opened the brightness of Dubai's desert sunlight overwhelmed the sensitivity of the image sensor and the four figures seemed to become thinner, insubstantial, lost in an aura of whiteness, but they were at that moment simultaneously captured on three exterior surveillance feeds, tiny characters stumbling on to a broad pavement.[33]

Moments later, "a small quadcopter drone was hovering fifty meters above them now, too quiet to be heard, and relaying its feed to a central monitoring station."[34] In these descriptions, the migrant family are rendered as objects of surveillance, which has itself become a full-spectrum activity, practiced by private corporations and security services, the state, and the camera-wielding tourist alike. By accident or by design, the world has become a place of total surveillance saturation. Moreover, the surveillance devices described in these passages are not only described objects in the novel but also sources of narrative point of view. In this way, Hamid illustrates the profound degree to which the world around us is now refracted most frequently through the eyes of the surveillance camera and the mobile phone. Such a view has been normalized and, as such, becomes narrative style.

White Masculinity and the Fictions of Citizenship

If the post-9/11 political and cultural landscape was populated by numerous examples of what Elaine Tyler May called "reinvigorated manhood," from George W. Bush and the figure of the fireman to Osama bin Laden and the leaders of the Taliban, it is equally the case that for many novelists, the events of September 11 produced a moment of crisis in which the more flexible forms of masculinity that had become valorized in the years prior to 9/11 came to be regarded as problematic. As such, for a significant number of novelists, 9/11 presented an opportunity to think through the new sociopolitical landscape in relation to the transformations of gender that it appeared in some ways to sweep aside. In this section, I argue that Joseph O'Neill's *Netherland* (2007) and Jess Walter's *The Financial Lives of the Poets* (2009) are two such novels. O'Neill and Walter alike represent protagonists whose masculinity, whiteness, and normative (global) citizenship are at odds with the increasingly diverse world that the events of 9/11 forces them to reckon with.

Like many of the first wave of 9/11-centered novels, O'Neill's *Netherland* (2007) – published just a few months after *The Reluctant Fundamentalist* – was largely written prior to the September 11 attacks and then heavily revised in their aftermath. O'Neill's novel tells the story of Hans, a Dutch banker living in New York. In the months after 9/11, Hans finds himself alone when his wife, Rachel, returns to the United Kingdom (where she is from) with their young son. The novel tells the story of Han's relationship with the city after the departure of his family and of his friendship with an enigmatic Trinidadian, Chuck Ramkissoon, whom he meets while playing cricket. Like *The Reluctant Fundamentalist* and many other post-9/11 novels, *Netherland* is concerned with the relationship between New York City and the nation, the recalibrations of citizenship and ethnicity after the attacks, and the relationship between patriotism and national identity. For example, speaking of national identity as it is portrayed in his novel, O'Neill has referred to the fact that its narrator is Dutch by birth as one of the most American things about it. "To have a Dutch narrator in the context of an American novel is almost to have the original American narrator," O'Neill argues, "because of course the Dutch were the first people here in New York . . . . So Hans is the most recent iteration of the original American presence in this part of the world."[35] O'Neill, moreover, has suggested in interviews that his status as both insider and outsider (he is Irish by birth but holds US citizenship) renders him ideally suited to think about the status of the United States after 9/11, observing, "you're quite well placed if you're an exotic American like me."[36]

The first-person narrator of *Netherland* holds a similarly exemplary position from which to observe his adopted country, which he does most frequently though the frame of cricket. Having rediscovered the sport, which he played in his youth, Hans joins the real-life Staten Island Cricket Club, which was founded in 1872. Cricket serves in *Netherland* as a means of examining both history and ethnicity. Hans's teammates hail from Trinidad, Guyana, Jamaica, India, Pakistan, and Sri Lanka. "I was the only white man I ever saw on the cricket fields of New York," he states.[37] White though he is, however, Hans also produces an equivalency between himself and his "exotic cricketing circle."[38] Describing the American men playing softball as he and his teammates await the use of the field, Hans describes them as "aging and overweight men much like ourselves, only white-skinned."[39] There is an elective affinity here, in which Hans positions himself as an outsider to the dominant, normative core of US identity norms. As a cricketer, he is Other. This perspective is confirmed a few pages later when Chuck (an umpire and not a player) gives a grand speech in front of two competing teams that he is trying to calm after a fight has broken out and a gun has been brandished. Admonishing the players to remember who they are and where they are playing, Chuck states:

> "Every summer the parks of this city are taken over by hundreds of cricketers but somehow nobody notices. It's like we're invisible. Now that's nothing new for those of us who are black or brown. As for those who are not" – Chuck acknowledged my presence with a smile – "you'll forgive me, I hope, if I say that I sometimes tell people, You want a taste of how it feels to be a black man in this country? Put on the white clothes of the cricketer. Put on white to feel black."[40]

Delivered early on in the novel, this speech suggests the degree to which O'Neill's novel is invested in thinking through the relationship between domestic US racial identities and those of the former colonies of the United Kingdom and Europe, from which the majority of Hans's cricketing teammates hail. But the novel also represents the difficult relationship between the city and the nation.

Like *The Reluctant Fundamentalist*, O'Neill's novel makes a distinction between New York City and the United States. The novel is an ode to the city of New York, but the New York it represents is a global city in which the usual allegiances of national identity have become frayed. Far from being unique to O'Neill's novel, this distinction was commonplace in the aftermath of the attacks – a period in which the symbolic meaning of the city, as of the nation, was being renegotiated. As Amy Kaplan observes, "it is hard to imagine New Yorkers referring to their city as 'the homeland.' Home, yes, but homeland? Not likely. Even in the upswelling of support for New York in the wake of 9/11, most Americans are unlikely to claim the city as part of the homeland, which has a decidedly anti-urban and anticosmopolitan ring to it."[41] In O'Neill's novel, New York is represented as both an affective site of nostalgia and a place of forward-thrusting futurism in step with neoliberal global capitalism. In the novel's first pages, and by way of example, Hans describes (on the day before he leaves for the bank's New York offices) a senior vice president whom he knows only in passing telling him that "New York's a very hard place to leave" and that he still misses it after twelve years.[42] Much later in the novel, Hans himself observes, the city "encourages even its most fleeting visitor to imagine for himself" a "nativity."[43]

The city also protects its citizens from the horrors of the nation at large. At one point, Hans and Rachel leave the city and make a trip upstate. Rather than the tranquil idyll they hope for, the couple is instead confronted with death and monstrosity. As Hans tells the reader,

> I strongly associate those trips with the fauna whose corpses lay around the road in great numbers: skunks, deer, and enormous indecipherable rodents that one never found in Europe. (And at night, when we sat on the porch, gigantic moths and other repulsive night-flyers would congregate on the screen, and my English wife and I would shrink back into the house in amazement and fear.)[44]

As this passage and others suggest, while the city is a place of affinity and opportunity, the nation from which it stands apart is a place of difference and threat. As a global citizen, moreover, Hans feels comfortable surrounded by the glitz and vulgarity of modern corporate life that characterizes the global city. As he admits: "Unfashionably, I liked Times Square in its newest incarnation .... Perhaps as a result of my work, corporations – even those with electrified screens flaming over Times Square – strike me as vulnerable, needy creatures, entitled to their displays of vigor."[45]

In passages such as these, the novel reveals the centrality of the global flows of capital and subjects that are central to its world. It is no surprise, moreover, that Hans is the only player on the Staten Island Cricket Club who lives in Manhattan and not one of the outer boroughs. A banker and a corporate lawyer, Hans and his wife have assets worth over $3 million and New York City is for him an opportunity to experience another part of the global world for a while and not – as it is for many of his fellow cricketers – a home not by choice but by necessity.

While many novelists make links between 9/11 and finance, with protagonists like Hans working in the financial industries, Jess Walter's *The Financial Lives of the Poets* (2009) is amongst the first novels to make direct and sustained connections between the global financial crisis of 2007 and the events of 9/11.[46] Like *Netherland*, *Poets* is narrated in the first person by its white, middle-class, male central protagonist; in both novels the narrator's capacity – and desire – to speak for himself is essential. Like *Netherland* (and *The Reluctant Fundamentalist*, albeit in a very different way) *Poets* is presented as an account, as the attempt of a man to explain his place in an altered world.[47] In Walter's novel, Matthew Prior is a financial journalist who has quit his job to "start an unlikely poetry-and-investment website."[48] Prior becomes a victim of the global recession when the fledgling website fails and he is at serious risk of losing not only the family home but also the family housed within it. In an opening chapter entitled "Another 7/11" the novel makes immediate reference to 9/11. The misnaming of 9/11 as 7/11 – a mistake made by the protagonist's mother who is dying of cancer and becomes "obsessed with the terrorist attacks in New York" in the months before her death (3) – produces a direct link between terrorism and finance that the novel pursues throughout. What 9/11 and the financial crisis produce in *Poets* is a radical recalibration of American prosperity, security, and opportunity. This is shown most clearly in the novel in its depictions of the unmooring of the middle classes from financial security, and nowhere more so than in its extended descriptions of the Prior's soon-to-be foreclosed house. As Prior observes of the house:

> we stopped thinking of the value of our home as a place of shelter and occupancy and family ... but as a kind of faith equation, theoretical construct, mechanism of wealth-generation, salvation function on a calculator, its value no longer *what it's worth* but some compound value that might exist given the continued upward tick of the market, because this was the only direction housing markets could ever go: up. (97–98)

In *Poets*, the family home is no longer – if it ever was – merely a place where the family lives, it has become both the measure of success and the engine of it. As such, when Prior's life begins to unravel, it is in the home that the most profound shifts are made visible. The world has begun to infiltrate the home in ways that Prior cannot control – not least in the virtual intrusion into the master bedroom by his wife's high school boyfriend with whom she has recently rekindled contact via social media.

As the 9/11 terrorist attacks produced anxiety about America's place in the world, the financial crisis (briefly) stopped a certain brand of American consumerism in its tracks. This transformation is encoded in the novel as an existential crisis of masculinity that Walter situates in a generational shift in which men have become increasingly unmoored from the security of properly masculine activity. This insecurity is represented in the novel in a number of ways, but most particularly in relation to work and physical labor. For example, about his father, the former manager of the automotive department at a Sears department store, Prior states,

> It was important that his necktie peer out of his shop clothes like that but I don't think it was something he consciously thought about; it was more like an innate Darwinian drive, a man in a tie and coveralls being the missing link in the evolution of my family's male drive from *lower-middle-class, rural blue collar* (Dad's dad worked on cattle ranches and in lumber mills) to *upper-middle class urban white collar*. (I've never worn a pair of coveralls; my private-school kids have never seen them.) (86)

The decline in capability through the four generations of Prior men is encoded as a loss of self-reliance twinned with a concomitant overreliance on the skills of others. For example, Prior goes on to suggest that something was lost when his father put on that tie, stating that his grandfather could "fix anything" but that he is only capable of changing a light bulb (86). What the protagonist of *Poets* must come to terms with is not only, as Prior puts it in the novel's penultimate paragraph, "the realization that the edge is so close to where we live" but also the understanding that his capacity to secure his family from that edge is attenuated by his own lack of physical skills (290). Like Hans in *Netherland*, Prior in *Poets* is forced to come to terms with the precarious nature of opportunity in a world that can no longer rely on long-held understandings of gender, race, and class that subtend traditional formations of national privilege.

In the final sections of *Exit West*, largely set on the West Coast of the United States, Mohsin Hamid likewise turns to contemporary transformations of ethnic and national identity, and nativism becomes a central subject. However, because of the radically altered sociopolitical context that the novel portrays, the ethnic/national makeup of the population Hamid represents is much changed. As the narrator describes: "In Marin there were almost no natives, these people having died out or been exterminated long ago, and one would see them only occasionally, at impromptu trading posts – or perhaps more often, but wrapped in clothes and guises and behaviours indistinguishable from anyone else" (195). While this description refers to American Indians, the concept of native identity is immediately troubled when the narrator claims that

> it was not quite true to say that there were almost no natives, nativeness being a relative matter, and many others considering themselves native to this country, by

which they meant that they or their parents or their grandparents or the grandparents of their grandparents had been born on the strip of land that stretched from the mid-northern Pacific to the mid-northern Atlantic, that their existence here did not owe anything to a physical migration that had occurred in their lifetimes. (196)

In addition to this passage's evocation of white ethnic nativity, what is perhaps most interesting here is the radical geographical compression of the United States of America to a thin "strip of land," thereby rescaling the country in relation to the rest of the world. No longer a beacon to the world, the United States becomes here one amongst many lands torn by conflict and migration. It is a spatial description that mirrors the psychic dislocation of those white-ethnic natives who find themselves "stunned by what was happening to their homeland" (196). It is important to note, moreover, that the narrator describes also a "third layer of nativeness," one, "composed of those who others thought directly descended, even in the tiniest fraction of their genes, from the human beings who had been brought from Africa to this continent centuries ago as slaves."[49] In the description of these three layers of nativeness – American Indian, white ethno-nationalist, African American – Hamid ties the long history of racial and ethnic violence in the United States to its contemporary forms.

Published during the first year of Donald Trump's presidency, at the height of the European migrant crisis, and following the United Kingdom's momentous decision to leave the European Union, *Exit West* both describes and anticipates the turn to isolationism and ethno-nationalism that have recently arisen around the world. As such – and like the other novels discussed in this chapter – the novel both represents the radical transformations of citizenship and national identity that took place in the aftermath of the 9/11 attacks and places them in longer histories of national identity and racial violence. As this chapter has shown, novel-length literary fiction that takes the terrorist attacks of 9/11 as its subject matter frequently does so via the complex and sophisticated negotiations of racial, gender, and ethnic identity that were the principal flashpoints around which the nation sought to make itself whole in the aftermath of the attacks. In the face of the overwhelmingly visual spectacle of the attacks, the novel found its relevance in the sorts of narratives of insecurity, home, and belonging that were often elided in the hyper-mediated clamor for meaning that arose in their immediate aftermath.

NOTES

1 See Timothy Melley, *The Covert Sphere: Secrecy, Fiction, and the National Security State* (New York: Cornell University Press, 2012).
2 Jay McInerney, "The Uses of Invention," *The Guardian*, September 17, 2005, 4.
3 Slavoj Žižek, *Welcome to the Desert of the Real* (London: Verso, 2002), 16.

4 Susan Buck-Morss, *Thinking Past Terror: Islamism and Critical Theory on the Left* (London: Verso, 2003), 73–74. For Buck-Morss and others, this dynamic echoed the conditions described by Jean Baudrillard in his influential work *The Gulf War Did Not Take Place* (Bloomington: Indiana University Press, 1995).

5 W. J. T. Mitchell, *Cloning Terror: The War of Images, 9/11 to the Present* (Chicago: The University of Chicago Press, 2011), 2.

6 Theodore Adorno, "Cultural Criticism and Society," in *Prisms* (Cambridge, MA: MIT Press, 1981), 35.

7 Richard Powers, "The Way We Live Now: 9-23-01: Close Reading: Elements of Tragedy; The Simile," *New York Times*, September 23, 2001.

8 Don DeLillo, "In the Ruins of the Future," *Harper's*, December 2001, 39.

9 Kristiaan Versluys, *Out of the Blue: September 11 and the Novel* (New York: Columbia University Press, 2009), 4.

10 Donald E. Pease, *The New American Exceptionalism* (Minneapolis: University of Minnesota Press, 2009), 5.

11 David Simpson, *9/11 The Culture of Commemoration* (Chicago: The University of Chicago Press, 2006), 4.

12 Randy Martin and Ella Shohat, "Introduction: 911 – A Public Emergency," *Social Text* 72, no. 3 (Fall 2002): 2.

13 Susan Willis, *Portents of the Real: A Primer for Post-9/11 America* (London: Verso, 2005), 46.

14 Elaine Tyler May, "Echoes of the Cold War: The Aftermath of September 11 at Home," in *September 11 in History: A Watershed Moment?*, edited by Mary L. Dudziak (Durham: Duke University Press, 2003), 50.

15 Fredric Jameson, "The Dialectics of Disaster," in *Dissent from the Homeland: Essays after September 11*, edited by Stanley Hauerwas (Durham: Duke University Press, 2003), 57.

16 Michael Rothberg, "A Failure of the Imagination: Diagnosing the Post-9/11 Novel: A Response to Richard Gray," *American Literary History* 21, no. 1 (Spring 2009): 152–158.

17 Richard Gray, "Open Doors, Closed Minds: American Prose Writing at a Time of Crisis," *American Literary History* 22, no. 1 (2009): 128–148.

18 Richard Gray, *After the Fall: American Literature Since 9/11* (London: Wiley-Blackwell, 2011), 30.

19 Catherine Morley, "'How Do We Write about This?': The Domestic and the Global in the Post 9/11 Novel," *Journal of American Studies* 45, no. 4 (November 2011): 719–721.

20 Leti Volpp, "The Citizen and the Terrorist," in Dudziak, *September 11 in History: A Watershed Moment*, 159.

21 For two important novels in which terrorists feature as central characters, see Don DeLillo, *Falling Man* (London: Picador, 2007); and John Updike, *Terrorist* (New York: Alfred A. Knopf, 2006).

22 Volpp, "The Citizen and the Terrorist," 147.

23 See, for example, Georgio Agamben, *Homo Sacer: Sovereign Power and Bare Life* (Stanford: Stanford University Press, 1998).

24 Mohsin Hamid, "My Reluctant Fundamentalist," in *Discontent and Its Civilizations: Dispatches from Lahore, New York and London* (London: Penguin, 2014), 67.

25 Mohsin Hamid, *The Reluctant Fundamentalist* (London: Hamish Hamilton, 2007), 1, 4.

26 It is worth noting that in her later novel *My Education*, Choi does directly reference the attacks of 9/11 with a sustained description of one of the novel's characters – a young boy of nine at the time – watching the bodies of those who fell or jumped from the upper stories of the Twin Towers of the World Trade Center. See Susan Choi, *My Education* (New York: Viking Books, 2013), 352–356.

27 For an account of the term "model minority" as it applies specifically to Asian Americans, see Paul Wong, Chienping Faith Lai, Richard Nagasawa, and Tieming Lin, "Asian Americans as a Model Minority: Self-Perceptions and Perceptions by other Racial Groups," *Sociological Perspectives* 41, no. 1 (1998): 95–118.

28 Susan Choi, *A Person of Interest* (New York: Penguin Books, 2008), 17.

29 Ibid., 17.

30 Ibid., 15.

31 Mohsin Hamid, *Exit West* (London: Hamish Hamilton, 2017), 189.

32 Ibid., 188.

33 Ibid., 86.

34 Ibid., 87.

35 Katie Bacon, "The Great Irish-Dutch-American Novel," *The Atlantic*, May 2008, www.theatlantic.com/magazine/archive/2008/05/the-great-irish-dutch-american-novel/306788/.

36 Ibid.

37 Joseph O'Neill, *Netherland* (New York: Pantheon Books, 2008), 10.

38 Ibid., 19.

39 Ibid., 11.

40 Ibid., 15–16.

41 Amy Kaplan, "Homeland Insecurities: Reflections of Language and Space," in Dudziak, *September 11 in History: A Watershed Moment?*, 62.

42 O'Neill, *Netherland*, 3.

43 Ibid., 181.

44 Ibid., 59–60.

45 Ibid., 21–22.

46 Jess Walters's previous novel, *The Zero* (New York: Regan, 2006), a finalist for the National Book award, took on directly the post-9/11 paranoia of the early years of the War on Terror.

47 For more on the subject of white male narrative voice, see Hamilton Carroll, "'Stuck Between Meanings': Recession-Era Print Fictions of Crisis Masculinity," in *Gendering the Recession: Media and Culture in an Age of Austerity*, edited by Diane Negra and Yvonne Tasker (Durham: Duke University Press, 2014), 203–222.

48 Jess Walter, *The Financial Lives of the Poets* (New York: Penguin Books, 2009), 5.

49 Hamid, *Exit West*, 196–197.

FURTHER READING

Short Fiction, Flash Fiction, Micro Fiction

Aldama, Frederick Luis. "Ana María Shua and the Shaping of a Planetary Republic of Flash Fiction Storytelling." *Alter/nativas* 4 (Spring 2015), https://alternativas.osu.edu/en/issues/spring-4-2015/miscelanea/aldama1.html.

"A Scientific Approach to the Teaching of a Flash Fiction." *Interdisciplinary Literary Studies* 16, no. 1 (2014): 127–144.

Blair, Peter, and Ashley Chantler, eds. *Flash: The International Short-Short Story Magazine*, Journal of the International Flash Fiction Association (IFFA). www1.chester.ac.uk/flash-magazine.

Fadda-Conrey, Carol. "Arab American Citizenship in Crisis: Destabilizing Representations of Arabs and Muslims in the US after 9/11." *MFS: Modern Fiction Studies* 57, no. 3 (Fall 2011): 532–555.

Hagedorn, Jessica, ed. *Charlie Chan Is Dead 2: At Home in the World*. New York: Penguin Books, 2004.

Hardy, Sarah, ed. "The Short Story: Theory and Practice." *Style* 27, no. 3, special issue (Fall 1993).

Hungerford, Amy. "McSweeney's and the School of Life." *Contemporary Literature* 53, no. 4 (Winter 2012): 646–680.

Kaldas, Pauline, and Khaled Mattawa, eds. *Dinarzad's Children: An Anthology of Contemporary Arab American Fiction*. Fayetteville: University of Arkansas Press, 2004.

Nelles, William. "Microfiction: What Makes a Very Short Story Very Short?" *Narrative* 20, no. 1 (January 2012): 87–104.

Patea, Viorica, ed. *Short Story Theories: A Twenty-First-Century Perspective*. Amsterdam: Rodopi, 2012.

Raley, Rita. "Reveal Codes: Hypertext and Performance." *Postmodern Culture* 12, no. 1 (September 2001): 106–135.

Samatar, Sofia. "Toward a Planetary History of Afrofuturism." *Research in African Literatures* 48, no. 4 (Winter 2017): 175–191.

Shapard, Robert, and James Thomas, eds. *Sudden Fiction: American Short Stories*. Salt Lake City: G. M. Smith, 1986.

Thomas, Sheree. *Dark Matter: A Century of Speculative Fiction from the African Diasopra*. New York: Aspect, 2000.

Thomas, James, Robert Shapard, and Christopher Merrill, eds. *Flash Fiction International: Very Short Stories from Around the World*. New York: W. W. Norton & Company, 2015.

Experimental Fiction

Aubry, Timothy. *Reading as Therapy: What Contemporary Fiction Does for Middle-Class Americans*. Iowa City: University of Iowa Press, 2011.
Boxall, Peter. *Twenty-First-Century Fiction: A Critical Introduction*. New York: Cambridge University Press, 2013.
Gladstone, Jason, Andrew Hoberek, and Daniel Worden, eds. *Postmodern/Postwar – and After: Rethinking American Literature*. Iowa City: University of Iowa Press, 2016.
Hoberek, Andrew. "Cormac McCarthy and the Aesthetics of Exhaustion." *American Literary History* 23, no. 3 (Fall 2011): 483–499.
Irr, Caren. *Toward the Geopolitical Novel: U.S. Fiction in the Twenty-First Century*. New York: Columbia University Press, 2013.
James, David. "Modern/Altermodern," in *Time: A Vocabulary of the Present*, edited by Amy J. Elias and Joel Burges, 66–81. New York: New York University Press, 2016.
    Modernist Futures: Innovation and Inheritance in the Contemporary Novel. New York: Cambridge University Press, 2012.
McLaughlin, Robert L. "Post-postmodernism," in *The Routledge Companion to Experimental Literature*, edited by Joe Bray, Alison Gibbons, and Brian McHale, 212–223. London: Routledge, 2012.
Rosen, Jeremy, *Minor Characters Have Their Day: Genre and the Contemporary Literary Marketplace*. New York: Columbia University Press, 2016.
Sykes, Rachel. *The Quiet Contemporary American Novel*. Manchester: Manchester University Press, 2017.

Speculative Fiction

Anderson, Reynaldo, and Charles E. Jones, eds. *Afrofuturism 2.0: The Rise of Astro-Blackness*. Lanham: Lexington Books, 2017.
Bahng, Aimee. *Migrant Futures: Decolonizing Speculation in Financial Times*. Durham: Duke University Press, 2018.
Bellamy, Brent Ryan, and Veronica Hollinger, eds. "Science Fiction and Climate Crisis." *Science Fiction Studies* 45, no. 3, special issue (November 2018).
Bould, Mark, ed. "Africa SF." *Paradoxa* 25 (2013).
Bould, Mark, and Rhys Williams, eds. "SF Now." *Paradoxa* 26 (2014).
Canavan, Gerry, and Andrew Hageman, eds. "Global Weirding." *Paradoxa* 28 (2016).
Canavan, Gerry, and Kim Stanley Robinson, eds. *Green Planets: Ecology and Science Fiction*. Middletown: Wesleyan University Press, 2014.
Castillo, Debra A., and Liliana Colanzi, eds. "Latin American Speculative Fiction." *Paradoxa* 30 (2018).
Dillon, Grace L., ed. *Walking the Clouds: An Anthology of Indigenous Science Fiction*. Tucson: University of Arizona Press, 2012.

Frelik, Paweł. "Of Slipstream and Others: SF and Genre Boundary Discourse." *Science Fiction Studies* 38, no. 1 (January 2011): 20–45.

Johns-Putra, Adeline. *Climate Change and the Contemporary Novel.* Cambridge: Cambridge University Press, 2019.

Lavender, Isiah, III, ed. *Black and Brown Planets: The Politics of Race in Science Fiction.* Jackson: University of Mississippi Press, 2016.

Merla-Watson, Cathryn Josefina, and B. V. Olguín, eds. *Altermundos: Latin@ Speculative Literature, Film, and Popular Culture.* Los Angeles: UCLA Chicano Studies Research Center Press, 2017.

Noys, Benjamin, and Timothy S. Murphy, eds. "Old and New Weird." *Genre: Forms of Discourse and Culture* 49, no. 2, special issue (2016).

Raulerson, Joshua. *Singularities: Technoculture, Transhumanism, and Science Fiction in the 21st Century.* Liverpool: Liverpool University Press, 2013.

Rieder, John, Grace L. Dillon, and Michael Levy, eds. "Indigenous Futurism." *Extrapolation* 57, nos. 1–2, special issue (2016).

Schmeink, Lars. *Biopunk Dystopias: Genetic Engineering, Society and Science Fiction.* Liverpool: Liverpool University Press, 2016.

Vint, Sherryl, ed. "The Futures Industry." *Paradoxa* 27 (2015).

Winter, Jerome. *Science Fiction, New Space Opera and Neoliberal Globalism: Nostalgia for Infinity.* Cardiff: University of Wales Press, 2016.

Yaszek, Lisa, and Isiah Lavender III, eds. *Afrofuturism through Time and Space.* Columbus: Ohio State University Press, 2019.

Graphic Fiction

Baetens, Jan, Hugo Frey, and Stephen E. Tabachnick, eds. *The Cambridge History of the Graphic Novel.* Cambridge: Cambridge University Press, 2018.

Ball, David M., and Martha B. Kuhlman, eds. *The Comics of Chris Ware.* Jackson: University of Mississippi, 2010.

Beaty, Bart, and Benjamin Woo. *The Greatest Comic Book of All Time: Symbolic Capital and the Field of American Comic Books.* New York: Palgrave Macmillan, 2016.

Bukatman, Scott. *Hellboy's World: Comics and Monsters on the Margins.* Oakland: University of California Press, 2016.

Chaney, Michael A., ed. *Graphic Subjects: Critical Essays on Autobiography and Graphic Novels.* Madison: University of Wisconsin Press, 2011.

El Refaie, Elisabeth. *Autobiographical Comics: Life Writing in Pictures.* Jackson: University Press of Mississippi, 2012.

Gabilliet, Jean-Paul. *Of Comics and Men: A Cultural History of American Comic Books.* Translated by Bart Beaty and Nick Nguyen. Jackson: University Press of Mississippi, 2013.

Gardner, Jared. *Projections: Comics and the History of Twenty-First-Century Storytelling.* Stanford: Stanford University Press, 2012.

Groensteen, Thierry. *Comics and Narration.* Translated by Ann Miller. Jackson: University Press of Mississippi, 2018.

Heer, Jeet, and Kent Worcester, ed. *A Comics Studies Reader.* Jackson: University Press of Mississippi, 2009.

Lyons, James, and Paul Williams, eds. *The Rise of the American Comics Artist: Creators and Contexts*. Jackson: University Press of Mississippi, 2011.

Mikkonen, Kai. *The Narratology of Comic Art*. New York: Routledge, 2017.

Miller, Ann, and Bart Beaty, eds. *The French Comics Theory Reader*. Leuven: Leuven University Press, 2014.

Pizzino, Christopher. *Arresting Development: Comics at the Boundaries of Literature*. Austin: University of Texas Press, 2016.

Schüwer, Martin. *Wie Comics erzählen: Grundriss einer intermedialen Erzähltheorie der grafischen Literatur*. Trier: Wissenschaftlicher Verlag Trier, 2008.

Tabachnick, Stephen E., ed. *The Cambridge Companion to the Graphic Novel*. Cambridge: Cambridge University Press, 2017.

Varnum, Robin, and Christina T. Gibbons, eds. *The Language of Comics: Word and Image*. Jackson: University Press of Mississippi, 2001.

Digital Fiction

Andersen, Christian Ulrik, and Søren Bro Pold. *The Metainterface: The Art of Platforms, Cities, and Clouds*. Cambridge: MIT Press, 2018.

Bell, Alice, Astrid Ensslin, and Hans Rustad. *Analyzing Digital Fiction*. New York: Routledge, 2016.

Bolter, Jay David. *Writing Space: Computers, Hypertext, and the Remediation of Print*, 2nd ed. Mahwah: Routledge, 2001.

Cayley, John. *Grammalepsy: Essays on Digital Language Art*. New York: Bloomsbury, 2018.

Douglass, Jeremy, Jessica Pressman, and Mark C. Marino. *Reading Project: A Collaborative Analysis of William Poundstone's Project for Tachistoscope {Bottomless Pit}*. Iowa City: University of Iowa Press, 2015.

Ensslin, Astrid. *Literary Gaming*. Cambridge: MIT Press, 2014.

Funkhouser, Chris. *New Directions in Digital Poetry*, 1st ed. New York: Bloomsbury Academic, 2012.

Hayles, N. Katherine. *Electronic Literature: New Horizons for the Literary*. Notre Dame: University of Notre Dame Press, 2008.

  How We Think: Digital Media and Contemporary Technogenesis. Chicago: The University of Chicago Press, 2012.

Johnston, David Jhave. *Aesthetic Animism: Digital Poetry's Ontological Implications*. Cambridge: MIT Press, 2016.

Joyce, Michael. *Of Two Minds: Hypertext Pedagogy and Poetics*. Ann Arbor: University of Michigan Press, 1996.

Kirschenbaum, Matthew G. *Mechanisms: New Media and the Forensic Imagination*. Cambridge: MIT Press, 2012.

Landow, George. *Hypertext 3.0: Critical Theory and New Media in an Era of Globalization*. Baltimore: Johns Hopkins University Press, 2006.

Mencía, María, and Katherine Hayles, eds. *#WomenTechLit*, vol. 8 of *Computing Literature*. Rochester: Computing Literature, 2017.

Murray, Janet H. *Hamlet on the Holodeck: The Future of Narrative in Cyberspace*. Cambridge: MIT Press, 1997.

Portela, Manuel. *Scripting Reading Motions: The Codex and the Computer as Self-Reflexive Machines*. Cambridge: MIT Press, 2013.

Pressman, Jessica. *Digital Modernism: Making It New in New Media*. New York: Oxford University Press, 2014.

Rettberg, Scott, Patricia Tomaszek, and Sandy Baldwin, eds. *Electronic Literature Communities*, vol. 6 of *Computing Literature*. Morgantown: Center for Literary Computing, 2015. https://elmcip.net/sites/default/files/media/critical_writing/attachments/elmcip_2_electronicliteraturecommunities.pdf.

Rettberg, Scott, and Sandy Baldwin, eds. *Electronic Literature as a Model of Creativity and Innovation in Practice: A Report from the HERA Joint Research Project*, vol. 4 of *Computing Literature*. Morgantown: Center for Literary Computing, 2014. https://elmcip.net/sites/default/files/media/critical_writing/attachments/rettberg_baldwin_elmcip.pdf.

Ryan, Marie-Laure. *Avatars of Story*. Minneapolis: University of Minnesota Press, 2006.

Ryan, Marie-Laure, Lori Emerson, and Benjamin J. Robertson, eds. *The Johns Hopkins Guide to Digital Media*. Baltimore: Johns Hopkins University Press, 2014.

Simanowski, Roberto. *Digital Art and Meaning: Reading Kinetic Poetry, Text Machines, Mapping Art, and Interactive Installations*. Minneapolis: University of Minnesota Press, 2011.

Tabbi, Joseph. *The Bloomsbury Handbook of Electronic Literature*. London: Bloomsbury Academic, 2018.

Wardrip-Fruin, Noah. *Expressive Processing: Digital Fictions, Computer Games, and Software Studies*. Cambridge: MIT Press, 2012.

Wittig, Rob. *Invisible Rendezvous: Connection and Collaboration in the New Landscape of Electronic Writing*. Hanover: Wesleyan University Press, 1994.

Afro-Futurism/Afro-Pessimism

Anderson, Reynaldo, and Charles E. Jones, eds. *Afrofuturism 2.0: The Rise of AstroBlackness*. Lanham: Lexington Books, 2016.

Carrington, André. *Speculative Blackness: The Future of Race in Science Fiction*. Minneapolis: University of Minnesota Press, 2016.

Commander, Michelle D. *Afro-Atlantic Flight: Speculative Returns and the Black Fantastic*. Durham: Duke University Press, 2017.

Dubey, Madhu. "Speculative Fictions of Slavery." *American Literature* 82, no. 4 (December 2010): 779–805.

Eshun, Kodwo. "Further Considerations on Afrofuturism." *CR: The New Centennial Review* 3, no. 2 (Summer 2003): 287–302.

Hartman, Saidiya. *Scenes of Subjection: Terror, Slavery, and Self-Making in Nineteenth- Century America*. New York: Oxford University Press, 1997.

Lose Your Mother: A Journey along the Atlantic Slave Route. New York: Farrar, Straus and Giroux, 2008.

Jackson, Sandra, and Julie E. Moody-Freeman, eds. *The Black Imagination: Science Fiction, Futurism and the Speculative*. New York: Peter Lang, 2011.

Keeling, Kara. *The Witch's Flight: The Cinematic, the Black Femme, and the Image of Common Sense*. Durham: Duke University Press, 2007.

Queer Times, Black Futures. New York: New York University Press, 2019.

Marriott, David. *Whither Fanon? Studies in the Blackness of Being*. Stanford: Stanford University Press, 2018.

"On Decadence: *Bling Bling*." *e-flux* no. 79 (February 2017), www.e-flux.com/journal/79/94430/on-decadence-bling-bling/.

Martinot, Steve, and Jared Sexton, "The Avant-Garde of White Supremacy." *Social Identities* 9, no. 2 (January 2003): 169–181.

Means Coleman, Robin. *Horror Noire: Blacks in American Horror Films from the 1890s to the Present.* New York: Routledge, 2011.

Moten, Fred. "Blackness and Nothingness (Mysticism in the Flesh)." *South Atlantic Quarterly* 111, no. 4 (October 2013): 737–780.

Patterson, Orlando. *Slavery and Social Death: A Comparative Study.* Cambridge: Harvard University Press, 1982.

Schalk, Sami. *Bodyminds Reimagined: (Dis)Ability, Race, and Gender in Black Women's Speculative Fiction.* Durham: Duke University Press, 2018.

Sexton, Jared. *Black Men, Black Feminism: Lucifer's Nocturne.* New York: Palgrave Pivot/Springer, 2018.

"People-of-Color-Blindness: Notes on the Afterlife of Slavery." *Social Text* 28, no. 2 (July 2010): 31–56.

Spillers, Hortense. "Mama's Baby, Papa's Maybe: An American Grammar Book." *Diacritics* 17, no. 2 (Summer 1987): 64–81.

Weheliye, Alexander. *Habeas Viscus: Racializing Assemblages, Biopolitics, and Black Feminist Theories of the Human.* Durham: Duke University Press, 2014.

Wilderson, Frank. *Incognegro: A Memoir of Exile and Apartheid.* Durham: Duke University Press, 2015.

Williamson, Terrion. *Scandalize My Name: Black Feminist Practice and the Making of Black Social Life.* New York: Fordham University Press, 2017.

Womack, Ytasha. *Afrofuturism: The World of Black Sci-Fi and Fantasy Culture.* Chicago: Lawrence Hill, 2013.

Transpacific Diasporas

Camacho, Keith. *Cultures of Commemoration: The Politics of War, Memory and History in the Mariana Islands.* Honolulu: University of Hawaii Press, 2011.

Cheung, King-Kok. *Chinese American Literature without Borders: Gender, Genre, and Form.* New York: Palgrave Macmillan, 2016.

Cruz, Denise. *Transpacific Femininities: The Making of the Modern Filipina.* Durham: Duke University Press, 2012.

DeLoughrey, Elizabeth. "The Myth of Isolates: Ecosystem Ecologies in the Nuclear Pacific." *Cultural Geographies* 20, no. 2 (April 2013): 167–189.

Espiritu, Yến Lê. *Body Counts: The Vietnam War and Militarized Refugees.* Oakland: University of California Press, 2014.

Espiritu, Yến Lê, Lisa Lowe, and Lisa Yoneyama. "Transpacific Entanglements," in *Flashpoints for Asian American Studies*, edited by Cathy Schlund-Vials, 175–189. Fordham: Fordham University Press, 2018.

Gonzalez, Vernadette. *Securing Paradise: Tourism and Militarism in Hawai'i and the Philippines.* Durham: Duke University Press, 2013.

Huang, Yunte. *Transpacific Imaginations: History, Literature, Counterpoetics,* Cambridge, MA: Harvard University Press, 2008.

Hsu, Hsu. *A Floating Chinaman: Fantasy and Failure across the Pacific.* Cambridge, MA: Harvard University Press, 2016.

Imada, Adria. *Aloha America: Hula Circuits through the US Empire*. Durham: Duke University Press, 2012.

Kim, Jodi. *Ends of Empire: Asian America Critique and the Cold War*. Minneapolis: University of Minnesota Press, 2010.

Man, Simeon. *Soldiering through Empire: Race and the Making of the Decolonial Pacific*. Oakland: University of California Press, 2018.

Nguyen, Mimi. *The Gift of Freedom: War, Debt, and Other Refugee Passages*. Durham: Duke University Press, 2014.

Ponce, Martin Joseph. *Beyond the Nation: Diasporic Filipino Literature and Queer Reading*. New York: New York University Press, 2012.

Roh, David S., Betsy Huang, and Greta A. Niu, eds. *Techno-Orientalism: Imagining Asia in Speculative Fiction, History & Media*. New Brunswick: Rutgers University Press, 2015.

Shigematsu, Setsu, and Comacho, Keith, eds. *Militarized Currents: Toward a Decolonized Future in Asia and the Pacific*. Minneapolis: University of Minnesota Press, 2010.

Sze, Julie. *Fantasy Islands: Chinese Dreams and Ecological Fears in an Age of Climate Crisis*. Oakland: University of California Press, 2015.

Watson, Jini Kim. "Postscript: On Transpacific Futurities." *Journal of Asian American Studies* 20, no. 1 (February 2017): 119–124.

Wilson, Rob, and Arif Dirlik, eds. *Asia/Pacific as Space of Cultural Production*. Durham: Duke University Press, 1995.

Yoneyama, Lisa. *Cold War Ruins: Transpacific Critique of American Justice and Japanese War Crimes*. Durham: Duke University Press, 2016.

Hemispheric Routes

Allen, Chadwick. *Transindigenous: Methodologies for Global Native Literary Studies*. Minneapolis: University of Minnesota Press, 2012.

Bales, Kevin. *Understanding Global Slavery: A Reader*. Berkeley: University of California Press, 2005.

Barronechea, Antonio. *America Unbound: Encyclopedic Literature and Hemispheric Studies*. Albuquerque: University of New Mexico Press, 2016.

Brickhouse, Anna. *The Unsettlement of America: Translation, Interpretation and the Story of Don Luis De Velasco, 1560–1945*. New York: Oxford University Press, 2014.

Chancy, Myriam. *From Sugar to Revolution: Women's Visions of Haiti, Cuba, and the Dominican Republic*. Ontario: Wilfrid Laurier University Press, 2012.

Dimock, Wai Chee. "Planetary Time and Global Translation: 'Context' in Literary Studies." *Common Knowledge* 9, no. 3 (Fall 2009): 488–507.

Levander, Caroline, and Robert Levine, eds. *Hemispheric American Studies*. New Brunswick: Rutgers University Press, 2008.

Mignolo, Walter. *Local Histories/Global Designs: Coloniality, Subaltern Knowledges and Border Thinking*. Princeton: Princeton University Press, 2000.

Naimou, Angela. *Salvage Work: U.S. and Caribbean Literatures amid the Debris of Legal Personhood*. New York: Fordham University Press, 2015.

Roach, Joseph. *Cities of the Dead: Circum-Atlantic Performance*. New York: Columbia University Press, 1996.

Saldívar, José David. *Trans-Americanity: Subaltern Modernities, Global Coloniality and the Cultures of Greater Mexico*. Durham: Duke University Press, 2012.

Taylor, Diana. "Remapping Genre through Performance: From American to Hemispheric Studies." *Publications of the Modern Language Association of America* 122, no. 5 (October 2007): 1416–1430.

Vazquez, Alexandra. *Listening in Detail: Performances of Cuban Music.* Durham: Duke University Press, 2013.

Vigil, Ariana. *War Echoes: Gender and Militarization in U.S. Latina/o Cultural Production.* New Brunswick: Rutgers University Press, 2014.

Waligora-Davis, Nicole A. *Sanctuary: African Americans and Empire.* New York: Oxford University Press, 2011.

Zamora, Lois Parkinson. *The Usable Past: The Imagination of History in Recent Fiction of the Americas.* Cambridge: Cambridge University Press, 1997.

Transgender and Transgenre Writing

Benaway, Gwen. "Holy Wild." *Room Magazine*, 2018. https://roommagazine.com/writing/holy-wild.

Boellstorff, Tom, Mauro Cabral, Micha Cárdenas, Trystan Cotten, Eric A. Stanley, Kalaniopua Young, and Aren Z. Aizura. "Decolonizing Transgender: A Roundtable Discussion." *TSQ: Transgender Studies Quarterly* 1, no. 3 (August 2014): 419–439.

edwards, kari. "A Narrative of Resistance," in *Troubling the Line: Trans and Genderqueer Poetry and Poetics*, edited by T. C. Tolbert and Trace Peterson, 317–325. Callicoon: Nightboat Books, 2013.

Edwards, Rebekah. "Trans-Poetics." *TSQ: Transgender Studies Quarterly* 1, nos. 1–2 (May 2014): 252–253.

Gill-Peterson, Julian. "Trans of Color Critique before Transsexuality." *TSQ: Transgender Studies Quarterly* 5, no. 4 (November 2018): 606–620.

Gossett, Reina, Eric A. Stanley, and Johanna Burton, eds. *Trap Door: Trans Cultural Production and the Politics of Visibility.* Cambridge, MA: MIT Press, 2017.

Green, Kai M., and Treva Ellison. "Tranifest." *TSQ: Transgender Studies Quarterly* 1, no. 2 (May 2014): 222–225.

Kuppers, Petra. "Trans-Ing Disability Poetry at the Confluence." *TSQ: Transgender Studies Quarterly* 1, no. 4 (November 2014): 605–613.

Ladin, Joy. "Trans Poetics Manifesto," in *Troubling the Line: Trans and Genderqueer Poetry and Poetics*, edited by T. C Tolbert and Trace Peterson, 299–307. Callicoon: Nightboat Books, 2013.

"I Am Not Me: Unmaking and Remaking the Language of the Self." *Lambda Literary*, December 28, 2014. www.lambdaliterary.org/features/12/28/unmaking-and-remaking-the-language-of-the-self/.

Link, Aaron Raz. "What Makes a Teaching Anthology in Minority Literature?" *TSQ: Transgender Studies Quarterly* 2, no. 3 (August 2015): 509–514.

Page/Odofemi, Morgan M. "Trans Women's Lit? An Interview with Trish Salah and Casey Plett." *Canadian Women in the Literary Arts*, February, 2014. http://cwila.com/trans-womens-lit-an-interview-with-trish-salah-and-casey-plett/.

Prosser, Jay. *Second Skins: The Body Narratives of Transsexuality.* New York: Columbia University Press, 1998.

Raha, Nat. "Transfeminine Brokenness, Radical Transfeminism." *South Atlantic Quarterly* 116, no. 3 (July 2017): 632–646.

Richardson, Matt, and Leisa Meyer. "Preface." *Feminist Studies* 37, no. 2, (Summer 2011): 247–253.

Rosenberg, Jordy, and Kay Gabriel. "Pleasure and Provocation: Kay Gabriel Interview with Jordy Rosenberg." *Salvage*, April 8, 2018. http://salvage.zone/online-exclusive/never-not-a-matter-of-taking-sides-kay-gabriel-interview-with-jordy-rosenberg/.

Salah, Trish. "In Lieu of a Transgender Poetics." *Open Letter* 13, no. 9 (Summer 2009): 34–36.

Stallings, L. H. *Funk the Erotic: Transaesthetics and Black Sexual Cultures.* Chicago: University of Illinois Press, 2015.

Tolbert, T. C., and Trace Peterson, eds. *Troubling the Line: Trans and Genderqueer Poetry and Poetics.* Callicoon: Nightboat Books, 2013.

Climate Fiction

Adamson, Joni. "Environmental Justice, Cosmopolitics, and Climate Change," in *The Cambridge Companion to Literature and the Environment*, edited by Louise Westling, 169–183. New York: Cambridge University Press, 2014.

Aravamudan, Srinivas. "The Catachronism of Climate Change." *Diacritics* 41, no. 3 (2013): 6–30.

Chakrabarty, Dipesh. "Anthropocene Time." *History and Theory* 57, no. 1 (March 2018): 5–32.

"Postcolonial Studies and the Challenge of Climate Change." *New Literary History* 43, no. 1 (2012): 1–18.

Craps, Stef, and Rick Crownshaw. "The Rising Tide of Climate Change Fiction." *Studies in the Novel* 50, no. 1, special issue (Spring 2018).

Fiskio, Janet, and Sophia Bamert. "New Directions in Ecocriticsm," in *American Literature in Transition, 2000–2010*, edited by Rachel Greenwood Smith, 291–308. New York: Cambridge University Press, 2018.

Heise, Ursula K. "Terraforming for Urbanists." *Novel* 49, no. 1 (May 2016): 10–25.

Heringman, Noah. "Deep Time at the Dawn of the Anthropocene." *Representations* 129, no. 1 (Winter 2015): 56–85.

Hulme, Mike. "'Telling a Different Tale': Literary, Historical and Meteorological Readings of a Norfolk Heatwave." *Climatic Change* 113, no. 1 (July 2012): 5–21.

Milkoreit, Manjana. "The Promise of Climate Fiction: Imagination, Storytelling, and the Politics of the Future," in *Reimagining Climate Change*, edited by Paul Wapner and Hilal Elver, 171–191. New York: Routledge, 2016.

Morton, Timothy. *Hyperobjects: Philosophy and Ecology after the End of the World.* Minneapolis: University of Minneapolis Press, 2013.

Oreskes, Naomi, and Erik M. Conway. *The Collapse of Western Civilization: A View from the Future.* New York: Columbia University Press, 2014.

Schneider-Mayerson, Matthew. "Climate Change Ficiton," in *American Literature in Transition, 2000–2010*, edited by Rachel Greenwood Smith, 309–321. New York: Cambridge University Press, 2018.

"The Influence of Climate Fiction: An Empirical Survey of Readers." *Environmental Humanities* 10, no. 2 (November 2018): 473–500.

Segal, Michael. "The Missing Climate Change Narrative." *South Atlantic Quarterly* 116, no. 1 (January 2017): 121–128.

Siperstein, Stephen, Shane Hall, and Stephanie LeMenager, eds. *Teaching Climate Change in the Humanities.* New York: Routledge, 2017.

Trexler, Adam, and Adeline Johns-Putra. "Climate Change in Literature and Literary Criticism." *Wiley Interdisciplinary Reviews: Climate Change* 2, no. 2 (March/April 2011): 185–200.

Convergence

Adam, Barbara. *Timescapes of Modernity: The Environment and Invisible Hazards.* New York: Routledge, 1998.

Bjornerud, Marcia. *Timefulness: How Thinking Like a Geologist Can Help Save the World.* Princeton: Princeton University Press, 2018.

Burges, Joel, and Amy J. Elias, eds. *Time: A Vocabulary of the Present.* New York: New York University Press, 2016.

Crary, Jonathan. *24/7: Late Capitalism and the Ends of Sleep.* London: Verso, 2014.

De Landa, Manuel. *A Thousand Years of Nonlinear History.* New York: Swerve Editions, 2000.

Dimock, Wai Chee. *Through Other Continents: American Literature across Deep Time.* Princeton: Princeton University Press, 2008.

Ermarth, Elizabeth Deeds. *Postmodernism and the Crisis of Representational Time.* Princeton: Princeton University Press, 1992.

Ernst, Wolfgang. *Chronopoetics: The Temporal Being and Operativity of Technological Media.* Translated by Anthony Enns. London: Rowan and Littlefield, 2016.

Ghosh, Amitav. *The Great Derangement: Climate Change and the Unthinkable.* Chicago: The University of Chicago Press, 2017.

Gould, Stephen Jay. *Time's Arrow, Time's Cycle: Myth and Metaphor in the Discovery of Geological Time.* New York: Penguin, 1988.

Hoffman, Eva. *Time.* New York: Picador, 2009.

Jameson, Fredric. *A Singular Modernity: Essay on the Ontology of the Present.* London: Verso, 2002.

Kern, Stephen. *The Culture of Time and Space, 1880–1918.* Cambridge, MA: Harvard University Press, 1983.

Koepnick, Lutz. *On Slowness: Toward an Aesthetic of the Contemporary.* New York: Columbia University Press, 2014.

Kubler, George. *The Shape of Time: Remarks on the History of Things.* New Haven: Yale University Press, 1962.

Martin, Theodore. *Contemporary Drift: Genre, Historicism, and the Problem of the Present.* New York: Columbia University Press, 2017.

Osborne, Peter. *The Politics of Time: Modernity and the Avant-Garde.* London: Verso, 1995.

Rosa, Hartmut. *Social Acceleration: A New Theory of Modernity.* Translated by Jonathan Trejo- Mathys. New York: Columbia University Press, 2013.

Sharma, Sarah. *In the Meantime: Temporality and Cultural Politics.* Durham: Duke University Press, 2014.

Steigler, Bernard. *Technics and Time, 1: The Fault of Epimetheus.* Translated by Richard Beardsworth and George Collins. Stanford: Stanford University Press, 1998.

Wajcman, Judy. *Pressed for Time: The Acceleration of Life in Digital Capitalism.* Chicago: The University of Chicago Press, 2015.

Weinstein, Cindy. *A Question of Time: American Literature from Colonial Encounter to Contemporary Fiction.* New York: Cambridge University Press, 2018.

Dissolution

Amar, Paul. *The Security Archipelago: Human-Security States, Sexuality Politics and the End of Neoliberalism.* Durham: Duke University Press, 2013.

Arendt, Hannah. *On Violence.* San Diego: Harcourt, Brace, and Jovanovich, 1970.

Bergoffen, Debra. "February 22, 2001: Toward a Politics of the Vulnerable Body." *Hypatia* 18, no. 1 (Winter 2003): 116–134.

Butler, Judith. *Precarious Life: The Powers of Mourning and Violence.* London: Verso, 2004.

   Frames of War: When Is Life Grievable? London: Verso, 2009.

Campbell, David. *Writing Security: United States Foreign Policy and the Politics of Identity.* Minneapolis: University of Minnesota Press, 1992.

Duggan, Lisa. *The Twilight of Equality?: Neoliberalism, Cultural Politics, and the Attack on Democracy.* Boston: Beacon Press, 2003.

Hesford, Wendy S., and Rachel A. Lewis, "Mobilizing Vulnerability: New Directions in Transnational Feminist Studies and Human Rights." *Feminist Formations* 28, no. 1 (Spring 2016): vii–xviii.

Jelly-Schapiro, Eli. "Security: The Long History." *Journal of American Studies* 47, no. 3 (August 2013): 801–826.

Lowe, Lisa. *The Intimacies of Four Continents.* Durham: Duke University Press, 2015.

Moore, Alexandra Schultheis. *Vulnerability and Security in Human Rights Literature and Visual Culture.* New York: Routledge, 2015.

Siebers, Tobin. *Disability Theory.* Ann Arbor: University of Michigan, 2008.

Sontag, Susan. *Regarding the Pain of Others.* New York: Picador, 2003.

Stockton, Kathryn Bond. "The Queer Child Now and Its Paradoxical Global Effects." *GLQ: A Journal of Lesbian and Gay Studies* 22, no. 4 (2016): 505–539.

Turner, Bryan S. *Vulnerability and Human Rights.* University Park: Pennsylvania State University, 2006.

Immobility

Acoli, Sundiata. *A Brief History of the New Afrikan Freedom Struggle.* Cumberland: Sundiata Acoli Freedom Campaign, 1992.

Brown, Sterling. "Southern Road," in *Southern Road, Poems by Sterling A. Brown; Drawings by E. Simms Campbell.* New York: Harcourt, Brace, 1932.

Bukhari, Safiya, ed. *The War Before.* New York: Feminist Press at the City University of New York, 2010.

Gaines, Ernest. *A Lesson before Dying.* New York: A. A. Knopf, 2004.

Herndon, Angelo. *Let Me Live.* New York: Random House, 1937.

Himes, Chester. *Yesterday Will Make You Cry.* New York: Norton, 1998.

Jackson, George. *Soledad Brother: The Prison Letters of George Jackson.* Chicago: Lawrence Hill Books, 1994.

   Blood in My Eye. New York: Random House, 1972.

King, Robert Hillary. *From the Bottom of the Heap: The Autobiography of Black Panther Robert Hillary King.* Oakland: PM Press, 2008.

Muntaqim, Jalil. *We Are Our Own Liberators.* Montreal: Abraham Guillen Press, 2003.

Nas. "One Love." Track 7 on *Illmatic*. Columbia, 1994.

Oshinsky, David. *"Worse Than Slavery": Parchman Farm and the Ordeal of Jim Crow Justice*. New York: Simon & Shuster, 1996.

Peltier, Leonard. *Prison Writings: My Life Is a Sundance*. New York: St. Martin's Press, 1999.

Sayles, James Yaki. *Meditations on Frantz Fanon's Wretched of the Earth: A Study Guide*. Chicago: Spear & Shield Publications, 2002.

Shakur, Tupac. "Soulja's Story." Track 3 on *2Pacalypse Now*. Interscope, 1991.

Williams, Robert Pete. "Prisoner's Talkin' Blues." Track 1 on *Angola Prisoners' Blues*. Arthoolie Productions, Inc., 1996.

Insecurity

Amoore, Louise, and Marieke De Goede. *Risk and the War on Terror*. London: Routledge, 2008.

Cherniavsky, Eva. *Neocitizenship: Political Culture after Democracy*. New York: New York University Press, 2017.

Crownshaw, Richard. "Deterritorializing the 'Homeland' in American Studies and American Fiction after 9/11." *Journal of American Studies* 45, no. 4 (November 2011): 757–776.

Fadda-Conrey. Carol. "Arab American Citizenship in Crisis: Destabilizing Representations of Arabs and Muslims in the United States after 9/11." *Modern Fiction Studies* 57, no. 3 (Fall 2011): 532–555.

Irr, Caren. *Toward the Geopolitical Novel: U.S. Fiction in the Twenty-First Century*. New York: Columbia University Press, 2014.

Martin, Andrew, and Patrice Petro. *Rethinking Global Security: Media, Popular Culture, and the "War on Terror."* New Brunswick: Rutgers University Press, 2006.

Martin, Randy. *An Empire of Indifference: American War and the Financial Logic of Risk Management*. Durham: Duke University Press, 2007.

McClanahan, Annie. *Dead Pledges: Debt, Crisis, and the Twenty-First-Century Culture*. Stanford: Stanford University Press, 2017.

McLaughlin, Robert D. "After the Revolution: US Postmodernism in the Twenty-First Century." *Narrative* 21, no. 3 (October 2013): 284–295.

Redfield, Marc. *The Rhetoric of Terror: Reflections on 9/11 and the War on Terror*. New York: Fordham University Press, 2009.

Shonkwiler, Alison. *The Financial Imaginary: Economic Mystification and the Limits of Realist Fiction*. Minneapolis: University of Minnesota Press, 2017.

Smith, Paul. *Primitive America: The Ideology of Capitalist Democracy*. Minneapolis: Minnesota University Press, 2007.

Stubblefield, Thomas. *9/11 and the Visual Culture of Disaster*. Bloomington: Indiana University Press, 2014.

Wegner, Phillip E. *Life between Two Deaths, 1989–2001: American Culture in the Long Nineties*. Durham: Duke University Press, 2009.

INDEX

28 Days Later, 72

Abdullah, Samiya Hameeda, aka "Goldii," 262
  "Trap Doors," 256–257
Abdur-Rahman, Aliyyah, 129
Abel, Jessica, *La Perdida*, 88
Abi-Karam, Andrea, 174–175
Aboriginal writers, 75–76
Abreu, Manuel Arturo, 174–175
Abu-Jamal, Mumia, 256–259
acceleration, 216–217, 221–223
Ace, Samuel, 174–175
Achebe, Chinua, *Things Fall Apart*, 36
Acker, Kathy, *Empire of the Senseless*, 104
Activision, 110
Adamson, Joni, 167
Adlard, Charlie, *The Walking Dead* comic, 72
Adorno, Theodor, 272–273
African American literature, 14–15, 26. *See also specific authors and genres*
  history and, 123–124
  science fiction and, 125–126
  temporality and, 123–124
African Americans, violence against, 123–125, 251–254, 259–260 (*see also* Black Lives Matter movement)
African American science fiction, 73–75, 125–126
Afrodiasporic wave, 74–76
Afrofuturism, 14–15, 74–76, 123–138
  black speculative fiction and, 124–125
  science fiction and, 128–129
Afro-Pessimism, 11–12, 14–15, 123–138
  African American literature and, 129–135
  methodologies and, 129
  slavery and, 126–127, 129–130, 138
  speculative nature of, 126–127

Agamben, Giorgio, 276
Alcalay, Ammiel, 4–5
Alexie, Sherman, 26, 75–76
Algren, Nelson, 104
alterglobalization movement, 65–66
alt-right, 3
alt-temporalities, 4–7
Alvar, Mia, 14–15
  In the Country, 7–8, 144–145
  "Esmeralda," 7–8
  "The Kontrabida," 144–145
Alvarez, Julia, 14–15, 26, 171
  Saving the World, 163–164
Amadahy, Zainab, 75–76
Amazon, 116
American exceptionalism, 237
Amerika, Mark, *Grammatron*, 106
Amis, Martin, *Time's Arrow*, 222–223
anachronism, 5–6
Anaya, Rudolfo, 26
Anders, Charlie, *Choirboy*, 187
Annales school, 221, 223
Anthony, Patricia, 65
the Anthropocene, 6–7, 13–14, 22–23, 59–60, 86–87, 198, 203, 208–209
Anthropocene storytelling, 199–200
anti-blackness, 126–129, 135–138, 177, 184–185, 253
anti-carceral hip-hop, 16–17
anti-prison narratives, 264
Anzaldua, Gloria, *BorderLands/La Frontera*, 182
Aoki, Ryka, 174–175
apocalypse, 217, 227–231
Appadurai, Arjun, 143
Apple, 102
The Apprentice, 10
Arab American literature, 26

Arellano, Robert, *Sunshine '69*, 107–108
Arnold, Matthew, 219–220
Arrhenius, Svante, 70–71
Arrighi, Giovanni, 221
artificial intelligence, 4
AR/VR environments, 115
Asian American literature, 14–15, 26, 76. *See also specific authors*
   Asian Americans, violence against, 151–155
   graphic fiction and narrative, 151–155
   transpacific turn, 143–146 (*see also* the transpacific)
Asian American Studies, 142–143
Asian Pacific Economic Cooperation (APEC), 142
Asimov, Isaac, 220–223
Askari X, 16–17, 253–255, 258–260, 262, 264
   "Gotta Go," 258–261
Atari, Inc., 8–10
Atwood, Margaret, 63–64
   Maddadam trilogy, 71–72
Auster, Paul, 103
   4 3 2 1, 4
autobiography
   Black radical prison autobiography, 257
   graphic narrative and, 89–91
   trans genre writing and, 186
autogynophilia, 189
Awkward-Rich, Cameron, 174–175, 178, 190–191
Ayles, James Yaki, 258–259

Bacigalupi, Paolo
   Shipbreaker trilogy, 71
   The Water Knife, 5–6, 71, 201–202, 204–205
   The Windup Girl, 71, 206–208
Baetens, Jan, 80–81, 94
Baker, Nicholas, *The Mezzanine*, 222–223
Bakhtin, Mikhail, 218
Baldwin, James, 16–17, 26, 253, 264
   The Fire Next Time, 7–8
   If Beale Street Could Talk, 262–263
Ballowe, Jeff, 100
Bambara, Toni Cade, 26
bande dessinée, 79
Banias, Ari, 174–175
Baraka, Amiri, 73–75
Barnes, Steven, 73–75
Barrett, Ulanday, 174–175

Barth, John, 103–104
   "Frame Tale," 104–105
   "Sentence," 104–105
Barthelme, Donald, 105
Barthes, Roland, 103–104
Baum, L. Frank, *The Patchwork Girl of Oz*, 104
Beatty, Christine, 187
Beatty, Paul, *The Sellout*, 242–243
Bechdel, Alison, *Fun Home: A Family Tragicomic*, 90, 94–95
Bechdel test, 178
Bell, Gabrielle, *Everything Is Flammable*, 90, 94–95
belonging, 286. *See also* citizenship
Benaway, Gwen, 174–175
Bender, George, 47
Bendorf, Oliver Baez, 174–175
Benford, Gregory, 65
Benveniste, Emile, 13
Bergman, S. Bear, 174–175
Berlant, Lauren, 123
Berners-Lee, Tim, 102
Berrout, Jamie, 174–175
Bérubé, Michael, 115
Bigelow, Alan, 109
   "Brainstrips," 109
   "How to Rob a Bank," 109
   "When I Was President," 109
Biko, Steven, 255
bildungsroman, 240–242
bimodality, 144
bin Laden, Osama, 281
Binnie, Imogen, 174–175
   Nevada, 188–190
biography, graphic narrative and, 89–91
biopolitics, 237
biotechnology studies, 206–208
Black Arts Movement, 260
Black Liberation Era, 258–259
Black Lives Matter movement, 14–15, 56–57, 75, 123–126, 240, 260
Black Mirror: Bandersnatch, 8–10
Black neoabolitionist narratives, 253–258
Black Panther, 124
Black Panther Party for Self-Defense (BPP), 260–261
Black Panthers, 256
Black radical prison autobiography, 257
Black radical temporality, 259
Black speculative fiction, 124–127
   Afrofuturism and, 124–125
   Black Lives Matter movement and, 124–126

Blanco, María del Pilar, 49–50
Boes, Tobias, 241–242
Bolaño, Roberto, 2666, 4
Bolter, Jay David, 100–102, 106
book, as physical object, 96–97
Borges, Jorge Luis, 26–27, 67, 229
  "The Aleph," 26–27, 38–39
  "forking path" narratives, 225
  "The Garden of Forking Paths,"
    107
Bornstein, Kate, 187
  Gender Outlaw, 176
Bose, Maria, 38
Bould, Mark, 14
Boyle, T. C., 63–64
Brady, Mary Pat, 6–7, 14–15
Branch, Michael, 204
Braudel, Fernand, 220–221, 223
Brecht, Bertholt, 26–27
Brexit, 286
Brickhouse, Anna, 157
Brite, Poppy Z., 187. See also Martin, Billy
Brolaski, Julian T., 174–175
Brooks, Max, World War Z, 72
Brown, John, 102
Bruchac, Joseph, 75–76
Buber, Martin, I and Thou, 13
Buckell, Tobias S.
  Arctic Rising, 71
  Hurricane Fever, 71
Buck-Morss, Susan, 272–273
Buddies in Bad Times Theatre, 180
Bui, Thi, 14–15
  The Best We Could Do, 151–155
Burgess, Tony, PontyPool Changes
  Everything, 72
Burns, Charles, Black Hole, 83
Bush, George W., 281
  administration of, 271
Bush, Vannevar, 101–102
Butler, Alec, 174–175
Butler, Judith, 239–240
Butler, Octavia, 49–50, 73–75
  Fledgling, 73–75, 125
  The Parable of the Sower, 70–71
  The Parable of the Talents, 70–71

Callison, Candis, 202
Calvino, Italo, 26–27
  If on a Winter's Night a Traveler, 8
Camus, Albert
  The Fall, 8
  The Stranger, 36

Cannizzaro, Danny, Pry, 115
capitalism
  globalization and, 238–239
  modernity and, 218–219
carceral scale, 168–171. See also
  incarceration; prison narratives
Cardenas, Micha, 177–178
Carroll, Hamilton, 16–17
Carroll, Jonathan, 64
Carruth, Allison, 204, 208
Carter, Alprentice "Bunchy," 260
catastrophe, 48–50, 68–73, 198, 202–203,
  237–238
causality, 6–7
CAVE environments, 115–116
Cayley, John, 116
Hak Kyung Cha, Theresa
  Dictee, 8
Chabon, Michael, 63–64
  The Amazing Adventures of Kavalier &
    Clay, 64
Chakrabarty, Dipesh, "The Climate of
  History," 198
Chamoiseau, Patrick, Texaco, 159
Chancy, Miriam, The Loneliness of Angels,
  159
Chang, Sucheng, 144
Charles, Jos, 174–175
Charlie Hebdo attack, Paris, 3
Chen, Ching-In, 174–175
Chiang, Ted, 7–8, 76
  "Story of Your Life," 6–8
Chicanxfuturism, 76
Childs, Dennis, 16–17
Cho, Tom, 174–175
Choi, Susan, 16–17, 271
  A Person of Interest, 276, 278–279
Choose Your Own Adventure series, 8–10,
  107, 112
Chronicle of Higher Education, 115
chronotopes, 218, 224–225, 229–230, 242
Chu, Wesley, Tao trilogy, 71
Chute, Hillary, 89–90
Cisco, Michael, 65–66
Cisneros, Sandra, 26
  Caramelo, 159
citizenship, 272–276, 279–281
  ethnicity and, 281–284
  fictions of, 281–286
  migration and, 285–286
  minority, 276–281
Clarke, Arthur C., 63–64
  Rendezvous with Rama, 63

class, 237
  climate fiction (cli-fi) and, 200–201
  trans genre writing and, 174
Clemmons, Zinzi, *What We lose*, 242–243
"cli-fi," 15–16
climate change, 2–4, 11, 14–16, 22, 67–73,
    157, 196–199, 202–207, 217–218,
    223–224. *See also* climate fiction (cli-fi)
  digital media and, 116
  protests and, 59–60
climate fiction (cli-fi), 71–72, 196–209
  class and, 200–201
  creaturely interventions, 206–209
  hacking crisis, 203–206
  realism and, 202–203
  space and, 201–202
  utopian, 203–206
climate fiction studies, 206–207
Clover, Joshua, 221
Clowes, Daniel, 83
Coates, Ta-Nehisi, *Between the World and
    Me*, 123–124
coevality, 3–4
COINTELPRO (Counterintelligence
    Program), 256
Colbert, Stephen, 2–3
Cole, Teju, 13–14, 33, 35
  "Hafiz," 37
  literary conceptualization of the internet,
    38
  Open City, 38
  "Seven short stories about drones," 33,
    35–39
collaborative authorship, graphic narrative
    and, 82–83
collective narrative, 113–115
coloniality, 74–75, 151, 177
combat, poetics of, 254–255
comics, 79, 89. *See also* graphic narratives
  reprint collections, 89
complexity, 50–56, 69, 107–110
computer code, 14
computer games, 110
conceptual writing, 100–101
contagion narratives, 72–73
Cooper, T., *Some of the Parts*, 187
Coover, Robert, 100–101
Coover, Roderick
  *Hearts and Minds: The Interrogations
    Project*, 116
  Toxi*City: A Climate Change Narrative,
    116
copyright law, 3

Cortázar, Julio, 26–27
  Hopscotch, 107
Cortés, Hernán, 171
cosmopolitanism, 26, 158
Crawford, Lucas, 174–175
creative nonfiction, 235–236
crip trans reading practices, 177–178
Critical Digital Media, 115–117
cross-media intertextuality, 13
Crucet, Jennine Capó, 14–15, 161–162, 164,
    171
Crumb, Robert, 79
cultural capital, 64
cybertexts, 113–114
cyber-utopianism, 106–107

Daniel, Sharon
  Inside the Distance, 116
  Public Secrets, 116
Danielewski, Mark Z., 43–44, 50, 104–105
  House of Leaves, 16, 48–49, 66–67
  Only Revolutions, 16
Danticat, Edwidge, 13–14, 26
  Brother, I'm Dying, 31
  "Children of the Sea," 31
  Claire of the Sea Light, 32
  The Dewbreaker, 32
  Krik?Krak! 32
  "A Wall of Fire Rising," 30
  "Without Inspection," 29–32
Da Silva, Denise Ferreira, 167
data aggregation, 4
Davis, Angela, 16–17, 253, 258–259
Davis, Lydia, 23
Davis, Ray, 63
Dead Prez, 16–17, 253, 255–258, 262, 264
  "Behind Enemy Lines," 256–257
  Let's Get Free, 254–256
decolonization, 177
deep time, 219–220
deincarceration, 261–262
Delany, Samuel R., 11–12, 73–75, 123,
    125–127
  Dhalgren, 63
  Through the Valley of the Nest of Spiders,
    73–75
Deleuze, Gilles, 179, 182
DeLillo, Don, 30, 63–64, 273
  Falling Man, 30, 274–275
  Ratner's Star, 63
  "Videotape," 10–11
Deline, Elliot, 174–175
depolicing, 261–262

deportation, 16–17
Derrida, Jacques, 104
Dery, Mark, 124
deterritorialization, 166, 180, 183–184
development, fictions of, 239–246
Díaz, Junot, 26, 50
    The Brief Wondrous Life of Oscar Wao,
      49–50, 64, 159, 242–243
Dibbell, Carola, *The Only Ones*, 72–73
Dick, Philip K., 67, 229
digital cinema, 116
digital fiction, 14, 22, 100–117
    critical digital media and, 115–117
    digital microfiction, 36–38 (*see also* Twitter
      fiction)
    digital technologies, literary
      experimentalism and, 24
    digital textualities, 14
    digital turn, 117
    interactive narrative and, 110–111
    intertextuality and, 105
    multi-authored, 113–115
    online, 113–115
    platforms, 7–10
digital interactivity, 8–10. *See also* interactive
    narrative
    second-person narrative perspectives, 8–10
digital literacy, 117
digital media, 3–5, 8–10, 105
    critical, 115–117
    literary potential of, 100
    second-person narrative perspectives and,
      12
digital poetry, animated, 109
disability, 14, 177–178
disaster preparedness, 22
disasters, 22
Disch, Thomas, 63–64
distraction, 4–5, 22
documentary naturalism, 10
documentary style, interactivity and, 116–117
dodd, jayy, 174–175
Dominguez, Cesar, 178–179, 186
Donaldson, Lou, 260–261
Doom Patrol, 176
Doroshow, Ceyenne, 174–175, 182
    Cooking in Heels, 181
Douglass, Frederick, 264
Drawn & Quarterly, 79
Du Bois, W.E.B., 264
Due, Tananarive, 73–75
duration, 219–222, 229–230. *See also*
    temporality

Earle, Harriet, 151
Eastgate Systems, 100–101, 106–107
Eastwood, Alexander, 177–178
ecocriticism, 15–16, 157–158, 196–199, 206–208
ecological disasters, 217–218, 223–224
economic downturns, 11
Edidi, Lady Dane Figuroa, 174–175, 182
    Yemaya's Daughters, 182
Edwards, Erica, 129
Edwards, Kari, 177–178
Egan, Jennifer, 7–8, 13–14, 50
    "Out of Body," 7–8
    A Visit from the Goon Squad, 5–8, 48–49,
      242–243
    "You (Plural)," 7–8
electronic literature (e-lit), 100
    future of, 117
    Network Writing, 113–115
Electronic Literature Collection, 100
Eliot, George, 68–69
Ellison, Ralph, 125
    Invisible Man, 36, 225–226
empire, 14–16, 22, 26, 151
encyclopedic novel, 22–23
environmental anxiety, global economies of,
    14–15
environmental disasters, 11, 21–22
environmentalism, 14–15
epistolary second-person, 7–8
Erdrich, Louise, 26, 196, 203
    Future Home of the Living God, 7–8, 205–207
    Love Medicine, 24
    Round House, 242–243
eschatology, 217, 227–231
Escobar, Arturo, 158–159
Espinosa, Joshua Jennifer, 174–175
ethnicity, citizenship and, 281–284
ethnic studies, 26
ethno-nationalism, 285–286
European migrant crisis, 286
Everett, Hugh III, 6–7
everyday life, 15–16
experimentalism, 13–14, 16, 43–60,
    102–103. *See also* innovation
    digital technologies and, 24, 37–38
    genre and, 48
    graphic fiction and, 83–88
    and its others, 44–48
    postmodernism and, 43–45
    realism and, 47–48, 50, 56–59, 242–243
    social media and, 37–38
"Extinction Rebellion" movement, 59–60
"extranarrative" elements, 221–222

fabula, 219–220

Facebook, 116

Familienroman, 88

Fanon, Frantz, 184–185, 190, 254–255

Fantagraphics, 79

fantasy, 123–124

Faulkner, William, 6–7, 219–220

Faust, Minister, 75

faux realism, 10

Federman, Raymond, 44–45

feminism, trans and, 178

feminist science fiction, 73–75

Ferguson, Missouri, 11–12

Ferré, Rosario, *The House on the Lagoon*, 159

Ferris, Emil, *My Favorite Thing Is Monsters*, 90

Fienberg, Leslie, *Stone Butch Blues*, 176

Finka, Marty, 177–178

Firewatch, 113

First Nations writers, 75–76. *See also* Native literature

Fitzpatrick, Cat, 174–175

flash fiction, 6–7, 13–14, 21–39

Fleischmann, T. Clutch, 174–175, 177–178

Foer, Jonathan Safran, *Extremely Loud and Incredibly Close*, 272–275

FOMO (Fear of Missing Out) syndrome, 115

forced migration, slavery and, 168

Foster, Sesshu, 7–8
    Atomik Aztex, 5–8, 76
    City of the Future, 4–5

Foucault, Michel, 103–104

Fountain, Ben, *Billy Lynn's Long Halftime Walk*, 35

Fowler, Karen Joy, 63–64
    The Jane Austen Book Club, 63–64

fragmentation, 16, 29, 102–103, 235–236, 240–243

Franzen, Jonathan, 45–46
    Freedom, 69

French New Wave, 10

Frey, Hugo, 80–81, 94

the future, 4–6. *See also* Afrofuturism; futurism
    new futures, 73–77

Futurians, 73

futurism, 5–6, 11–12
    Afrofuturism, 14–15, 74–76, 123–138
    Chicanxfuturism, 76
    Indigenous futurism, 75–76
    as literature of the present, 11–12

Gabriel, Kay, 174–175

Gallagher, Catherine, 229

gaming, 8–10, 113

Garber, Marjorie, 187

gay/lesbian fiction. *See* queer fiction

Geha, Joseph, 26

gender, 237. *See also* queer theory; trans genre writing
    gendered alterities, 14
    white masculinity, 183–184, 281–286

genderqueer writing, 175–176, 182. *See also* queer fiction; trans genre writing

Gendertrash, 176

Genette, Gérard, 219, 221–222

genre. *See also* slipstream; *specific genres*
    adaptations of, 88–91
    adapted in graphic narrative, 88–91
    experimentalism and, 48
    genre blurring, 14 (*see also* multi-genre techniques)
    genre turn, 123–124
    innovation and, 48–51
    multi-genre techniques, 8, 23–24
    "non-genre genre story," 64

genre fiction and narrative, 22
    increasing prominence of, 123–124
    racial homogeneity of conventional, 124

Gen X, 3–4

Gen Z, 2–4

Ghosh, Amitav, 59–60, 68–69, 71–72, 197–198

Gibbons, Dave, *Watchmen*, 79

Gibson, William, 16, 71, 218–219
    The Peripheral, 6–7, 229–231

Gideon, Siegfried, 221

gig economy, 3

Gillespie, William, 104
    The Unknown, 108, 114

Gilroy, Paul, 157

Glaser, Rachel B., 13–14
    "Pee on Water," 28–29

global climate change (GCC). *See* climate change

global crises, 11. *See also* catastrophe; *specific crisis*

global financial crisis of 2007, 284–285

globalization, 13–15, 160
    capitalism and, 238–239

global militarized atmospherics, 32–39

global novel, 22–23

global racial capitalism, 22

global south, 237–238

global warming, 70–71. *See also* climate change

Gloeckner, Phoebe, *The Diary of a Teenage Girl*, 90, 95–96
Gloss, Molly, 63–64
The Jump-Off Creek, 63–64
Goble, Mark, 6–7, 16
Goh, Jaymee, 76
Goines, Donald, 253
Goldberg, Ariel, 174–175
Goldman, Francisco, *The Ordinary Seaman*, 159
Gomel, Elana, 136
Gomez, Jewelle, 73–75
Gone Home, 113
Goodie Mob, 254–255
Google, 4, 8, 116
Google Books, 8
Goranson, Alicia, *Supervillainz*, 187
Gorman, Samantha, *Pry*, 115
Grande, Reyna, 16–17, 252–253
graphic fiction and narrative,
    14, 79–97, 154
  adaptations of literary genres in, 88–91
  Asian American, 151–155
  (auto)biographical works, 89–91
  collaborative authorship and, 82–83
  in contemporary mediascape, 96–97
  experimentalism and, 83–88
  hybrid language and, 91–96
  interactive narrative and, 81–83
  long-form, 82–83, 97
  meaning in, 91–94
  metaphoricity and, 94–96
  serialization and, 83
  spatiality and, 85–86
  temporality and, 85–88
  visual qualities of, 91–95
graphic reportage, 90–91
Gray, Richard, 274–275
Great Acceleration, 199–200
Great Recession 2008, 199–200, 202–203, 237
greenhouse effect, 70–71
Grewal, Inderpal, 239
Grusin, Richard, 106
Guantánamo Bay, 239
Guattari, Félix, 182
Gutkind, Lee, 235–236

Hairston, Andrea
  Mindscape, 74
  Redwood and Wildfire, 74
  Will Do Magic for Small Change, 73–75
Hamer, Fannie Lou, 264

Hamid, Mohsin, 16–17, 271
  Exit West, 276, 279–281, 285–286
  How to Get Filthy Rich in Rising Asia, 7–8
  The Reluctant Fundamentalist, 276–283
Hampton, Fred Jr., 256–257, 260
Hampton, Fred Sr., 255–257, 260
Hanafi, Amira, 116–117
  A Dictionary of the Revolution, 116–117
Haraway, Donna, 104, 203
Harrison, M. John, 65–66
Hartman, Saidiya, 126
Hatfield, Chalres, 80–81
Hawthorne, Nathaniel, *Twice Told Tales*, 25
Hayles, N. Katherine, 100–101, 105–106
Heartscape, Porpentine Charity, Twine works, 12–13
Heise, Ursula K., 22–23
  Imagining Extinction, 198
  Sense of Place and Sense of Planet, 197
Heller, Joseph, *Catch-22*, 35
Hemingway, Ernest, 21
hemispheric literature, 14–15, 157–171
hemispheric turn, 157
Hemon, Aleksandar, *The Lazarus Project*, 5–6
Henry, Imani, 187
Hernandez, Jaime, 76
Hernandez brothers, *Love & Rockets*, 79
Herndon, Angelo, 253
highbrow, 13, 64
Himes, Chester, 16–17, 253
hip-hop narratives, 16–17, 251–253, 262–264
  anti-carceral, 253–258
  imprisoned intellectual, 258–261
historical fiction, 5–6, 217–219
history, 15–16, 151–155, 217–219
  African American literature and, 123–124
  historical causality, 6–7
Hoberek, Andrew, 50
Hodgson, William Hope, 65–66
Hogan, Ernest, 76
Hogan, Linda, 14–15, 171
  Dwellings, 160–161
  People of the Whale, 166–169
home, 281–286
  'turn to the domestic' and, 274–275
Hoover, J. Edgar, 256
Hopkinson, Nalo
  Brown Girl in the Ring, 73–75
  Midnight Robber, 73–75
  The New Moon's Arms, 73–75
  The Salt Roads, 73–75
  Sister Mine, 73–75

Hoskins, Janet, 142–143
Houser, Heather, 15–16
Howe, Daniel, 116
HTML (Hypertext Markup Language), 102, 106–109
Huggins, Ericka, 260
Huggins, John, 260
Hurricane Katrina, 237–238
Hutton, Lil' Bobby, 260
hybrid language, graphic narrative and, 91
HyperCard, 102, 106–107
hyperfiction, 102–103
hypermedia, 101–102, 116
hypersecuritization, 279–281
hypertext, 14, 101–102, 116
    interactivity and, 109–110, 112
    intertextuality and, 104
    narrative potentiality of, 107
    postmodernism and, 102–107
hypertext fiction, 107–110
    hypertext technology and, 101–102
    postmodernism and, 109–110
    web hypertext novels, 107–110

Ibomu, Khnum Muata "stic.man," 254–255, 257
illness, 14
immigration, 143–145, 235, 239, 252–253
Immigration and Customs Enforcement (ICE), 239
Immigration and Nationality Act of 1965, 143–144
immigration policy, 143–144
imperialism, 159–160
incarceration, 16–17, 251–260, 262–264
    imprisoned intellectual narratives, 263–264
    slavery and, 132, 251–258, 262–264 (*see also* neoabolitionism; neoslavery narratives)
    social, 257–258
Indigenous futurism, 75–76. *See also* Native literature
Infocom, 110
information, 4, 14–15
    age of, 4
innovation, 46
    genre and, 48–51
    neoliberal capitalism and, 50
    realism and, 44–48
    volatility and, 56
Interactive Fiction (IF), 110–111
interactive narrative, 8–10, 14, 113–114, 116
    digital fiction and, 110–111
    documentary style and, 116–117

graphic narrative and, 81–83
hypertext and, 109–110, 112
interactive movies, 8–10
internet, 38, 106–107
    electronic literature (e-lit) published on the, 113–115
interruption, 16, 235–236, 242–243
intersectionality, 22
intersubjectivity, limits of, 12–13
intertextuality, 5–6, 22, 102–104
    cross-media intertextuality, 13
    digital fiction and, 105
    hypertext and, 104
    postmodernism and, 104
Invincible (aka III Weaver), 16–17
    "The Door," 257–258
Invisible Seattle, 114
In Your Face, TNT: Transsexual News Telegraph, 176
Ishatela, Omali, 255
isolation, 16, 235–236
isolationism, 286

Jackson, George, 16–17, 253, 258–259, 262–264
Jackson, Pamela, *The Doll Games*, 108–109
Jackson, Shelley
    The Doll Games, 108–109
    My Body & a Wunderkammer, 103
    Patchwork Girl, 100–101, 103–104
    Riddance: or the Sybil Joines Vocational School for Ghost Speakers & Hearing-Mouth Children, 108–109
Jackson, Shirley, 67
    "The Lottery," 25–26
Jacobs, Harriet, 264
James, David, 13–14
Jameson, Fredric, 274
    The Antinomies of Realism, 217–219
    Postmodernism, 4
Jaramillo, Ann, 16–17, 252–253
Jayo Felony, 253, 262, 264
Jeffers-Cooper, Eve Jihan ("Eve"), "Gotta Man," 257
Jemisin, N.K., 14–15, 75, 127–128, 135–138
    Broken Earth trilogy, 7–8, 75, 125, 135
    "The City Born Great," 27–28
    Dreamblood series, 75
    The Fifth Season, 11–12, 75
    Inheritance trilogy, 75
    The Stone Sky, 75
Jenkins, Andrea, 174–175
Jenkins, Candice, 11–12, 14–15

The Jersey Shore, 10
Jim Crow apartheid, 253
Johnson, Charles, 73–75
Johnson, Denis, 47
Johnson, Marsha P., 179–180
Johnson, Mat, *Pym*, 5–6, 125
Jones, Gayl, 26
  Mosquito, 159
Jones, Stephen Graham, 75–76
  Mapping the Interior, 75–76
Jones, Tavari, *An American Marriage*,
  242–243
Jordan, June, 260
Jorgenson, Christine, 176
journalism, 10, 15–16, 235–236
  graphic narrative and, 90–91
Joyce, James, 219–220
  Ulysses, 36, 102–104
Joyce, Michael, 102
  afternoon, a story, 100–104
Justice Now, *The We That Sets Us Free*,
  257–258

Kafka, Franz, 26–27
  The Trial, 36
Kaopio, Matthew
  Up Among the Stars, 75–76
  Written in the Sky, 75–76
Kaplan, Amy, 282–283
Katchor, Ben, 82
  Hand-drying in America, 88
Kavaney, Roz, 174–175
Kelly, Adam, 58–59
Kelly, James Patrick, 63–64
Kepnes, Caroline, *You*, 8–10
Kerouac, Jack, 104
Kessel, John, 63–64
Keyes, Cheryl, 257
Kiernan, Caitlín R., *The Drowning Girl:
  A Memoir*, 67
Kincaid, Jamaica, 26
  Autobiography of My Mother, 159
  A Small Place, 8
King, Martin Luther, Jr., 138
King, Stephen, 65, 67
  Dark Tower, 64
Kingsolver, Barbara, *Flight Behavior*, 69, 196,
  202–205
Kirkman, Robert, *The Walking Dead* comic,
  72
Kittler, Friedrich, 221–222
Klimas, Chris, 112
Kokomo, 174–175

Konstantinou, Lee, 225
Koselleck, Reinhart, 216–217
Koshy, Susan, 26
KRS-One, 253–255, 259–260
Krugman, Paul, 221
Kumarasamy, Akil
  "At the Birthplace of Sound," 7–8
Kuppers, Petra, 177–178
Kwastek, Katja, 216–217

labor
  gig economy, 3
  global economies of, 14–15
  transnational, 22, 29–32
La Cour, Erin, 216–217
Ladin, Joy, 174–175, 178
Lahiri, Jhumpa, 26
  Unaccustomed Earth, 242–243
Lamar, Kendrick, 16–17, 264
  "Untitled 3," 251–254
Lamb, Sybil, 174–175
Landow, George, 100–101
land rights, 22
language
  Anthropocene resistance to, 59–60
  hybrid, 91
  materiality of, 48–49
Lara, Ana-Maurine, 14–15, 171
  Erzulie's Skirt, 167–169
Latin@ literature, 26, 76. *See also specific
  authors*
Latin American Boom generation, 26–27
Latini, Lilith, 174–175
Latinxfuturism, 76
LaValle, Victor, 75
  The Ballad of Black Tom, 5–6
  Big Machine, 125
  The Changeling, 125
  The Devil in Silver, 125
Law, John, 158–159
Laymon, Kiese, *Long Division*, 125
Leckie, Ann, *The Raven Tower*, 12–13
Lee, Chang-rae, 196
  On Such A Full Sea, 200–202, 204–207
Lee, Don, *Country of Origin*, 145–146
Lee, Julia, 14–15
Lee, Min Jin, 14–15
  Pachinko, 146, 152
Lee, Yoon Ha, 76
Lefebvre, Henri, 158
Le Guin, Ursula, 63–64
Le-Khac, Long, 26
Lepucki, Edan, *California*, 71–72

Lerner, Ben, 50
  10:04, 4–6, 11, 48–49, 198
Lethem, Jonathan, 13–14, 63–64
LGBTQ identity language, 175–176
LGBTQ writing, 174–191. *See also* queer
  fiction
life-writing, 8
Lightspeed magazine, 76–77
Ligotti, Thomas, 65–66
Link, Kelly, 65–66
literary prizes, short fiction and, 23–24
"little" magazines, 25
Liu, Ken, 76
the local, 158
Lohafer, Susan, 25–26
López de Gómara, Francisco, 171
Lord, Karen, 75
Lorde, Audre, 16–17
Lorey, Isabell, 239
Love, Monifa, 16–17, 253
  Freedom in the Dismal, 262–264
Lovecraft, H.P., 27–28, 65–66, 220
Lucero, Evelina Zuni, 14–15, 171
Luiselli, Valeria, 16, 239
  Lost Children Archive, 5–8
  *Tell Me How It Ends: An Essay in Forty
    Questions*, 2, 234–235, 247–248
Lukács, György, 218–219
Lutz, Gary, 47
lynching, 260–262
"lyrical realism," 46–47

Machen, Arthur, 65–66
Macintosh computer, 102
MacLeod, Alistair, 47
magical realism, 123–124
Mahfouz, Naguib, 26–27
Main Source, 16–17, 253, 259–260, 264
  "Just a Friendly Game of Baseball,"
    260–261
Malamud, Bernard, 26
Malcolm X, 16–17, 255–256, 264
Malloy, Judy, *Uncle Roger*, 100–103
Malm, Andreas, 203
Malzberg, Barry, 67
Mandel, Emily St. John, *Station Eleven*,
  72–73
Mannheim, Karl, 3–4
"many-worlds" theory, 229. *See also* the
  multiversal
Maori writers, 75–76
Maracle, Aiyyana, 187
Marclay, Christian, *The Clock*, 5–6

Marcus, Ben, 13–14, 45–48, 50–51
Marino, Mark, 114–115
  #Behindyourbak, 115
  The Ballad of Work Study Seth, 114
  I Work for the Web, 115
  The Loss Wikiless Timespedia, 114
  Occupy MLA, 115
Marquardt, Frank, 104
  The Unknown, 108, 114
Marshall, Kate, 197–199
Marston, Sallie, 158
Martin, Billy, *Lost Souls*, 187
Martin, Randy, 273–274
Martin, Trayvon, 251–252
Marxism, 217–218
masculinity, white, 183–184, 281–286
mass culture, 13
mass incarceration. *See also* incarceration
maximalist novel, 22–23
May, Elaine Tyler, 274, 281
Mayworks Festival of Working People and
  the Arts, 180
McCarthy, Cormac, 13–14, 50
  The Road, 49–50, 64
McCloud, Scott, 153–154
McGuire, Richard, 14, 222–223
  Here, 16, 83, 85–88, 215–219, 222,
    227–229, 231
McGuire, Seanan (Mira Grant), *Newsflesh*
  series, 72
McGurl, Mark, 197–199, 220
McHugh, Maureen F., 63–64
McInerney, Jay, 272–273
  Bright Lights, Big City, 8
  The Good Life, 274–275
McLuhan, Marshall, 105
McPhee, John, *Basin and Range*, 219–220
McSweeney's, 79
media environment
  graphic narrative and, 96–97
  reading in, 96–97
media specificity, 105–106
Melley, Timothy, 272
Melville, Herman, 67–69
  "Benito Cereno," 12–13
  Moby Dick, 36
memex, 101–102
Memmot, Talan, *Lexia to Perplexia*, 106
Messud, Claire, *The Emperor's Children*,
  274–275
metafiction, 5–6
metaphoricity, graphic narrative and, 94–96
MFA workshops, short fiction and, 23

microfiction, 13–14, 21–39
    digital, 36–38 (*see also* Twitter fiction)
    in translation, 26–27
micro-generations, 3–4
microtemporalities, 6–7
Miéville, China, 13–14, 65–66
    Embassytown, 5–6
    This Census-Taker, 7–8
migration, 14–15, 146, 239, 252–253,
    279–281. *See also* immigration;
    Transpacific diasporas
    citizenship and, 285–286
    forced, 168
    international, 22, 274
    migration crises, 2–3, 16–17, 274
    narratives of, 29–32
militarism, 32–37
Millenials, 2–4
Millhauser, Steve, 63–64
minifictions, 29
minoritarian critique, 26
minority citizens, as Other, 276–281
"minority cosmopolitanism," 26
minority literature, 179. *See also specific
    literatures*
Mirajelo, Carlos, 76
Misha, 75–76
Mitchell, David, *Cloud Atlas*, 227–228
Mitchell, William (aka "Large Professor"),
    260–262
Mitchell, W.J. T., 272–273
Mock, Janet, 174–175
modern epic, 22–23
modernism, 6–7, 102–103, 220–221
    acceleration and, 216
    modernist Twitter poetics, 37
modernities, 14–15
    capitalism and, 218–219
Mohanraj, Mary Anne, 76
monoworlds, 14–15, 158–159
Monterroso, Augusto, "El Dinosaurio,"
    21
Montfort, Nick, 110–111
Moody, Rick, "Boys," 28
Moore, Alan, *Watchmen*, 79
Moore, Jason, 203
Moore, Lorrie, *Self Help*, 8
Moore, Tony, *The Walking Dead* comic, 72
Morales, Alejandro, 76
Moreno-Garcia, Silvia, 76
Moretti, Franco, 241
Morley, Catherine, 275
Morris, Jan, 176

Morrison, Toni, 16–17, 26, 49–50, 253, 262
    Beloved, 134, 137
    A Mercy, 159
Morrissey, Judd, *The Last Performance*, 114
Moseley, Walter, 73–75
Moshfegh, Ottessa, 13–14, 56–58
    McGlue, 56
Moulthrop, Stuart, 105
    Hegirascope, 105
    Pax: An Instrument, 105
    Reagan Library, 105
    Victory Garden, 100–101
Mouly, Françoise, 85
mourning, 273–274
Mukherjee, Bharati, 26
multiethnic US literature, 26, 241
multi-genre techniques, 8, 23–24
multimediality, 108–109
multimodality, 113–114
    reading and, 96–97
multitemporality, 13
the multiversal, 159–164, 171. *See also*
    pluriversal fiction
Mumford, Lewis, 221
Munro, Alice, 24, 47
Murakami, Haruki, *1Q84*, 4
Murphy, Gretchen, 157
Muzumdar, Sucheta, 143

NAFTA (North American Free Trade
    Agreement), 159–160
Naimou, Angela, 6–8, 13–14
Namaste, Viviane, 177, 184, 187
narration, description and, 94
narrative experimentation, 6–7
narrative structure, fantasies of,
    242–243
natal alienation, 256–257, 262
Nathanaël, 174–175, 177–178
"national-historical time," 242
National Transgender Theatre Festival, 180
Native American writers, 75–76
Native literature, 6–7, 14–15, 26, 75–76,
    160–161, 166–169, 171
nativist nationalism, 278, 285–286
natural disasters, 22, 237–238
naturalism, 10
navigation, reading and, 107–108
Nayeri, Dina, "The Ungrateful Refugee," 26
Nelson, Jason
    Game, Game, Game and Again Game, 113
    *I Made This. You Play This. We Are
    Enemies*, 113

Nelson, Jason (cont.)
Nothing You Have Done Deserves Such Praise, 113
Nelson, Ted, 101–102, 104
Nelson, Theodor Holm, 101–102
neoabolitionism, 253–260
neo-ethnonationalisms, 16–17
neoliberalism, 238
  neoliberal capitalism, 50
  neoliberal optimism, 123
neoslavery narratives, 253, 258–259, 262–264
Netflix, 8–10
Netprov (network improve literature), 114–116
Network Writing, 113–115 ED: Style varies
New Criticism, 25
Newton, Huey P., 260
New Wave science fiction, 73–75
New Weird, 65–68
New Yorker, 25–26, 29, 34, 36, 38, 63–64
New York Review of Science Fiction, 63
New York Times, 36
Ng, Celeste, 16
  Everything I Never Told You, 242–247
Ngram, 8
Ngugi wa Thiong'o, 254–255
Nguyen, Viet Thanh, 13–14, 23–24, 142–143, 154
  The Displaced: Refugee Writers on Refugee Lives, 24
  Nothing Ever Dies, 24
  The Refugees, 242–243
  The Refugees, 23–24
  The Sympathizer, 23–24
A Night at the Movies, or, You Must Remember This, 105
Nishimoto, Arthur, *Hearts and Minds: The Interrogations Project*, 116
Nixon, Rob, 21, 199–200, 203, 222–223
  Slow Violence and the Environmentalism of the Poor, 197, 201
nonfiction, 235–236. *See also* creative nonfiction
nonlinear temporality, 6–7
non-Western cosmology, 124
Norgaard, Kari Marie, 202
"novel of education," 240–242
nuclear proliferation, 16–17
NWA, 259–260

Obama, Barack, 2–3, 138, 252–253
Obejas, Achy, "You," 7–8

O'Brien, Tim, *The Things They Carried*, 34–35
Occupy Movement, 240
O'Connor, Flannery, 26
The Office, 10
Okorafor, Nnedi
  Akata Warrior, 74–75
  Akata Witch, 74–75
  The Book of the Phoenix, 74–75
  Lagoon, 74–75
  The Shadow Speaker, 74–75
  Who Fears Death, 74–75, 125
  Zahrah the Windseeker, 74–75
O'Leary, Patrick, 64
Olugbala, Mutulu "M-1," 254–256
Olukotun, Deji Bryce, 75
O'Neill, Joseph, 16–17, 271
  Netherland, 281–285
Optic Nerve series, 88–89
Orange, Tommy
  There There, 6–8
orature, 254–255, 262–264
Orbán, Katalin, 6–7, 14
Otlet, Paul, 101–102
Ozeki, Ruth, 1, 6–8, 13–16, 43–44, 218–219
  A Tale for the Time Being, 5–8, 49–50, 145–149, 151, 154, 206–209, 223–229, 231, 242–243

Packard, Edward, "Adventures of You," 8–10
Palmer, Dexter, 75
paranoia, 100, 105
Parikh, Crystal, 16
Paris, 254–255
parody, 104
participatory reading, space of, 81–83
patriotism, 274, 281–282
Patterson, Orlando, 126
Patterson, Richard North, 2–3
Pease, Donald E., 273–274
Peele, Jordan, *Get Out*, 124
Peña, Daniel, 171
  Bang, 170–171
Perec, Georges, *A Void*, 185
"peripheral realism," 241
Perry, Phyllis, 73–75
personal computing, 8–10
perspectival shifts, 14
pessimism, 123
Peters, Torrey, 174–175
Peterson, Trace, 174–175, 177–178
Phan, Aimee, *We Should Never Meet*, 26
Philip, M. NourbeSe, *Zong!*, 185

Philips, Tom, 105
  A Humument, 105
Phillipa, Xanthra, 187
Pita, Beatrice, 76
Plenitude, 174–175
Plett, Casey, 174–175
pluriversal fiction, 14–15, 158–161
Poe, Edgar Allen, 25, 104
point-of-view shifts, 102–103
police violence, 16–17, 251–254, 258–260, 264. *See also* Black Lives Matter movement
political polarization, 4–5
politics, 4–5, 10
Pollack, Rachel, 176, 187
Poor Righteous Teachers, 254–255
popular culture, 15–16
populism, 3
Porpentine Charity Heartscape (Porpentine), 112–113
  Howling Dogs, 112–113
  With Those We Love Alive, 113
post-9/11 fiction, 16–17, 30–31, 33–34, 272–286
  "failure of the imagination" and, 274–275
  'turn to the domestic' and, 274–275
postcolonial theory, 8
"post-genre" writers, 64–67
postmodernism, 4, 13–14, 16, 100–104, 106–107
  experimental fiction and, 43–45
  hypertext and, 102–107
  hypertext fiction and, 109–110
  intertextuality and, 104
  reflexivity and, 105
postmodernities, 14–15
post-privacy era, 10
"post-racial" ethos, 124–125
"post-Seattle fiction," 65–66
post-structuralism, 103–104
Powers, Richard, 16, 218–219, 272–273
  The Overstory, 223–229, 231
precarity, 3–4, 16, 50–51, 54, 59, 235–239, 271
the present
  historicizing, 3–4
  obliteration of, 4–5
  presentness, 6–7
  present tenses, 14–15
print fiction, hypertext and, 105–106
prison blues, 253
prison industrial complex (PIC), 252, 255–256, 261. *See also* incarceration

prison narratives, 253, 262–264. *See also* incarceration
privacy, technology and, 100
privilege, 284–285
progress, 138, 216, 240–242
  myth of, 259
  traditional narratives of, 129
Proust, Marcel, 221–222, 225–226
Public Enemy, 16–17, 253–255, 259–260
Pynchon, Thomas
  Against the Day, 64
  Gravity's Rainbow, 63

Queen Latifah, 254–255
queer fiction, 15–16, 73–75, 165, 174–191. *See also* specific authors; trans genre writing
queer theory, 15–16, 177, 187
QuickTime VR, 105–107

Rabassa, José, 159–160
Rabiyah, Amir, 174–175
race, 15–16, 237–238. *See also* anti-blackness; whiteness
  post-9/11 racial logics, 276–281
  racial alterities, 14
  trans genre writing and, 174, 176, 179–181, 183–184, 189–190
racial profiling, 251–252
racism. *See also* alt-right; anti-blackness; racialized violence; racial profiling
  against Asian Americans, 149
  post-9/11 racial logics, 278–279
  racialized violence, 14–15, 251–254, 256, 258–259 (*see also* police violence)
  white masculinity, 183–184, 281–286
  white nationalism, 3
  white supremacism, 253–255, 259, 263–264
Raha, Nat, 174–175
Raj, Rupert, 187
Rand, Ayn, 8
Rankine, Claudia, 7–8
  Citizen, 4–5, 7–8, 123–124
Ravine, Jai Arun, 174–175
RAW magazine, 85
Raymond, Janice, 186
reading. *See also* screen and device interactivity
  conceptual reading strategies, 107–108
  graphic narrative and, 97
  in media environment, 96–97
  multimodal texts and, 96–97
  navigation and, 107–108

RealAudio, 106–107
realism, 13–14, 16, 69
    climate fiction (cli-fi) and, 202–203
    experimentalism and, 44–48, 50, 56–59,
        242–243
    "lyrical realism," 46–47
    "peripheral realism," 241
Redmond, Shana, 259–260
reflexivity, 109–110
    authorial, 103–104
    four forms of, 102–106
    generic or formal, 104–105
    intertextual, 104
    medial, 105–106
    postmodernism and, 105
regenerative violence, 273–274
regionalist fiction, 26
relationality, 158–161
"remediation," theory of, 106
Rettberg, Scott, 7–10, 12–14, 100, 102–104
    Hearts and Minds: The Interrogations
        Project, 116
    Toxi*City: A Climate Change Narrative,
        116
    The Unknown, 108, 114
Rich, Nathaniel, Odds Against Tomorrow,
    71–72
Ricoeur, Paul, 223
Rivera, Gabby, 14–15, 166–167, 171
    America Chavez, 164–165
    Juliet Takes a Breath, 165
Riviera, Sylvia, 179–180
Robinson, Eden, 75–76
Robinson, Kim Stanley, 70–71, 203
    2312, 4, 70–71
    Aurora, 70–71
    Galileo's Dream, 70–71
    Green Earth, 70–71
    Icehenge, 70–71
    Mars trilogy, 22, 70–71
    New York 2140, 4, 70–71, 203–206
    Pacific Edge, 70–71
    Science in the Capital trilogy, 70–71
Robinson, Marilynne, 13–14, 43, 45–48
    "Gilead" series, 54
    Lila, 54–56
Robson, Justina, 65–66
Rodriguez, Dylan, 237–238
Romantic writers, 219–220
Rosario, Nelly, Song of the Water Saints, 159
Ross, Mirha-Soleil, 180, 187
    Yapping Outloud: Contagious Thoughts of
        an Unrepentant Whore, 180–181

Rothberg, Michael, 274–275
Rubin, Henry, 177
Russ, Joanna, The Female Man, 63
Russian formalism, 219–220
Ryman, Geoff, 65

Sacco, Joe, 90–91
Salah, Trish, 15–16, 174–175
Salinger, J.D., "A Perfect Day for
    Bananafish," 25–26
Salvídar, José David, 157
Salvídar, Ramón, 124–125
Samatar, Sofia, 75
Sánchez, Rosaura, 76
Sánchez Gómez, José Miguel, 76
Sanders, William, 75–76
satire, 10
Saunders, Charles R., 73–75
Saunders, George, 7–8, 13–14, 16, 47, 63–64
    "Home," 7–8, 33–35
    Lincoln in the Bardo, 35, 48–49
Sayrafiezadeh, Saïd, "Paranoia," 33–34
"scaffold imaginary," 158–159
scale, 157–171
    circulation of large spatial and temporal
        scales, 22–25
    as imperial and colonial tool, 158
    long scales, 22–25
    nested hierarchies of, 160
    oceanic, 166–168
    scaling, 24–25
    writing against scalar structure, 159–164,
        171
scene-to-scene transitions, graphic narrative
    and, 153–154
Scholz, Carter, 63–64
Schulman, Helen, A Day at the Beach,
    274–275
Schutt, Christine, 47–48, 51–54
    Florida, 52–54
science, 69–71
science fiction, 14, 16, 63–64, 123–124, 127,
    222–223, 229. See also speculative
    fiction
    African American literature and, 73–75,
        125–126, 128–129
    Afrofuturism and, 128–129
    climate change and, 67–73 (see also climate
        fiction (cli-fi))
    diversity in, 76–77
    feminist, 73–75
    new futures, 73–77
    New Wave science fiction, 73–75

the New Weird and, 65–68
sf fandom, 63
Scott-Heron, Gil, 260
Scranton, Roy, 198–199
screen and device interactivity, 4–5, 11–12,
    96–97
second-person narrative perspectives, 7–13,
    35
    20th-century predecessors of, 8
    digital fiction platforms and, 7–8
    digital interactivity, 8–10
    digital media and, 12
    precursors of, 8
    rise of, 8
    social media and, 12
    transgender narrative and, 12–13
security, 236–239. See also insecurity
    fictions of, 239–246
    securitization, 239
security state, rise of, 100, 239–246
self-citation, 29–32
self-consciousness, 102–103, 109–110
Senna, Danzy, New People, 242–243
September 11, 2001, 16–17, 30, 100, 105,
    236–237
    "failure of the imagination" and, 274–275
    fiction published since, 285–286
    post-9/11 fiction, 271–286
    post-9/11 racial logics, 276–281
    'turn to the domestic' and, 274–275
serialization, graphic narrative and, 83
Sexton, Jared, 123, 126–127, 135
sex workers, trans, 179–181
Seymour, Nicole, 204
SF Eye, 64
Shakir, Evelyn, 26
Shakur, Assata, 16–17, 253, 255–259,
    263–264
Shakur, Mutulu, 258–259
Sharpe, Christina, 129
Shawl, Nisi, 75
Shelley, Mary, 103
Shephard, Lucius, 63–64
Shipley, Ely, 174–175
Shockwave, 106–107
Shohat, Ella, 273–274
Short, Emily
    Counterfeit Monkey, 111
    Galatea, 111–112
    Savoir-Faire, 111
short fiction, 13–14, 21–39
    brief history of, 25–27
    devaluation of, 23

literary prizes and, 23–24
long scales and, 22–25, 27
MFA workshops and, 23
short-short fiction, 13–14 (see also flash
    fiction)
short story cycle, 26
in translation, 26–27
short-range vision, 32–39
Shraya, Vivek, 174–175
Silko, Leslie Marmon, 26, 75–76
    Almanac of the Dead, 159
Simpson David, 273–274
simultaneity, 38–39
sincerity, 225
Singh, Vandana, 76
Siraganian, Lisa, 37
Sista Souljah, 253
slave narratives, 253
slavery, 8, 56–57, 74–75, 251–259, 262–264.
    See also neoabolitionism; neoslavery
    narratives
    Afro-Pessimism and, 126–127, 129–130,
        138
    forced migration and, 168
    incarceration and, 132, 251–258, 262–264
    violence and, 74–75
slipstream, 13–14
slipstream fiction, 64
Slotkin, Richard, 273–274
slowness, 216–217, 221–223, 226–227
Small, David, Stitches, 90, 94–96
Smith, Justin E.H., 3
Smith, Zadie
    "Meet the President!," 33, 38–39
    "Two Directions for the Novel," 46–47
Snorton, C. Reilly, 177–178, 184, 191
social media, 8–10, 33, 35–38, 116. See also
    specific platforms
    literary experimentation and, 37–38
    Netprov (network improve literature) and,
        114–115
    second-person narrative perspectives and,
        12
social networks, 115. See also social media
Soderbergh, Steven, sex, lies, and videotape,
    10
space, climate fiction (cli-fi) and,
    201–202
space-times, multipolar, 14–15
spatiality, graphic narrative and, 85–86
the speculative, 14, 63–77, 123–125, 128
    black speculative fiction, 124–127
speculative pessimism, 123–124, 128, 138

"speculative realism," 124–125
speed(s), 4–5, 216–217, 221–223, 226–227.
    See also acceleration; slowness
Spiegelman, Art, 85
    Maus: A Survivor's Tale, 79
Spillers, Hortense, 126, 190
Spoon, Rae, 174–175
Stafford, Barbara Maria, 104
Stapledon, Olaf, 220
state violence, 16–17. See also police violence
"status fiction," 45–46
Stephenson, Neal
    Cryptonomicon, 64–65
    Seveneves, 69–70
Sterling, Bruce, 14, 64
Stewart, Kathleen, 51
Stewart, Sean., 65
Stoler, Ann, 26
Stone, Robert, Dog Soldiers, 63
Stone, Sandy, "The Empire Strikes Back:
    A Posttranssexual Manifesto," 176–177,
    182–186
Storyspace software, 100–102, 104, 106–107
storytelling, spatialized, 102–103 (see also
    graphic narrative)
storyworlds, 81
Stratton, Dirk, The Unknown, 104, 108, 114
Straub, Peter, 65
    Koko, 64–65
stream of consciousness, 102–103
Stryker, Susan, 177
Sukenick, Ronald, 44–45
Sullivan, Caitlin, Nearly Roadkill, 187
surveillance, 10–11, 38–39, 279–281. See also
    securitization
suspense, 16, 235–236, 242–243, 245
Suzuki, Erin, 143
Swainston, Steph, 65–66
Sze, Julie, 197–198

Taliban, 281
Tan, Amy, The Joy Luck Club, 24
technology, 3, 22, 100–102, 106–107, 115.
    See also screen and device interactivity
    acceleration and, 216
    consciousness and, 106
    experimentalism and, 24, 37–38
    hypertext (see hypertext)
    internet and (see internet)
    iPad apps, 115
    screens, 4–5, 11–12, 96–97
    speed and, 4–5
    text technologies, 109–110 (see also hypertext)

teleology, 129, 138
    temporal nonlinearity, 6–7
    temporal shifts, 13
temporality, 4–7, 13. See also timescales
    accelerating, 217
    African American literature and, 123–124
    Black radical temporality, 259
    games with, 222–227
    geologic, 12–13
    graphic narrative and, 85–88
    multitemporality, 13
    timescales, 22, 219–222
Tender Claws studio
    Tendar, 115
    Virtual Virtual Reality, 115
Tepper, Sheri S., 65
terror, 16–17, 276. See also violence
    in post-9/11 novel, 272–276
    unrepresentability of, 16–17
    war on terror, 32–33, 236–237, 252, 271,
    273–274, 279–281
Them, 174–175
Theonia, Charles, 174–175
The Third Alterative, 65–66
Thirteenth Amendment, U.S. Constitution,
    252, 259–260
Thom, Kai Cheng, 174–175, 182
    Fierce Femmes and Notorious Liars:
    A Dangerous Trans Girl's Confabulous
    Memoir, 181–182
Thomas, Angie, The Hate You give, 242–243
Thomas, Lindsay, 22
Thomas, Sheree R.
    Dark Matter: A Century of Speculative
    Fiction from the African Diaspora,
    73–75
    Dark Matter: Reading the Bones, 73–75
Thompson, Craig, Blankets, 90
Thornton, Jeanne, 174–175
thresholds between worlds, crossing, 160–161
Tierce, Merritt, 13–14
    Love Me Back, 51–52
time. See temporality
Tinsley, Omise'eke Natasha, 167
Tolbert, TC, 174–175
Tolstoy, Leo, 68–69
Tomine, Adrian, 88–89
    "A Brief History of the Art Form Known as
    'Hortisculpture'," 89
    Killing and Dying, 88
    Summer Blood, 154
Toomer, Jean, 125
Topside Press, 174–175, 189–190

Topside Workshop, 178
Tran, GB, *Vietnamerica*, 90–94
transgenderism, "queer paradigmed," 177
transgender studies, 176–177
transgender writing, 15–16, 174–191. *See also* trans genre writing
conditions of emergence, 178–185
feminism and, 178
in late 20th century, 176–178
second-person narrative perspectives and, 12–13
trans autobiography, 189
trans canon, 178
trans poetics, 178, 190–191
trans politics, 178, 180
trans subjects, 15–16, 179–180, 185
trans genre writing, 15–16, 174–191
autobiography and, 186
decolonization and, 177
as disruption and interference, 178–179
as minor literature rather than emergent, minority literature, 179, 181–182, 185–188
normative constraints of, 185–187, 189
queerly inflected, 183
race and, 179–181, 183–184, 189–190
subalterned, 181–184, 189–190
trans genres, 178, 185
untimely genres, 186–188
trans inscription, 178–179, 181, 185
transition memoirs, 175–176, 181–182, 186
normative temporality and, 189
translation, 26–27
trans literary criticism, 174
trans literature, 15–16
emergence of, 177, 179 (*see also* trans genre writing)
transnationalism, 143
transnational labor, 22, 29–32
"transnational turn," 143, 242–243
trans normativity, 184
the transpacific, 142–143, 146–151
transpacific diasporas, 142–155
transpacific shift, 143–146
Trans-Pacific Partnership (TPP), 142–143
transsexual critique, 187
transsexuality
discourses on, 176
genres of, 189
medicalization of, 186
transsexual memoir, 186
transsexual writing, 175–176. *See also* trans genre writing

TransSisters, 176
Trans Studies, 177
trauma, 273–275
Trevor, William, 47
Trexler, Adam, 69, 72–73
Anthropocene Fictions, 196–197
Trump, Donald, 4, 59–60, 100, 123, 278
2016 presidential campaign and, 10
presidency of, 2–3, 10–11, 286
undocumented immigrants and, 252–253
"truthiness," 2–3
Tsing, Anna, 208
Tsoupikova, Daria, *Hearts and Minds: The Interrogations Project*, 116
Tsukayama, John, 116
Tung, Charles, 220
Twine, 112–113
Twitter, 11. *See also* Twitter fiction
Twitter fiction, 33, 35–38
Ty, Eleanor, 144

undocumented immigrants, 252–253
Up the Yangtze, 197–198
USA Patriot Act, 273–274
US imperialism, 252–253
US militarism, 32–37
utopianism, 242

Valerio, Max Wolf, 191
Van Dam, Andries, 102
VanderMeer, Ann, *The Weird*, 65–66
VanderMeer, Jeff, 65–66, 196
Acceptance, 7–8, 67–68
Annihilation, 67–68
Authority, 67–68
Borne, 206–208
Southern Reach trilogy, 67–68
The Strange Bird, 206–209
The Weird, 65–66
Versluys, Kristiaan, 273
Vetch, 174–175
Victorian writers, 219–220
Vida, Vendela, *The Diver's Clothes Lie Empty*, 7–8
video gaming, 8–10, 14
Village Voice, 63
violence, 14, 16–17. *See also specific kinds of violence*
against African Americans, 123–125, 251–254, 259–260 (*see also* Black Lives Matter movement)
against Asian Americans, 151–155
colonial, 74–75

violence (cont.)
  slavery and, 74–75
  against trans subjects, 183–184
  police violence, 16–17, 251–254, 258–260,
    264 (*see also* Black Lives Matter
    movement)
  racialized violence, 14–15, 251–254, 256,
    258–259 (*see also* police violence)
virtual reality, 14, 116
visual metaphors, 14
visual qualities, of graphic narrative, 91–95
visual textuality, 108–109. *See also* graphic
  narrative
Vizenor, Gerald, 75–76
Volpp, Leti, 276
Vonnegut, Kurt, 103
  Breakfast of Champions, 104
Vourvoulias, Sabrina, 76
vulnerability, 16, 51–56, 236–240
"vulnerability thesis," 237
Vuong, Ocean, *On Earth We're Briefly
  Gorgeous*, 7–8

wake work, 129
Waldman, Amy, *The Submission*, 242–243,
  274–275
Walker, Alice, 26
Wallace, David Foster, 43–44, 103–105
Wallerstein, Immanuel, 221
Walter, Jess, 16–17, 271
  The Financial Lives of the Poets, 281,
    284–285
Ward, Jesmyn, 14–16
  Salvage the Bones, 198
  Sing, Unburied, Sing, 125, 132–135, 137,
    242–243
Ware, Chris, 14
  Building Stories, 83–85, 88
  *Jimmy Corrigan, or the Smartest Kid on
    Earth*, 88–89
warfare, 16–17, 22, 32–33, 271–274
war fiction, 33–37
war on terror, 32–33, 236–237, 252, 271,
  273–274, 279–281
Warren, Calvin, 129
Watergate, 11
Watkins, Claire Vaye, 196
  Gold Fame Citrus, 71–72, 201–202, 204
Webbelies, 115
web hypertext novels, 104, 107–110. *See also*
  hypertext; hypertext fiction; internet
Weird Tales pulp magazine, 65–66
Wells, H. G., 220

What Remains of Edith Finch, 113
White, Curtis, *Memories of My Father
  Watching TV*, 105
Whitehead, Colson, 13–15, 50, 64
  The Underground Railroad, 56–59, 64,
    125, 129–130, 242–243
  Underground Railroad, 5–6
  Zone One, 48–49, 56–57, 72, 125,
    129–132, 135
white masculinity, 183–184, 281–286
white nationalism, 3
whiteness, 189–190, 237–238
white supremacism, 253–255, 259, 263–264
Whyte, Kyle Powys, 206
Wilderson, Frank, 126–128, 131–132, 134
wildness, 208–209
Wilhelm, Kate, 63–64
Williams, Joy, 13–14, 47
Williams, Thomas, *The Hair of Harold Roux*,
  63
Williams, Thomas Chatterton, 56–57
Willis, Connie, 63–65
Willis, Susan, 274
Willyboy, 176
Wilson, Daniel H., 75–76
Wilson-Yang, Jia Qing, 174–175
Wittig, Rob, 114–115
  #Behindyourbak, 115
  Blue Company, 114
  The Fall of the Site of Marsha, 114
  Invisible Seattle, 114
  I Work for the Web, 115
  Occupy MLA, 115
Wolfe, Gary K., 64–65
Wolfe, Gene, 63–64
Wolfe, Tom, 8
women of color, carceral experience of, 257–258
Woolf, Virginia, 6–7, 219–221
  Mrs. Dalloway, 6–7, 36
Wordsworth, William, 219–220
work songs, 253
world literary systems, 22
world-systems theory, 221
World Wide Web, 102, 106–107. *See also*
  internet
Wortman, Jennifer, "Theories of the Point-of-
  View Shift in AC/DC's 'You Shook Me
  All Night Long'," 13
Wynter, Syvlia, 179, 183–185

Yamashita, Karen Tei, 14–15, 76, 166–167, 171
  I Hotel, 165–166
Yolen, Jane, 65

Yoss. *See* Sánchez Gómez, José Miguel
You, 8–10
You vs Wild, 8–10

Zavala, Lauro, 29
Zemeckis, Robert, *Back to the Future*, 5–6
zines, transsexual and transgender, 176

Ziser, Mike, 197–198
Žižek, Slajov, 272–273
Zola, Emile, 68–69
zombie narratives, 72
Zork series, 110
Zuni Lucero, Evelina, *Night Sky, Morning Star*, 169–170